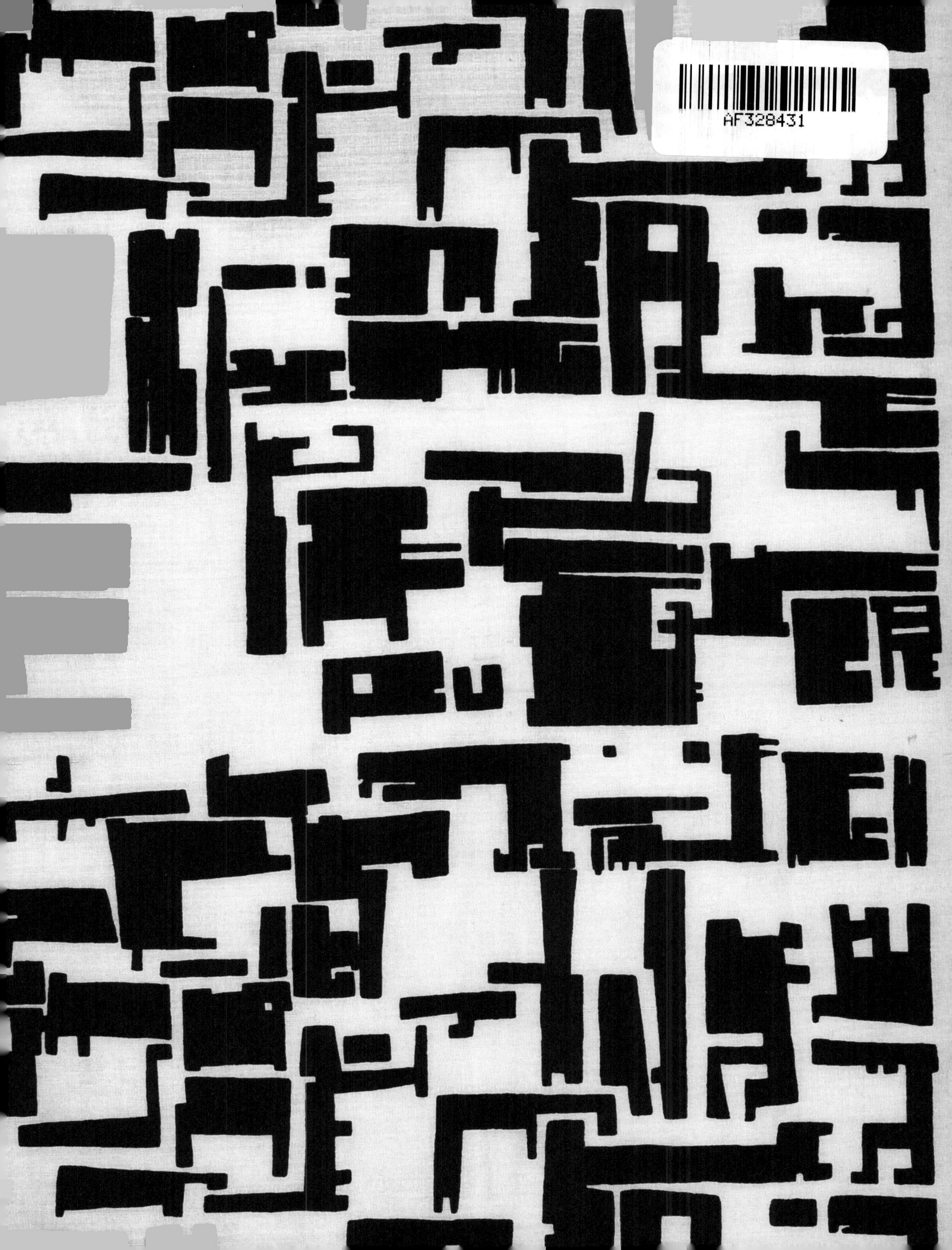
AF328431

CONRAN
QUANT

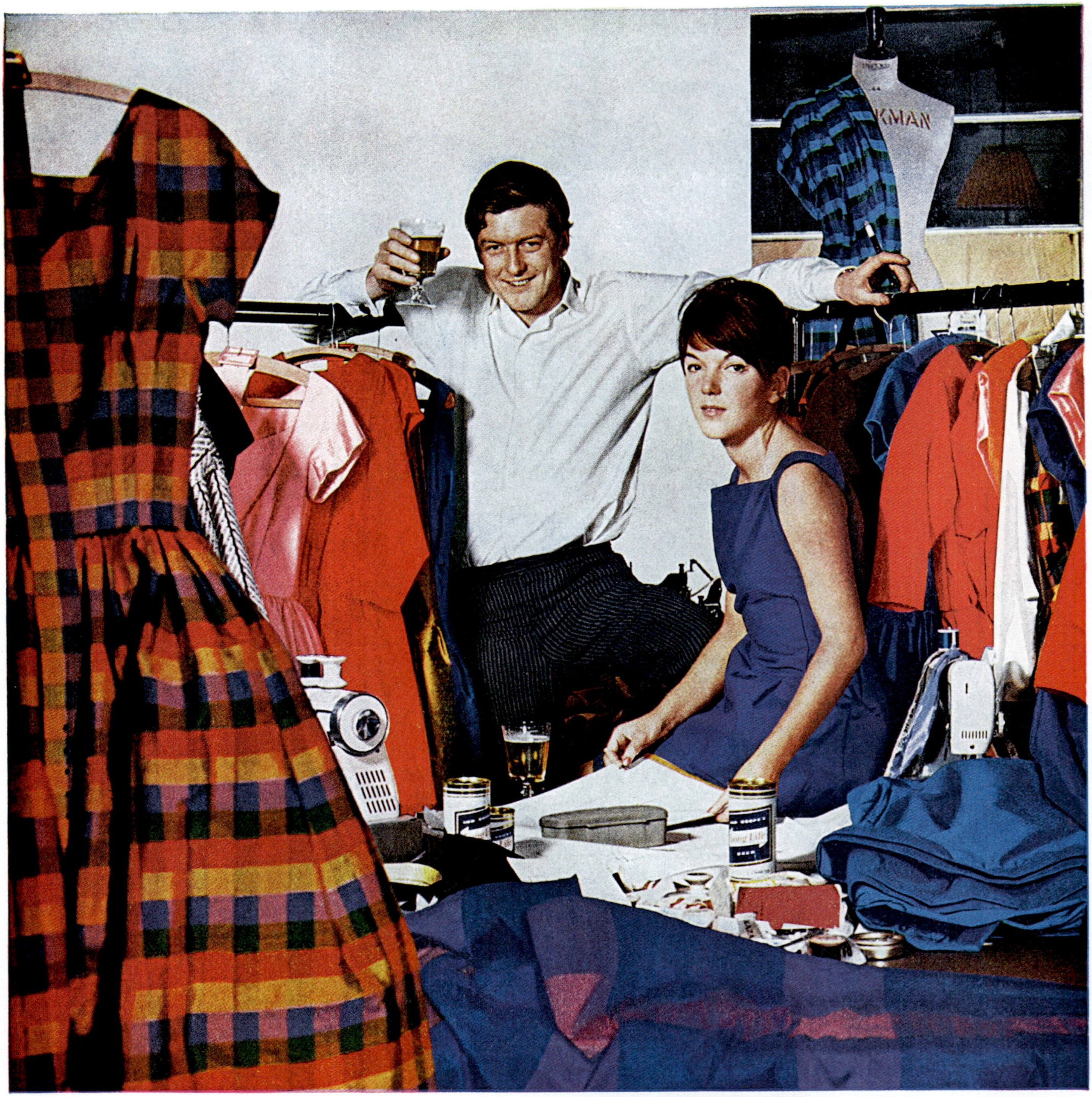

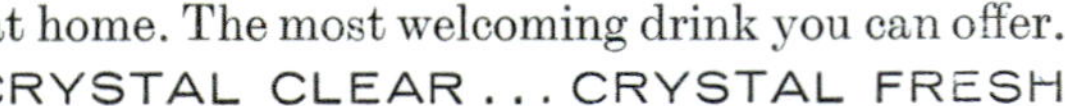

ALEXANDER & MARY PLUNKET GREENE, whose BAZAAR sets new fashion trends in London, relax after hours in their Chelsea workroom with a glass of Long Life.

PEOPLE WHO SET TODAY'S TRENDS DRINK Long Life

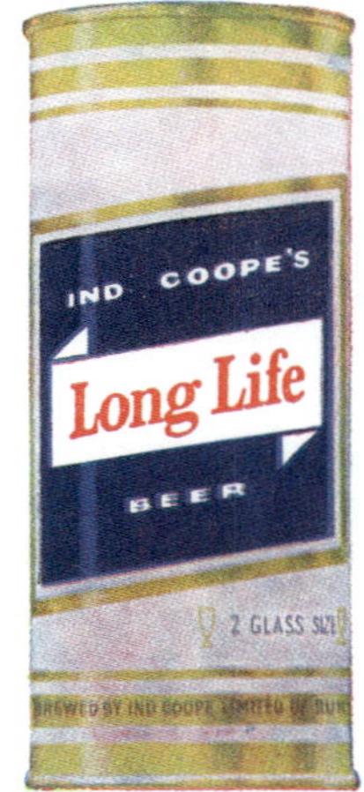

Drink the beer that suits today's taste—LONG LIFE. Refreshingly light, with a clear, clean taste. Easy to cool, easy to store, and no empties to bother about. Keep a supply of LONG LIFE at home. The most welcoming drink you can offer.

CRYSTAL CLEAR . . . CRYSTAL FRESH

CONRAN
QUANT

Swinging London
A Lifestyle Revolution

ACC ART BOOKS

ISBN: 978 178884 011 8

British Library Cataloguing-in-Publication Data
A catalogue record for this book is available from the British Library

ENDPAPERS: Textile, 'Plaza,' screen-printed cotton, designed by the architect John Sayers and printed by Bernard Ashley for Ashley Mountney, c.1955. (© John Sayers)

FRONTISPIECE: Advertisement for Long Life Canned Beer, 1960. The first canned beer in Britain, Long Life represented modernity, youth and the new affluent celebrity lifestyle, as epitomised by Mary Quant and her husband Alexander Plunket Greene.

BACK COVER: (Left) Terence Conran at his first exhibition, 1952. (Photo by Michael Wickham. © Denny Wickham); (Right) Mary Quant outside Bazaar, 1963. (Terence Pepper Collection)

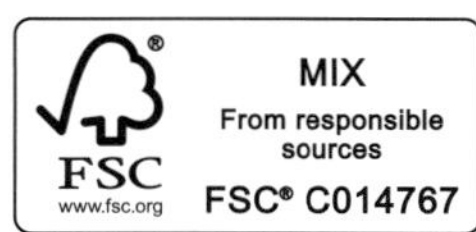

Printed by Graphius Belgium
for ACC Art Books Ltd., Woodbridge, Suffolk, England

www.accartbooks.com

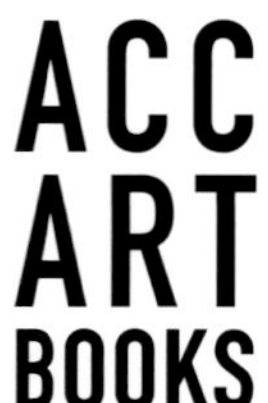

Table of Contents

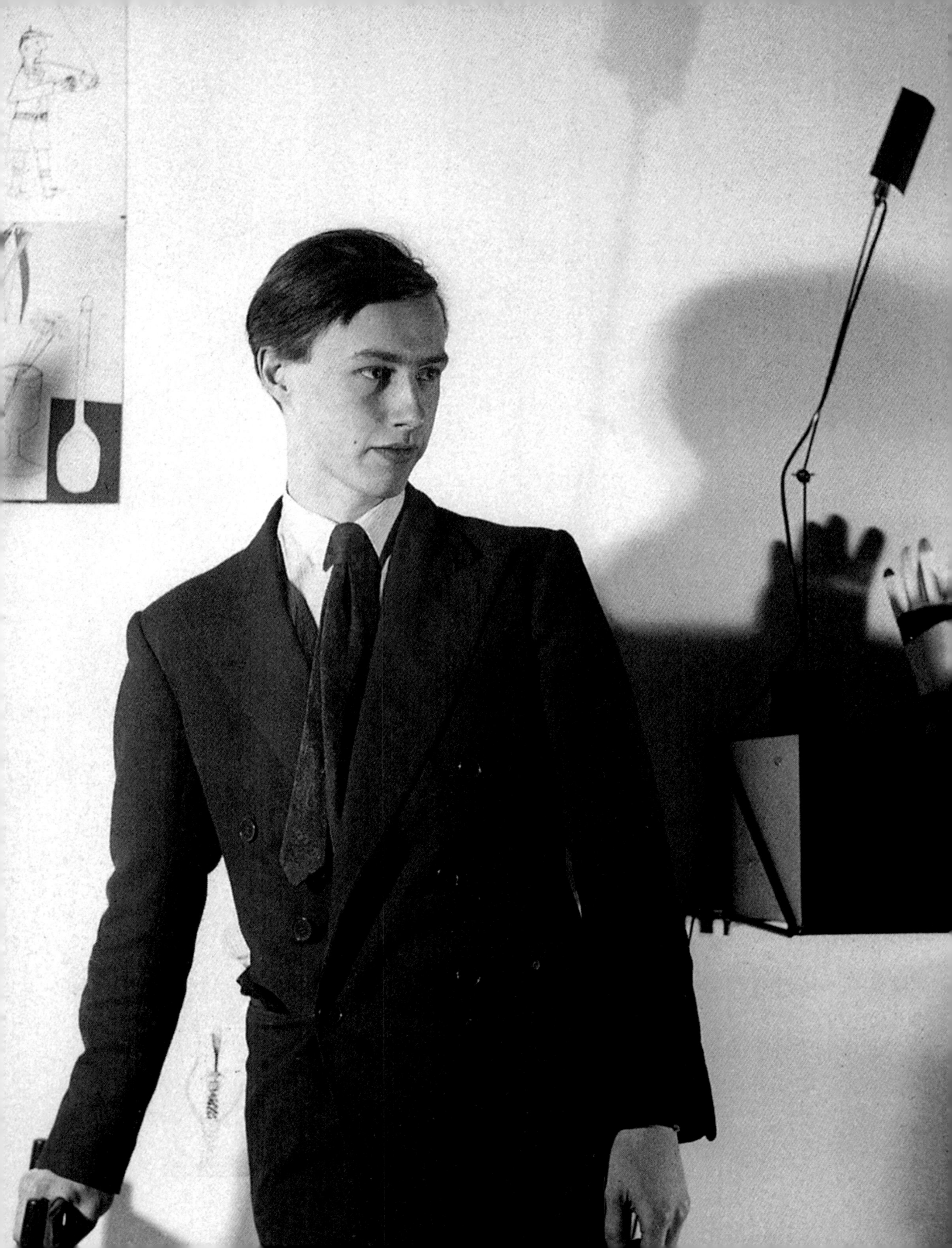

Introduction

'BLISS WAS IT IN THAT DAWN TO BE ALIVE BUT TO BE YOUNG WAS VERY HEAVEN!'

William Wordsworth, *The Prelude*

OFTEN CALLED the 'Youth Quake', the Pop revolution's primary forms of expression were fashion, music and art, with fashion and music setting the pace. The opening of the boutique Bazaar by revolutionary young fashion designer Mary Quant, in November 1955, was a seminal moment in the evolution of the cultural and social phenomenon that subsequently became known as 'Swinging London'.

THE REBELLIOUS YOUNG QUANT, however, was not alone in her questioning of the established order and the status quo. Throughout the 1950s many others also contributed to the irresistible momentum for cultural and social change, which eventually came to fruition in the 1960s amid the energy and excitement of Pop culture. From the late 1940s onwards, the work and ideas of Quant's friend and associate, the enterprising young designer, future retail entrepreneur and restaurateur, Terence Conran, was also at the forefront of this growing desire amongst the young for fundamental change. Conran eventually realised his vision of bringing the 'Good life' to Britain when he set up Habitat in 1964, a new type of 'lifestyle' store, which, at its inception, had something of an egalitarian idealism about it.

BAZAAR and the unveiling of Quant's radical new fashion designs fortuitously coincided with the release in 1955 of the film *Blackboard Jungle*, a tale of troubled and delinquent teenagers. Bill Haley's iconic song from the film's soundtrack, *Rock Around the Clock*, coalesced with the arrival of Elvis Presley and full-blown Rock 'n' Roll the following year to herald the advent of the Pop era. In Britain a proto-Pop culture had initially evolved in the early post-war years among a loosely knit group of radical young architects, designers, photographers, film makers, musicians, and 'arty' dilettantes, who mainly lived and worked in and around the environs of Chelsea, then a somewhat faded and passé bohemian area of London, long the haunt of artists and intellectuals.

THE SUBTLE network of relationships that developed between the key members of this informal group formed an essential part of the substratum which later underpinned Pop culture in 1960s London. Quant and her husband Alexander Plunket Greene, who both came of age in the early 1950s amidst the vitality and enthusiasm generated by the young in the post-war era, were prominent personalities in this group of influential young bohemians. Among significant others in what became known as the 'Chelsea Set' were Plunket Greene's former school friend Terence Conran and his then-wife Shirley, the future novelist. Yet another talented and ambitious young couple to emerge from this fertile mélange to achieve exceptional acclaim and commercial success were the textile and fashion designer and retailer Laura Ashley, and her husband and business partner Bernard, who achieved international fame in the later 1960s and 1970s. Trying to define exactly who or what the Chelsea Set comprised, is as difficult as trying to comprehend the protean nature of Pop culture itself. When attempting to explain the phenomenon in her 1966 autobiography, Quant wrote:

'Nobody has ever been able to make up his mind precisely what 'The Chelsea Set' was but I think it grew out of something in the air which developed into a serious effort to break away from the 'Establishment'. It was the first real indication of a complete change of outlook. The fact that this gathered momentum so much more quickly than anyone ever imagined was unpredictable.'[1]

The young Conran photographed by Michael Wickham at his exhibition, held at Simpsons of Piccadilly, 1952.

A MORE INDIRECT but important influence on this nascent Pop culture were the work and theories of the members of the Independent Group, an informal association of young avant-garde artists, architects, intellectuals and critics, who based themselves in London at the then recently formed Institute of Contemporary Arts, the ICA. The sculptor Eduardo Paolozzi, Terence Conran's great friend and mentor, took, in tandem with his colleague the avant-garde photographer Nigel Henderson, a major part in the Independent Group's activities.

MANY OF THE GROUP'S ideas were more widely disseminated through exhibitions such as Paolozzi's and Henderson's 'Parallel of Life and Art', organised in collaboration with the Brutalist architects Peter and Alison Smithson at the ICA in 1953. Members of the Group also created the seminally important exhibition 'This is Tomorrow', held at the Whitechapel Art Gallery in 1956. Another of the group, the artist Richard Hamilton, famously used the word Pop in his well-known photomontage for the cover of the exhibition's catalogue. However, it was Paolozzi who first coined the term for his collage of 1947, *I Was a Rich Man's Plaything*. Now generally considered the first work of Pop Art, it was originally part of *BUNK*, the ground-breaking series of collages he presented at the inaugural meeting of the Independent Group in 1952. Within the Group, Paolozzi and Henderson made a considerable contribution to the development of Pop aesthetics and theory. The products of their Hammer Prints workshop, set up in the mid 1950s for the design and production of applied art, gave a foretaste of the often surreal and ironic elevation in Pop design of the mundane and everyday as objects of desire.

THROUGHOUT THE 1950s, an all-pervasive but subtle change was in the air; one which manifested itself not only in the growing phenomenon of the King's Road and the Chelsea Set, but more significantly in the eruption of coffee bars, bistros, trattorias and other such alien eateries which began to appear on the nation's high streets at this time. The successful intrusion of these distinctly foreign types of establishments in traditional British street life was, in part, the result of a growing familiarity with continental culture, largely gained through the increasing availability of inexpensive foreign package holidays, the rapid growth of TV ownership and the impact of movies with exciting European settings and romantic story lines. Outstanding among such films were Audrey Hepburn's highly acclaimed debut in 1953 in the film *Roman Holiday* and later, in 1963, *Summer Holiday*, starring the pop idol Cliff Richard in a teen romance set against the backdrop of Athens and the Parthenon, complete with chart-topping pop songs and the cast decked out in the latest youth fashions. Partly down to these various influences, throughout the later 1950s and early 1960s many young Britons, wanting a more permanent piece of the action on their home turf, began to flirt with such exotic comestibles as spaghetti Bolognese or the drinking of 'frothy coffee' in coffee bars from transparent Pyrex cups, invariably accompanied by the somewhat sticky consumption of such delicacies as rum babas or apfelstrudels.

YET, WHATEVER the influence of inexpensive foreign travel or the exciting romantic locations of movies, such as Rome or Athens, without doubt the origins of these somewhat suspect extraneous activities amongst the young in newfangled coffee bars and bistros, also owed something to the widespread success and popularity of the books of the remarkable cookery writer Elizabeth David: *A Book of Mediterranean Food* and *French Country Cooking*, published in 1950 and 1951 respectively. By the later 1950s her message was being ably propagated through the advocacy of a coterie of influential cookery writers, either in their columns for leading national newspapers or by the successful co-option in the culinary cause of the then fairly recent medium of television.

REFERRING MORE generally to the dynamism, energy and enthusiasm generated amongst the young in those early post-war years, the furniture and industrial designer Robin Day wrote:

> *'We were dedicated, competitive and filled with evangelical zeal. Living standards were rising dramatically, the austerities and rationing of the war years were lifting and there was a growing feeling of optimism and confidence and anticipation of a bright new world.'*[2]

Mary Quant, Knightsbridge, 1961.

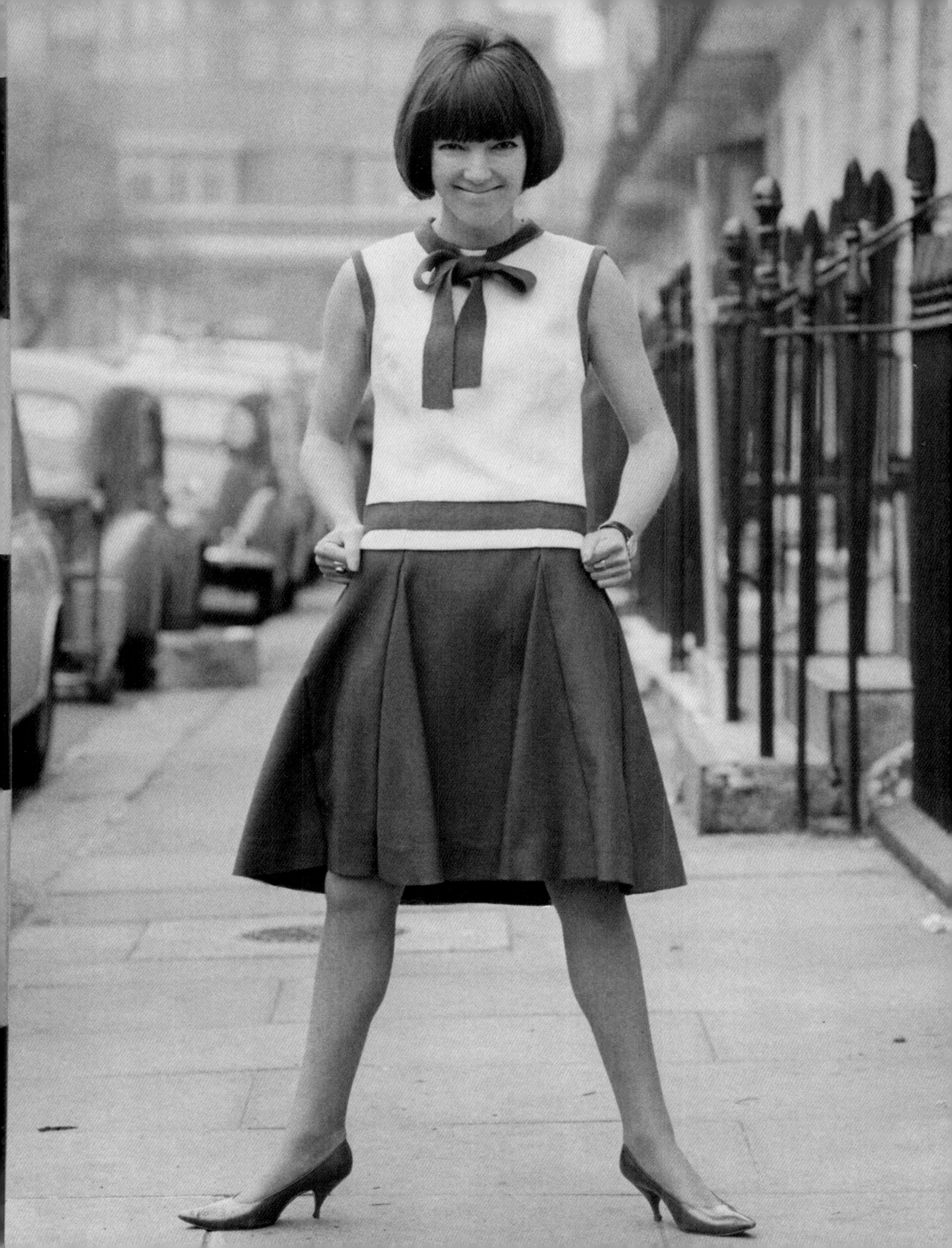

MARY QUANT: BEGINNINGS

THE FASHION GURU Ernestine Carter wrote of Mary Quant in 1973 that:

'It is given to a fortunate few to be born at the right time, in the right place, with the right talents. In recent fashion there have been three: Chanel, Dior and Mary Quant... It took two bloody wars to create the right atmosphere for Chanel and Dior. The revolution that prepared the way for Mary Quant was bloodless – the revolt of the young.' [3]

BORN IN 1934 in London, Mary Quant was the eldest child of aspirational Welsh teachers 'who were earnest believers in the merits of plain living and high thinking.' [4] She was brought up in the Shooters Hill area of London, which adjoins Blackheath, then south London's intellectual and artistic equivalent of Hampstead in the north of the city. Other than being evacuated with her family during the Second World War, she continued to live there with her parents until leaving Goldsmiths College in the early 1950s.

HER PARENTS were determinedly ambitious for Quant and her brother to achieve and further themselves, and, with their strong belief in the value of professional qualifications and the virtues of hard work and study, she had great difficulty in convincing them to allow her to take a course in Illustration at Goldsmiths. They eventually agreed, but only as the course would consequently lead to the Diploma in Art and Design, which would qualify her as an art teacher.

QUANT HAD originally wanted to study fashion: 'I was obsessed by fashion. I always had been... I wanted to go to fashion school. My parents were dead against it. "There is no future in fashion", they said, and from their perspective they were probably right... But I longed to design clothes. My parents and I settled on a compromise, I enrolled at Goldsmiths.' [5]

IN THE EVENT, Quant failed to get an art teachers' diploma, probably an act of sabotage on her part against her parents' ambitions for her. She wrote that:

'My relationship with my parents was appalling... In spite of the never-ending rows at home, I was determined I was not going to be a teacher.' [6]

HOWEVER, FATE intervened when Quant met at college her soul mate, future husband and business partner, Alexander Plunket Greene, who became the most significant person in her life and the greatest influence. Their meeting was a remarkable conjunction of mind and spirit, as no one's social background and upbringing could have been more different from Quant's than Plunket Greene's.

Mary Quant outside Bazaar, 1963.

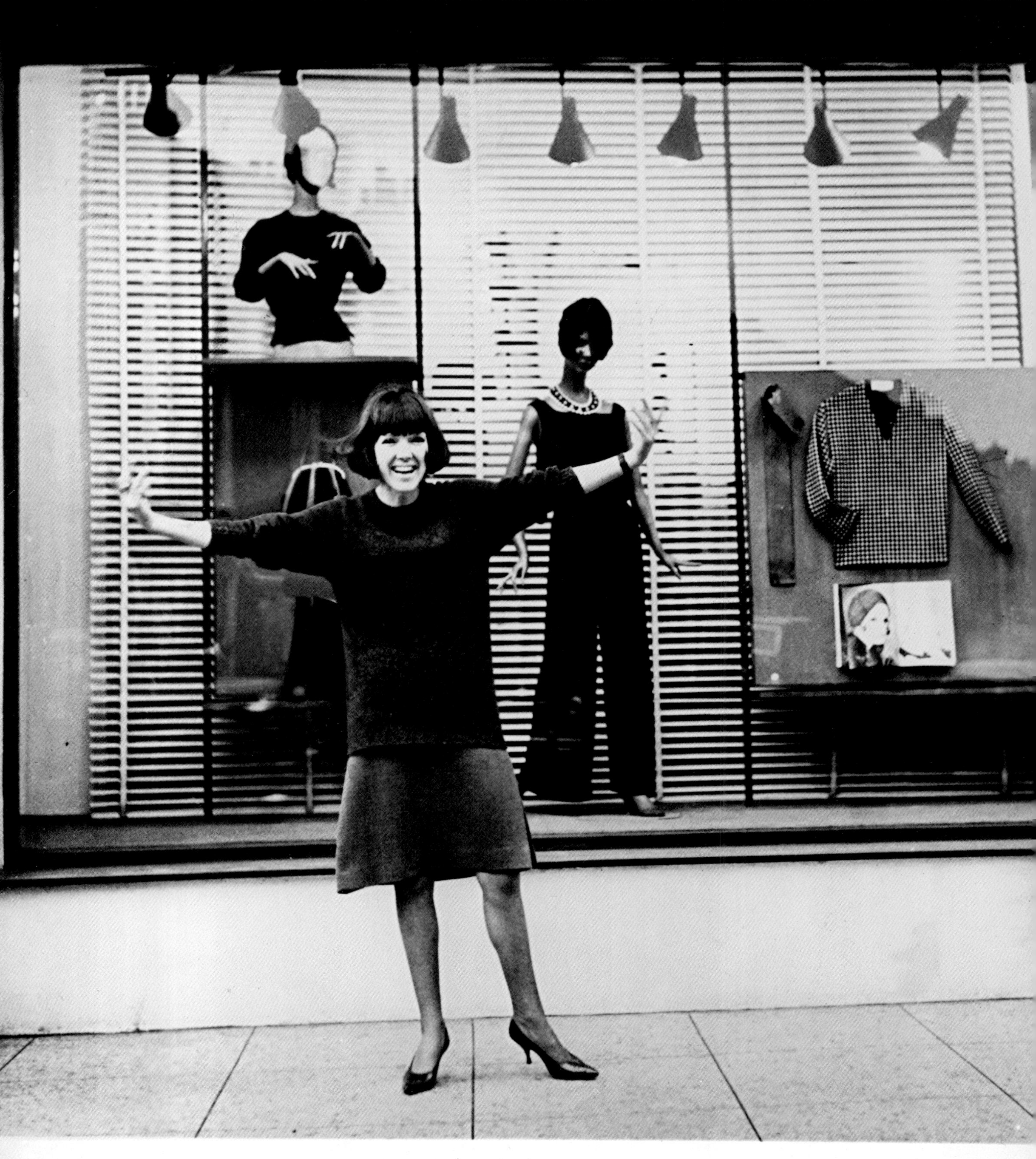
BAZAAR

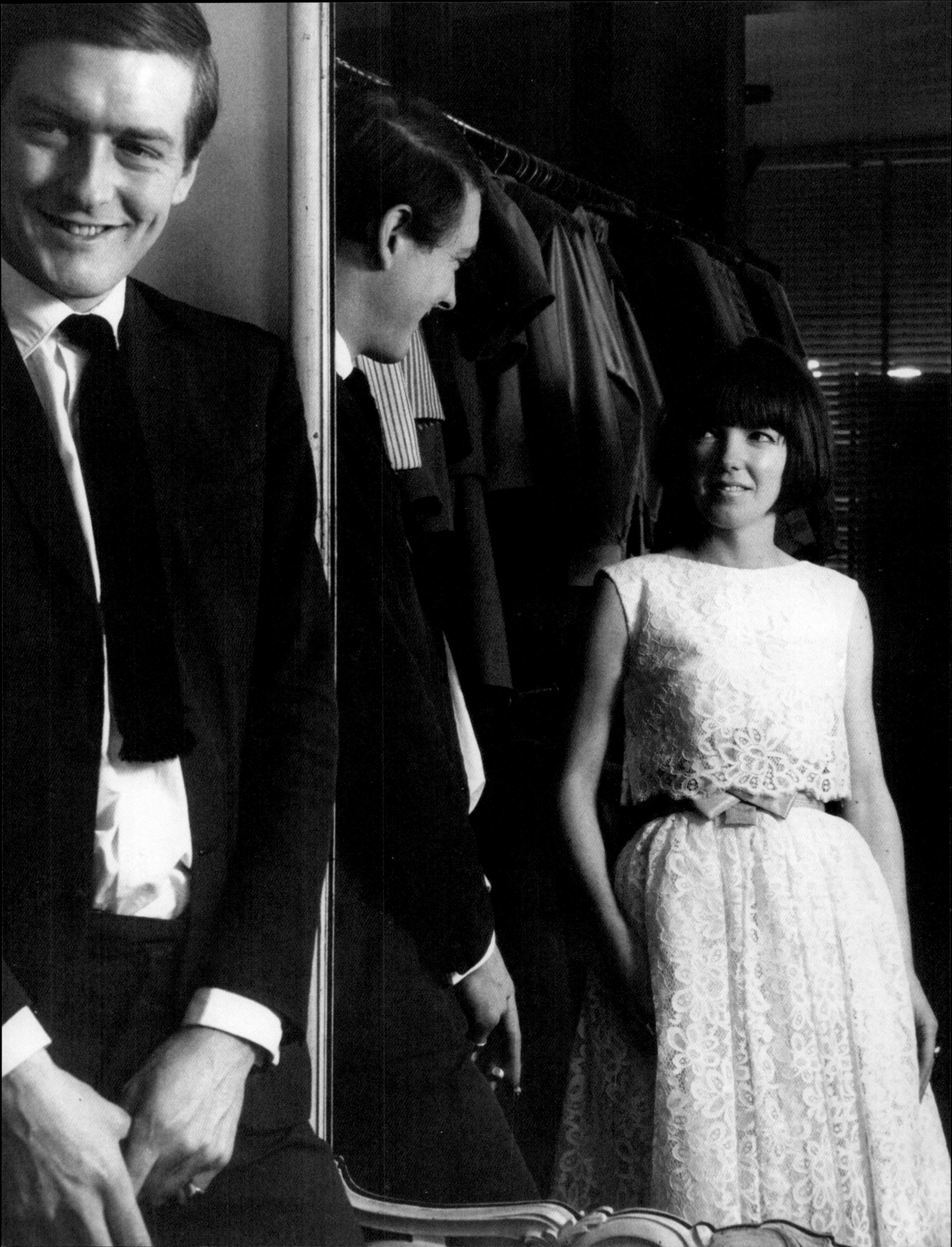

ENTER ALEXANDER PLUNKET GREENE

BORN IN 1932, Plunket Greene was the scion of a somewhat eccentric upper class family with influential aristocratic connections, being cousins of the Duke of Bedford and the Russell family, among them the philosopher Lord Bertrand Russell. In the 1920s his parents, Richard Plunket Greene and Elizabeth Russell, had moved in the orbit of the 'Bright Young Things', Richard being described by Evelyn Waugh, his friend from his Oxford days, as 'piratical in appearance, sometimes wearing ear-rings, a good man with a boat, a heavy smoker of dark strong tobacco.'[7]

PLUNKET GREENE'S parents divorced when he was eight and he lived mainly with his grandmother, rarely seeing his father, whom he remembered as 'an exciting stranger, a tall, handsome, buccaneering man in naval uniform who turned up out of the blue at rare intervals'.[8]

HE THEN BECAME a boarder at a preparatory school in the Boxgrove area of Guildford. It was while there that he first encountered Terence Conran, a fellow pupil. As a teenager he attended Bryanston, a public school radically different to the likes of Eton and Harrow. The school had a strong reputation in the arts, with an emphasis on the creative and the practical and encouraged pupils to develop their individuality and personal abilities. It was particularly popular with parents who had artistic connections. Lucian Freud was a pupil in the late 1930s and among Plunket Greene's peers were the artists Howard Hodgkin and Anthony Hill, and, once more, his long-term friend Terence Conran, a significant relationship in the growth of Pop culture. Plunket Greene later recalled that:

'Terence was less of a child than the rest of us and I was rather in awe of him; he was a surly lad with some very strong ideas. He still is if you don't know him.'[9]

AFTER LEAVING BRYANSTON he appeared somewhat lost and unfocused. Doing something vaguely artistic at Goldsmiths College was probably seen as an acceptable way to pass the time. His mother apparently showed little concern or interest in his future, other than occasionally saying, 'Really, Alexander, I think you ought to have a go at something soon'. Following his sojourn at Goldsmiths, and living on an allowance from his family, he pretended to be a photographer for a while, but seems to have fooled nobody. Because of this early history, he later felt strongly that to spoil one's children in childhood and adolescence is the worst thing any parent can do.[10]

Alexander with Mary in the second Bazaar, 1961.

A LANDSCAPE OF PLEASURE: COFFEE BARS, BISTROS AND BRASSERIES

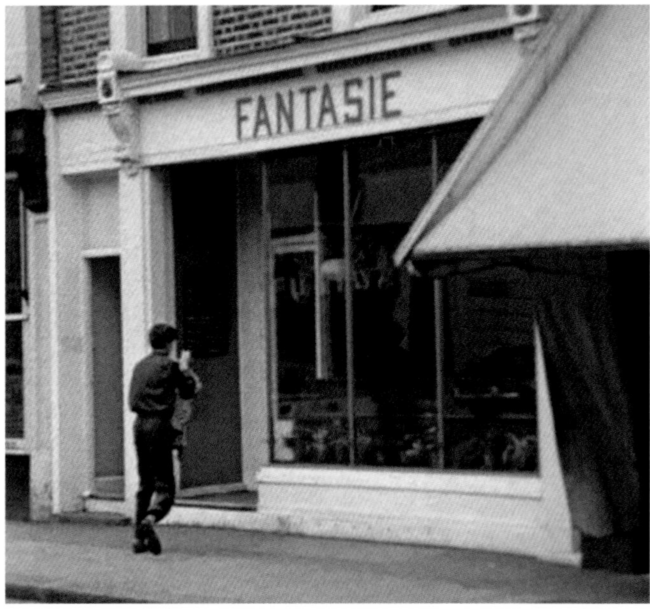

The exterior of Archie McNair's Fantasie, one of the first coffee bars on the King's Road, 1954.

By 1954, Plunket Greene and Quant were feeling, at the very least, somewhat alienated from their families and thoroughly rebellious; the scene was set for mischief and general high jinks, something they appear to have pursued with relish. It was while following this hedonistic career path, after returning from an impromptu excursion to the South of France (financed by the sale of a pair of cufflinks for £350, a bequest from Plunket Greene's uncle) that they first encountered Archie McNair, eventually to be the third vital ingredient in the phenomenon that became Bazaar. They were introduced to him in the bar of Finches, a popular watering hole in the King's Road, much frequented by members of the Chelsea Set. McNair's influence was to prove immense, not only for the success of the future Bazaar, but for the whole Chelsea revolution. He was an ex-solicitor turned photographer, who still retained an umbrella and briefcase, and spoke in the 'precise and pedantic way that one associates with solicitors ... he seemed oddly out of place in his photographic studio and this in itself was odd, as it was there that the whole Chelsea revolution was conceived ... The coffee bars, the restaurants and even Bazaar would not have happened if he had not spotted the talent of the people who sat around his studio drinking his coffee. Nor would they have happened without his flair for property and his knowledge of the law and business.' [11]

At that time, 1954, McNair was about to open the Fantasie, one of the first coffee bars on the King's Road. 'It became the centre of the social life of Chelsea ... the whole Chelsea thing really brewed up there ... between the Fantasie, Finches and Archie's studio.' [12]

One of the photographers McNair then employed in his studio was Antony Armstrong-Jones, who a little later became the Earl of Snowdon when he married The Queen's sister, Princess Margaret. As chance would have it, Terence Conran, not long returned from his first visit to France, was then also in the process of opening a coffee bar in the King's Road, The Orrery. This, however, was not Conran's first sortie in the food and drinks industry, as the previous year, 1953, he and a friend, Ivan Storey, had opened the Soup Kitchen, a very stylish but inexpensive eatery in the Covent Garden area of London, which is probably best described as an early British attempt at a bistro. It is here the origins of Conran's later career as a restaurateur are first discernible.

The principal influence on this new style of eating, meeting and greeting places was France, particularly the open, relaxed cafe culture of Paris and the rich, generous cuisine of Provence. In essence, the Soup Kitchen and The Orrery coffee bar were early attempts by the young Conran to recreate, amid the general drabness of post-war London, environments both emotionally and atmospherically allied to what the art critic Robert Hughes called, in his description of the influence of the south of France on the sensual pleasures of Picasso's art and the brilliantly coloured designs of Matisse, 'visions of harmony and delight ... a landscape imagined as Arcadia ... a landscape of Pleasure.' [13]

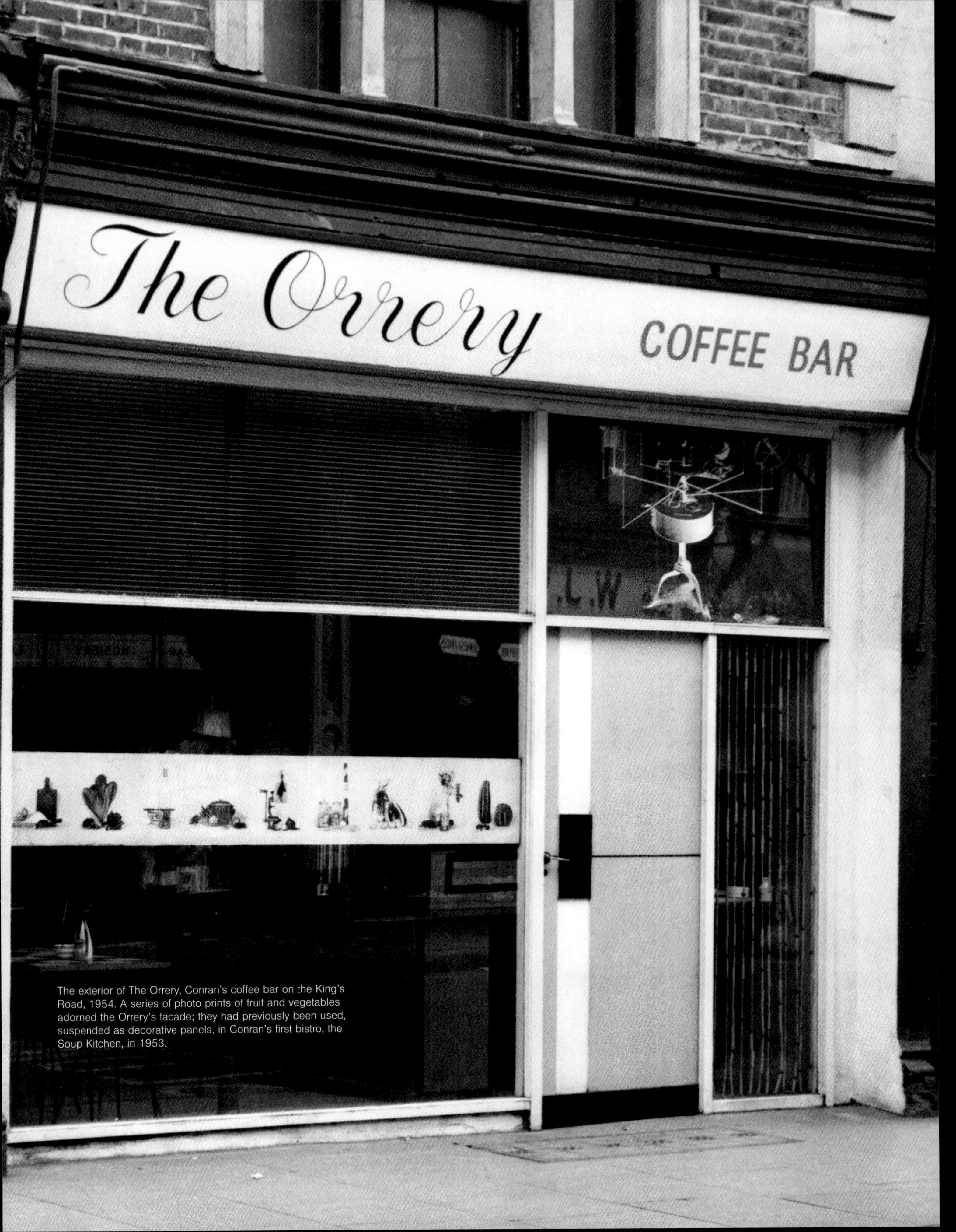

The exterior of The Orrery, Conran's coffee bar on the King's Road, 1954. A series of photo prints of fruit and vegetables adorned the Orrery's facade; they had previously been used, suspended as decorative panels, in Conran's first bistro, the Soup Kitchen, in 1953.

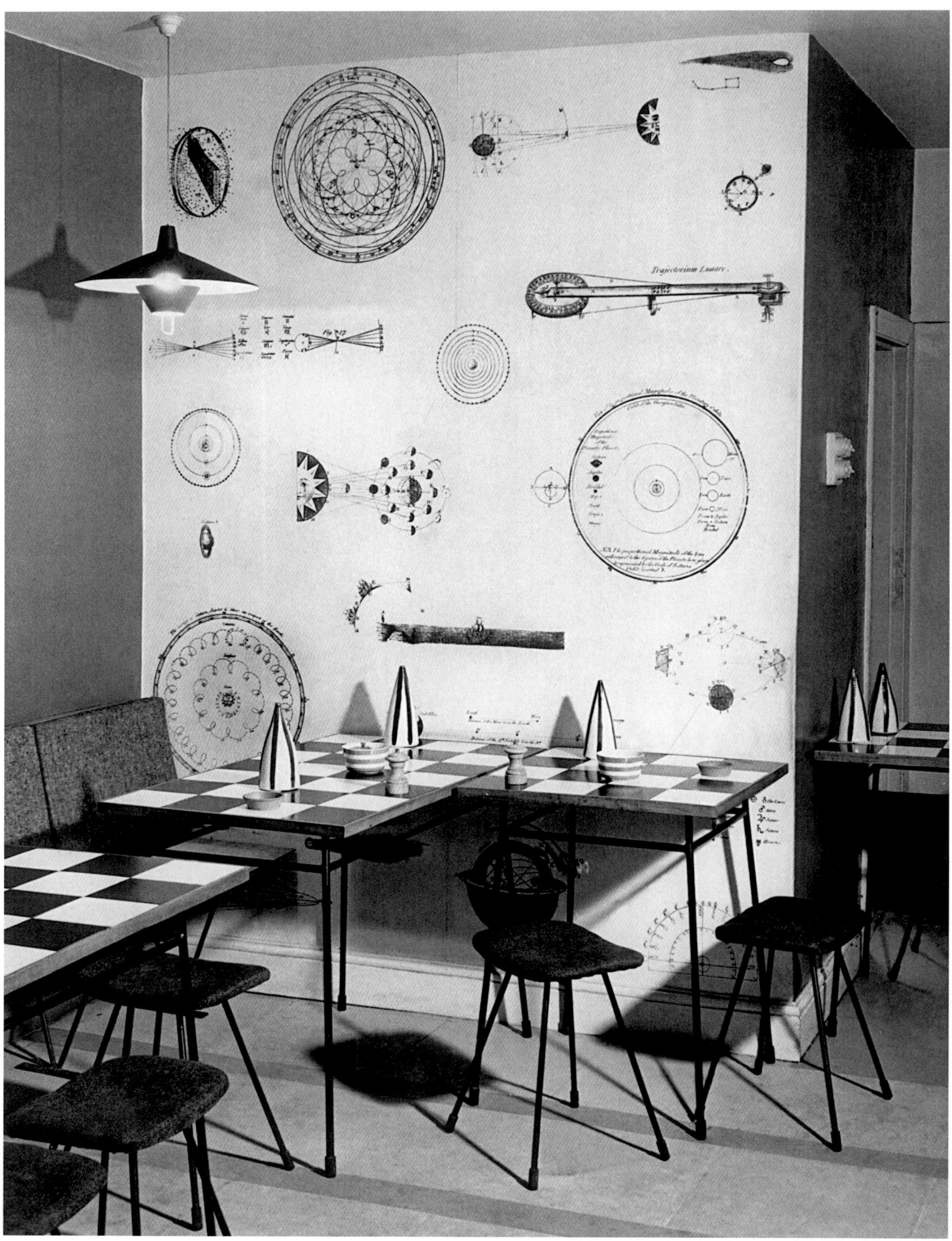

Opposite: Interior of The Orrery coffee bar, 1954.

Below: Wicker chair designed by Conran used in the Soup Kitchen, 1953. The frame of welded steel rod would have been made by him.

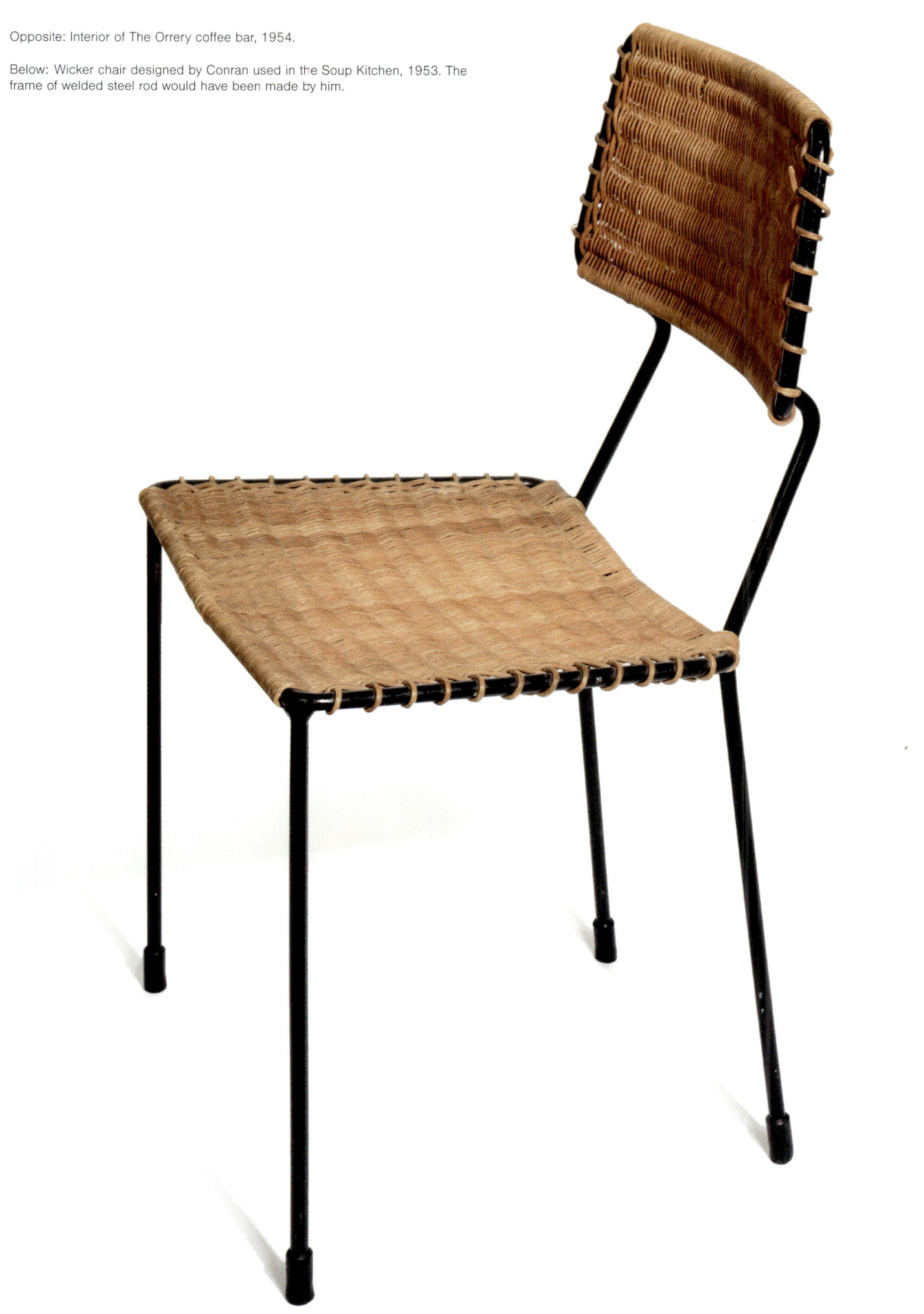

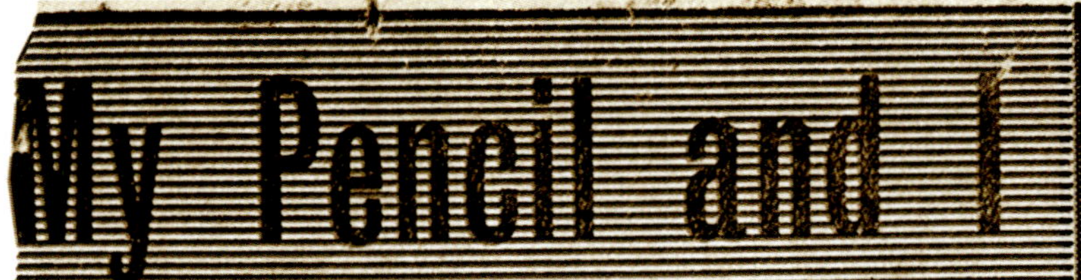

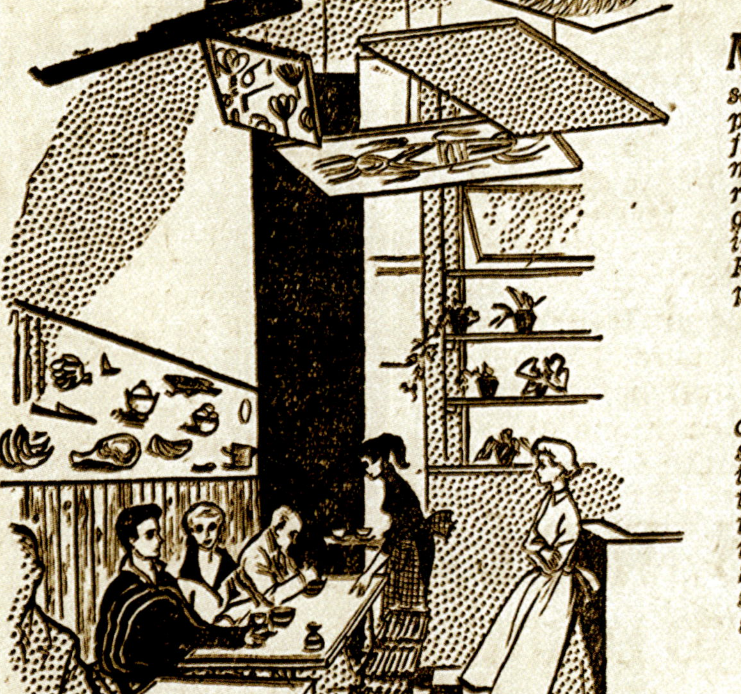

SOUP KITCHEN, 1953

NOT far from Trafalgar-square I found the sou kitchen with a difference—it doesn't serv soup only and it's madly contemporary. First sur prise is a vivid red wall. The ceiling is black, th floor chequered black and white. Lights ar masked by suspended boards coloured white, gre red and thunder blue, or covered with huge photo graphs of egg whisks and decorative old engrav ings. Eighteenth-century engravings from an ol French cookery book make an unusual mural— piles of prawns, joints of meat, artichokes. . . . .

☆

On the long bench seat below are zebra-stripe cushions. The light wood tables and cane-toppe stools have the slim, black iron legs seen so muc in Italy lately. They were designed, with the in terior, by Terence Conran, a young designer c textiles and furniture, who runs the soup kitche with two friends. Theatre folk come from nearb St. Martin's-lane to enjoy the French chef's onio soup or minestrone, served up in blue and whit striped bowls.

Drawing by Vivien Hislop of the Soup Kitchen's interior.
Published in *The Evening News*, 1953.

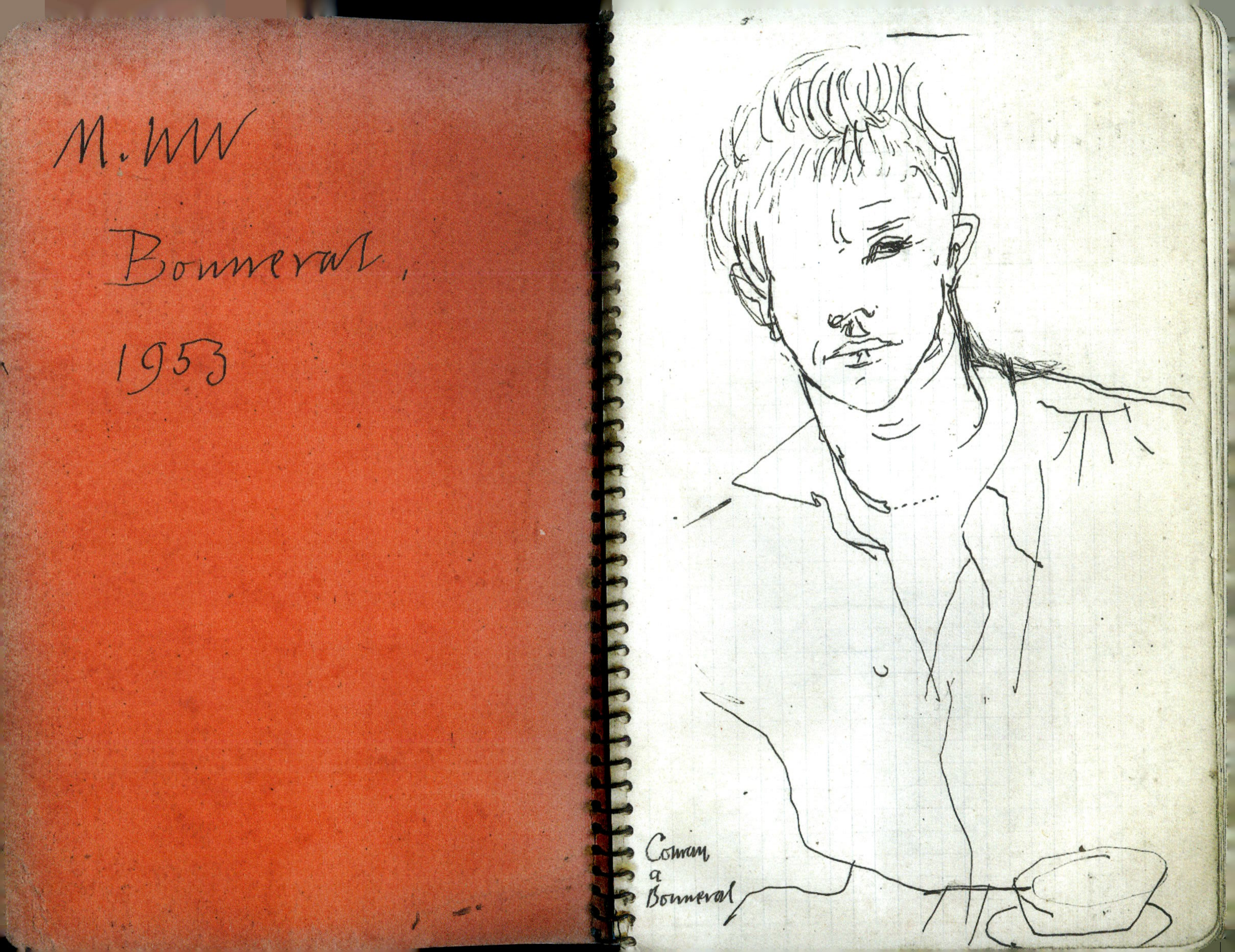
M.W
Bonneval,
1953
Cosman
a
Bonneval

BOOKS
AND
COOKS

DESPITE ITS HORRORS, many young British serving overseas in the Second World War were afforded glimpses of, or even experienced brief encounters with, fascinating cultures and sun-drenched lifestyles completely alien to the Protestant rectitude of their own chillier northern climes. Such wartime experiences later exerted a considerable influence on the mushroom growth of the post-war phenomena of inexpensive Mediterranean holidays and travel.

A PARTICULARLY EARLY expression of this post-war desire for hedonistic escapism was the publication in 1948 of *Time Was Away: A notebook in Corsica*. Written by the poet Alan Ross and illustrated by the Neo-romantic painter John Minton, the book is a paean to Mediterranean culture. Minton's drawings, a tour de force of images of the island's sun-baked landscapes, rich fecundity and laissez-faire lifestyle, were subsequently a major influence on the style of travel posters in the 1950s.

MINTON CAME AGAIN TO the fore of popular attention in 1950, when he illustrated what is possibly one of the most influential books in British post-war cultural history, Elizabeth David's *A Book of Mediterranean Food*. In parts anecdotal, a travelogue and an etiquette and recipe book full of wry humour, its publication was the opening shot in the revolution in British culinary skills, eating habits and lifestyle, which occurred in post-war Britain. Later, in the 1960s, spurred on by the popularity of Terence Conran's Habitat stores, David followed up the spectacular success of her books by opening a shop in Pimlico, on the fringes of Chelsea, selling kitchen equipment, for which, largely due to her own good offices, there was a growing demand. All of the stock sold in the shop was personally selected and approved by her.

THE WRITER Auberon Waugh once said of Elizabeth David that she would get his vote as the single person most responsible for improving British life in the twentieth century. The success of *A Book of Mediterranean Food* and her later books such as *French Country Cooking* (1951) – also illustrated by Minton – influenced the style and reinforced the popularity of not only coffee bars but also the multitude of bistros, brasseries and trattorias that spread out across the country from the King's Road in the later 1950s and 1960s.

IN ELIZABETH DAVID'S wake followed the American Robert Carrier, whose influential ideas on food and lifestyle were initially brought to the public's awareness through his weekly cookery column for the ground-breaking *Sunday Times Colour Section*. The first such by any British newspaper, it was said to have broken the mould of weekend newspaper publishing. The cover of the *Colour Section's* first issue, on 4 February 1962, featured a photograph by David Bailey of the iconic 1960s model Jean Shrimpton wearing a Mary Quant dress – a microcosm of early Pop culture.

THE SUPPLEMENT was not officially called *The Sunday Times Magazine* until 1963. That same year Carrier's cookery writings for it were published as *Great Dishes of the World*, the success of which was followed up in 1965 by the *Robert Carrier Cookbook*. The social changes brought about, in part, by all this sudden, somewhat frenetic, culinary activity were reinforced by Egon Ronay's *Guide to British Eateries*, the first of which was published in 1957. To be mentioned in a Ronay guide subsequently became a much sought-after mark of distinction among increasingly competitive and ambitious British restaurateurs.

THE ESTABLISHMENT OF Conran's and McNair's coffee bars and, a little later, Plunket Greene's proto-brasserie, Alexander's, are very early examples of this change in lifestyle and attitude which signalled the emergence of the King's Road as the fulcrum of Pop culture in Swinging London. The Soup Kitchen and The Orrery coffee bar were directly inspired by Conran's first visit to France in 1953. One of the great turning points in his life, it was for him a revelatory moment. Like many British, both before and since, he was ravished by the ambiance of the country, its style and culture.

'I was overwhelmed by the sensual quality of everyday French life, the markets, the food in roadside cafes, the simple unpretentious but abundant displays on stalls and in shops. The food was always delicious, washed down with carafes of rough red wine generously thrown in for free...' [14]

'My thinking at the time – whether to do with furniture or food – was "why shouldn't good things be available at a price ordinary people could afford?" Anything that was good in England at that time was out of reach for ordinary people. In France, food and other everyday things – stoneware, terracotta, pottery, pots and pans – were affordable for all.' [15]

IT WAS PROBABLY then that Conran first conceived of something he later gave expression to in the setting up of Habitat, his major contribution to the post-war revolution in British culture and lifestyle.

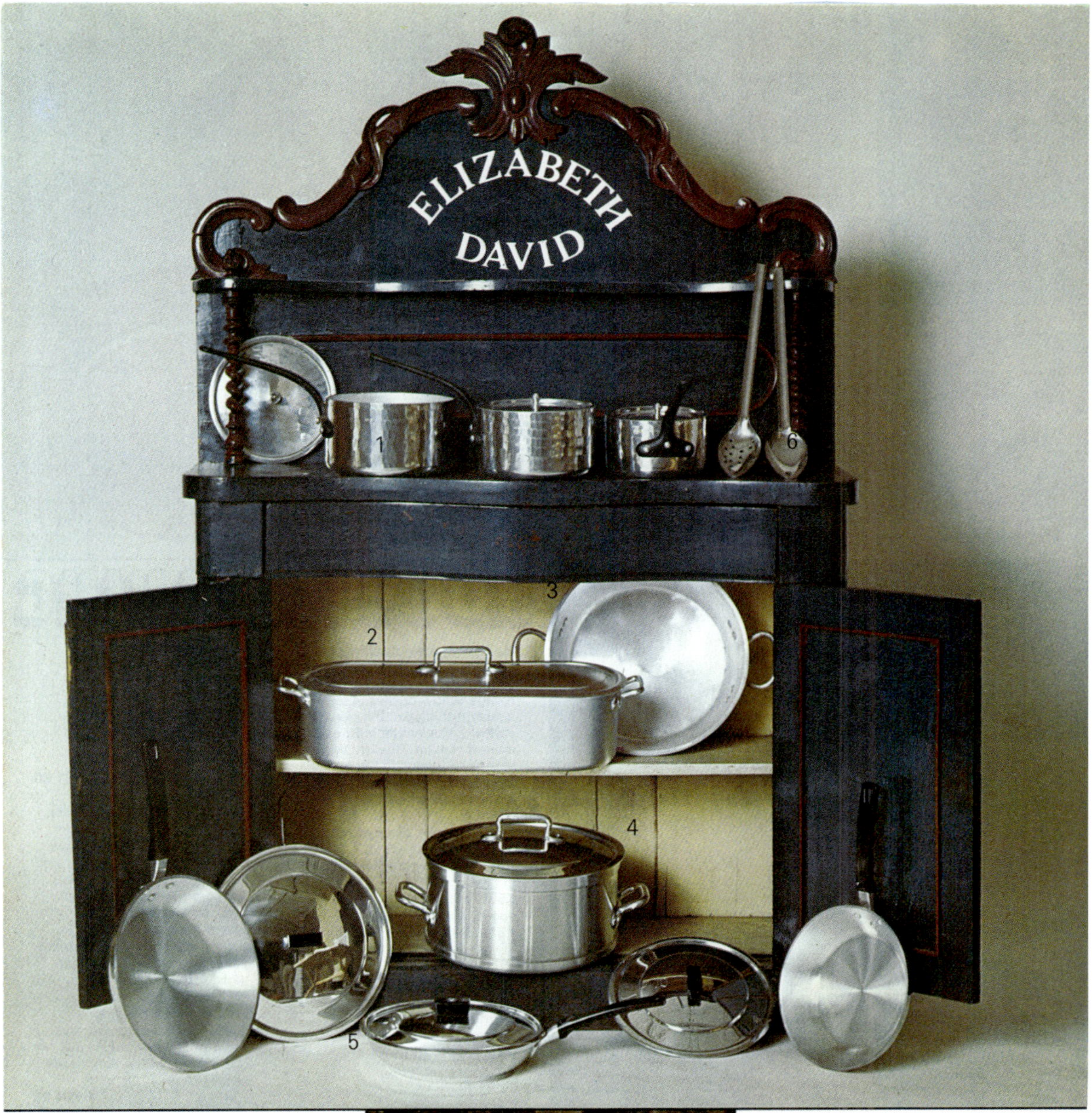

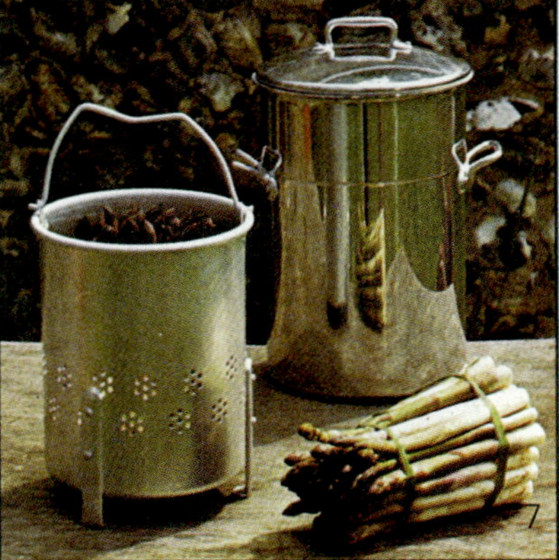

This year we have asked Elizabeth David, probably the world's most authoritative food and cookery writer, to contribute her own section to the Habitat catalogue. She has been entirely free to make her own choice and has selected for Habitat customers a basic *batterie de cuisine* from the very best equipment made in France and all over the world. Often the items are not cheap but, as readers of her books will know, Mrs. David has sound reasons for her preferences and explains them with conviction. Over the years Mrs. David has been responsible for introducing many people to the fundamental equipment of cookery, to the pots and pans of provincial France and to the once neglected English traditions. We now make this range available to an even wider audience in a form which could almost be regarded as an illustrated appendix to her own books.

We regret it is not possible to hold orders pending a delivery date or delivery address

A display of Elizabeth David's *Batterie de Cuisine* in a Habitat Catalogue, 1971.

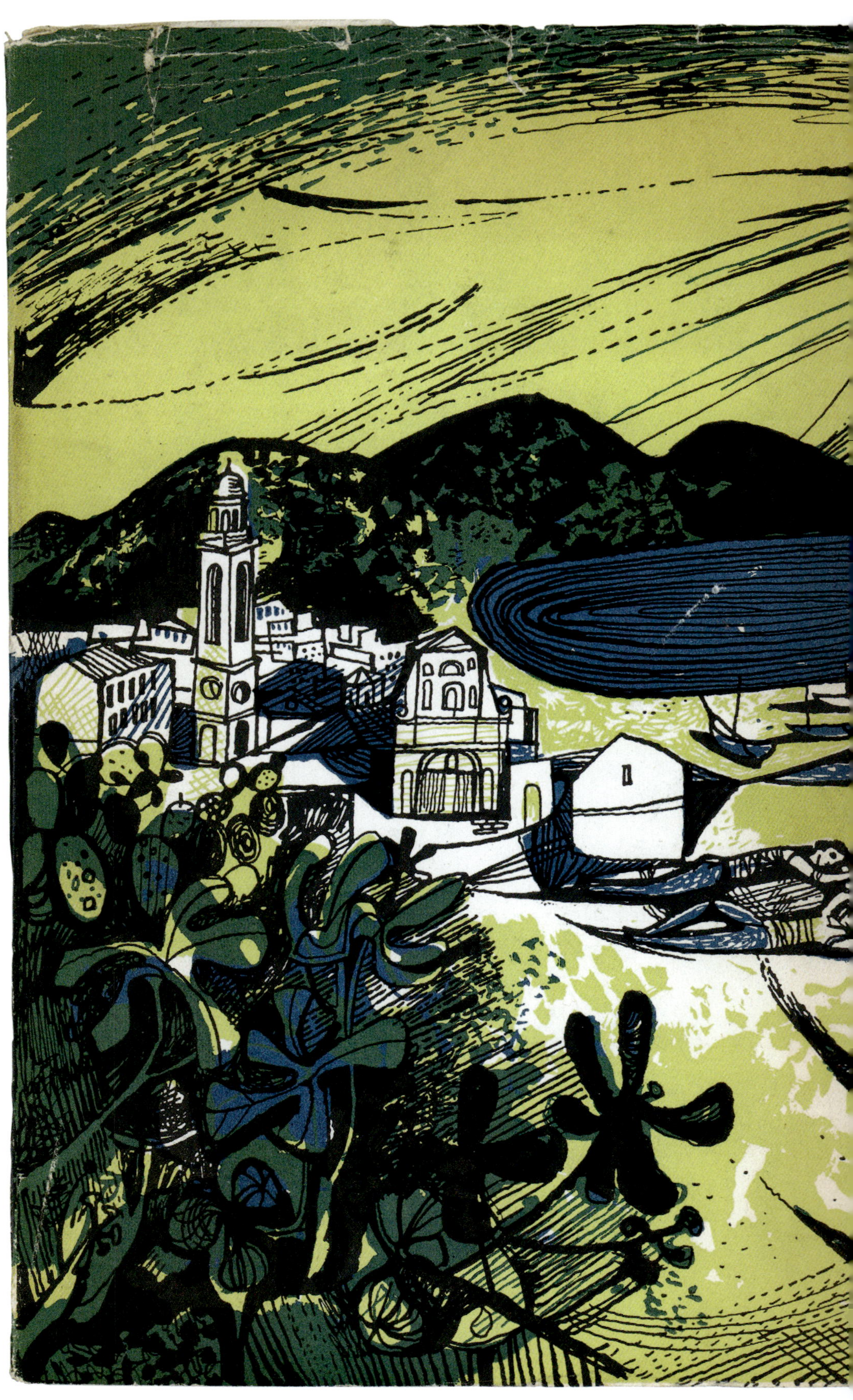

The dust jacket of *Time Was Away* by the poet Alan Ross, illustrated by John Minton, 1948.

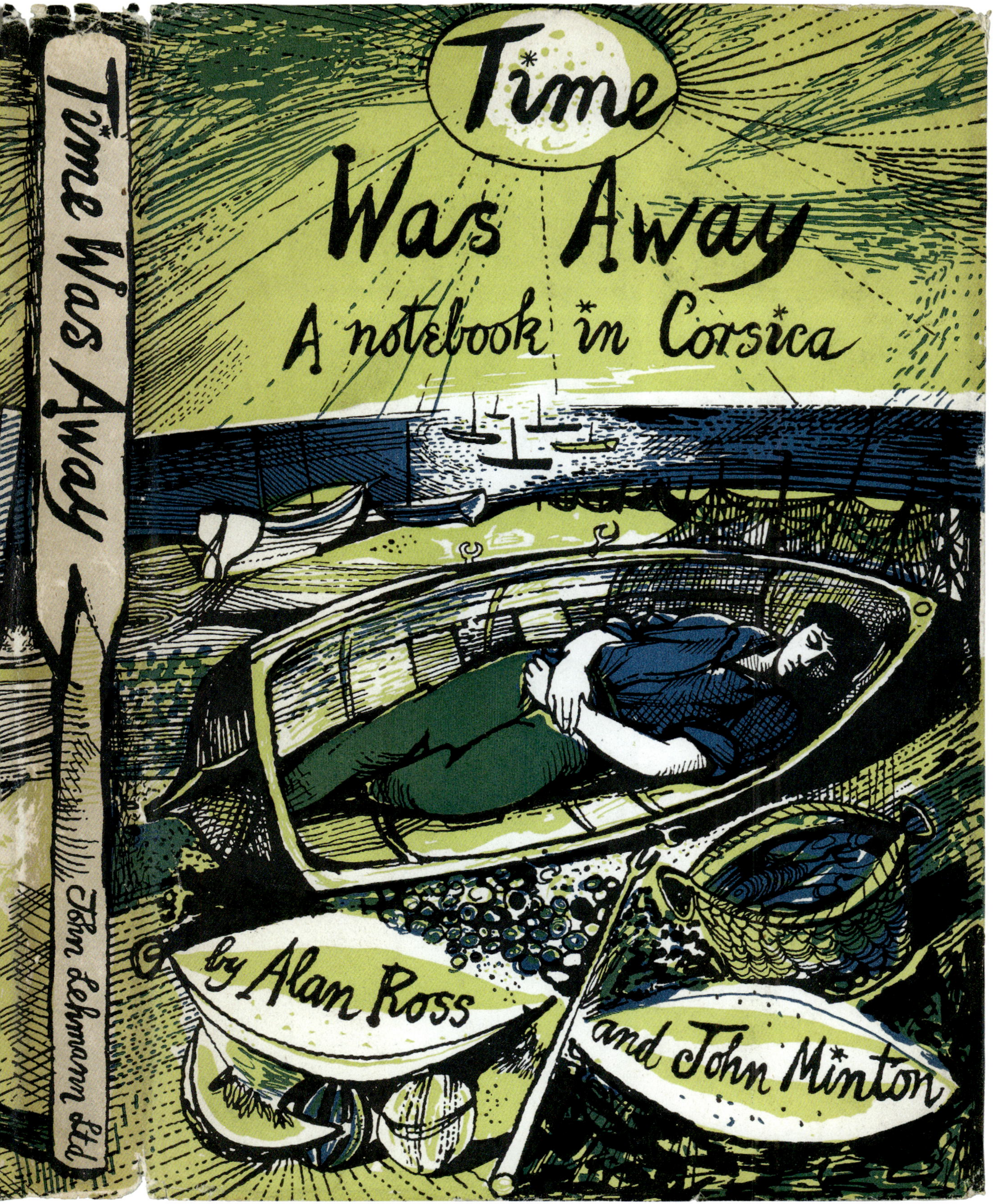
Time
Was Away
A notebook in Corsica
by Alan Ross
and John Minton
Time Was Away · John Lehmann Ltd

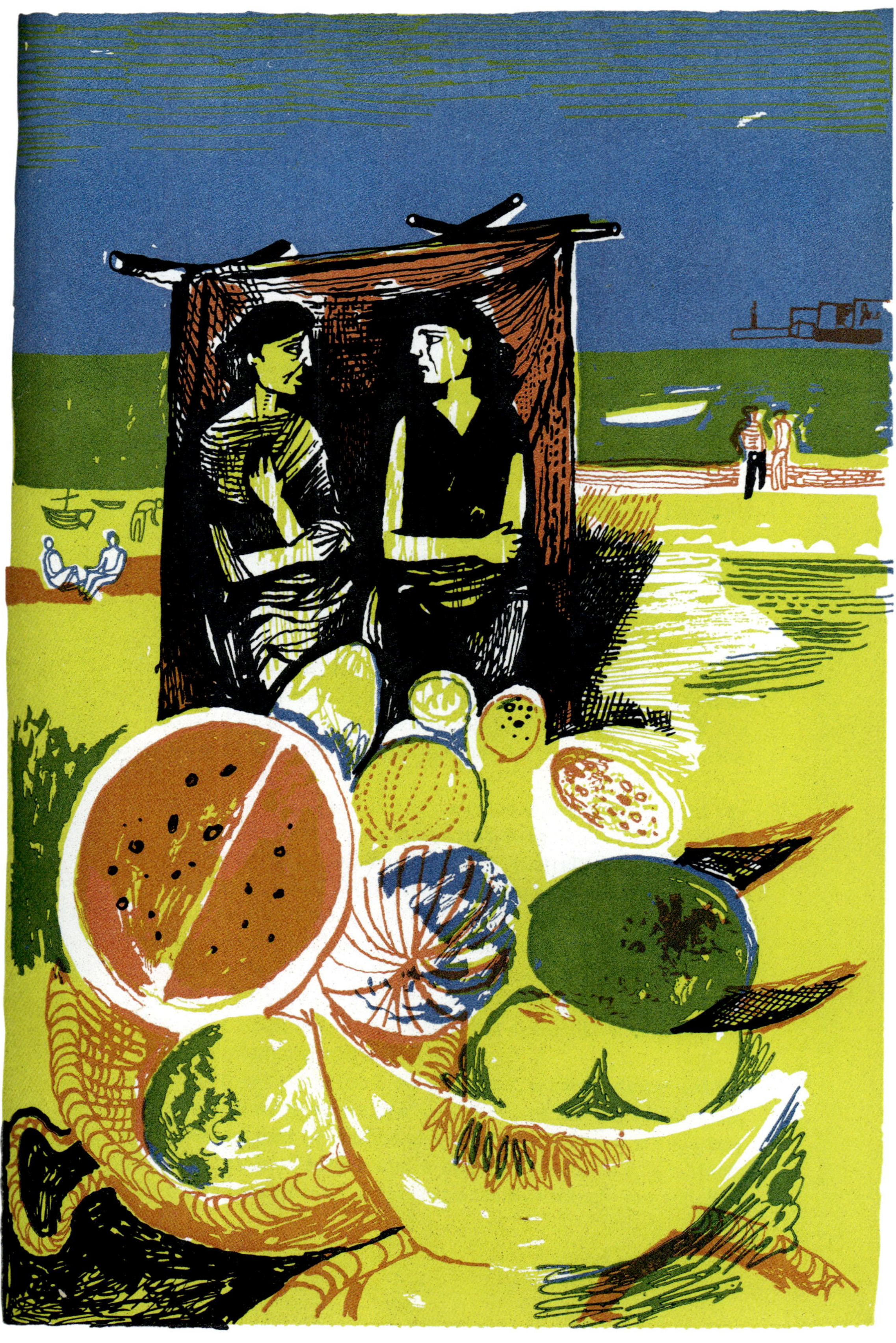

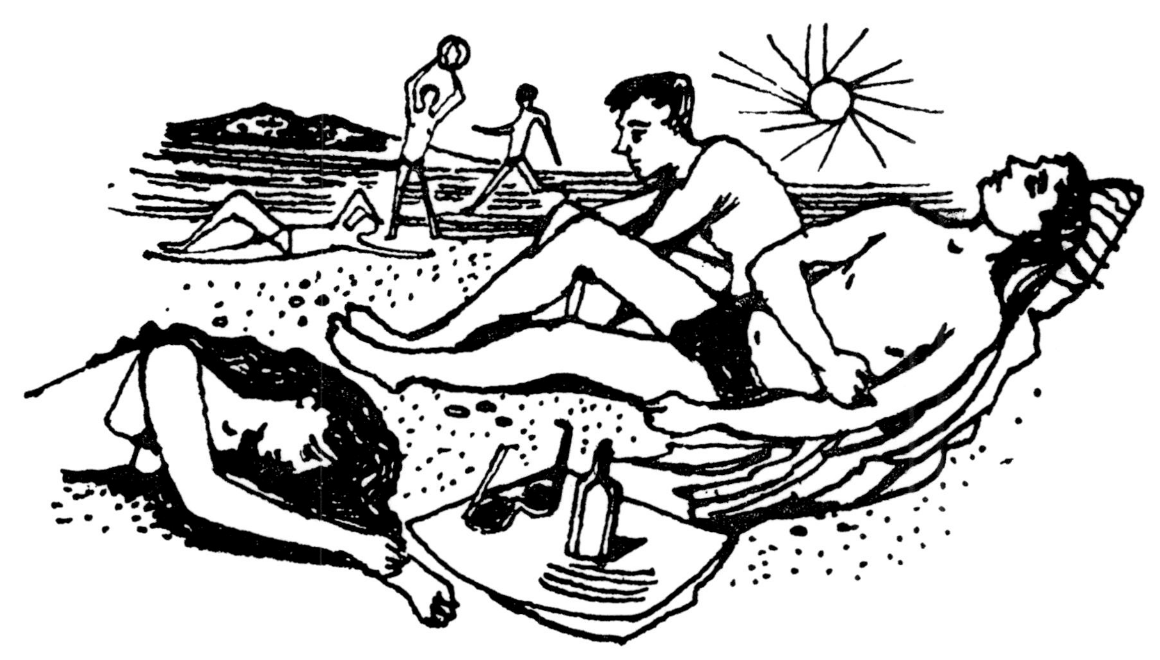

A vignette from *Time Was Away* succinctly anticipates the hedonistic dreams of millions in the following decades.

Opposite: Illustration from *Time Was Away*. The artist John Minton's illustrative style subsequently influenced the design of many travel posters in the 1950s.

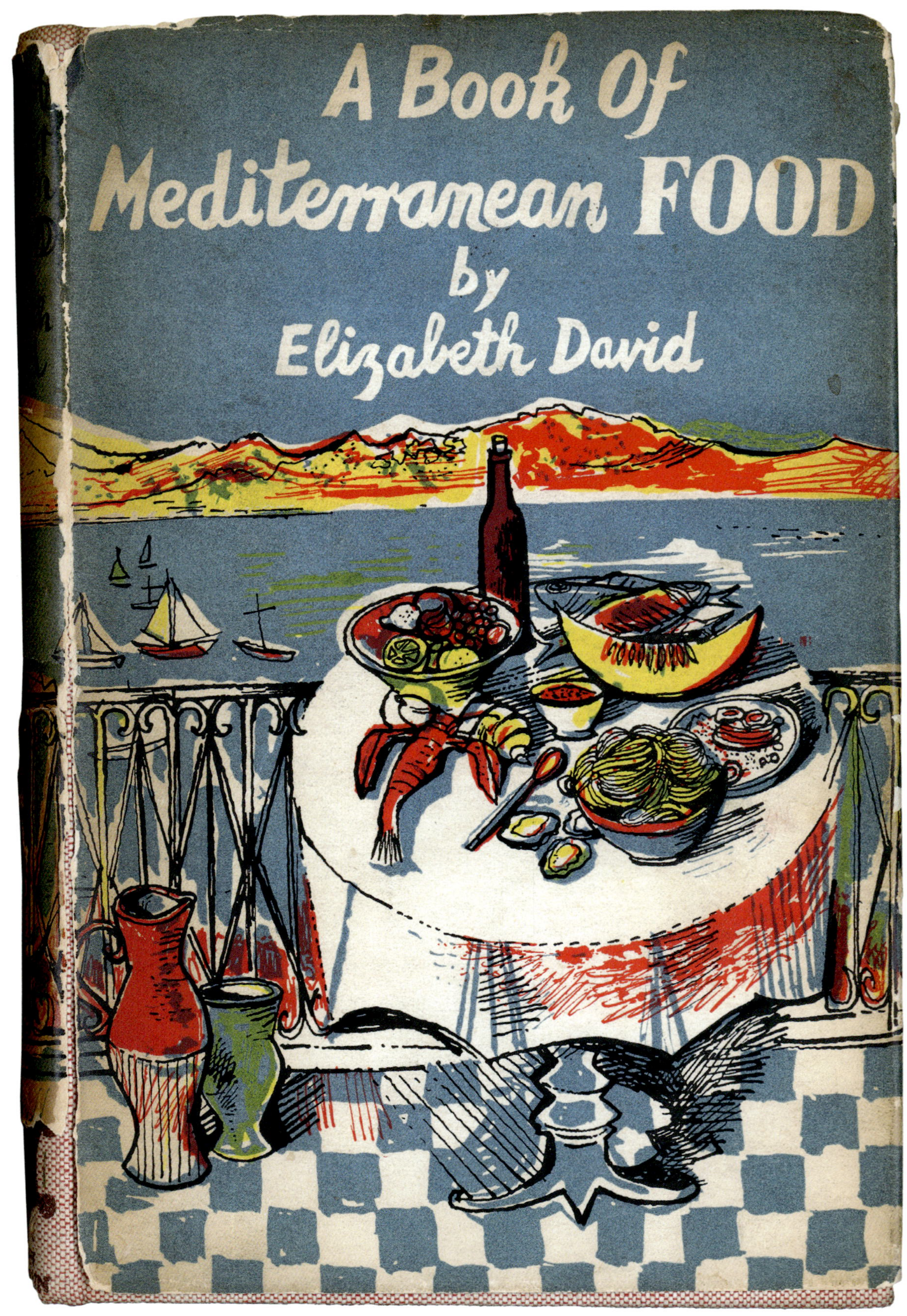

The dust jacket of A Book of Mediterranean Food, by Elizabeth David, illustrated by John Minton, 1950. The book is Elizabeth David's major contribution to the radical change of lifestyle in post-war Britain.

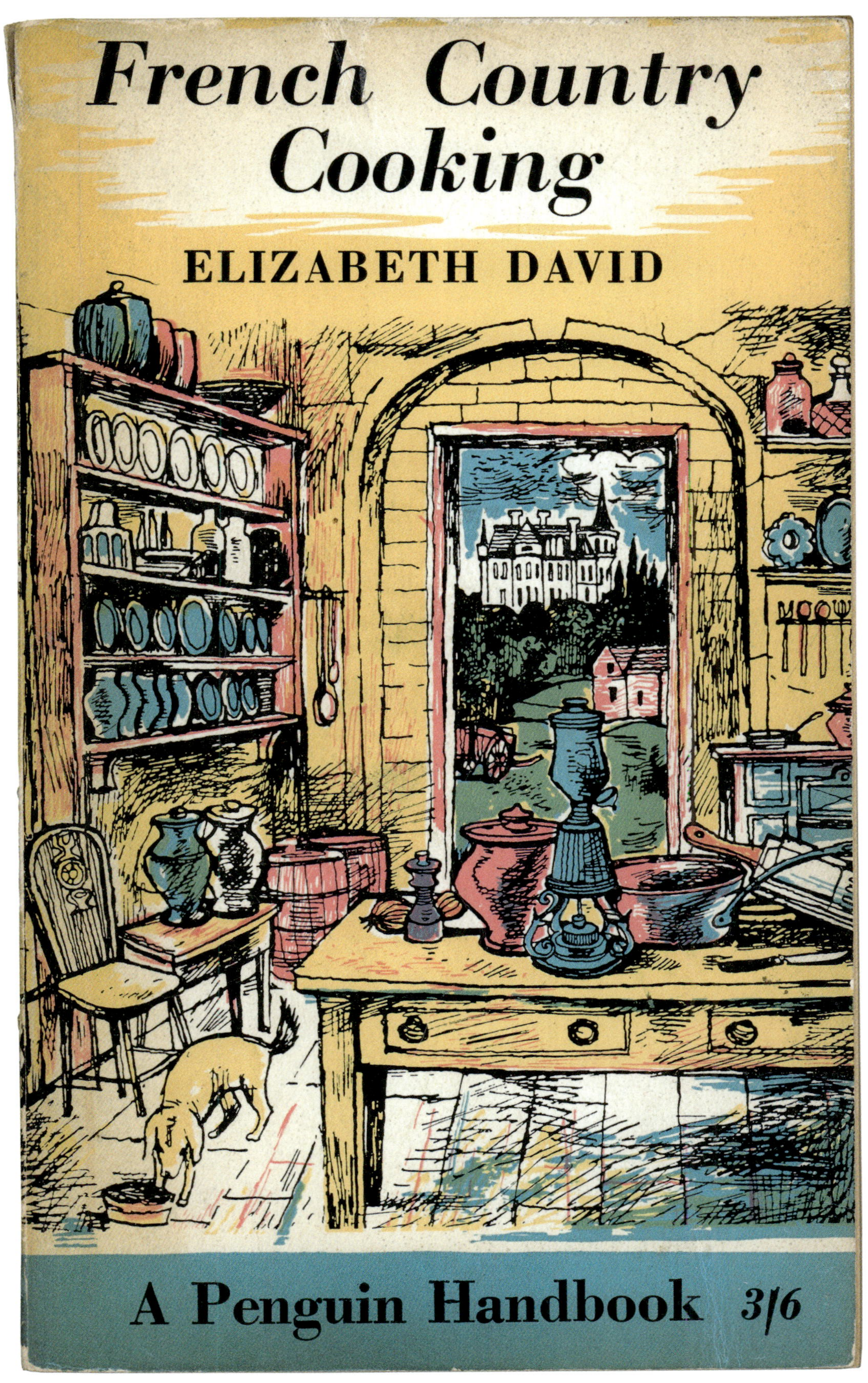

The cover of Elizabeth David's *French Country Cooking*, illustrated by John Minton.
First Penguin edition, 1959.

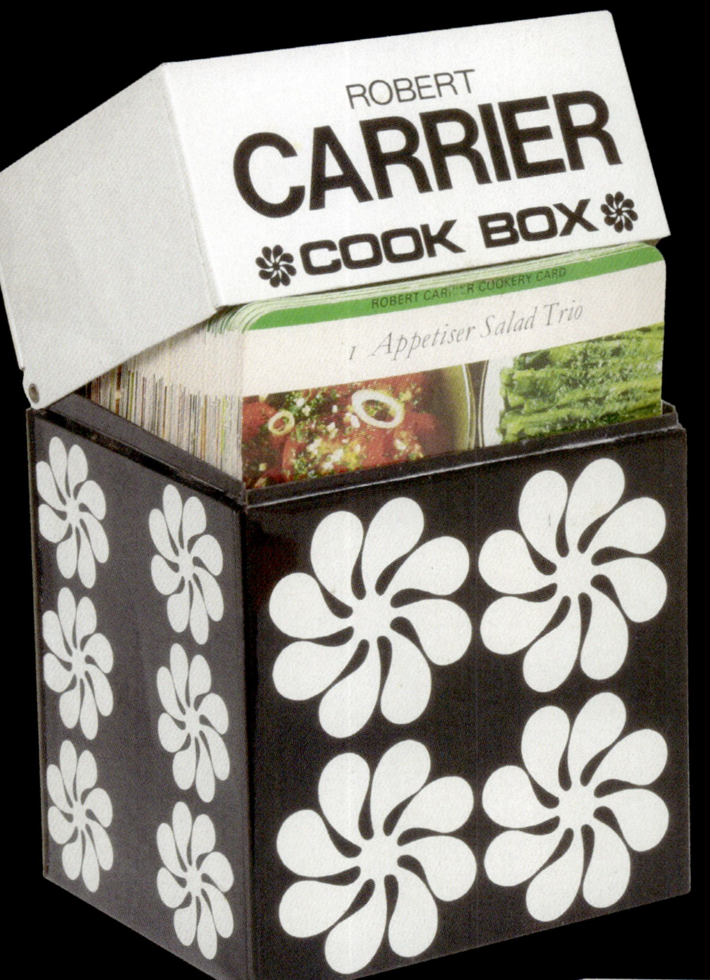

Left: Robert Carrier's tin
'Cook Box', 1967. Below:
The two-volume boxed set of
Carrier's *Great Dishes of the
World*, 1963, and *The Robert
Carrier Cookbook*, 1965.

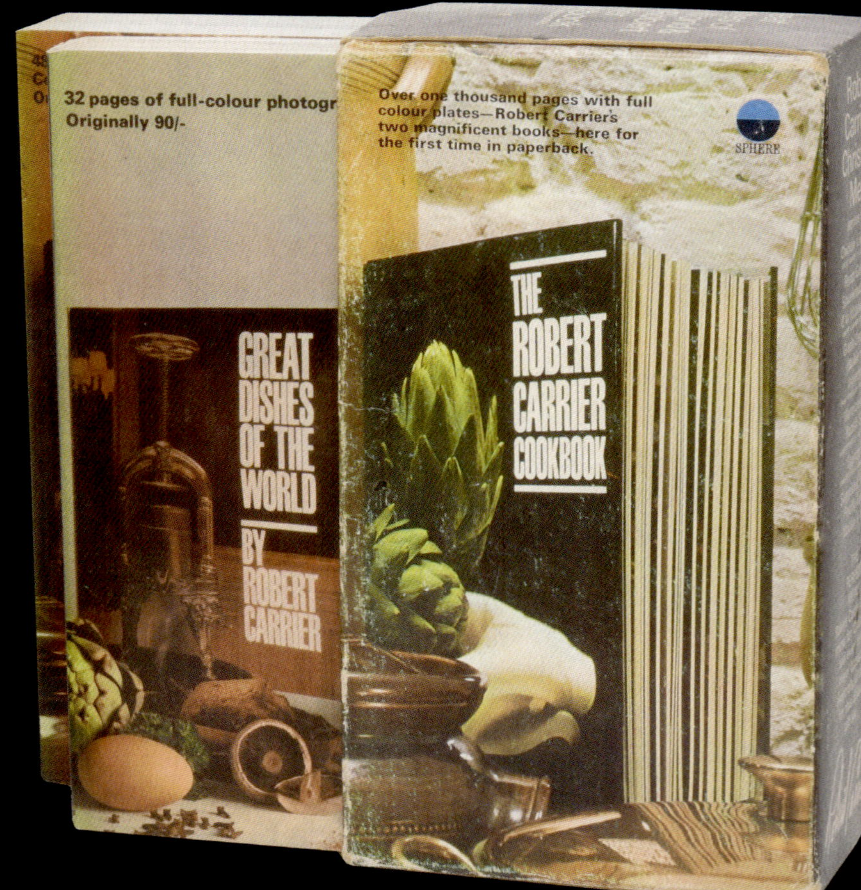

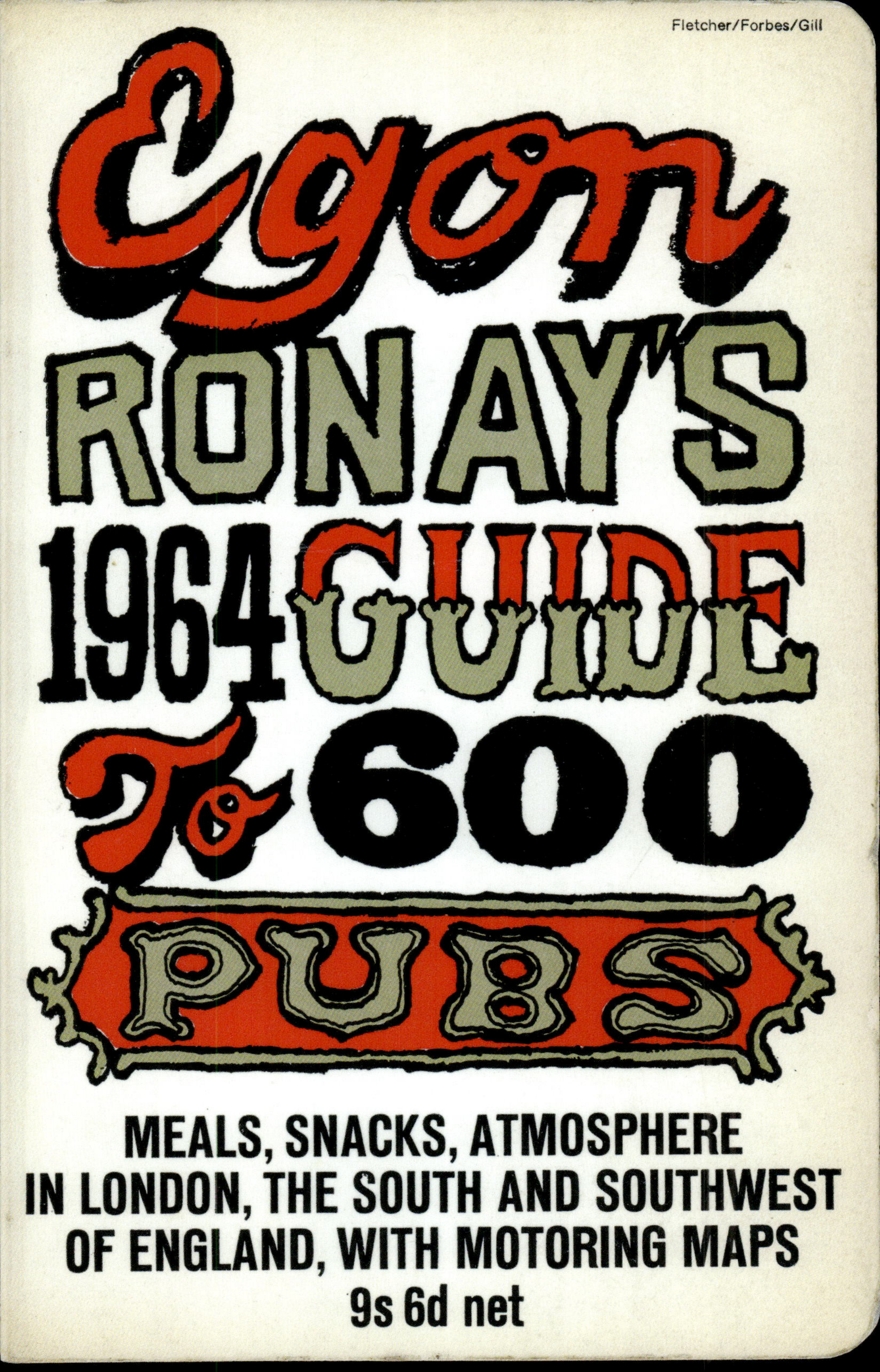

Egon Ronay's

1964 GUIDE TO 600 PUBS

MEALS, SNACKS, ATMOSPHERE IN LONDON, THE SOUTH AND SOUTHWEST OF ENGLAND, WITH MOTORING MAPS

9s 6d net

To be mentioned in a Ronay guide was a much sought-after mark of distinction

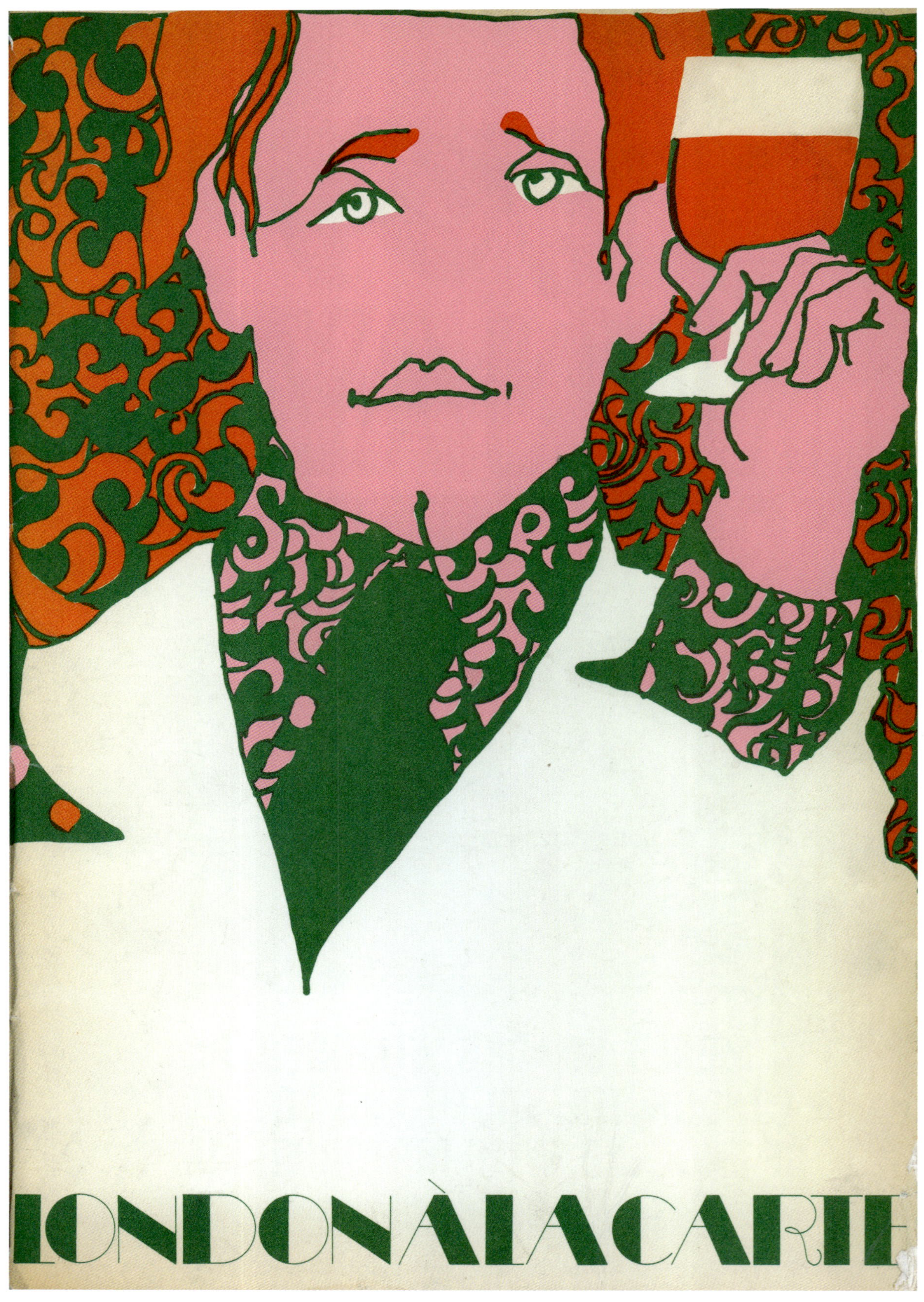

Cover of the folder *London: À la Carte*, the Habitat restaurant guide. Designed by
Agneta Neroth, compiled by Caroline Conran, 1967.

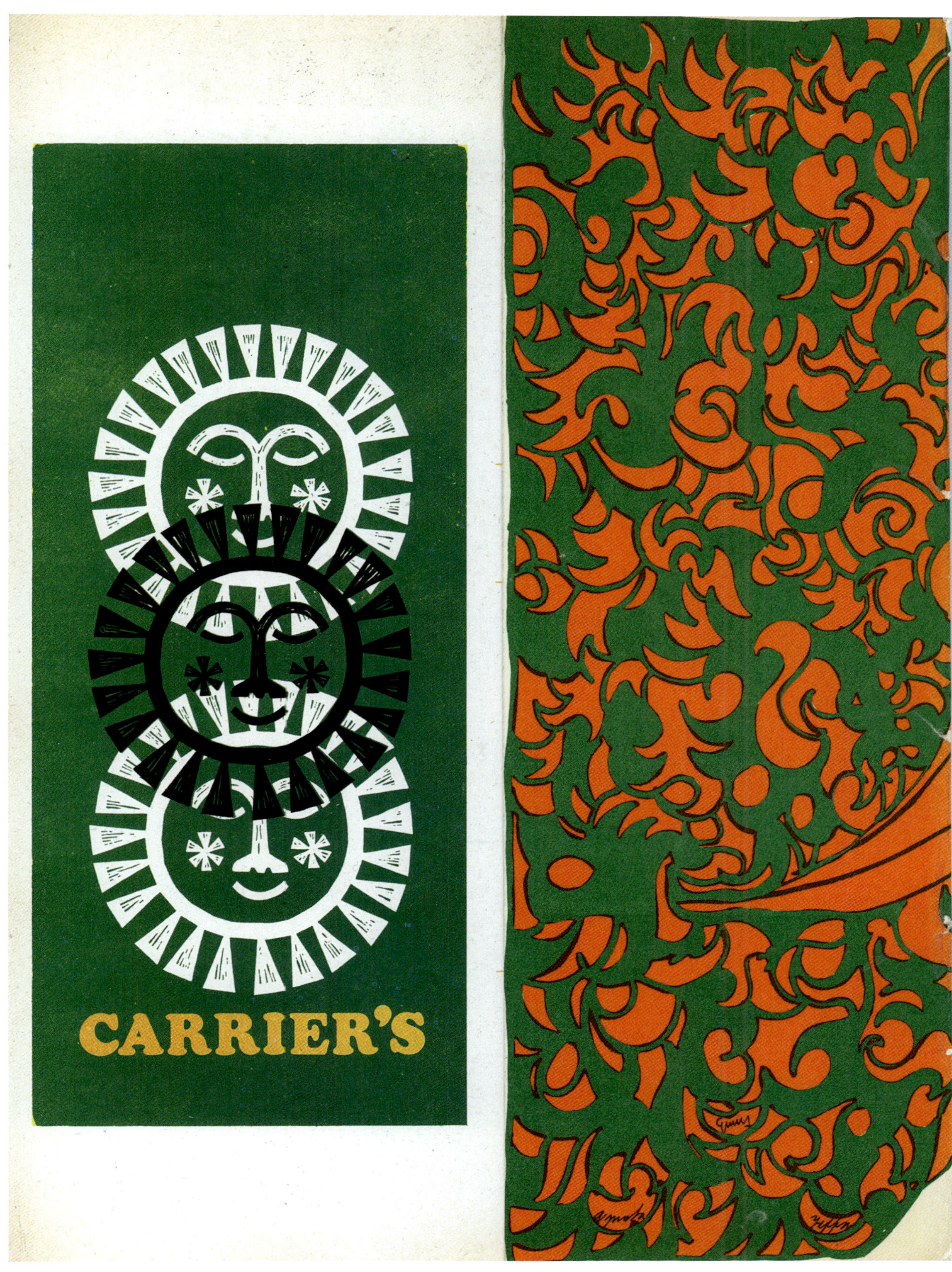

Menu for Robert Carrier's restaurant in Islington, from *London: À La Carte*, 1967.

MARY QUANT:
BAZAAR NO.1

ALTHOUGH INITIALLY thwarted by her parents in her desire to be a fashion designer, and having finished her course at Goldsmiths somewhat ingloriously, Quant managed to obtain employment making hats for Erik, a Mayfair-based society hat designer, for the covetable wage of £2.10 shillings a week (£2.50), but, as always, she continued to either create or adapt her clothes to her own designs. However, her tenacity and determination, coupled with her undeniable, if somewhat wacky and off-beat talent, obviously impressed Archie McNair sufficiently for him to propose that she, with himself and Plunket Greene, set up in the fashion business. Fortunately, Plunket Greene had just inherited £5,000 on his twenty-first birthday, which McNair was prepared to match.

> *'We would open a shop. It was to be a bouillabaisse of clothes and accessories ... sweaters, scarves, shifts, hats, jewellery and peculiar odds and ends. We would call it Bazaar. I would be the buyer... This was something I desperately wanted to do.'* [16]

EVEN AS A CHILD, Quant had always held very distinct ideas on fashion, particularly for young people like herself. She rejected the dominant fashionable styles of the 1950s, which were essentially a continuation or variations of the 'New Look' created by the Parisian couturier Christian Dior, which he'd launched in 1947. The concepts and philosophy behind the New Look and haute couture fashion in general represented everything that not only Quant, but many other young women, rejected from the mid 1950s onwards.

AN INTEGRAL FEATURE of the New Look was the return of the hourglass figure, which necessitated women being once more encased in heavily boned and tightly laced corsetry, something which had already been banished by the early 1920s under the influence of the couturiers Paul Poiret and Coco Chanel. In yet another apparently retrograde step, unlike the shorter skirts associated with Chanel and her ilk in the pre-war era, the very full skirts of many New Look dresses, supported by layers of stiffened petticoats, often dipped almost to the ankles; others, nearly as long, were extremely tight-fitting and either known as 'Pencil' or, more appropriately, 'Hobble' skirts.

PROBABLY, IN PART, a societal reaction to the relatively free and increasingly independent lifestyles that many women had, through necessity, experienced during the war, fashion and style in the immediate post-war years echoed those of the Edwardian era in a reinforcement of 'the obligatory yokes of husband and family insisted upon during the post-war reconstruction.' [17]

FASHION WAS THEN largely determined by male couturiers for their mainly middle-aged elite clientele. The needs of the average young woman were hardly, if ever, considered. Teenagers, a distinctly new life form from a world as alien to the fashion establishment as the planet Mars, were not considered at all. It was this situation that Quant was, almost unwittingly, preparing to take on when she opened Bazaar.

WITH THE ESTABLISHMENT of Bazaar, Quant irreversibly altered the traditional approach to both fashion design and retailing; predictably, the all-powerful French fashion establishment was initially outraged and dismissive. When, in 1959, Pierre Cardin – then the *enfant terrible* among the Parisian couturiers – designed his first *prêt-a-porter* collection under licence for the Printemps department store in Paris, the exclusive haute couture trade was so threatened that he was ignominiously expelled from the all-powerful Chambre Syndicale de la Couture Parisienne. He was reinstated not long after, however, and by the end of the 1960s most of the Paris fashion houses, having sense enough to recognise a losing battle when they saw one, had set up their own boutique outlets with more affordable *prêt-a-porter* collections. Quant subsequently voiced the

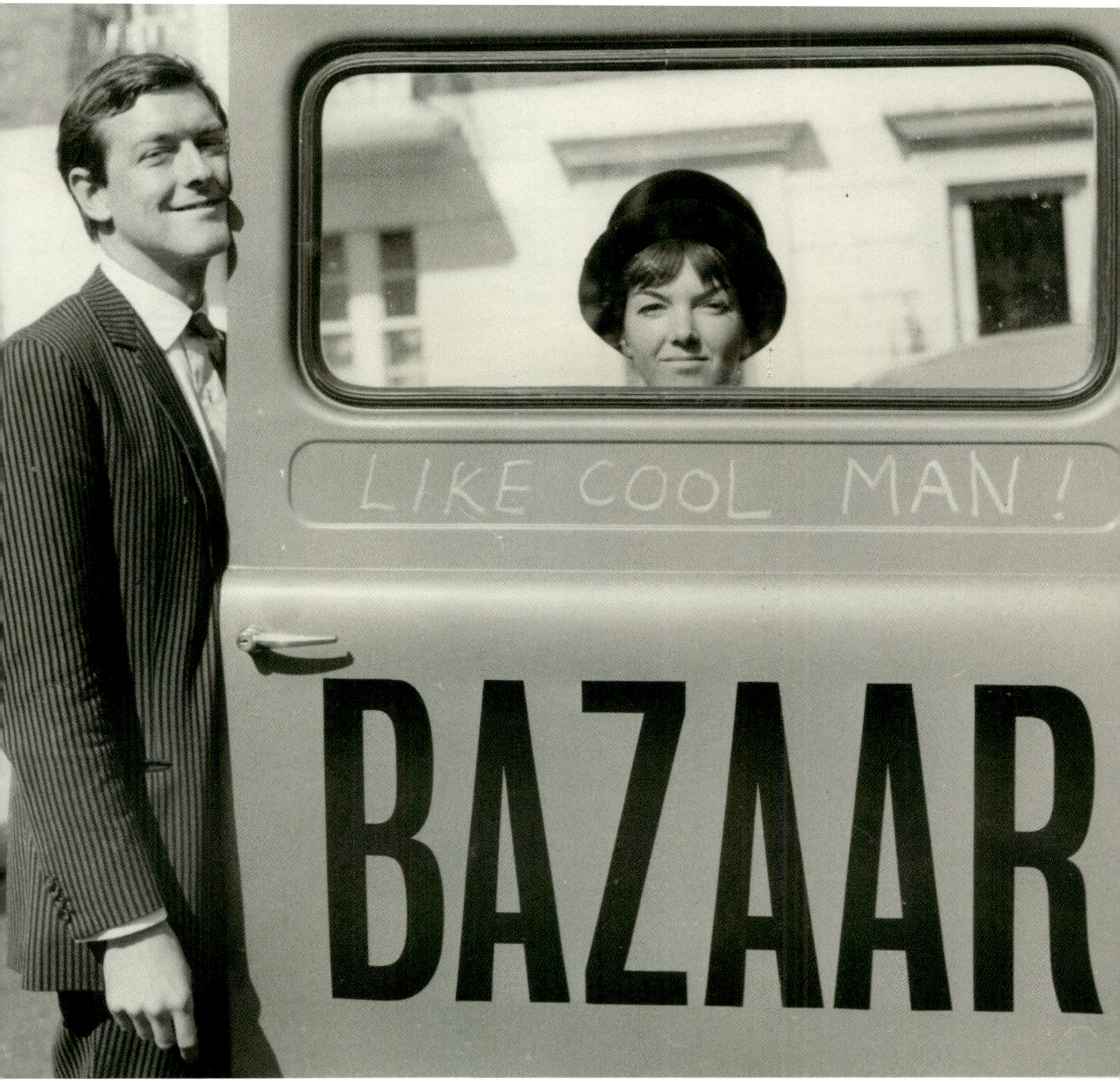

Mary Quant with Alexander Plunket Greene, 1961.

distress caused her by the snobbish and spiteful reception of her work by the French couture trade, when she wrote that:

'The Paris couture world did not like all this attention going to London and a British designer. So when the press told Coco Chanel that I admired her beyond all others, she said, "From her, it is a very small compliment." ...Other French couturiers said my designs were vulgar or gimmicky and some said I was "a flash in the pan". I began to call myself "a flash in the pan", but I was in fact pretty upset.' [18] *'Oh la la, this presumptuous little English girl spells Chic as Cheek.'* [19]

IT IS HARDLY overstating the case to say that with the opening of Bazaar in November, 1955, the concept of Swinging London first saw the light of day. However, it had not been an entirely painless procedure, having involved a lengthy and somewhat fraught tussle with the local planning authority and the Chelsea Society, concerning the conversion of the ground floor and basement of Markham House, a Georgian building on the King's Road, into a shop for Bazaar and the basement as a suitable venue for Alexander's, Plunket Greene's proposed brasserie and jazz bar.

HAVING WON THE struggle to physically establish Bazaar, Quant next faced the problem of what stock it should contain. She could find virtually nothing to buy that met her high expectations and soon came to the conclusion that she would not only have to design, but also make the stock herself, or find others prepared to make it for her. She installed a couple of sewing machines in her small flat and found a professional dress maker to work alongside her. Describing her early inexperienced and improvised method of work she wrote:

'I brought Butterick paper patterns and cut out pieces where I didn't want them and added more paper where I did ... I brought the materials from Harrods as no one had told me about buying cloth wholesale ... It was an extremely crude method of working ... I had to sell one day's

output before I had the money to go out and buy more material ... The dresses would be sold that evening so I'd be able to dash along to Harrods again in the morning with more money to spend ... because I was buying my cloth over the counter at Harrods, there wasn't a great deal of profit.' [20]

WHATEVER THE INITIAL teething problems, Bazaar was an immediate success. Most of the clientele were friends and acquaintances of Quant's and Plunket Greene's from among the Chelsea Set, the habitués of the King's Road scene of coffee bars, bistros and pubs, who all shared similar ideas of how they wanted to dress and look.

ELABORATE FULL-SKIRTED 'posh' frocks in luxurious fabrics and their poorer high street derivatives, often weighed down with jewellery, real or not, and unnecessary accessories – one of Quant's *bêtes noires* – were defiantly 'out'. Practical workhorse textiles such as grey flannel, rough textured tweeds and oddly – coloured cotton or wool jersey were used to realise radically plain and unadorned designs. Unstructured tunics or simple pinafore dresses with dropped waistlines, often worn with coloured stockings, were decidedly 'in'. Importantly, all were completely inappropriate attire for well-heeled ladies. Writing in the *New York Times Magazine* in 1967, the journalist Maureen Cleave succinctly summed up this essential aspect of the Quant philosophy: 'The young should look like the young ... The old could, if they wished, look like the young, but the young must not on any account look like the old.'

QUANT'S SIMPLE EASY youthful style originated in the numerous art colleges, like Goldsmiths, that sprung up around Britain after 1945. The primary influences on the art school look were American casuals and sportswear, especially the use of jersey and denim, and the easy styles affected by San Francisco's and New York's Beat generation. The gamine look, popular among the artists and intelligentsia of Paris's Left Bank bohemian cafe society, epitomised by the style of the singer Juliette Greco, was also de rigueur among students in general. All of this was regurgitated by Quant in a highly original fusion that also referenced the earlier work of Coco Chanel and the emancipated fashions of the 1920s. This was probably the first time that youthful street fashion both directly inspired and set the pace of international avant-garde style, something which has since become a leitmotif of British fashion.

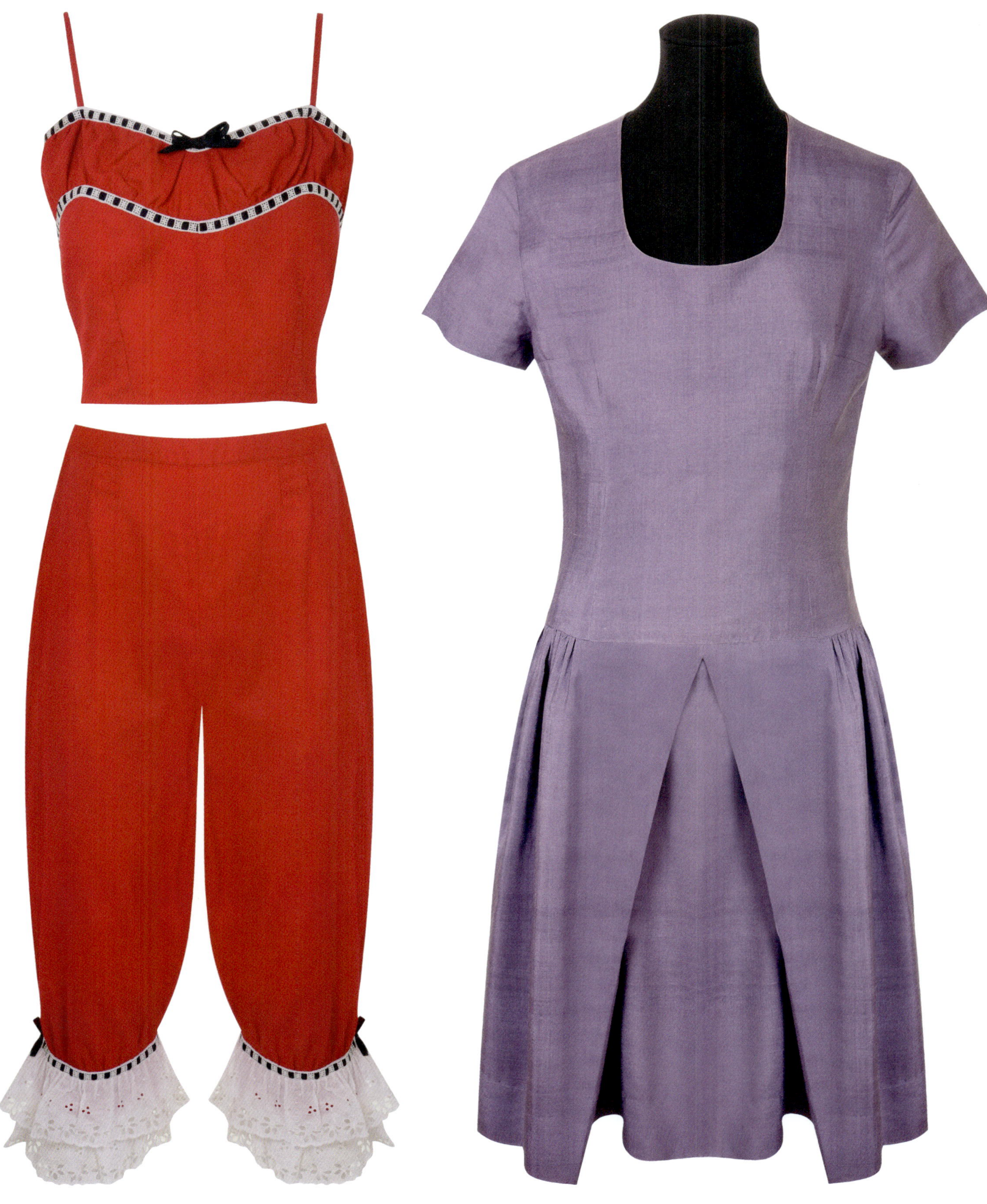

Lounging Pyjamas, c.1955-1956. Quant designed and sold sets of 'mad Lounging Pyjamas' on the occasion of Bazaar's opening in November 1955. The design of this set from the early Bazaar period clearly references late Victorian underwear and the risqué costumes worn by 'Saloon Gals' in Western movies and Edwardian 'Gaiety Girls'. They are remarkable items of early Pop fashion.

A lilac silk dress c.1957. In this example of a dress from the earliest period of Bazaar, the essence of the Quant style is already clearly defined.

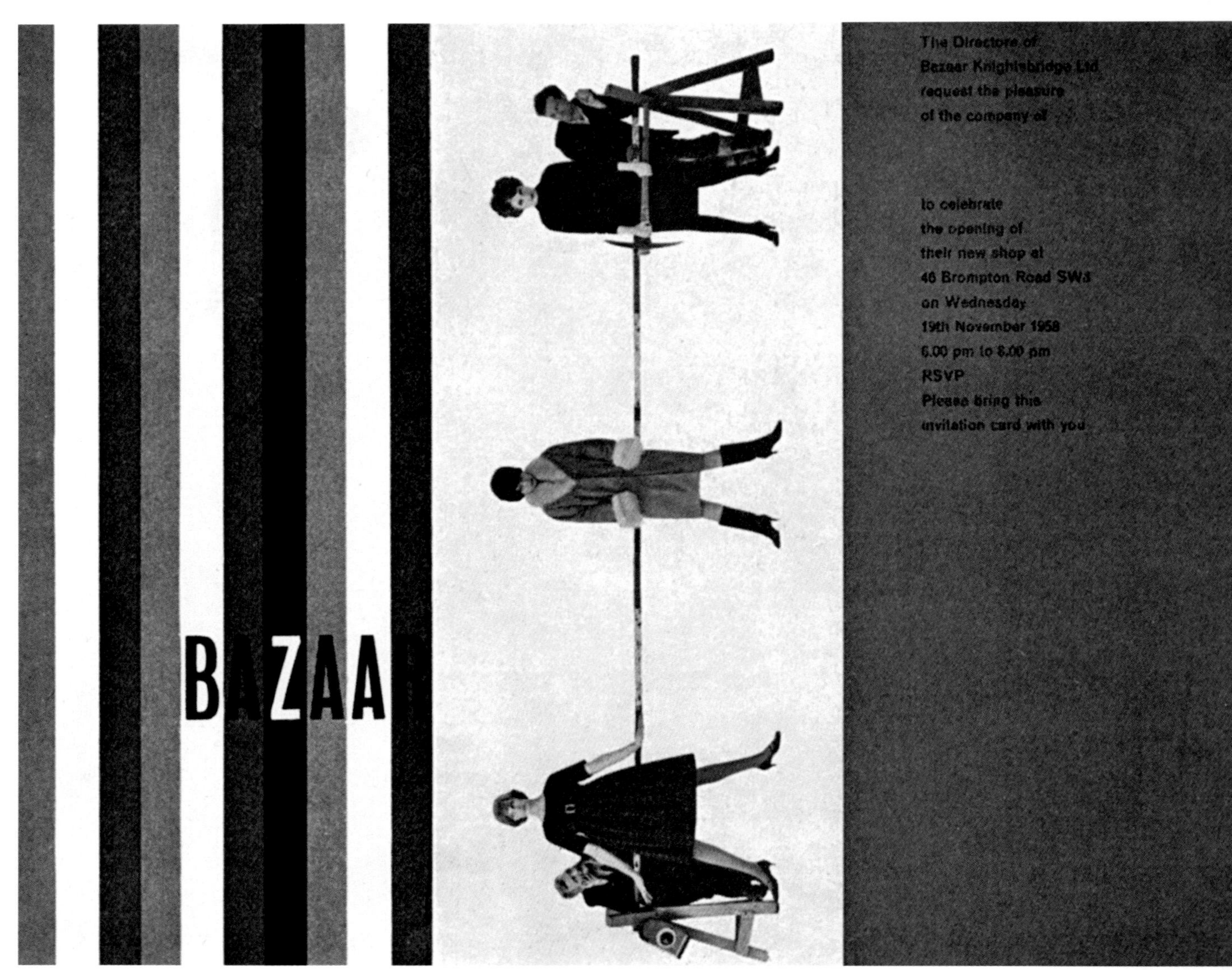

An invitation to the official opening of Bazaar No. 2 on the 19 November 1958, although the shop had been open for business since late 1957. The invitation is the work of Conran's long-term friend and professional advisor, the graphic designer Ian Bradbery, a former lecturer at Conran's alma mater, London's Central School of Art and Design.

BAZAAR NO.2
THE CONRAN
CONNECTION

WITH THE HELP of Archie McNair's shrewd business acumen and Plunket Greene's newly discovered flair for witty publicity and cheeky public relations, Bazaar flourished. So much so, that a little less than two years after its opening in November 1955, a second boutique was opened on Brompton Road in the Knightsbridge area of London. Initially an empty shell in a completely new build, Plunket Greene's long-term friend Terence Conran was engaged to design both the frontage and interior of the second Bazaar from scratch.

THE ORIGINAL IDEA was for Quant, Plunket Greene and McNair to form a joint company with Conran and his second wife Shirley, both of whom were, besides much else, textile designers. Known among themselves as 'Plunket's Proposition,'[21] the concept was for the Conrans to design the textiles and Quant the clothes, but, as so often, such enthusiastic youthful plans were to remain unrealized. Quant later recalled that:

'Terence had a gilded feeling of success about him before anybody else. There used to be page after page written about the Conrans in 'House & Garden', in their Regent's Park Terrace house.

Terence and Shirley never arrived anywhere except on the run.'[22]

ALTHOUGH CONRAN'S design for Bazaar No. 2 was very simple, but extremely elegant in a somewhat austere modernist style, it was also very dramatic. The shop's frontage, entirely glass from floor to ceiling, was kept clear of any window display, while an open staircase floated down, apparently unsupported, through the centre of the shop from a mezzanine floor. When a fashion show was held, somewhat akin to a 1960s 'Happening,' it could be seen from the street in its entirety, the models changing in full view on the mezzanine before dancing down the staircase to the sounds of a Modern Jazz combo. When combined with Quant's radical fashion designs, it's not difficult to imagine the impact such extraordinary 'goings on' had in London in the late 1950s. At one point in the proceedings, in something oddly prescient of Swinging London, an extremely youthful Andrew Loog Oldham – later 'discoverer' and highly original, if somewhat controversial, manager of The Rolling Stones – managed to attach himself, after much persistence, to Quant's entourage in the role of part-time window dresser and self-appointed 'jack of all trades', before suddenly 'swanning' off – without due notice – to France some nine months later.[23] Plunket Greene and Quant personally celebrated the opening of the second Bazaar by regularising their relationship and getting married that same year; 1957 was an important milestone for them.

FOR THE INTERIOR of Bazaar No. 2, Conran selected lighting by the sculptor and designer Bernard Schottlander, an associate of Conran's from his time at the Central School of Art. Schottlander's lighting designs, some of which rival, and often predate, the best by his French and Italian contemporaries, were among the coolest available in Britain in the late 1950s.[24] Somewhat prescient of the future Habitat style, Conran chose for some of the boutique's seating relatively inexpensive elegant black lacquered chairs with rush seats, which he'd been importing from Italy since at least 1955. Among other accessories in period photos of the interior are what appear to be examples of Fornasetti waste bins, although they may also have been by Conran himself, or even products of Paolozzi and Henderson's Hammer Prints workshop.

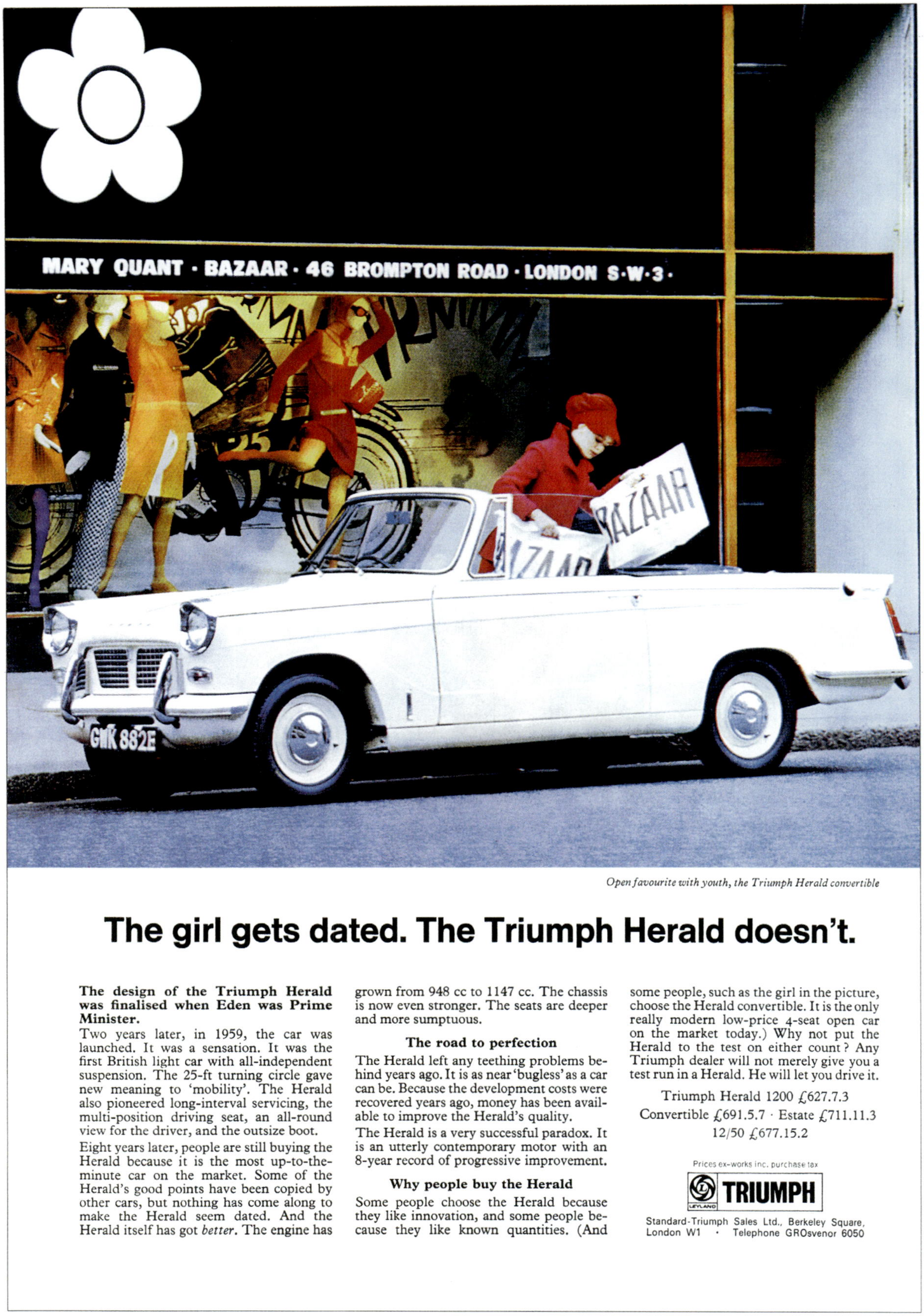

Open favourite with youth, the Triumph Herald convertible

The girl gets dated. The Triumph Herald doesn't.

The design of the Triumph Herald was finalised when Eden was Prime Minister.

Two years later, in 1959, the car was launched. It was a sensation. It was the first British light car with all-independent suspension. The 25-ft turning circle gave new meaning to 'mobility'. The Herald also pioneered long-interval servicing, the multi-position driving seat, an all-round view for the driver, and the outsize boot.

Eight years later, people are still buying the Herald because it is the most up-to-the-minute car on the market. Some of the Herald's good points have been copied by other cars, but nothing has come along to make the Herald seem dated. And the Herald itself has got *better*. The engine has grown from 948 cc to 1147 cc. The chassis is now even stronger. The seats are deeper and more sumptuous.

The road to perfection

The Herald left any teething problems behind years ago. It is as near 'bugless' as a car can be. Because the development costs were recovered years ago, money has been available to improve the Herald's quality.

The Herald is a very successful paradox. It is an utterly contemporary motor with an 8-year record of progressive improvement.

Why people buy the Herald

Some people choose the Herald because they like innovation, and some people because they like known quantities. (And some people, such as the girl in the picture, choose the Herald convertible. It is the only really modern low-price 4-seat open car on the market today.) Why not put the Herald to the test on either count? Any Triumph dealer will not merely give you a test run in a Herald. He will let you drive it.

Triumph Herald 1200 £627.7.3
Convertible £691.5.7 · Estate £711.11.3
12/50 £677.15.2

Prices ex-works inc. purchase tax

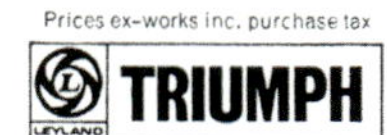

Standard-Triumph Sales Ltd., Berkeley Square, London W1 · Telephone GROsvenor 6050

An advertisement for a Triumph Herald convertible, c.1966. Then considered the height of style among trendy young women drivers, the car is knowingly displayed against the background of Bazaar No. 2.

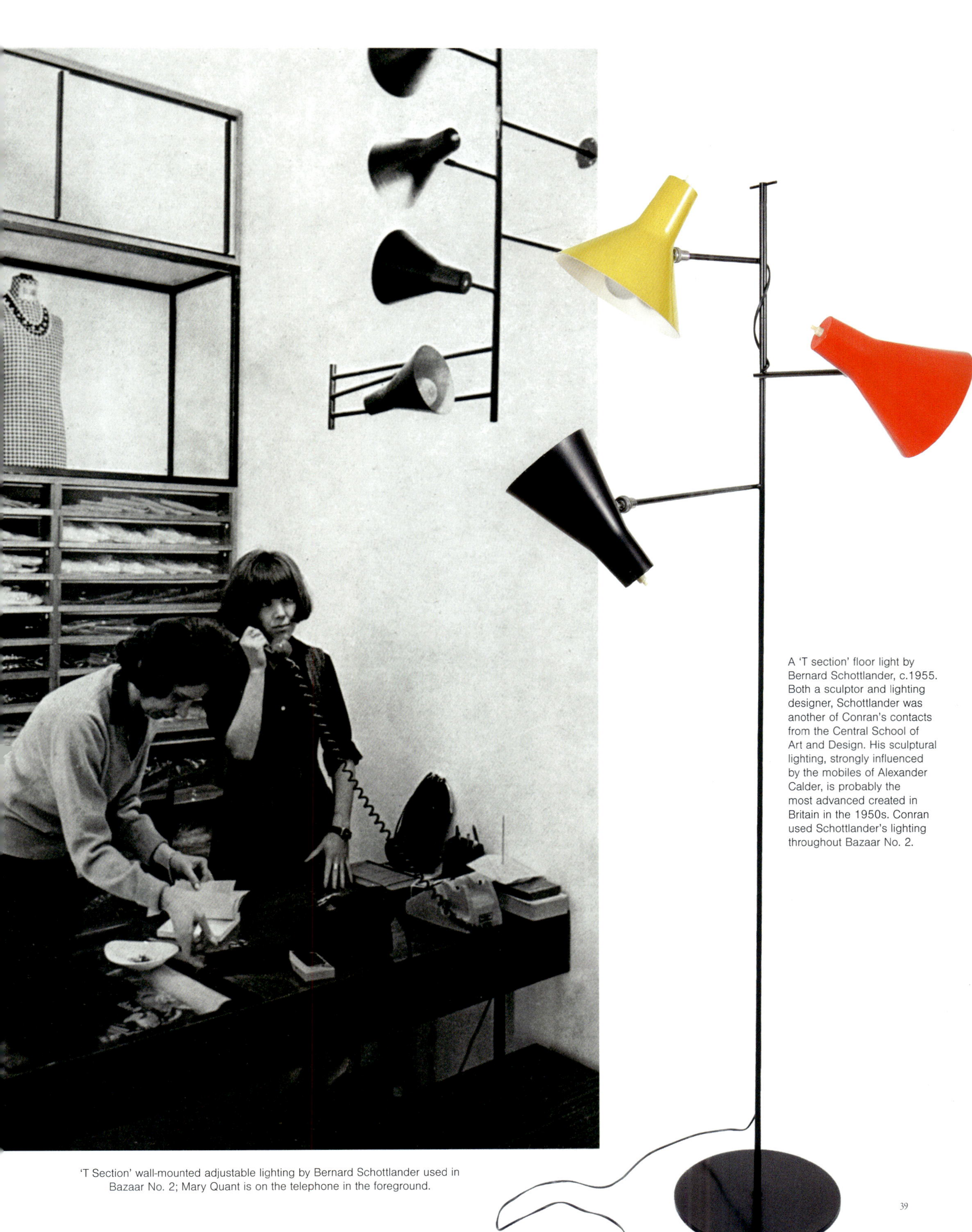

A 'T section' floor light by
Bernard Schottlander, c.1955.
Both a sculptor and lighting
designer, Schottlander was
another of Conran's contacts
from the Central School of
Art and Design. His sculptural
lighting, strongly influenced
by the mobiles of Alexander
Calder, is probably the
most advanced created in
Britain in the 1950s. Conran
used Schottlander's lighting
throughout Bazaar No. 2.

'T Section' wall-mounted adjustable lighting by Bernard Schottlander used in
Bazaar No. 2; Mary Quant is on the telephone in the foreground.

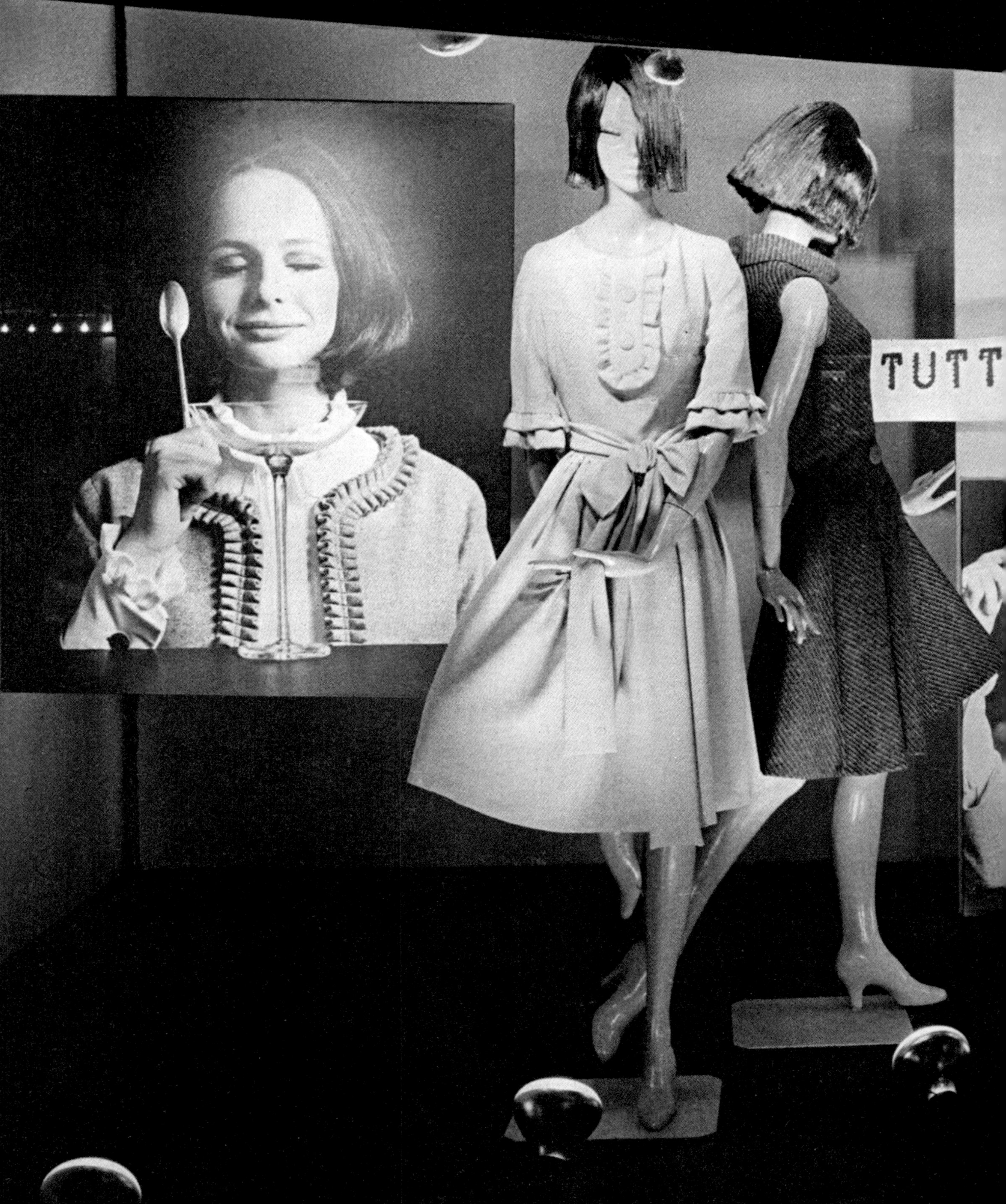
TUTT

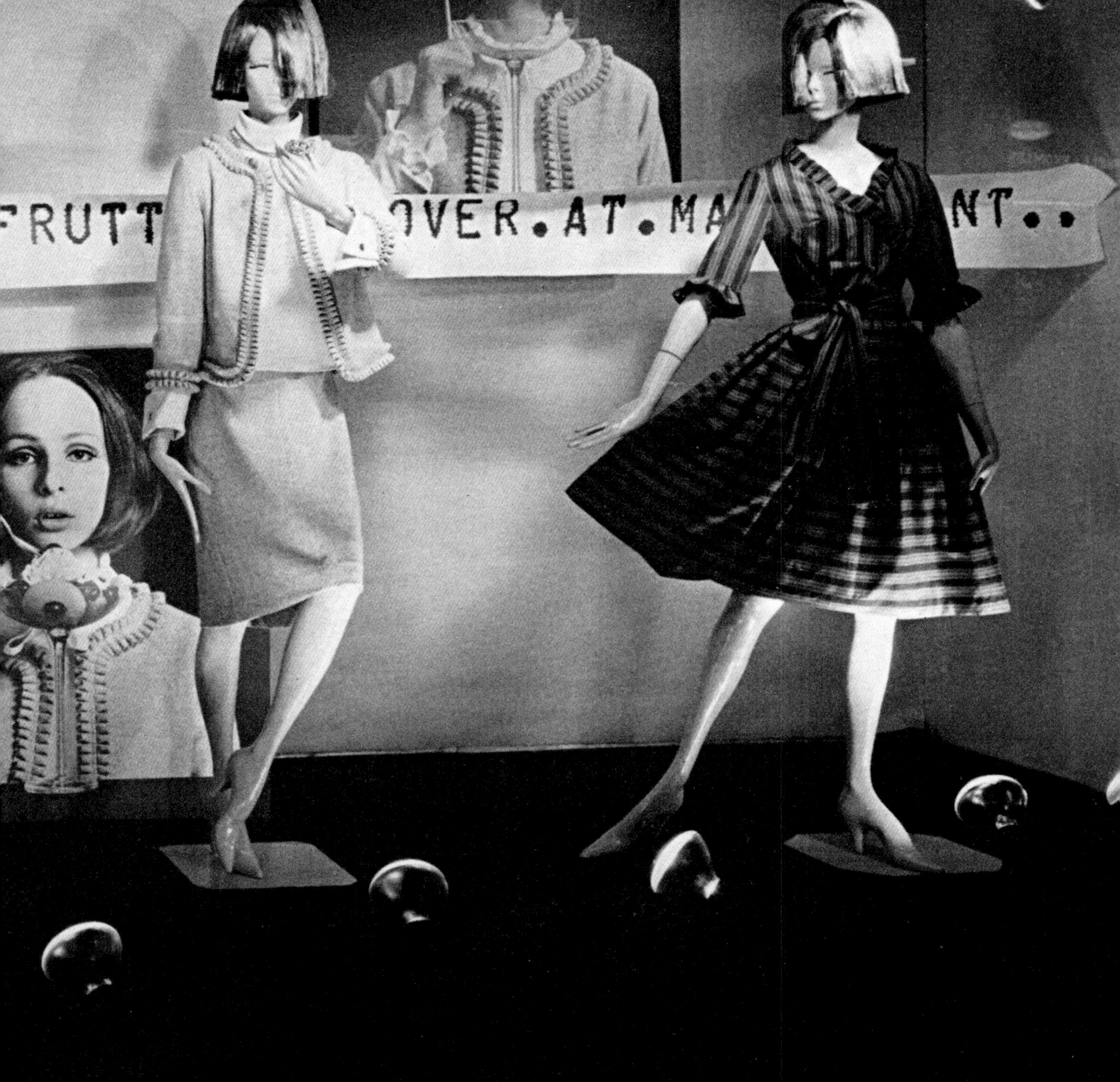

A window display at Bazaar No. 2, 1962

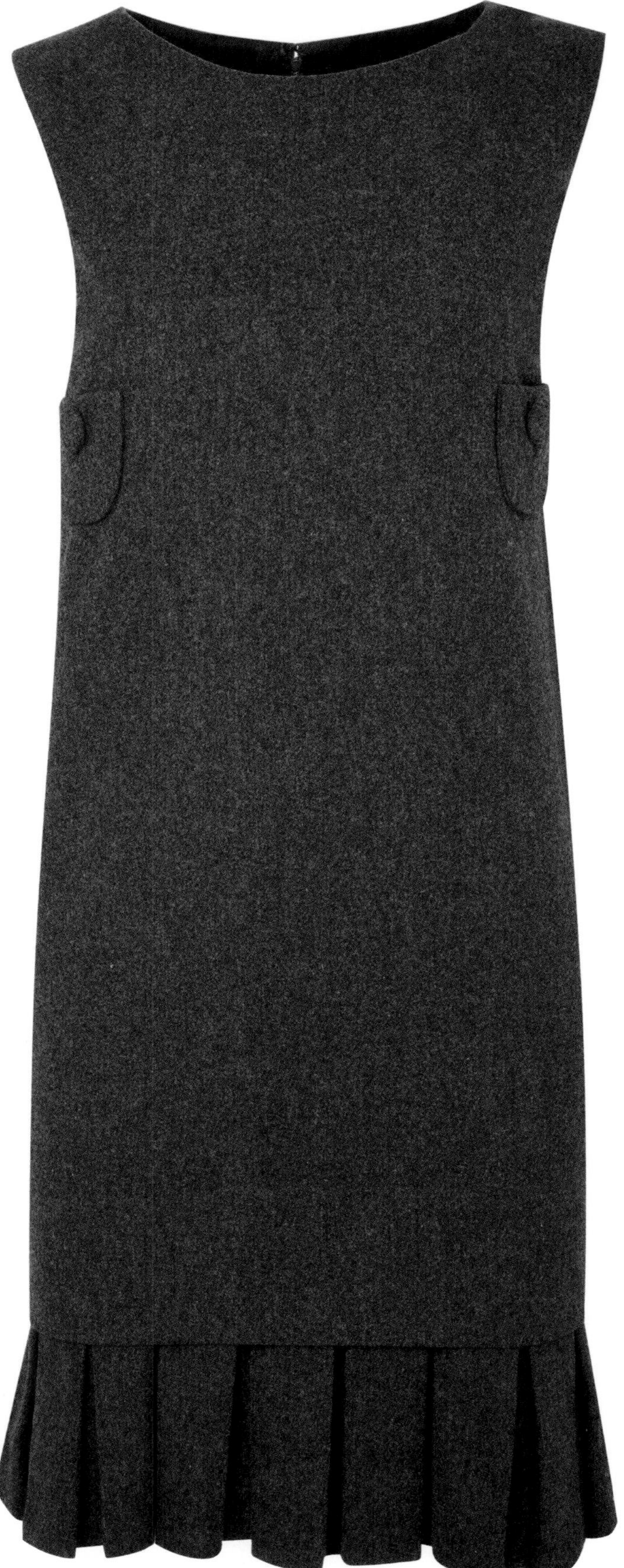

Pinafore Pleats, 1958. An example in grey flannel of an unstructured Sac dress, which that year signalled the most radical change of direction in women's fashion since Dior introduced the 'New Look' in 1947. It is an important design that led to the liberating fashions of the 1960s.

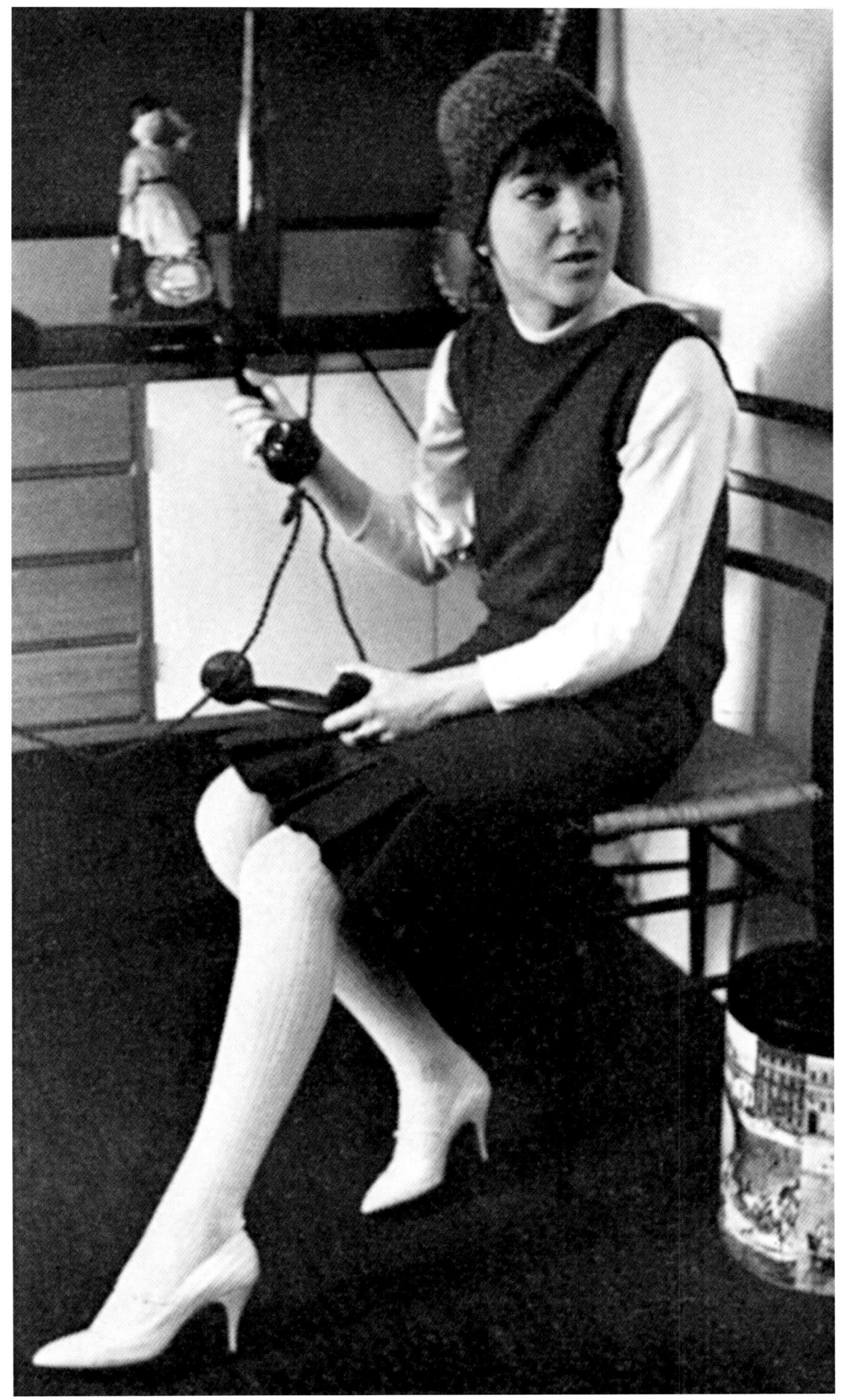

Quant wearing an example of Pinafore Pleats, 1958.

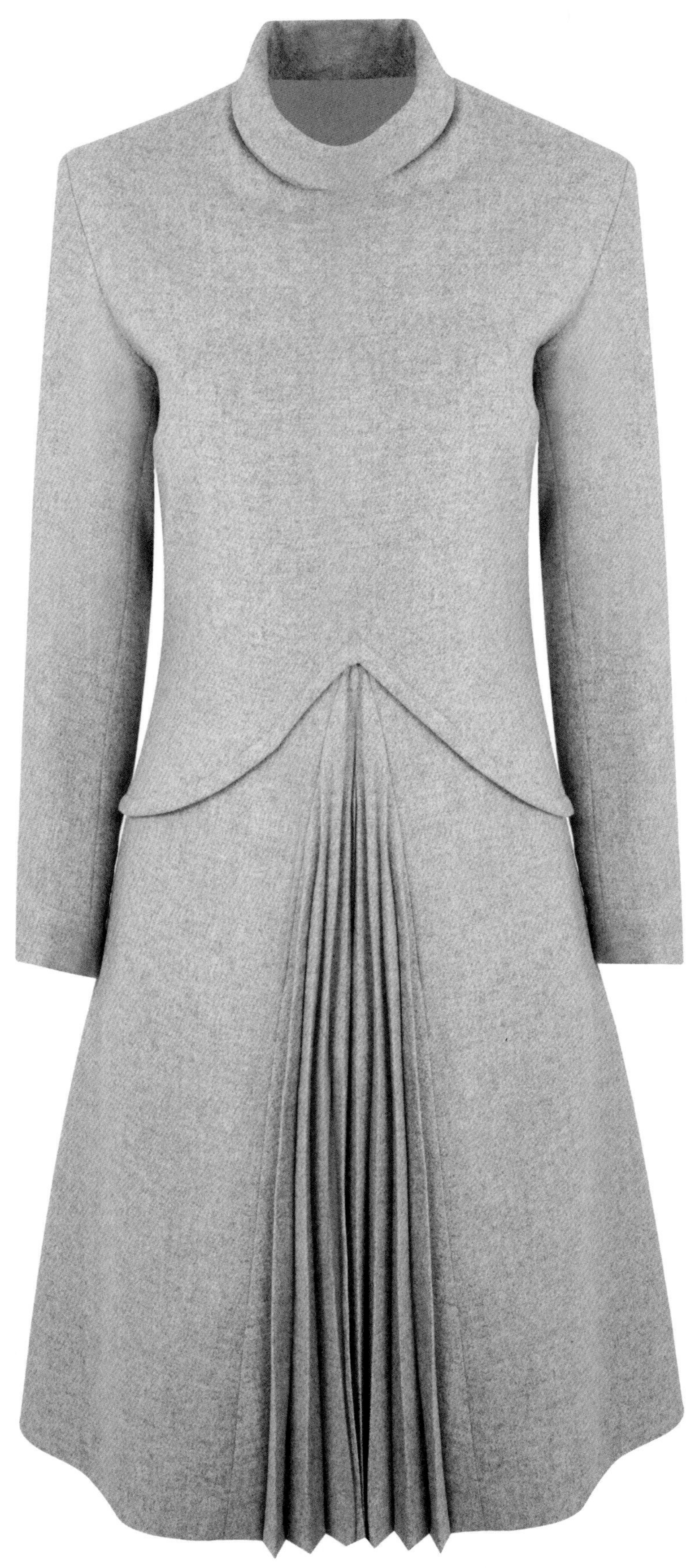

A grey flannel dress, c.1959-1960, its pared-down functional elegance the
quintessence of the Quant style and philosophy.

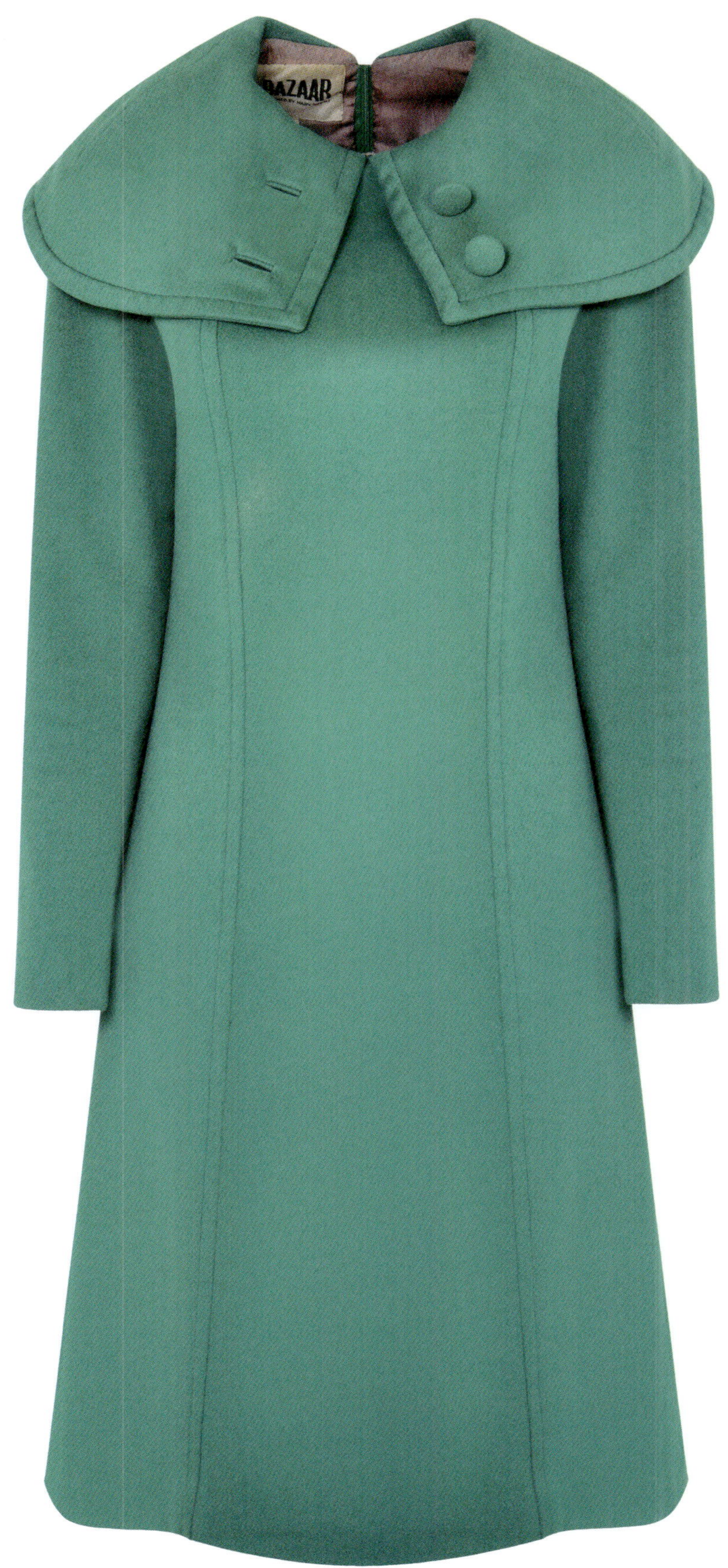

A jade green woollen dress by Quant, c.1959-1960.

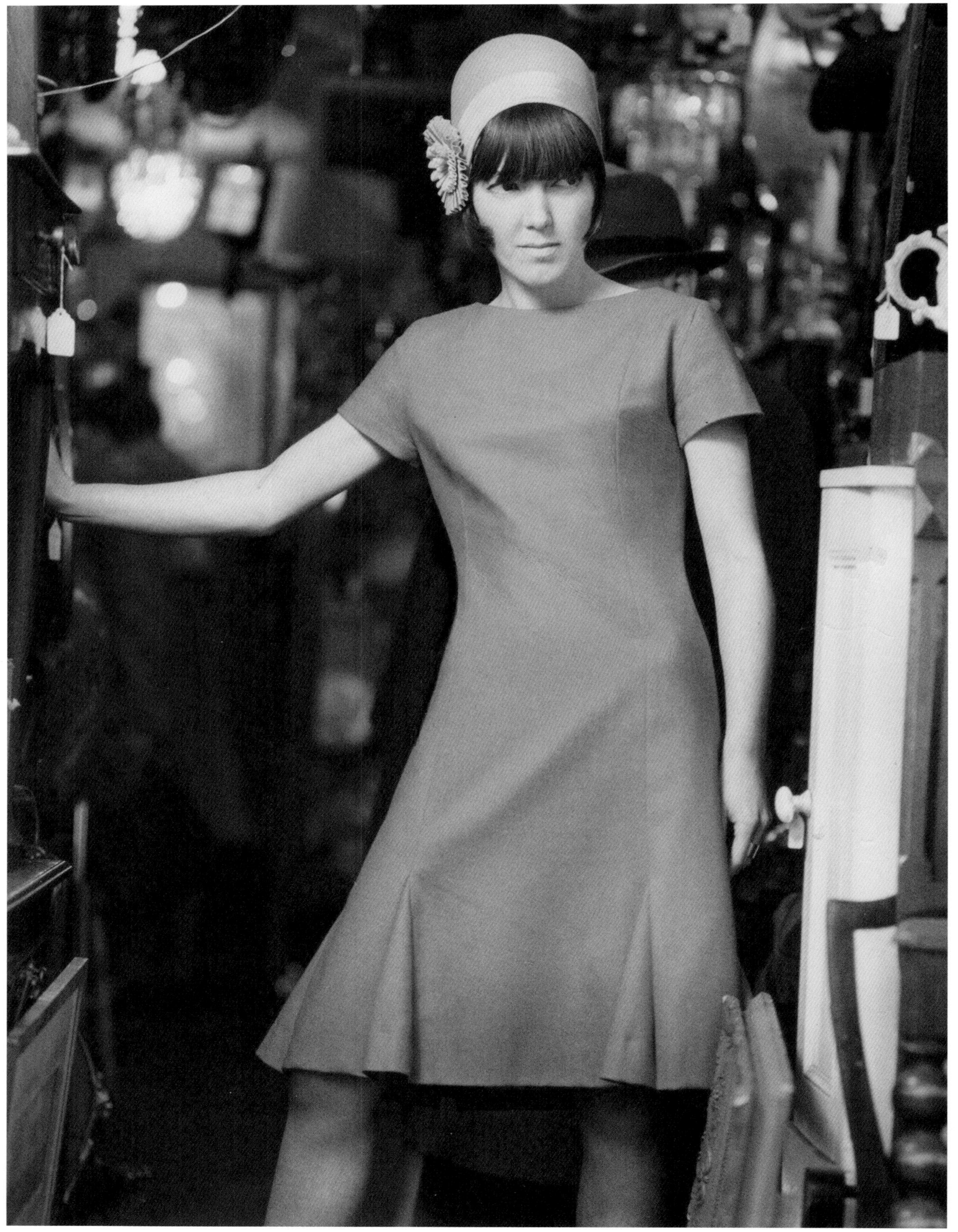

Mary Quant, 1961.

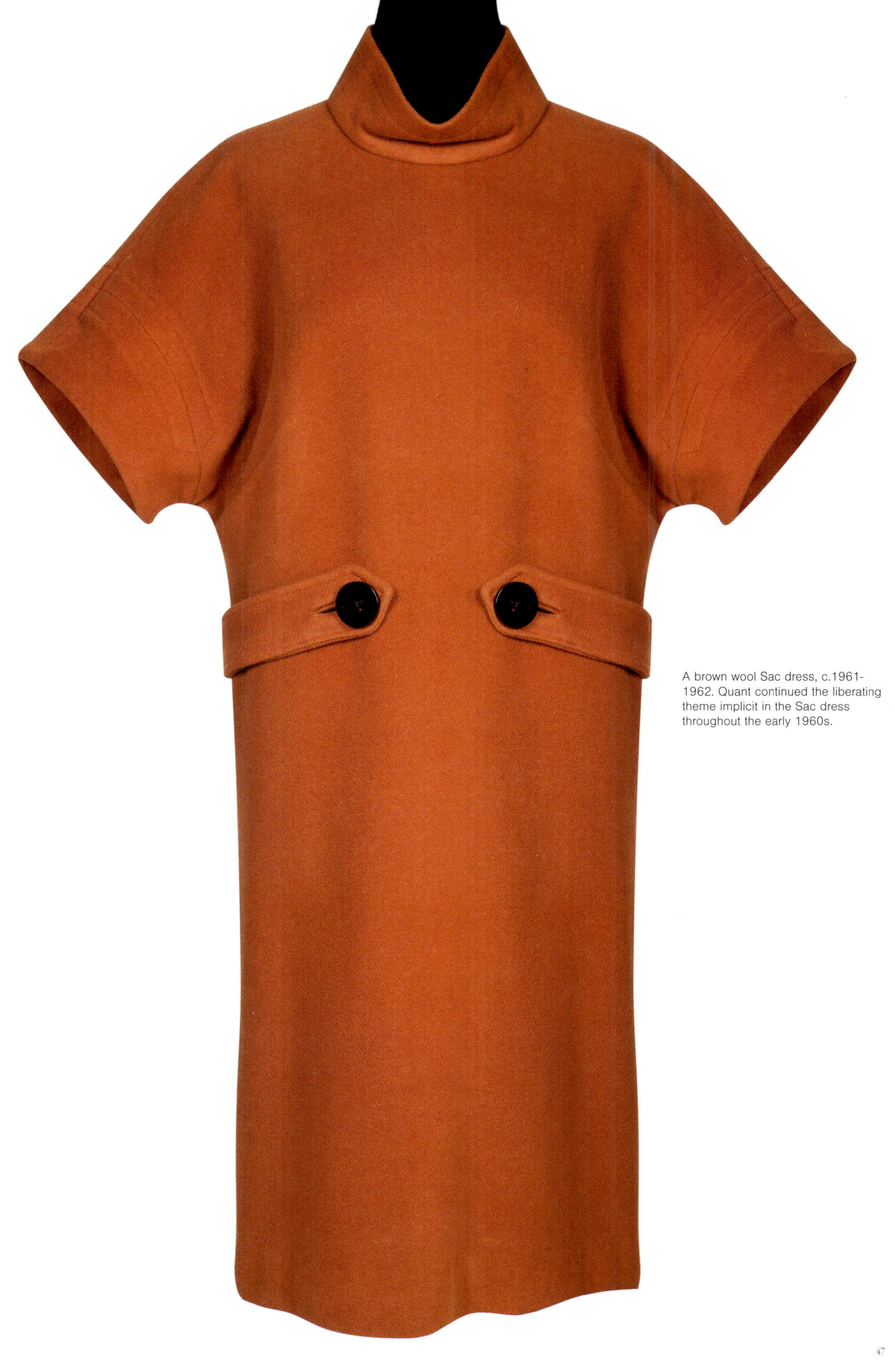

A brown wool Sac dress, c.1961-1962. Quant continued the liberating theme implicit in the Sac dress throughout the early 1960s.

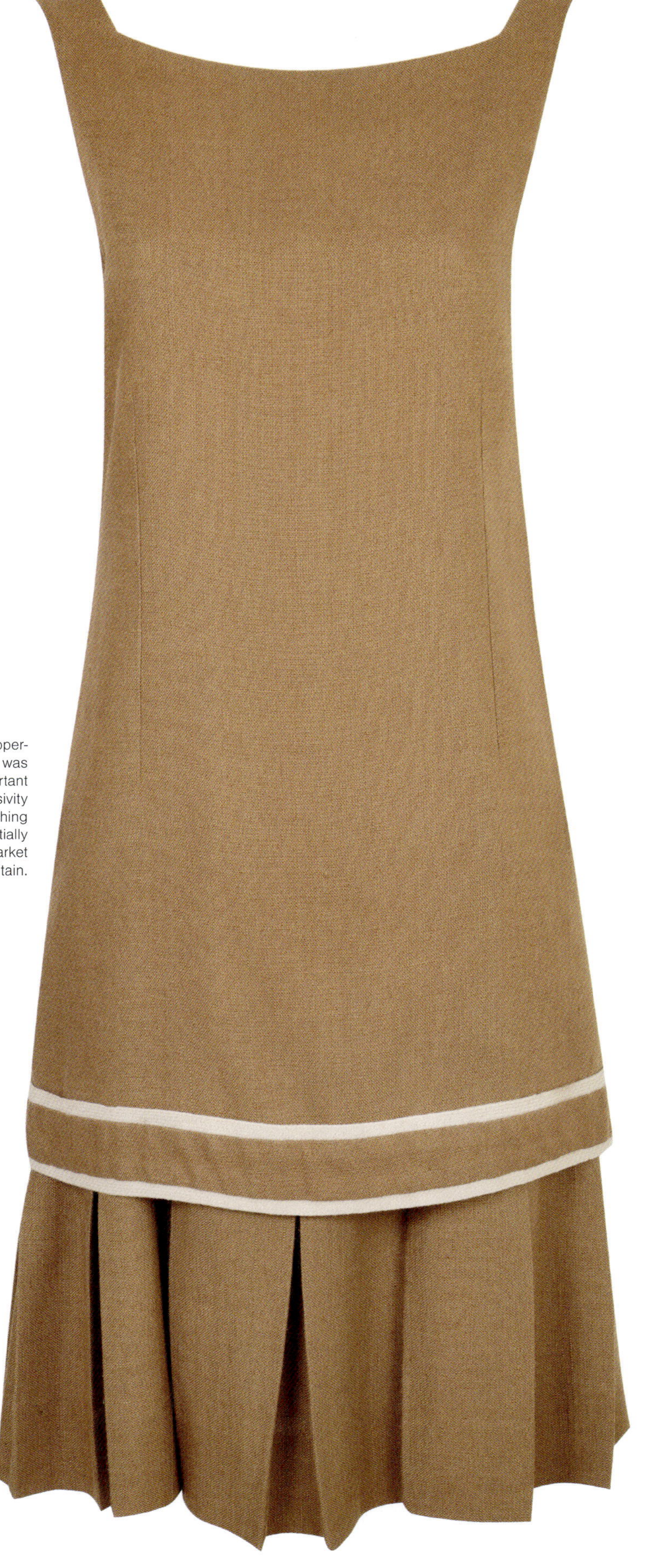

Opposite: Editorial in *Seventeen* magazine, April 1961, featuring the Flapper dress, photographed in Chelsea against a veteran Phoenix car. The feature announced the arrival in the USA of 'The Big Look, the Kooky Look in Chelsea'. The image equates the liberated Flapper of the 1920s with the modern young woman of the early 1960s.

A pale coffee and cream linen Flapper-style dress, 1960-1961. This dress was designed on the cusp of the important change in 1961 from the exclusivity of Bazaar to the wholesale clothing company Mary Quant Ltd, which initially had up to 30 outlets in upmarket department stores throughout Britain.

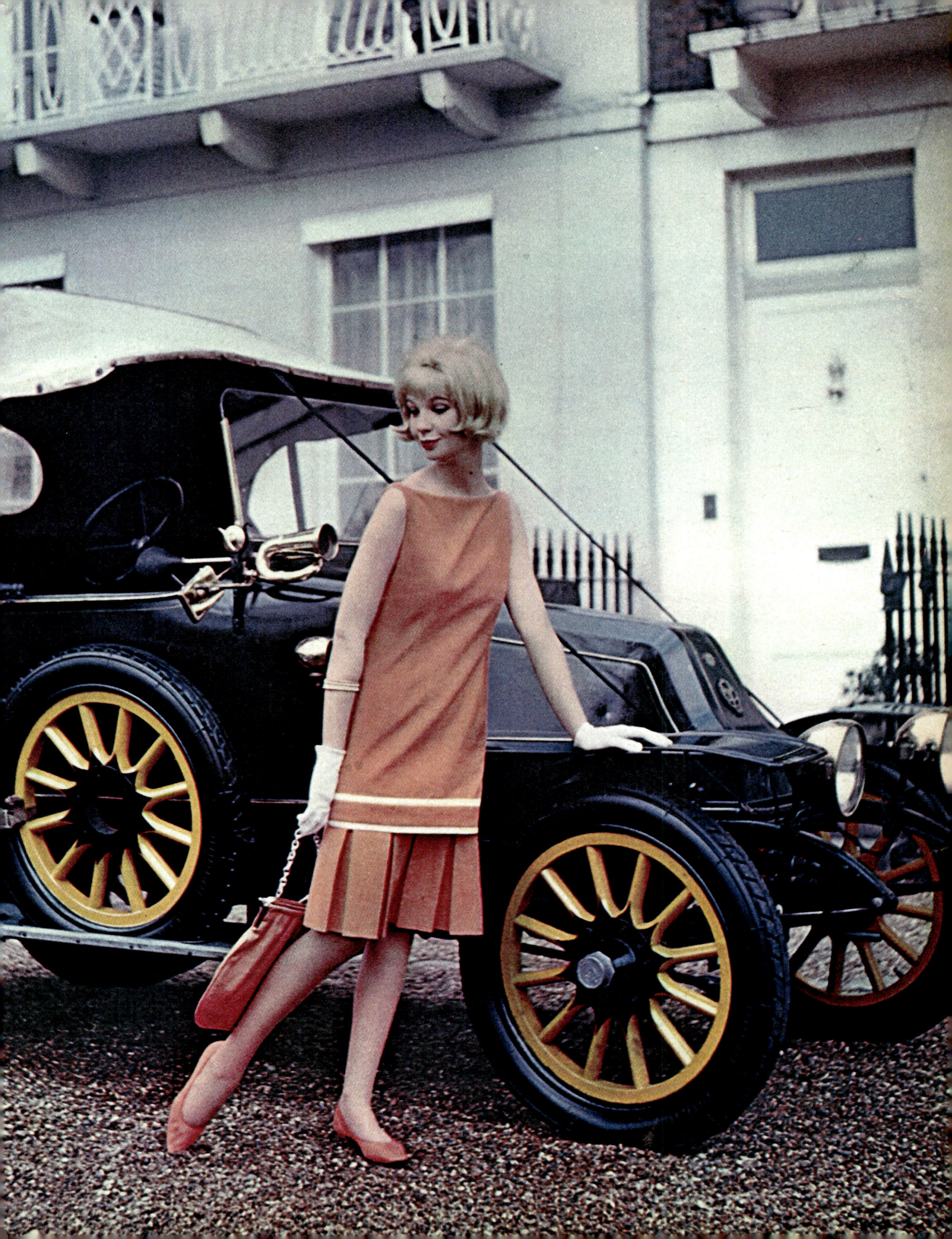

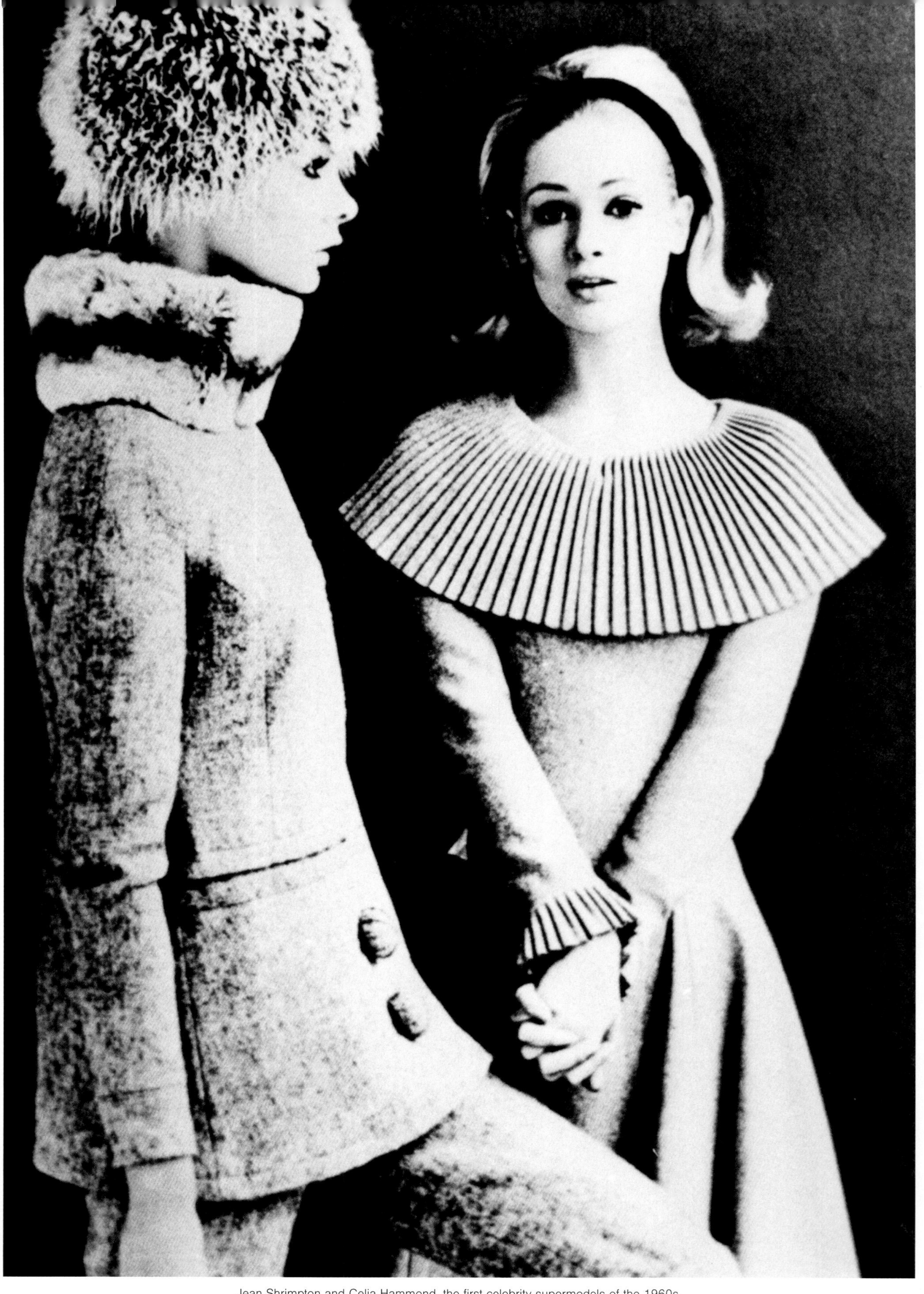

Jean Shrimpton and Celia Hammond, the first celebrity supermodels of the 1960s, showing off Mary Quant ensembles in 1962.

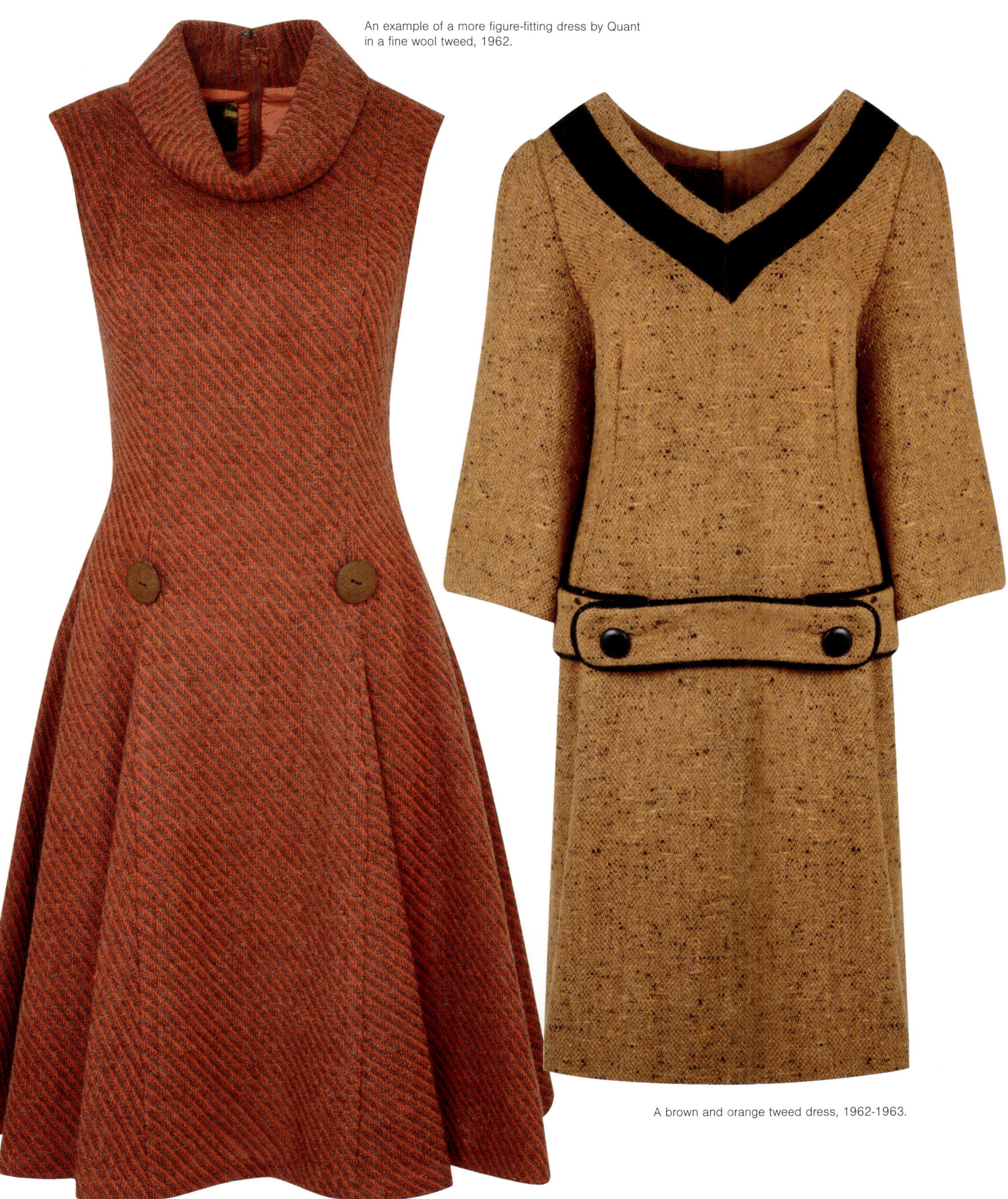

An example of a more figure-fitting dress by Quant in a fine wool tweed, 1962.

A brown and orange tweed dress, 1962-1963.

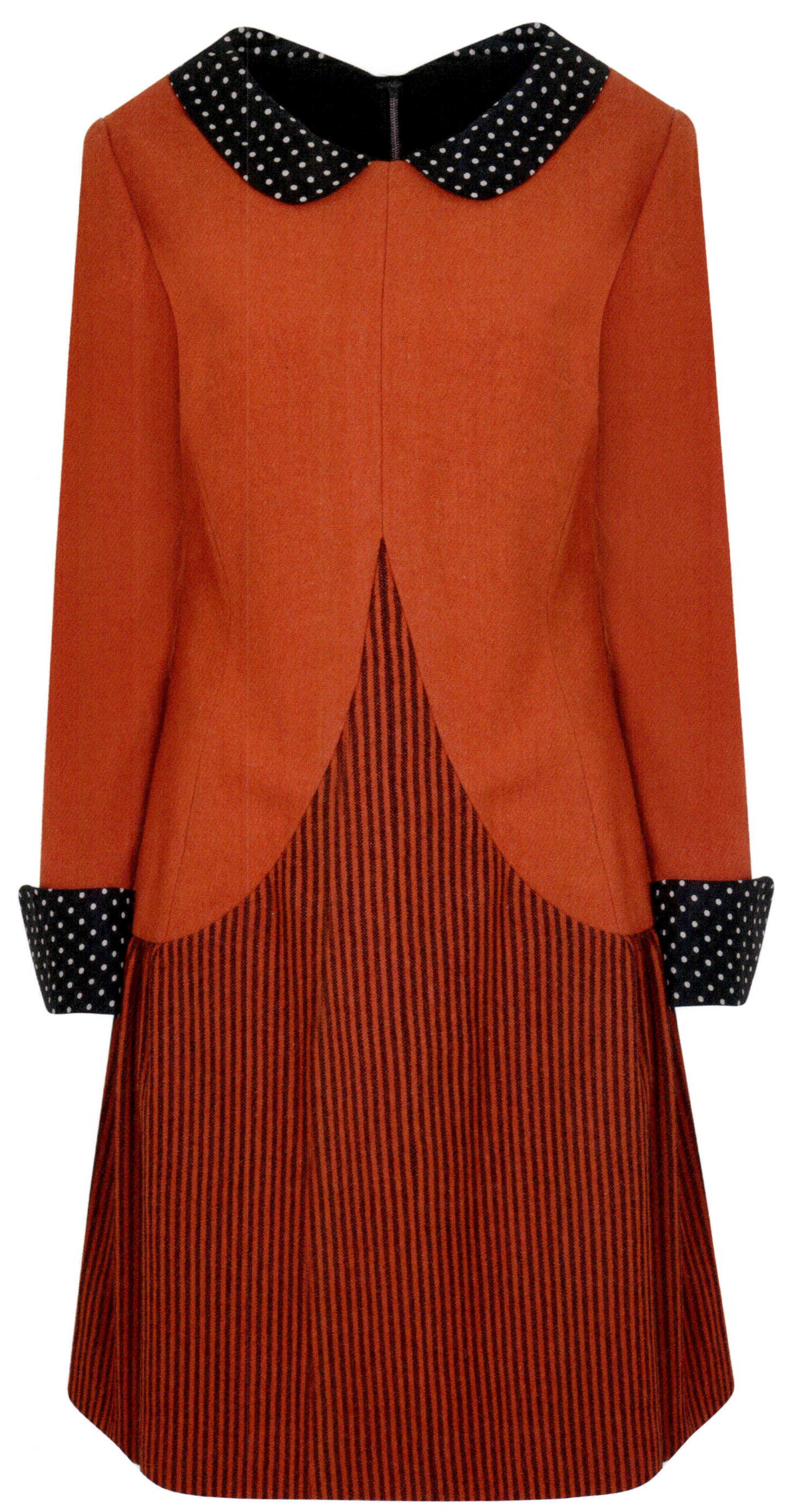

A red wool dress with polka dot silk cuffs and Quant's signature Peter Pan collar,
1964.

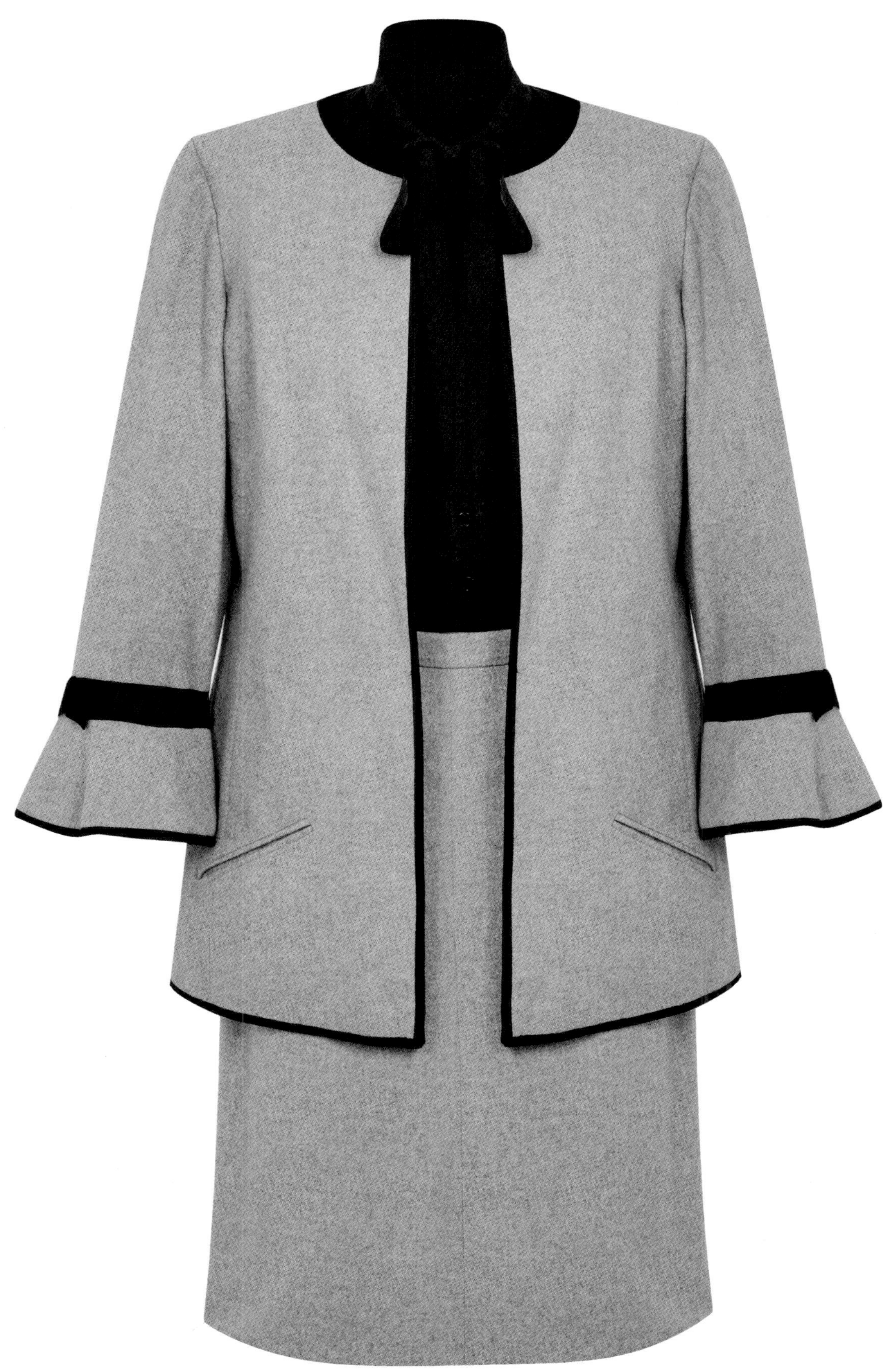

A grey flannel two-piece suit with black trimming, worn with a black silk blouse, both designed by Quant, c.1964. The suit mirrors the collarless grey suits worn by The Beatles on their debut the previous year. Ironically, The Beatles' original suits were inspired by the work of possibly Quant's only real equal, the French couturier Pierre Cardin.

HARBINGERS OF POP

THE APPLIED ART of the Italian surrealist Piero Fornasetti – often composed from collaged images of mundane objects wittily and somewhat bizarrely conflated with antique prints of Classical subjects – exerted a great influence on Paolozzi's and Henderson's decorative art and the design of their early exhibitions with the Independent Group, such as the 1953 'Parallel of Life and Art'. Conran, who illustrated a number of Fornasetti's designs in his 1957 book *Printed Textile Design*, not only showed something of Fornasetti's influence in his work, but also that of Fornasetti's mentor and close collaborator, the architect Gio Ponti. Their influence is not only apparent in certain of Conran's textile designs, but also more generally in the subtly elegant and refined combinations of colours and materials he used in his early furniture and interior design schemes.

IN 1955, Conran and his second wife Shirley returned from their honeymoon in Italy with 'a car load' of variations of the generic black-lacquered and rush-seated Chiavari chair, seven of which he then began to import and market.[25] Earlier, in 1952, the Chiavari had provided the model from which Gio Ponti derived his now classic chair, the much more exclusive, extremely elegant, black lacquered and lightweight Leggera. Much approved of by Conran, he used several of these as dining chairs in his own flat and also sold them through his company, Conran Furniture.

IN THE LATER nineteenth century William Morris had provided a well-known precedent for Ponti's reworking of the Chiavari chair as the Leggera, when his original company, Morris, Marshall, Faulkner & Co, reworked and retailed a simple rush-seated country chair

as the Sussex. Morris sold at least three variations of it, the original standard model, thought to be designed by the architect Philip Webb and a second variation attributed to the Pre-Raphaelite artist Dante Gabriel Rossetti. The third was the work of the painter Ford Madox Brown, a close associate of the Pre-Raphaelite Brotherhood and an early partner in Morris's original company. Conran apparently approved of the Sussex range, as in the early 1950s he appears to have personally owned a three-seated version of the Ford Madox Brown model, which he also occasionally used as a prop in advertisements and promotional material. In 2014 the display of the National Portrait Gallery's exhibition 'Anarchy and Beauty: William Morris and His Legacy, 1860 – 1960', opened with an example of the original Philip Webb version of the Sussex chair and concluded with one of Conran's wicker Cone chairs, a neat pair of bookends for the exhibition.

LATER, ONE OF the items of furniture most closely associated with Habitat in the 1960s was Vico Magistretti's 1959 reinterpretation of a sturdy rush-seated Italian country chair, the Carimate, which became one of the store's best sellers. Throughout his professional career Conran has valued the unpretentiousness, warmth and functional qualities of such simple traditional furniture and domestic implements, which he has consistently stocked, and, with respect, occasionally reworked.

IN SOME WAYS similar to Gio Ponti's transformation of the workaday Chiavari into the sophisticated and elegant Leggera and Superleggera, Fornasetti's elevation and often surprisingly glamorous reinterpretation of the mundane and the everyday, is prescient of much Pop design in the 1960s. Paolozzi wrote in 1957:

> *I admire the overall approach of Piero Fornasetti, who rattles through every subject as an inspiration... I feel that this designer is influencing new design in every aspect of applied art and that students can learn a great deal from similar rhythmical groupings of quite ordinary objects.*[26]

WHEN QUANT WROTE of the 'mad' window displays at Bazaar No. 1, with particular reference to the quirky use of Penny-farthing bicycles, old Victorian prams, painted horses from carousels and 'other fairground things', she was clearly describing elements of the newly emerging Pop aesthetic, then not only being explored by Paolozzi and Henderson in their applied art, but also in a fine art context by the painter and designer Peter Blake. One of Blake's teachers and mentors at the Royal College of Art was Barbara Jones, an early authority on popular culture. In 1951 she curated the groundbreaking exhibition 'Black Eyes & Lemonade', held at the Whitechapel Art Gallery as part of the Festival of Britain. It was one of the first, if not the first, exhibitions to focus on the popular arts as a subject deserving of serious study. She was also author of the influential books *The Unsophisticated Arts* and *Follies and Grottos*. Blake described her as 'a treasure trove of information about popular culture.'[27]

FROM EARLY ON, the incongruous and often provocative Dadaist and Surreal inclusion of Victoriana and disassociated commonplace objects became a feature of Conran's interiors. Sometimes he would, for instance, utilise a defunct metal tractor seat as a fruit bowl or 'catch-all', and perhaps introduce in the same interior, apparently purposelessly, elongated Victorian glass confectioners' jars, pointlessly suspend a fisherman's keep net from the ceiling or prominently exhibit a somewhat battered nineteenth-century milliner's dummy's head. Later, Habitat displays often subtly suggested how a Pop interior might be put together. For instance, by perhaps incongruously placing a Victorian street vendor's bright red and gold painted tin heater, clearly marked for 'Saveloy sausages', on a strictly Modernist room divider, which stood, in turn, against a vividly coloured Pop-inspired textile hung against a background of raw brick or untreated pale wood.

ALMOST AN ICONOCLASTIC reaction to the then all-pervasive and somewhat stultifying dominance of Modernism, such quirky Pop juxtapositions brought a necessary flare and sense of humour to the predominantly Scandinavian-influenced 'good taste' of much British modernity, which was otherwise becoming increasingly predictable and routine. The Habitat style particularly appealed to 'the young and switched on', echoing their own attitude to clothes – for instance, 'expensive shirts worn with un-pressed denims.'[28]

'It is hard to imagine a greater contrast to the ordered background anonymity of the modernist interior. The Pop domestic interior was

theatrical, an environment in which to enact the Pop lifestyle of action, fun and change.'[29]

A MAGAZINE FEATURE on an early pre-Pop interior by Conran already noted that:

'Although this is not everyone's design for living, it is not extravagantly modern: old furniture is mixed with new, paintings range from Reynolds to Reg Butler, and the unit furniture is cleverly designed and not, as it often is, too clinical looking'.[30]

CONRAN'S COMMISSIONS for unequivocally commercial companies such as David Whitehead and W.R. Midwinter, were designed specifically for the popular mass market, which, together with his early use of Pop objects in interior designs, would not have necessarily endeared him to the Modernist design elite. Many of the elite's strongly held views were epitomised by the purist activities of the Council of Industrial Design, who widely disseminated and reinforced Modernist design orthodoxy through their influential magazine *Design*. Shirley Conran later recalled that:

'Right from the start I noticed there was a negative attitude towards Terence. I think it was professional jealousy – real envy and hatred towards this young man ... Terence was very unpretentious; he just got on with it.'[31]

CONRAN'S WARMER AND inclusive approach to modern design, and his sincerely held belief that it should be widely available and affordable for all, was closer to the ideas of the British design reformists in the later nineteenth century than it was to the design snobbery and Bauhausian rectitude espoused by many of his contemporaries in the 1950s.

'In his adult life the idea of making a design which many people would buy would be far more exciting than the plaudits of his fellow designers.'[32]

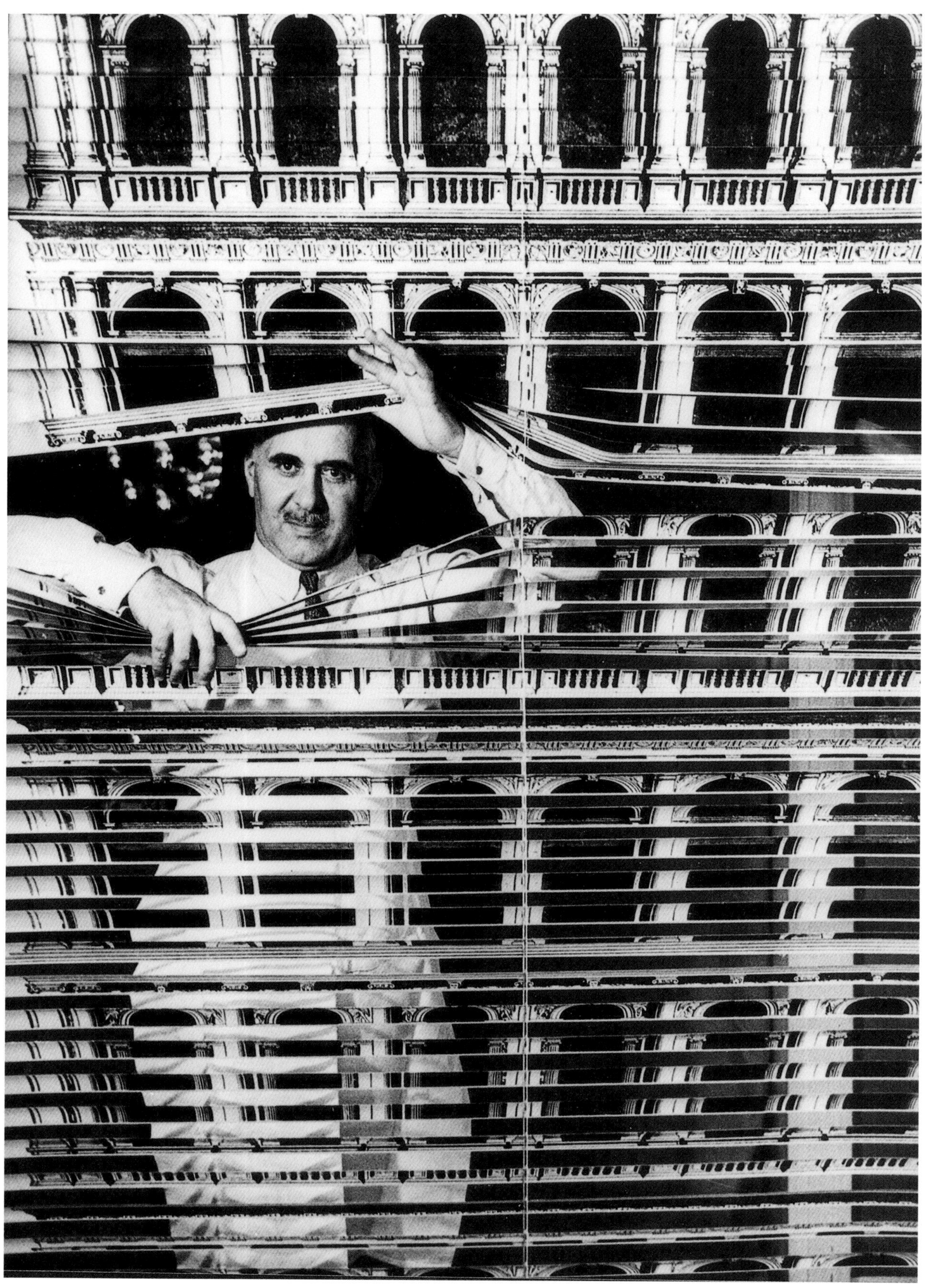

A Venetian blind by Piero Fornasetti, 1950s. The witty and playfully subversive work of the Italian Surrealist artist and designer Piero Fornasetti – pictured – had a considerable influence on the applied designs of a group of British proto Pop designers and artists in the mid 1950s, which included Terence Conran and his close friend and mentor, the sculptor, artist and designer Eduardo Paolozzi. (Above – Permission of Fornasetti. Photographer Ugo Mulas.)

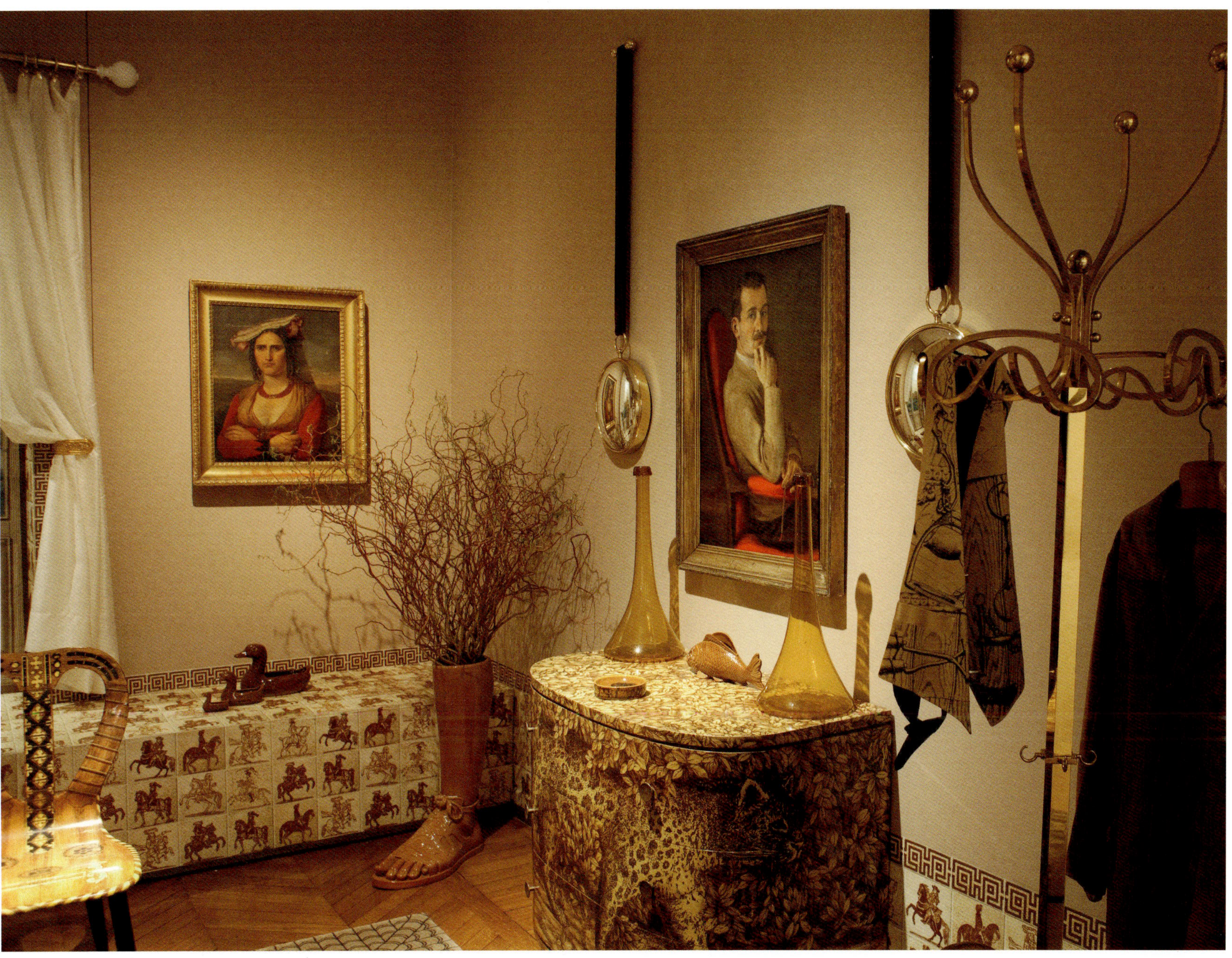

A Fornasetti interior c.1955. Exhibited in 'La Folle Practique', The Musée des Arts Décoratifs, Paris, 2015. (Permission of Fornasetti.)
Among these examples of Fornasetti's work is his disembodied 'Roman Foot', considered the most surreal of his creations.

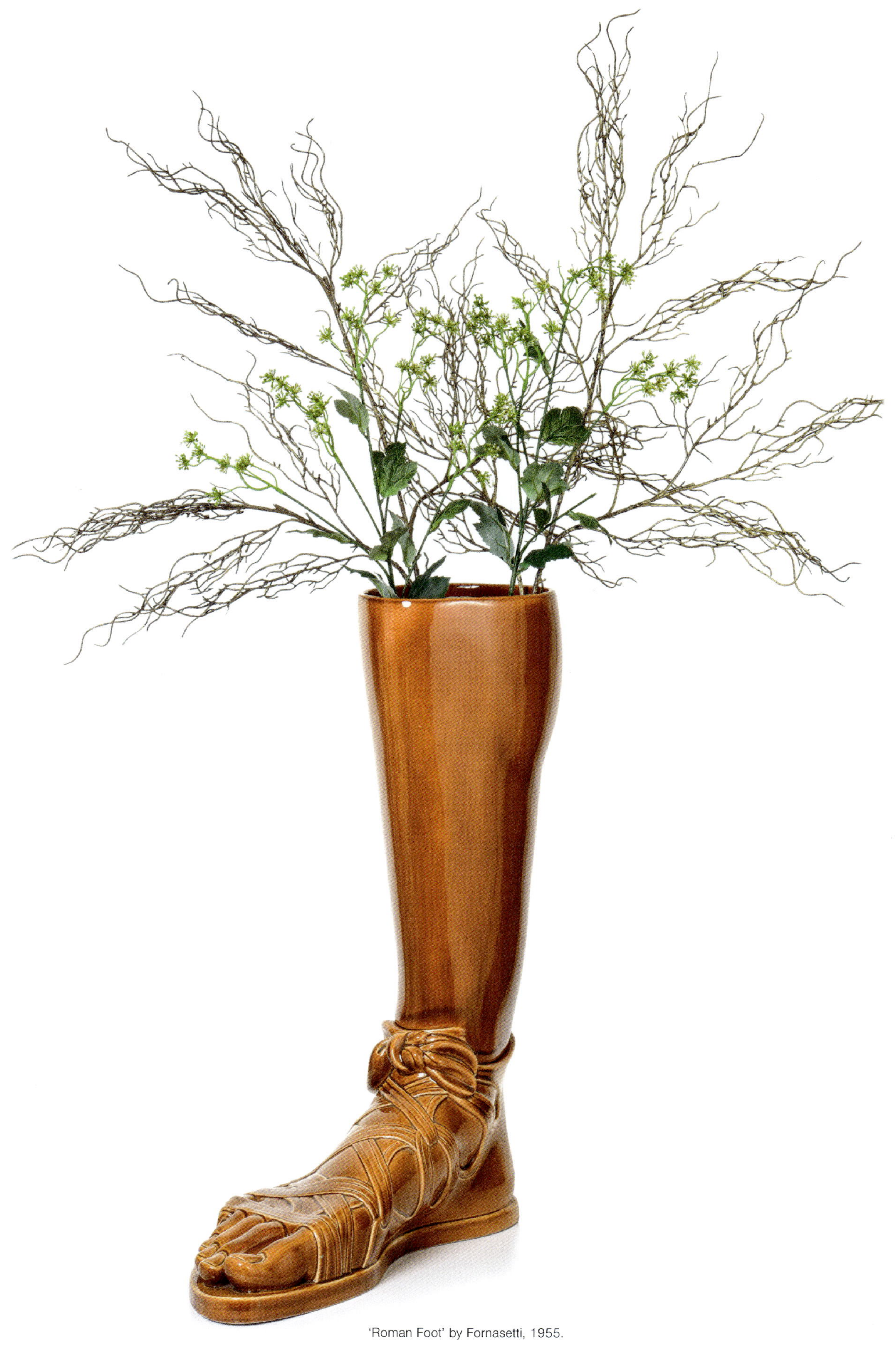

'Roman Foot' by Fornasetti, 1955.

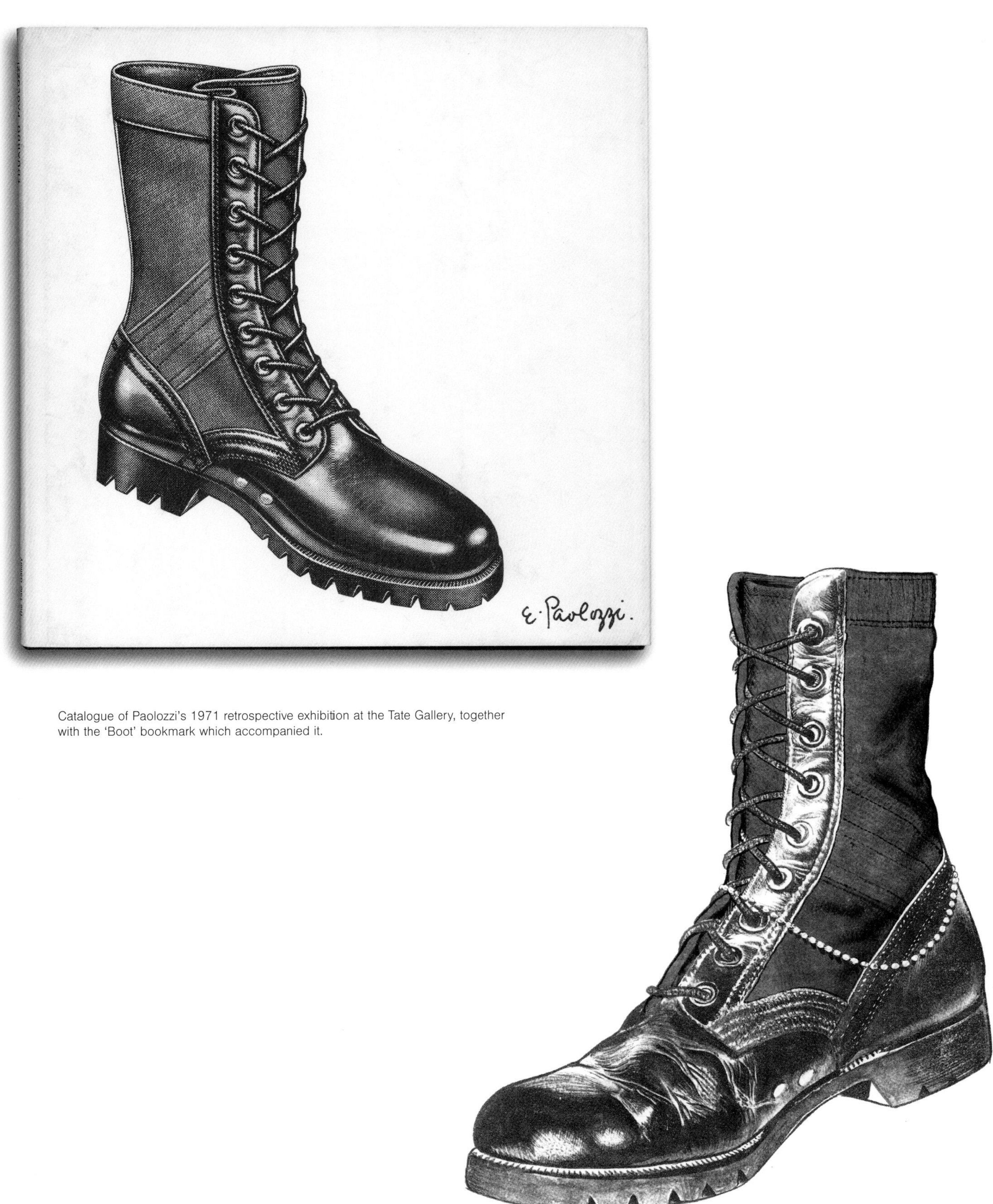

Catalogue of Paolozzi's 1971 retrospective exhibition at the Tate Gallery, together with the 'Boot' bookmark which accompanied it.

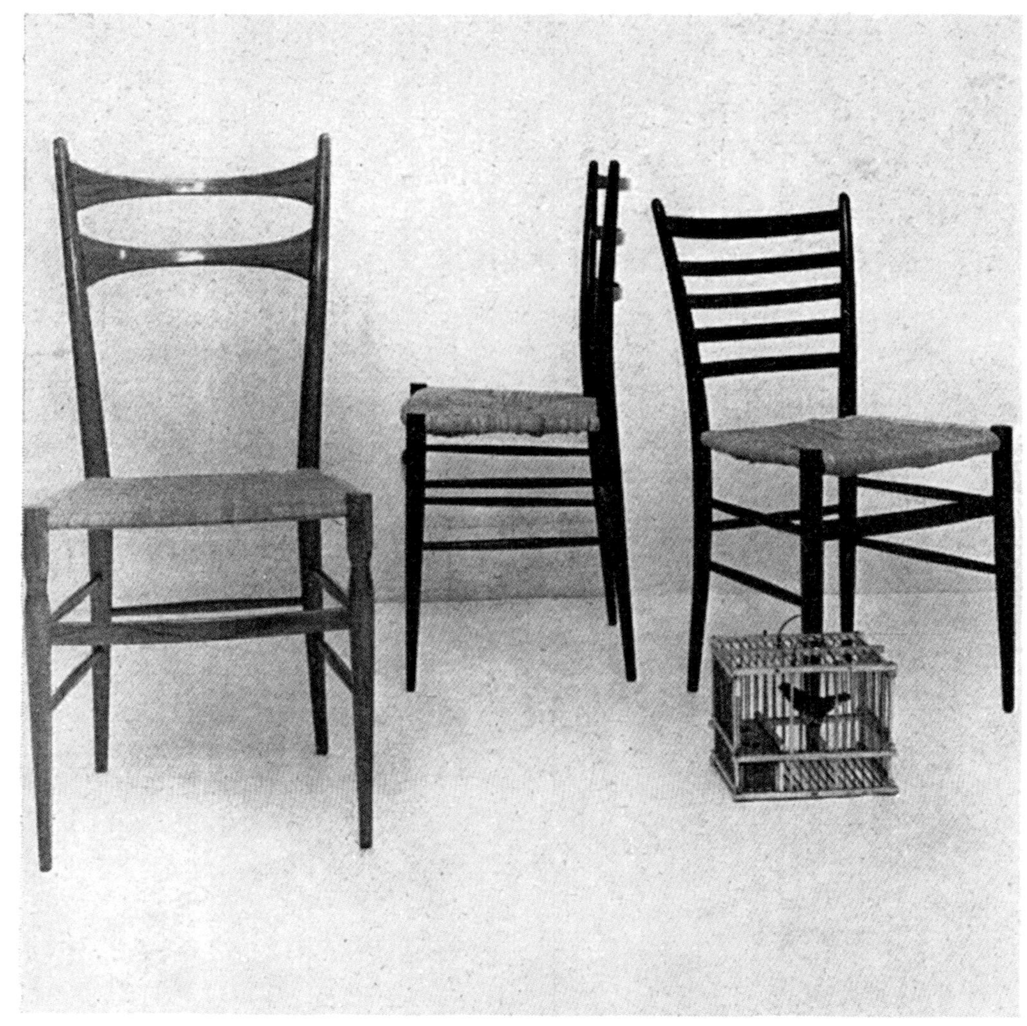

CONRAN FURNITURE 6 Cadogan Lane, London, S.W.1

The most elegant hand-made Italian chairs. Obtainable at Peter Jones and all John Lewis branches.

IC 3 in pale cherry 9 gns. IC 2 ebonised ash with three bars £5 19s. 6d. IC 1 with five bars £4 19s. 6d.

Conran advertisement for Italian Chiavari chairs, 1956. Greatly influenced by the work of Fornasetti's sometime collaborator, the architect Gio Ponti, Conran imported and sold seven variations of the Chiavari chair. Ponti had earlier reworked the Chiavari as the classic Leggera.

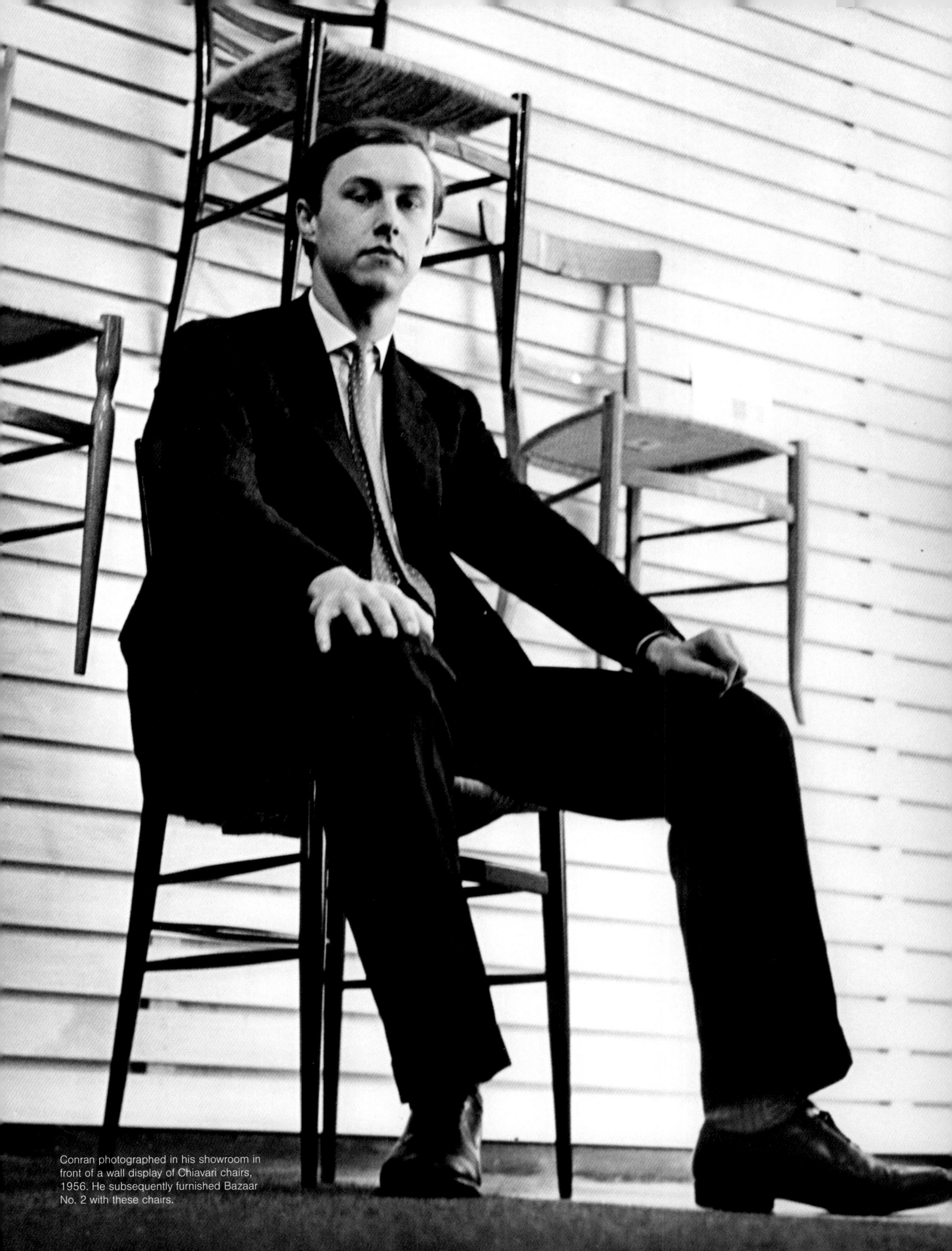

Conran photographed in his showroom in front of a wall display of Chiavari chairs, 1956. He subsequently furnished Bazaar No. 2 with these chairs.

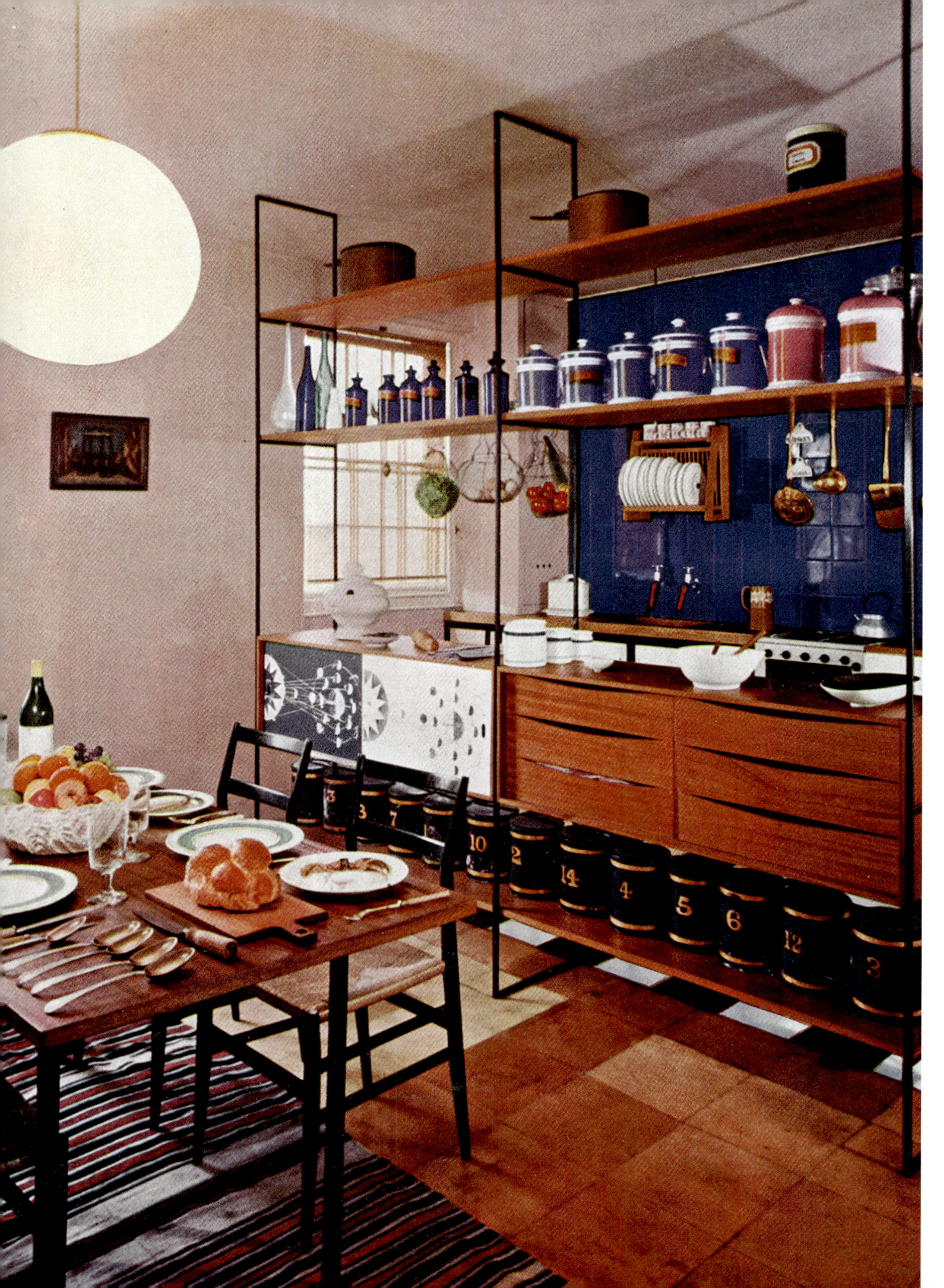

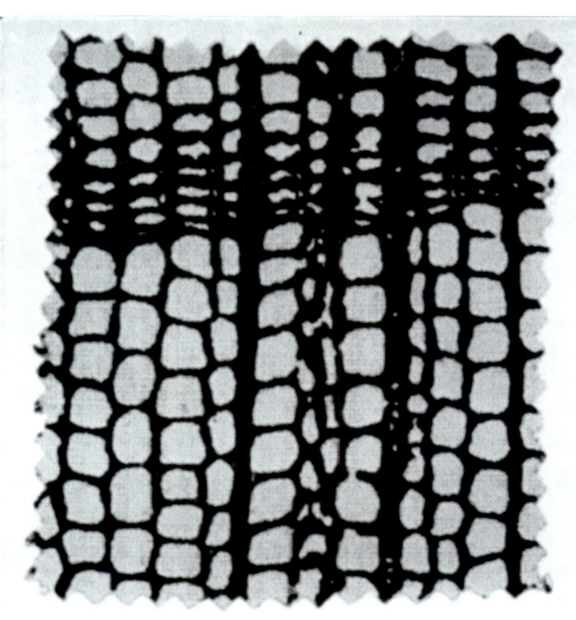

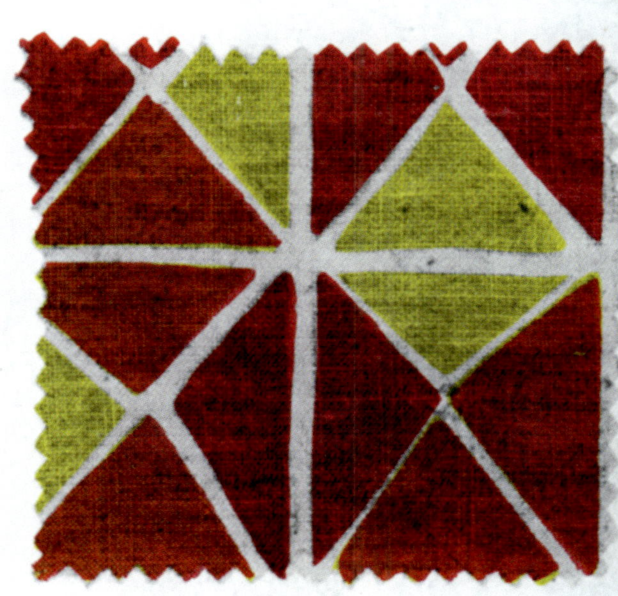

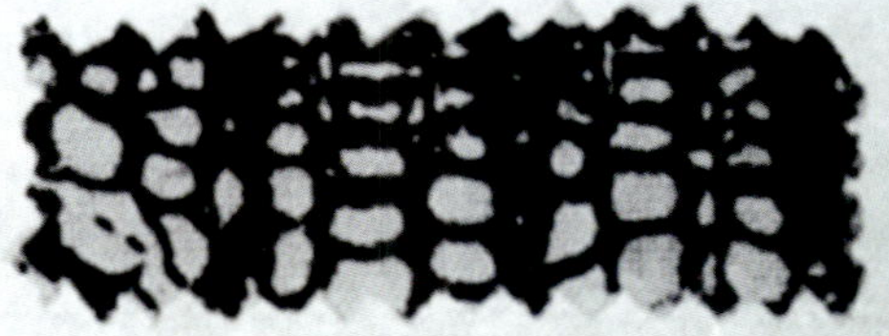

The cover of Conran's book *Printed Textile Design*, 1957. The influence of both Fornasetti and Paolozzi, Conran's former textile teacher, is apparent throughout the book.

Opposite: The interior of Terence and Shirley Conran's home, Regent's Park Terrace, 1957. Examples of Gio Ponti's Leggera can be seen around the table.

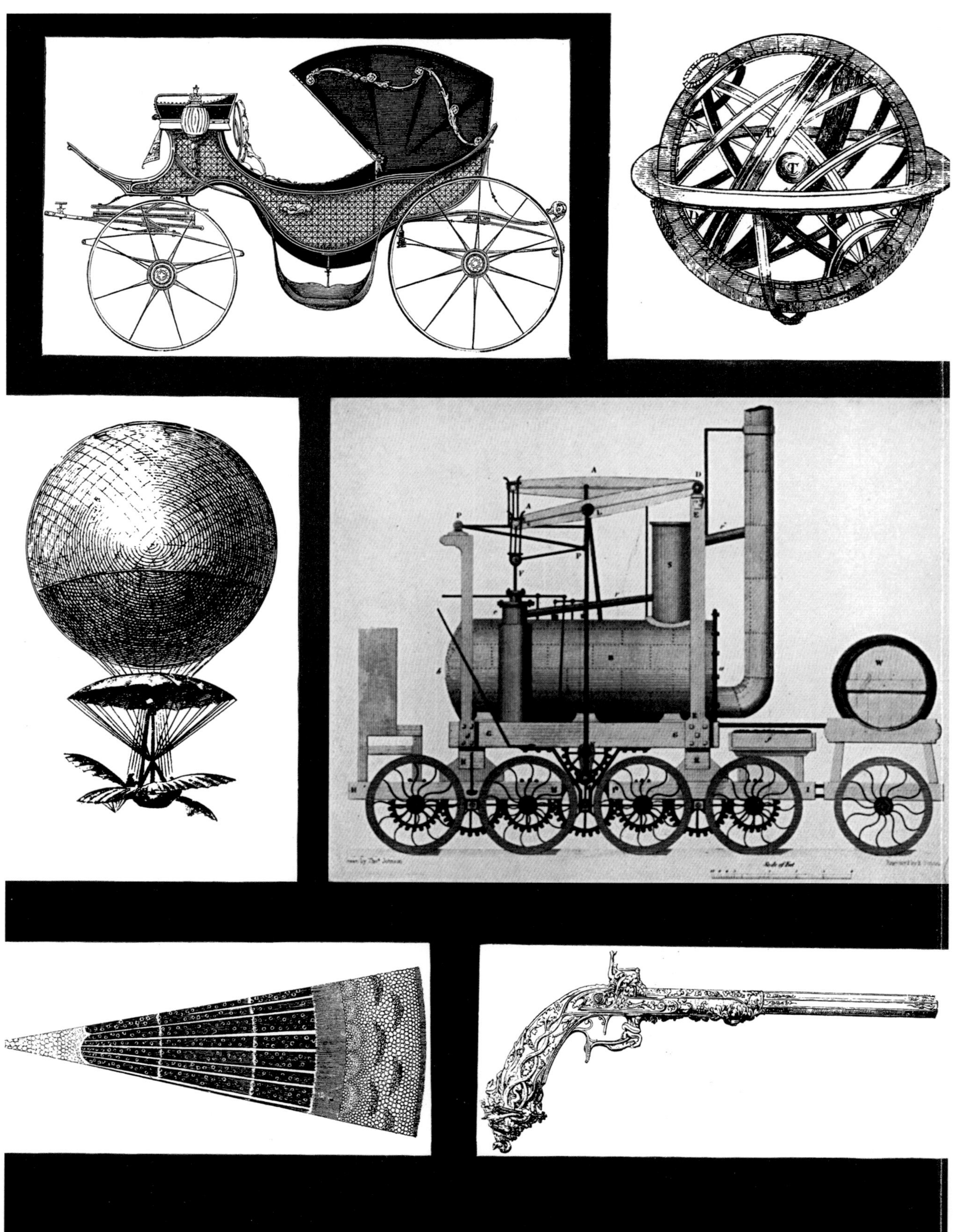

A page of eighteenth- and nineteenth-century prints, suggested by Conran as design sources in *Printed Textile Design*.

Opposite: Textile, 'Curiosity', by Terence Conran, c.1957. The design clearly shows the influence of Fornasetti.

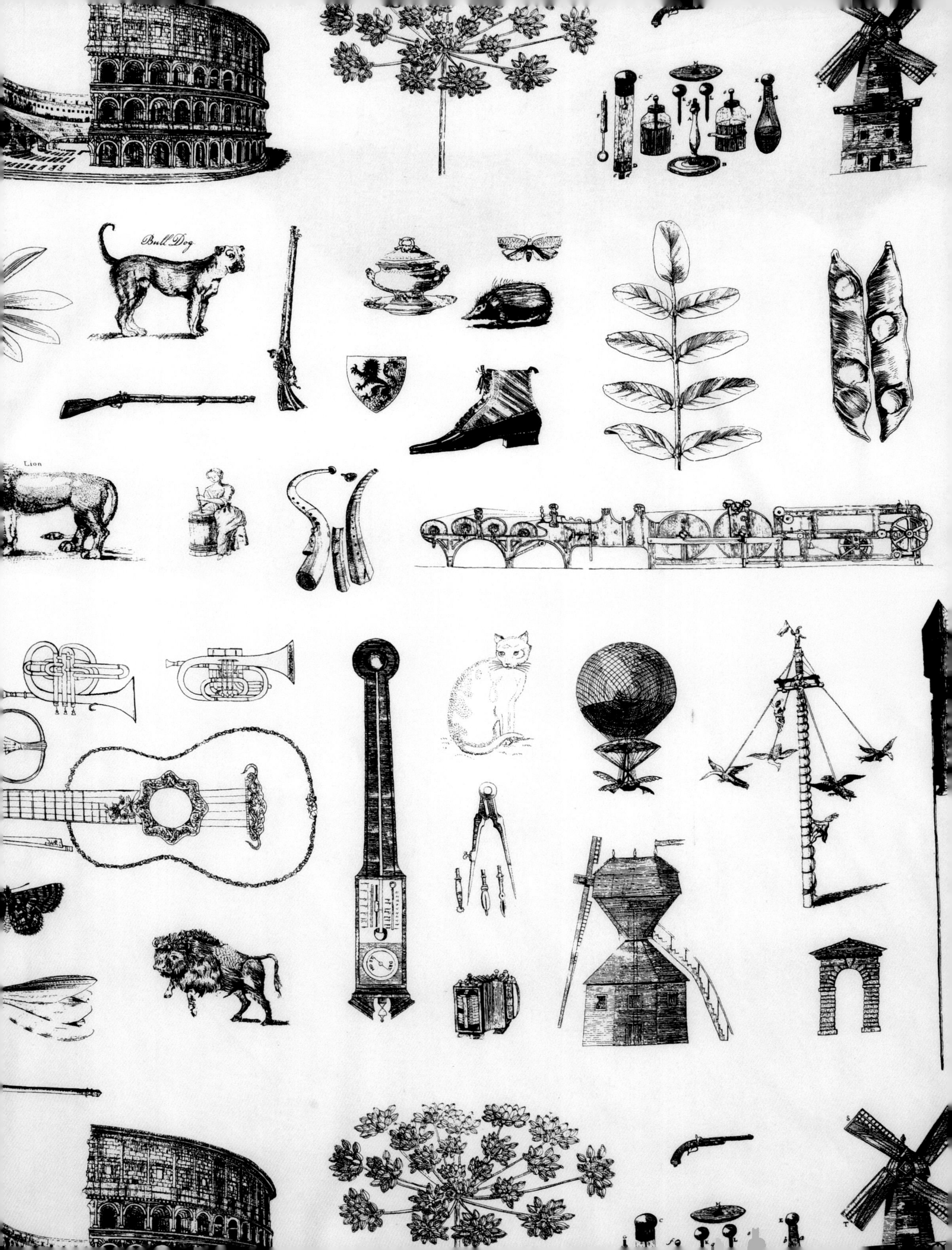
Bull Dog
Lion

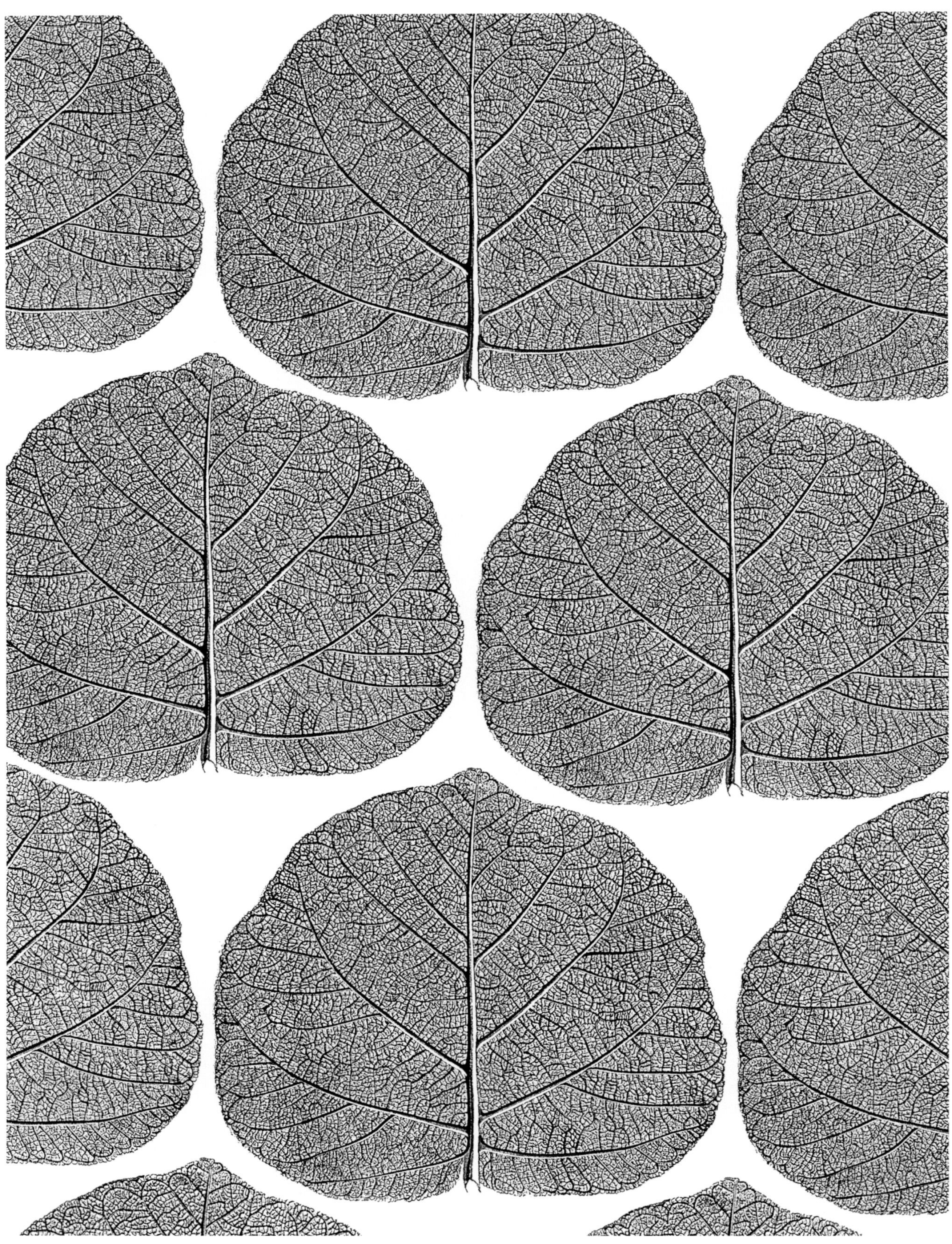

Textile, 'Leaf', designed by Terence Conran, produced by the newly created Conran Fabrics, 1956. The design, derived from an eighteenth-century botanical print, is illustrated in *Printed Textile Design*. Earlier in the 1950s Conran used enlarged single images of this 'leaf' print mounted as wall panels in interior design schemes.

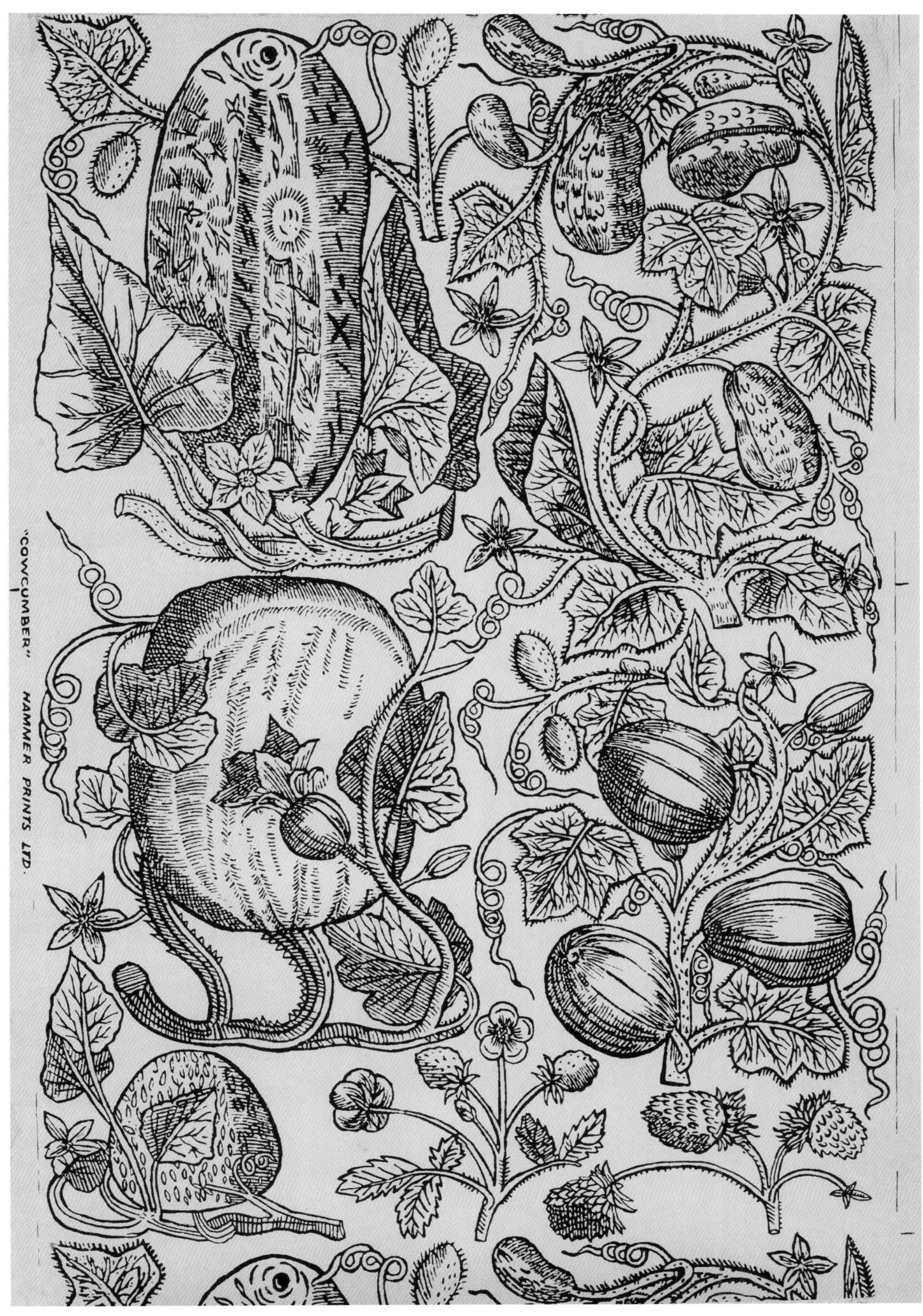

Wallpaper, 'Cowcumber', Hammer Prints, 1956. Produced as both a wallpaper and a textile design. It is derived from a seventeenth-century botanical print. Most prcbably designed by Eduardo Paolozzi and showing Fornasetti's influence, of whom Paolozzi wrote in *Printed Textile Design*: 'I admire the overall approach of Piero Fornasetti who rattles through every subject as an inspiration.'

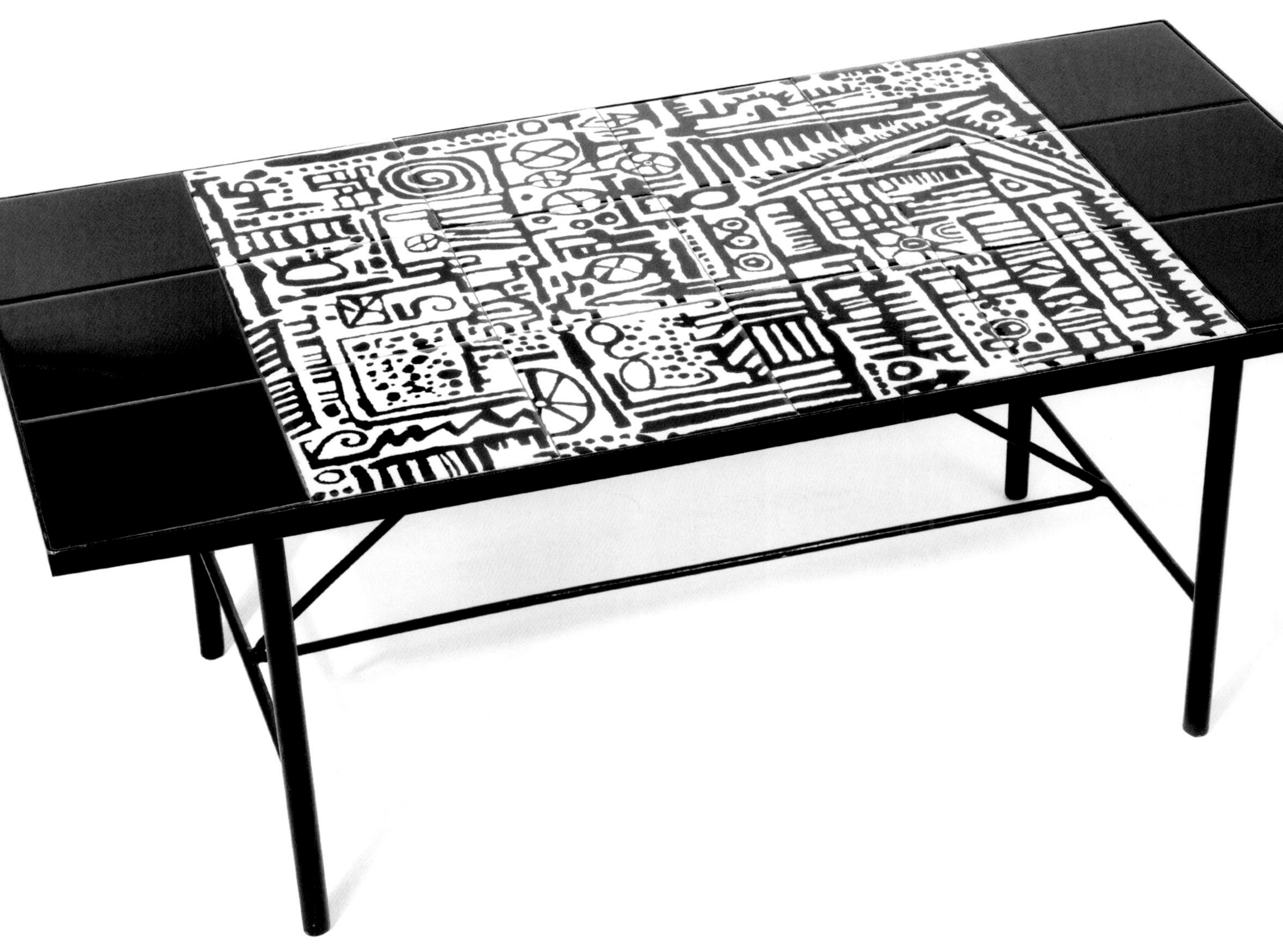

A coffee table with a 'Barkcloth' patterned tiled top for Hammer Prints, c.1956. The table's welded metal frame was designed and produced for Hammer Prints by Paolozzi's friend and former student, Terence Conran. The pattern was screen-printed by Paolozzi and his colleague Nigel Henderson onto H.R. Johnson blanks.

Opposite: Textile 'Barkcloth' for Hammer Prints, 1956. Screen-printed cotton twill. The pattern is inspired by Paolozzi's great personal interest in ethnographical art. A variation exists in which Paolozzi's name is an intregal part of the design.

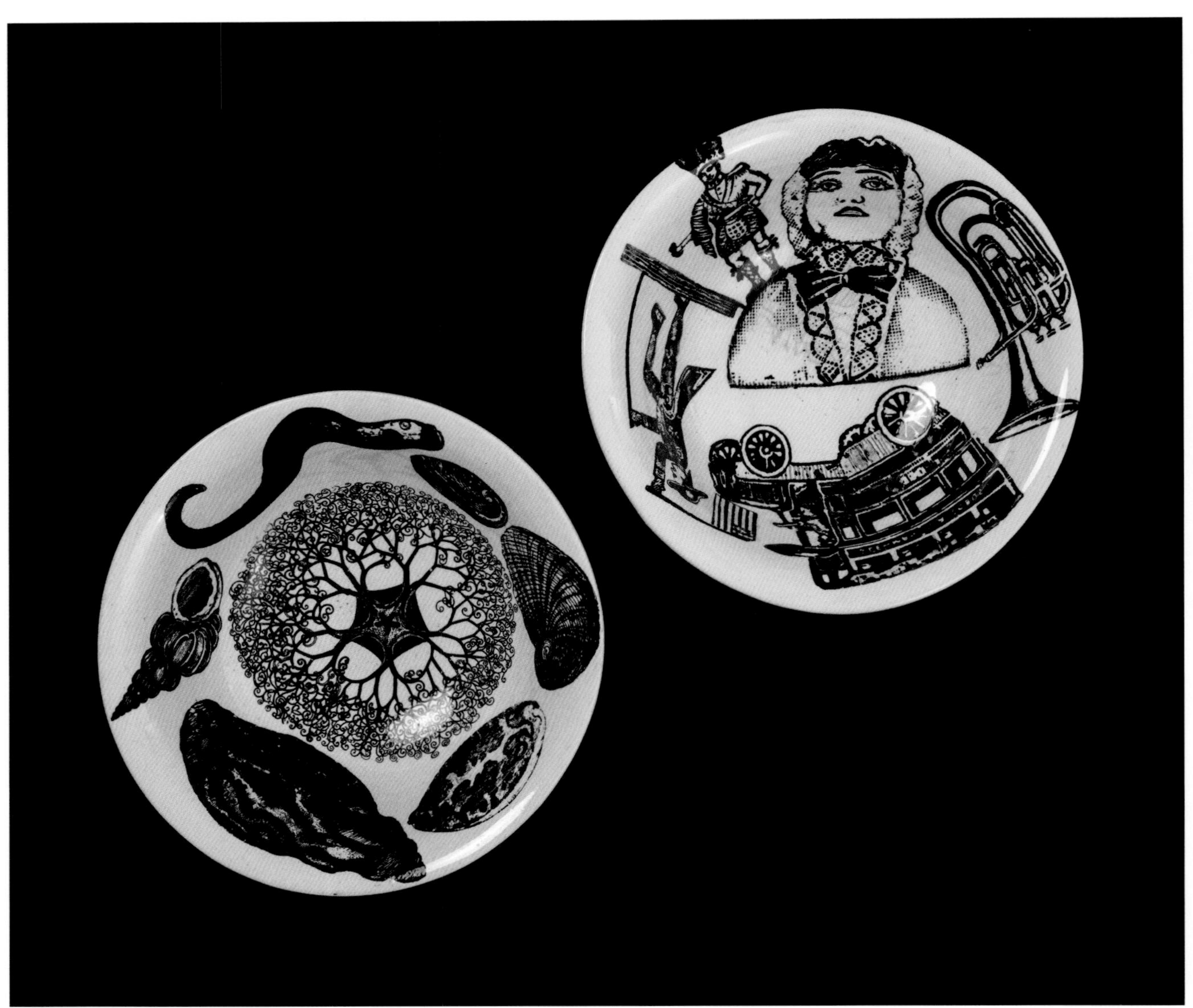

Two bowls by Hammer Prints, screen-printed onto Ridgway Pottery blanks, c.1956. The patterns 'Sea beasts' and 'Toys', influenced by Fornasetti's work, are derived from eighteenth- and nineteenth-century prints.

Opposite: A printed rayon textile designed by Paolozzi, manufactured by David Whitehead Ltd, c.1953. The design is thought to have been purchased by Whitehead's from the exhibition 'Painting Into Textiles', held in London at the Institute of Contemporary Arts in 1953.

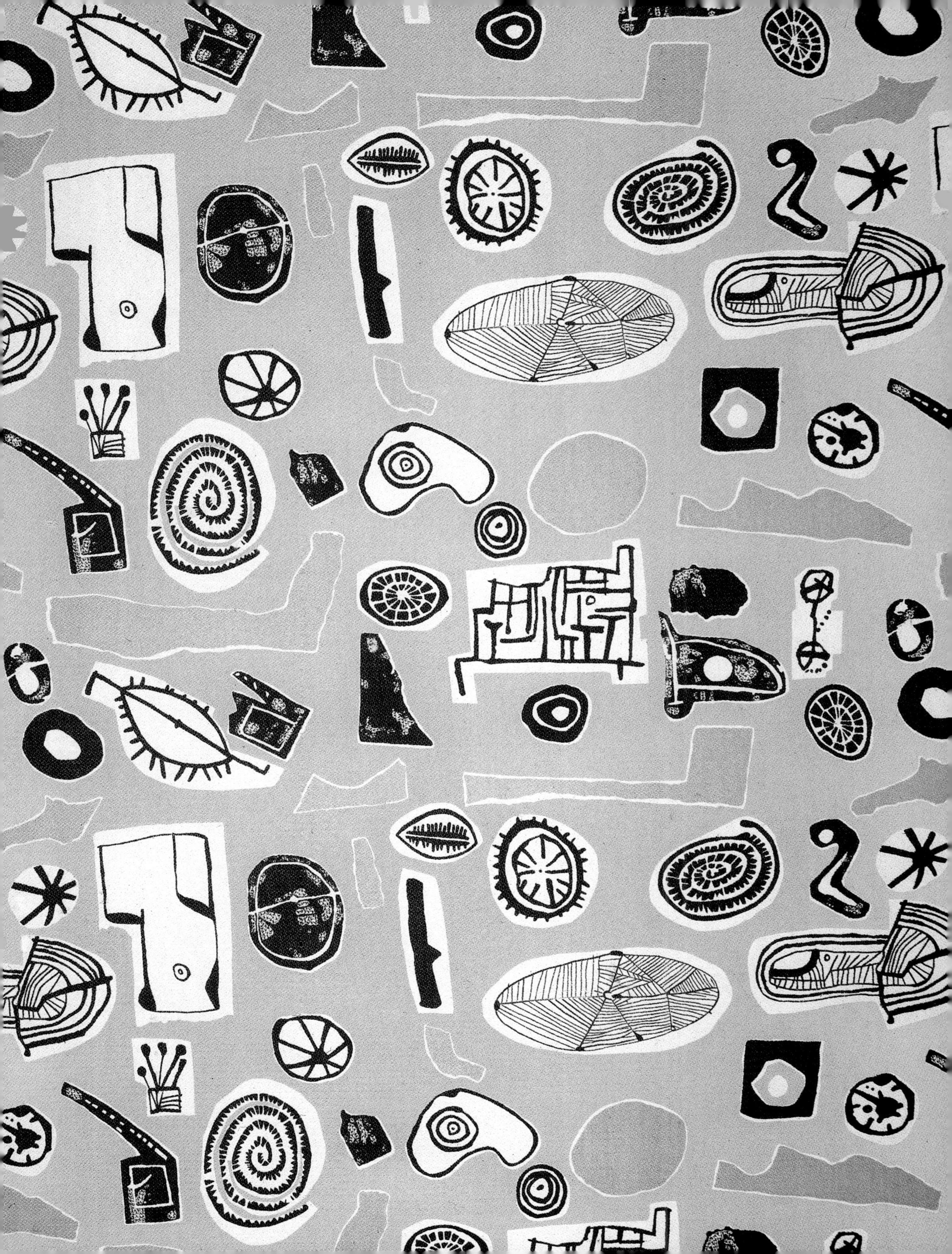

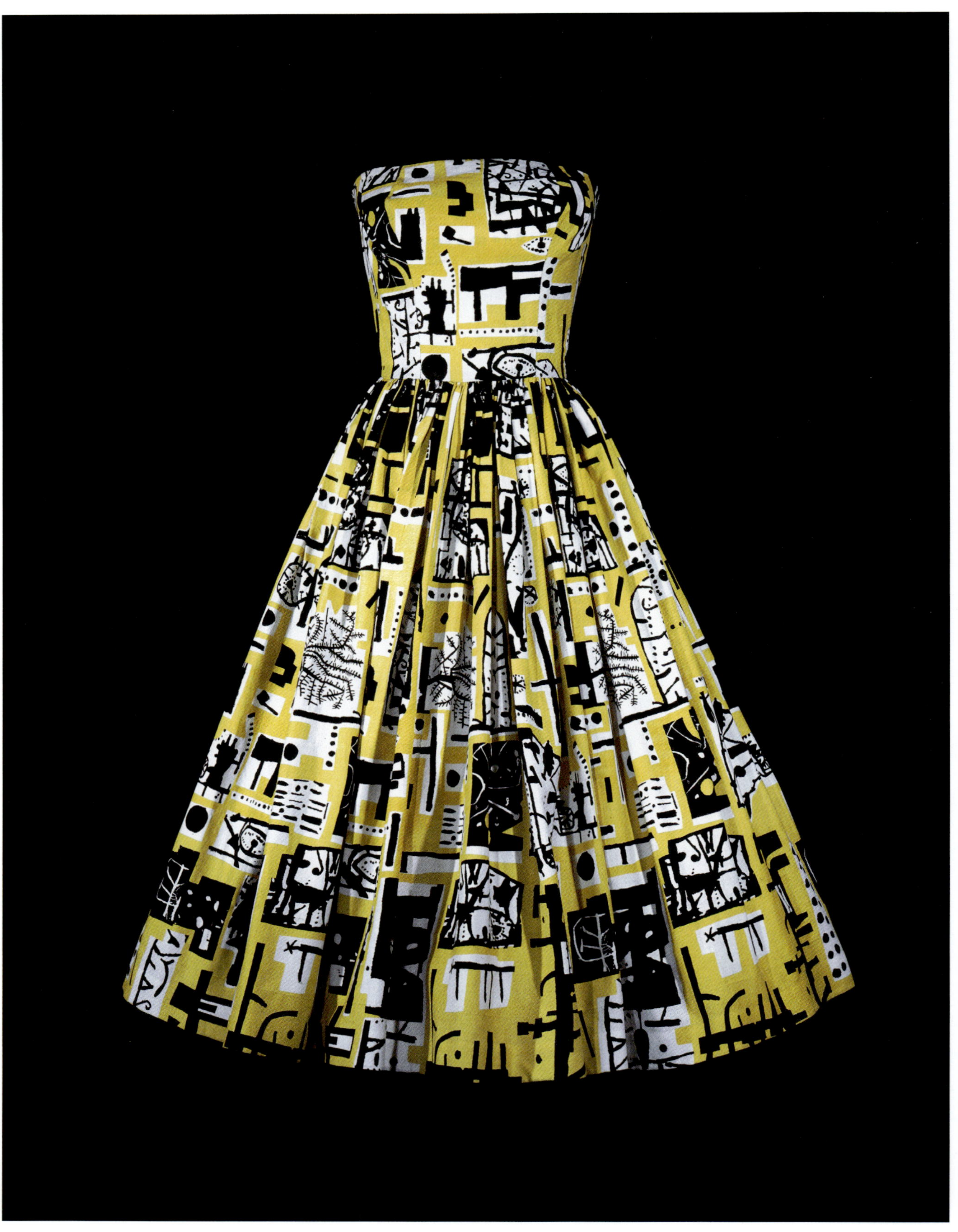

Dress, the textile for which was designed by Paolozzi and exhibited at 'Painting Into Textiles', 1953. This dress, designed by John Tullis for Horrockses Fashions, was part of a group of dresses created for The Queen to select from for her coronation tour of the Commonwealth in 1953.

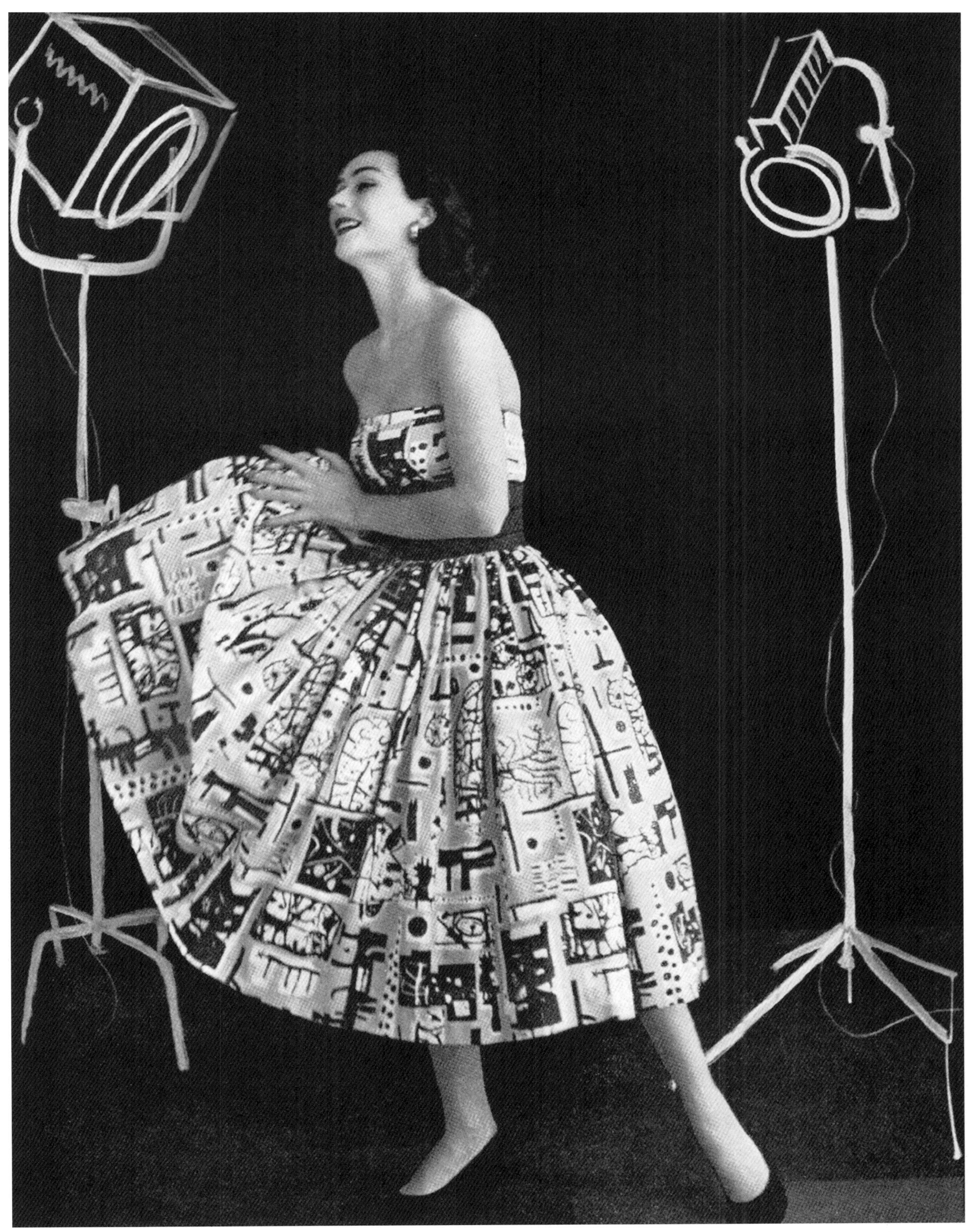

The 'Paolozzi' dress photographed by 'Jay' (Elsbeth Juda) for the *Ambassador Magazine*, 1953.

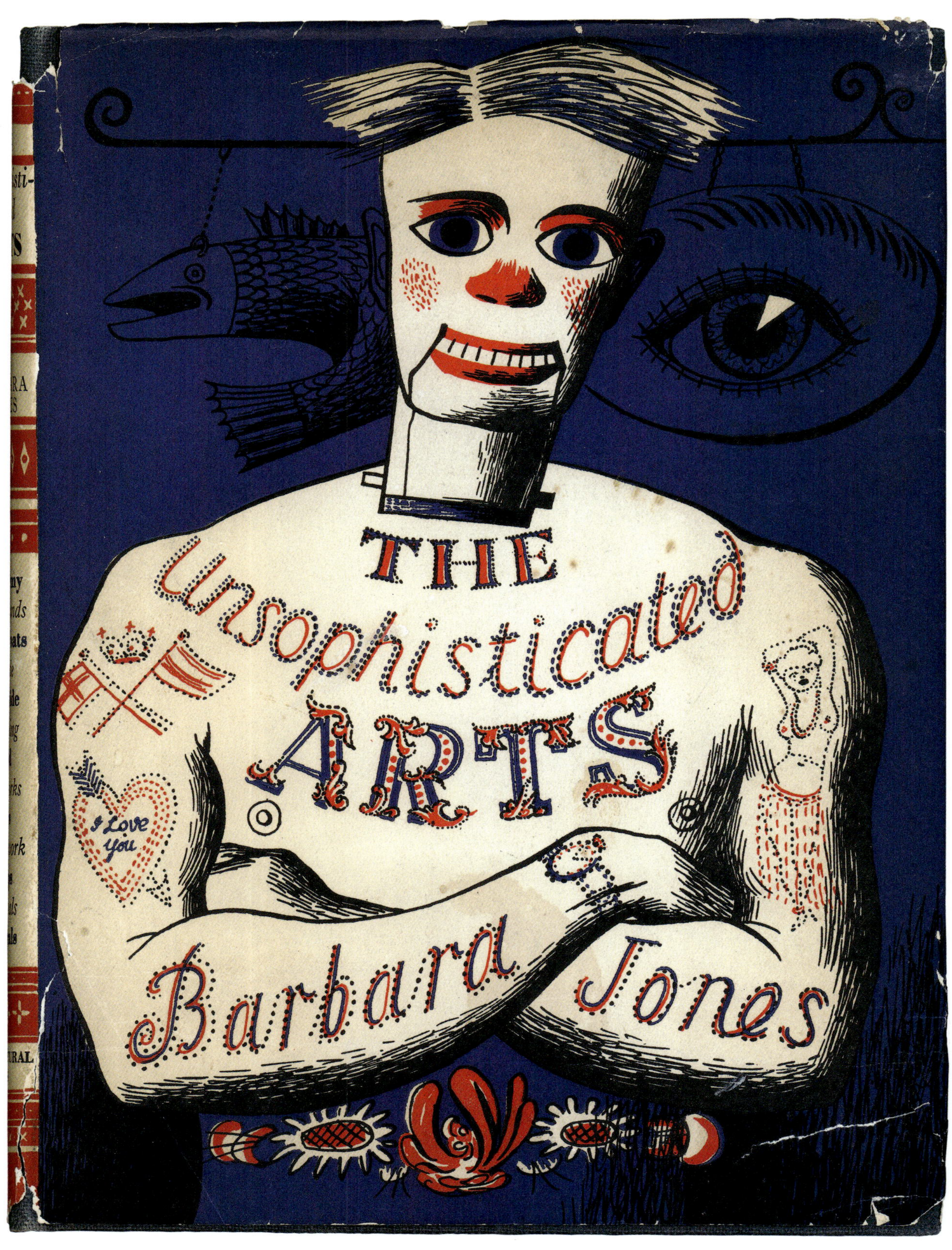

The artist and designer Barbara Jones' dust jacket for her book *The Unsophisticated Arts,* 1951.
Jones, an authority on the Popular arts, was an influential teacher at the Royal College of Art in the
1950 and 1960s. Among her students was the Pop artist Peter Blake.

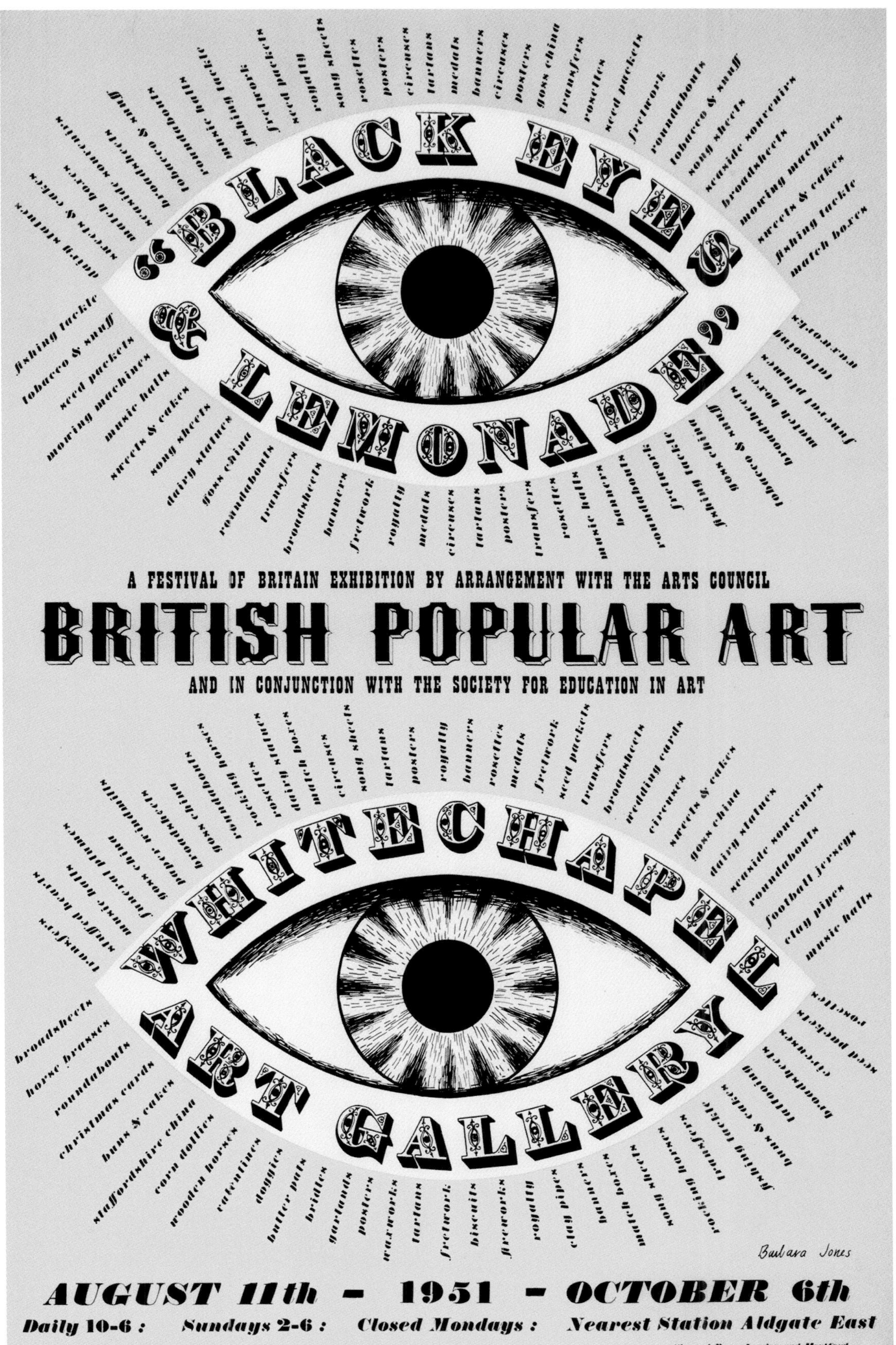

Barbara Jones' poster for her exhibition 'Black Eyes & Lemonade', held at the Whitechapel Art Gallery as part of the Festival of Britain in 1951.

TERENCE CONRAN: 'MEETINGS WITH REMARKABLE MEN'[33]

BETWEEN LEAVING SCHOOL in the summer of 1948, still only 16 years old, and marriage to his second wife Shirley in 1955, Conran's many, often fortuitous, encounters with a succession of remarkable men and women contributed to a fecund abundance of ideas and experiences, which formed a rich primordial soup from which Habitat later emerged.

ON LEAVING SCHOOL he started a course in textile design at London's Central School of Arts and Crafts. He decided, in part, to study textile design on the advice of an exceptional teacher at Bryanston, the art historian Charles Handley-Read. One of the first to seriously study and collect later nineteenth- and early twentieth-century British design, Handley-Read was an authority on the work of the Gothic revival architect William Burges. Tragically, both he and his wife Lavinia committed suicide in 1971. An important memorial exhibition of their collection, 'Victorian and Edwardian Art, the Handley-Read Collection,' was held in London at the Royal Academy of Arts in 1972. Handley-Read's influence is particularly evident in Conran's interest in the ideas and work of the nineteenth-century textile designer, pattern maker and socialist entrepreneur, William Morris. Others have also drawn attention to the correspondence between the aims and ambitions of these two. This was made particularly clear in Fiona MacCarthy's 2014 exhibition at the National Portrait Gallery, 'Anarchy and Beauty, William Morris and His Legacy', which concluded with a photographic enlargement of the young Conran lounging engagingly in his Cone chair, which in turn was displayed beside an example of the chair itself.

ONE OF THE EARLIEST of Conran's meetings with particularly singular people occurred at the Central School, where his teacher in textile design was the sculptor and leading member of the Independent Group, Eduardo Paolozzi, who became his lifelong friend and mentor. Conran's studies at the Central School came to an abrupt end in the second year of his course, however, when he was talent-spotted by the architect and interior designer Dennis Lennon, who, while on a visit to the Central School, was so impressed by Conran's work and ideas that he offered him a job in his design practice. Conran sensibly accepted the offer and, more or less immediately commenced work in Lennon's office, where he gained both much practical experience and his first wife, the architect Brenda Davison. She was a divorcee some five or six years older than him and, he later wrote, taught him a lot on both 'interior design and sensuality'.[34] The highpoint of Conran's work with Lennon was for the Festival of Britain in 1951, where he made many contacts important for the success of his future career. One of the most significant was with John T. Murray, director of furnishing fabrics for the textile manufacturer David Whitehead Ltd, a company then producing some of the most exciting, yet affordable, ranges of avant-garde textiles in Britain. Conran was still working under Lennon's umbrella when he recycled his earlier design 'Chequers' for Whitehead's display at the Festival, one of the most successful textiles of the era.

AFTER LEAVING Dennis Lennon's practice, following the closure of the Festival in late 1951, Conran was able to sign a formal contract with Whitehead's, for whom he designed a well-known series of textiles which epitomize the 'Contemporary' aesthetic. One extraordinary off-shoot of Conran's brief sojourn with Whitehead's was the premature development in 1952 of an advanced but ill-fated range of printed denim, conceived for the teen market some twenty years ahead of a fashion which eventually took off in the late 1960s. Over the course of the following decade he also created several extremely successful patterns for the pottery manufacturer W.R. Midwinter's 'Stylecraft' range of tableware. For a dinner service in the Midwinter 'Fashion' shape, he re-used his textile design 'Chequers', and, drawing on his great personal interest in natural history, created for another entitled 'Nature Study'. His culinary pursuits found expression in the design 'Salad Ware' and his interest in both gardens and interior design was acknowledged in 'Plant Life', all of which have since become popular icons of Contemporary design.

IT WAS PARTLY through Conran's involvement with Midwinter that his friend, the industrial designer and later Professor of Ceramics at the Royal College of Art, David, Marquis of Queensbury, became involved with the company. It was he who successfully brought Midwinter ceramics into the 1960s with his new 'Fine' shape, later known as MQ1, which he successfully followed with his second design for the company, MQ2. It was also Queensbury who inadvertently introduced Conran to Shirley, the girl who would become his second wife (although at that time she was still Queensbury's girlfriend). Another former Royal College student then also taken up as a designer by Midwinter was the sculptor Colin Melbourne, Queensbury's friend and former partner in Drumlanrig Melbourne, Queensbury's first commercial ceramic venture. Melbourne created for Midwinter a range of now celebrated ceramic animal figures, very much the post-war equivalents of John Skeaping's animalier for Wedgwood in the 1930s.

CONRAN ALWAYS HAD a particular interest in furniture design, and while working with Dennis Lennon, he designed and made a group of metal and plywood furniture commissioned for the Ridgeway Hotel, Lusaka, now the capital of Zambia. He made the chairs in a lockup workshop he was renting with Paolozzi in a railway arch in Bethnal Green, where, having learnt the craft of metal welding while at Bryanston School, he initiated Paolozzi into the mysteries of that useful skill.

AN EARLY FEATHER in Conran's cap was the purchase by Picasso of several examples of an extraordinary chair he'd designed, a sort of grand Contemporary-style statement. This was accomplished through his friend Toby Jellinek, who was then living in France and making furniture in a workshop opposite Picasso's studio in Vallauris. Among the furniture he produced was this sculptural throne-like design of Conran's. Jellinek's girlfriend Sylvette became Picasso's model for a while, and it was through this connection that Jellinek made him a gift of Conran's chair. Picasso was so pleased with it that he ordered two more. Picasso's mistress Françoise Gilot later recalled in her biography *Life with Picasso*, that:

'It was such an abstraction of an idea of a chair that it reminded Pablo of certain paintings he had done during the 1930s ... a chair made up of a skeleton framework much like this one.' [35]

DURING THIS TIME, 1950-53, Conran lived in a series of rented rooms in the houses of various friends, which seem to have run on the lines of artists' collectives, that remarkably presage the communes of the later 1960s. Living this way, he made many good friends who became fans and supporters of his work. The first of his landlords, Ivan Storey, was a former boyfriend of Conran's first wife Brenda. It was with him that Conran later set up the Soup Kitchen. Conran's friend Toby Jellinek was also a tenant there for a short while. More importantly for the success of Conran's excellent long-term relationship with the influential magazine *House & Garden*, was Olive Sullivan, the magazine's decoration editor, who lived on the top floor. Living close by, Paolozzi also spent much time at the house, often working alongside Conran in a room in the basement they had utilised as a sort of studio. Paolozzi also mainly ate there as 'where he lived was so horrid'. [36]

A FELLOW TENANT of Conran at Storey's house was the writer and poet Den Newton, who became a major influence on him and an important mentor. When Newton and his wife subsequently moved to a house of their own in South Kensington, Conran moved with them. His friend, the sculptor William Turnbull, a member of the Independent Group, also had rooms there, as did a former lecturer at the Central School, the typographer and exhibition designer Ian Bradbery. It was Bradbery who later encouraged Conran to offer a complete professional exhibition and interior design service which became, in 1956, the Conran Design Group. Bradbery was also responsible for the design of some of Conran's early catalogues and other graphic design work.

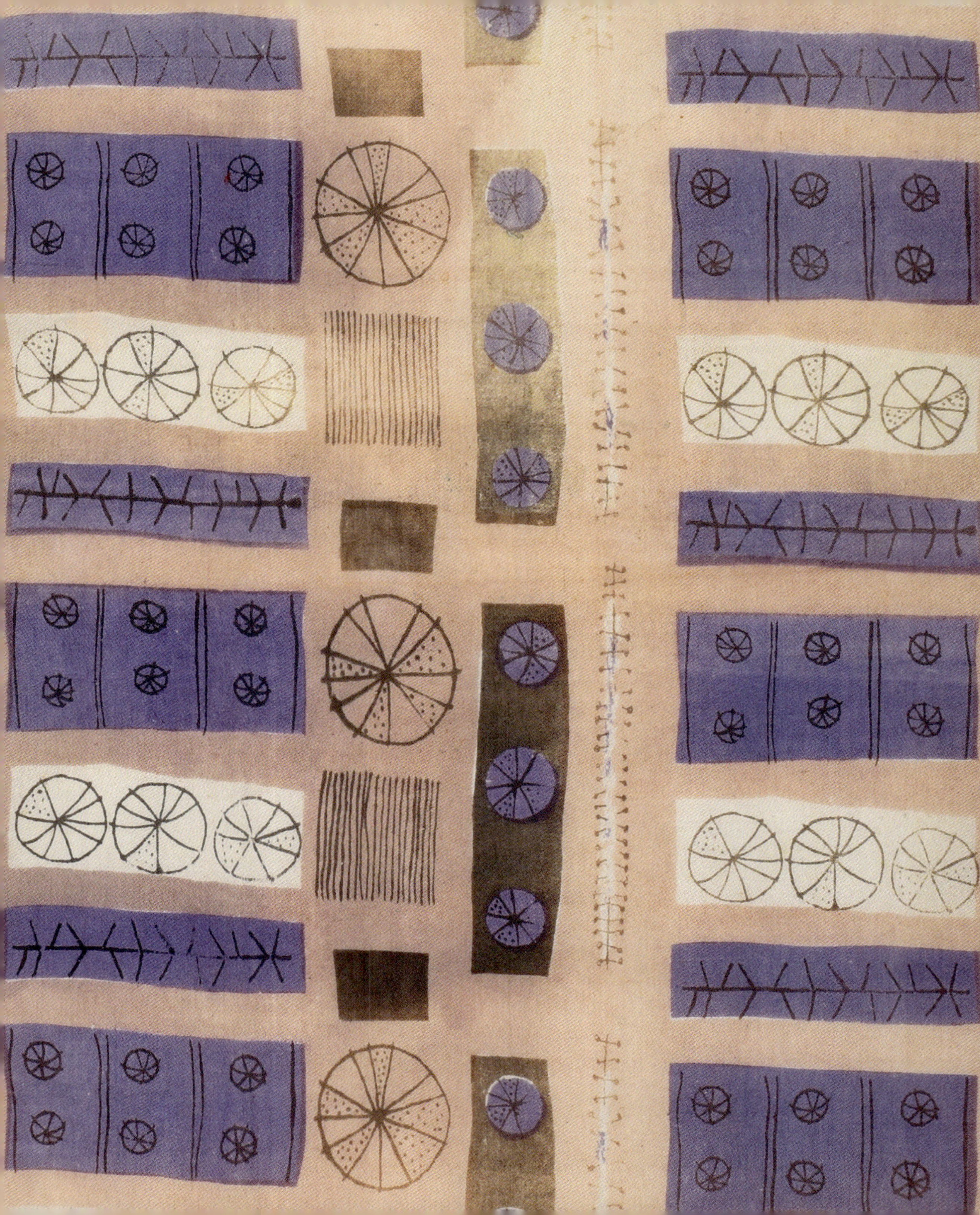

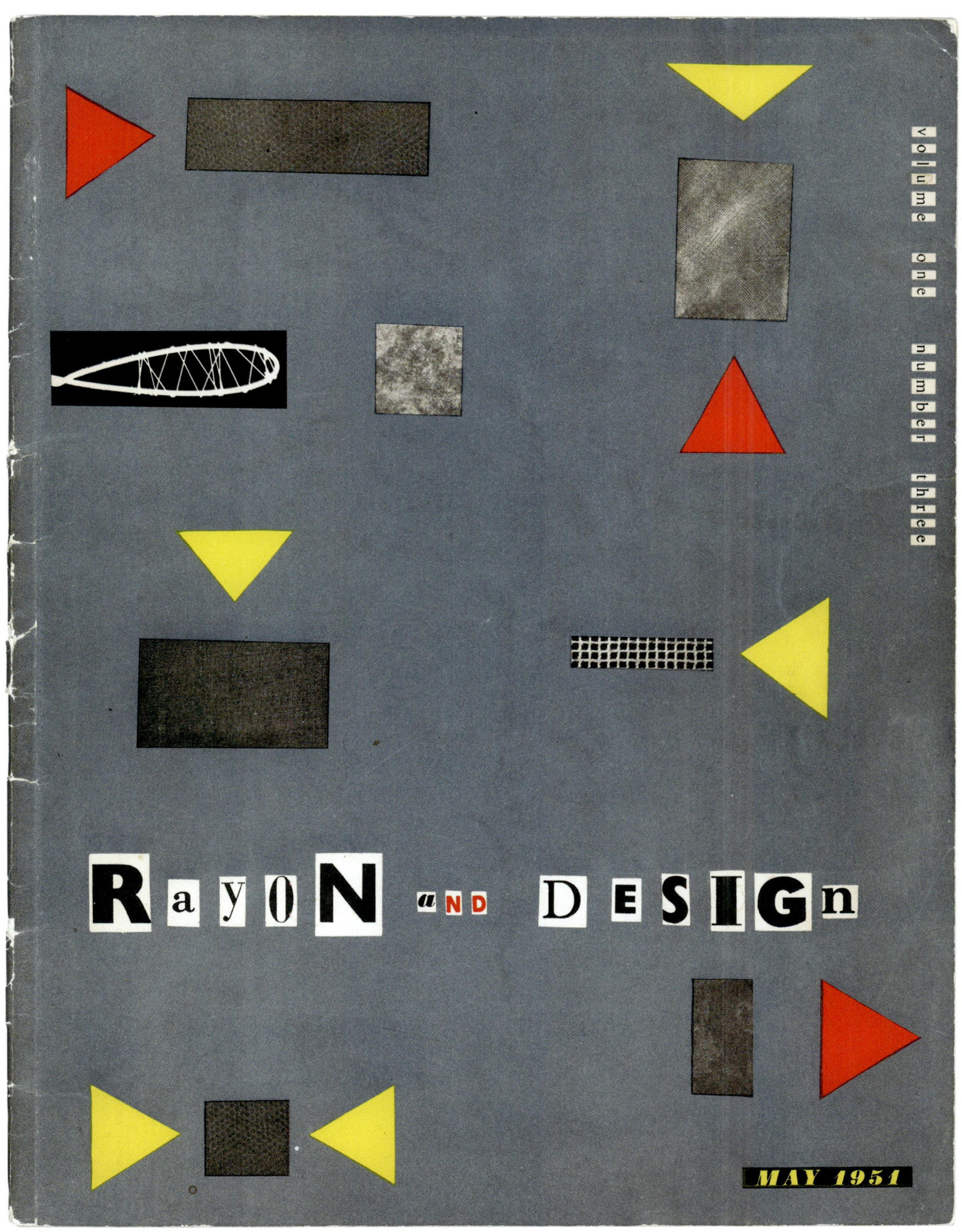

Conran's cover for *Rayon and Design* magazine, May 1951.

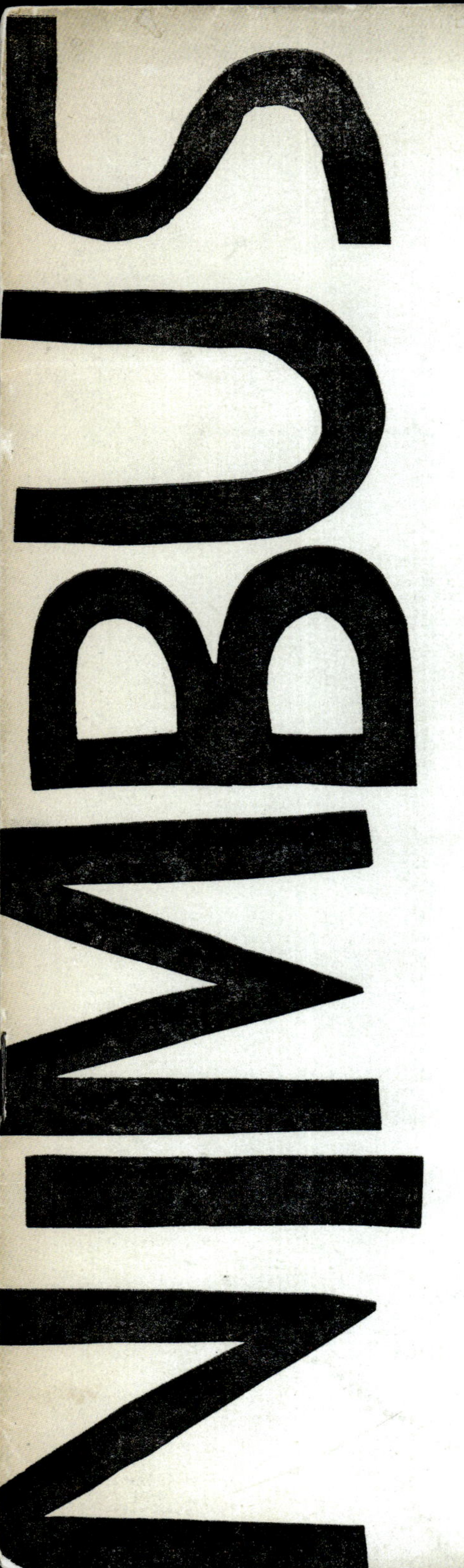

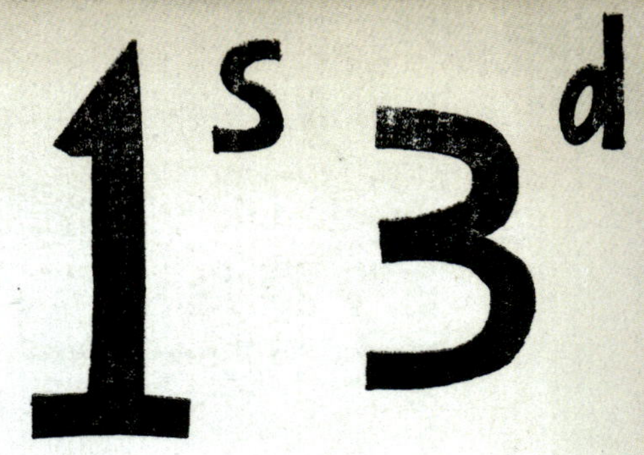

FRANCES BELLERBY

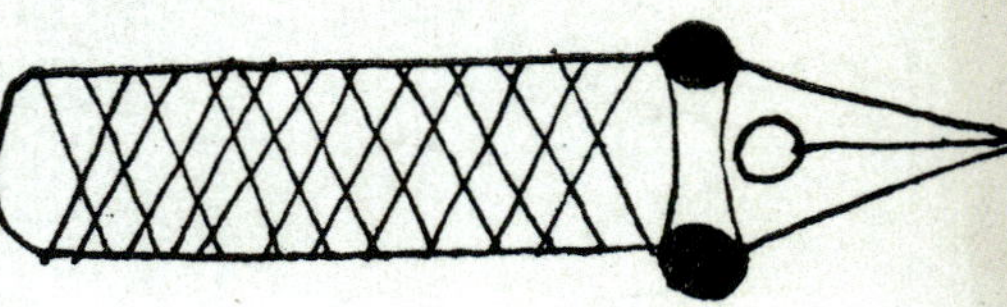

R. F. C. HULL

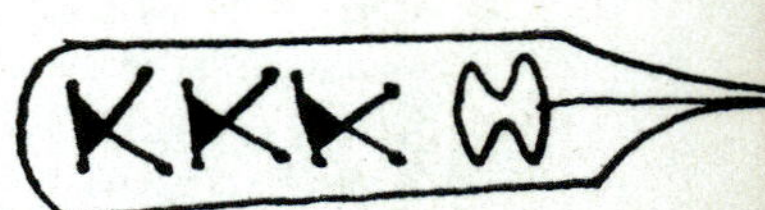

CLIVE SPENCER

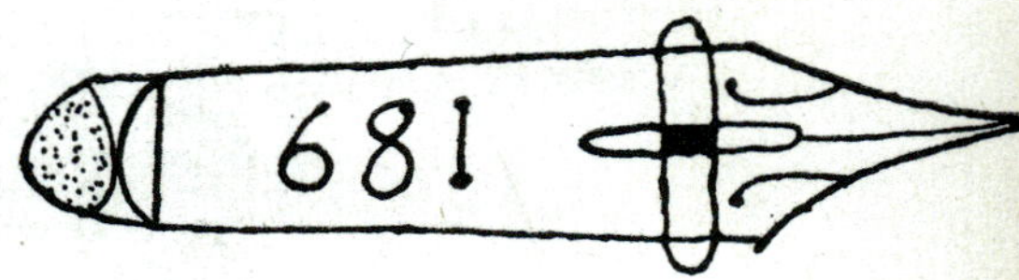

& OTHERS

No. 1   December 1951

The cover of *Nimbus*, a quarterly magazine, No.1, December 1951.
Designed by Terence Conran, edited by Tristram Hull, with an essay by Conran's friend,
Toby Jellinek.

Opposite: Textile, 'Mobile', designed by Terence Conran for Edinburgh Weavers.
Screen-printed cotton, 1950.

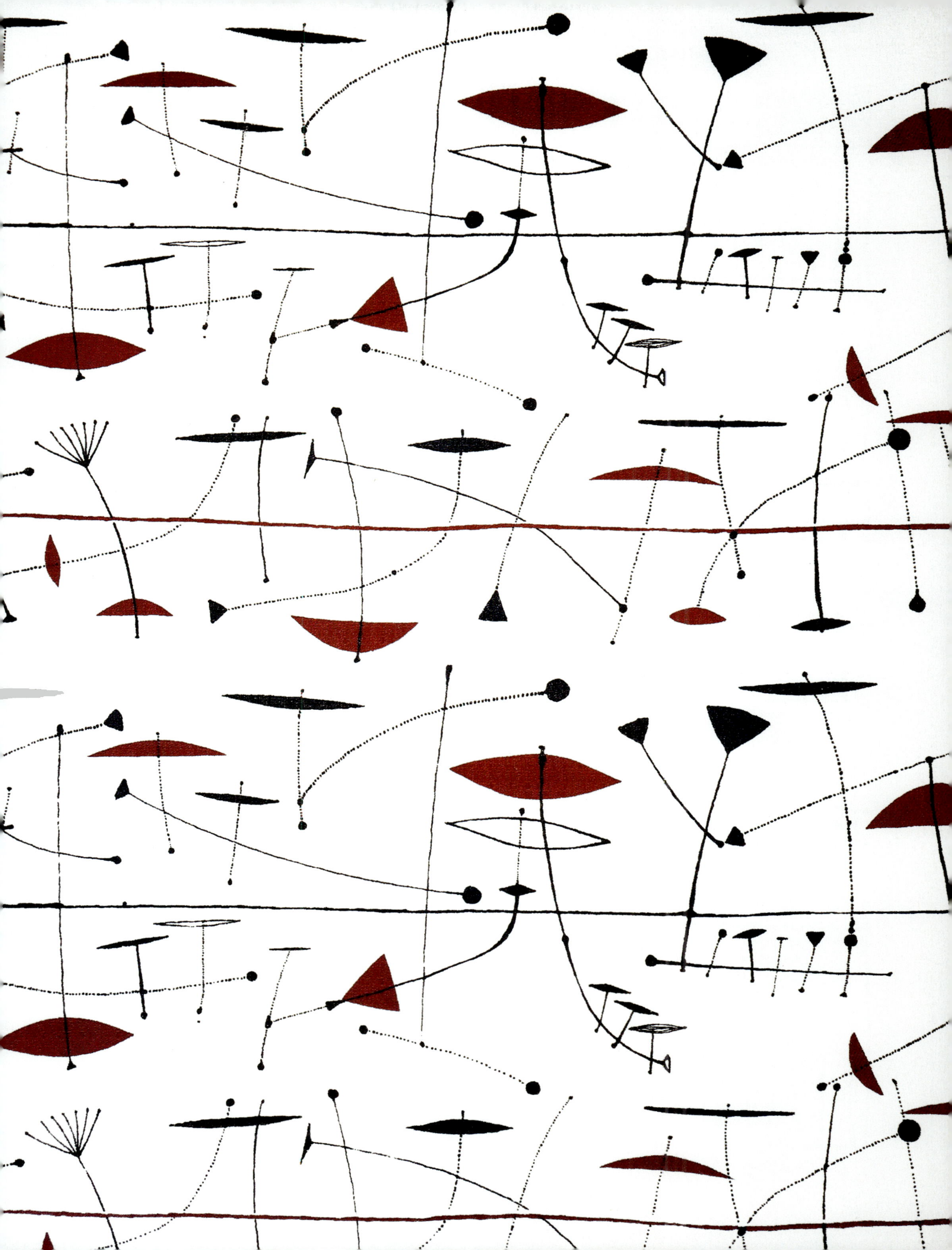

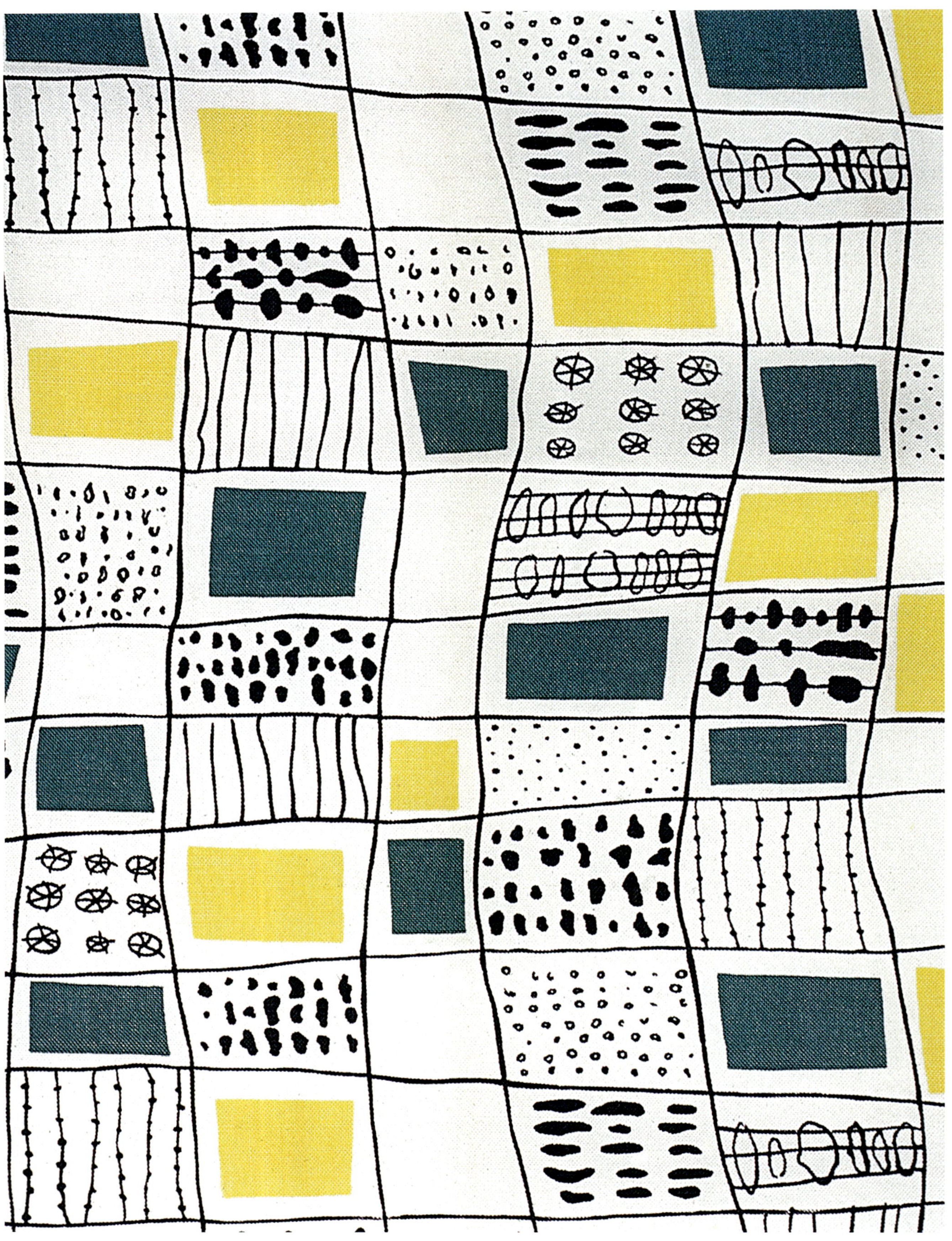

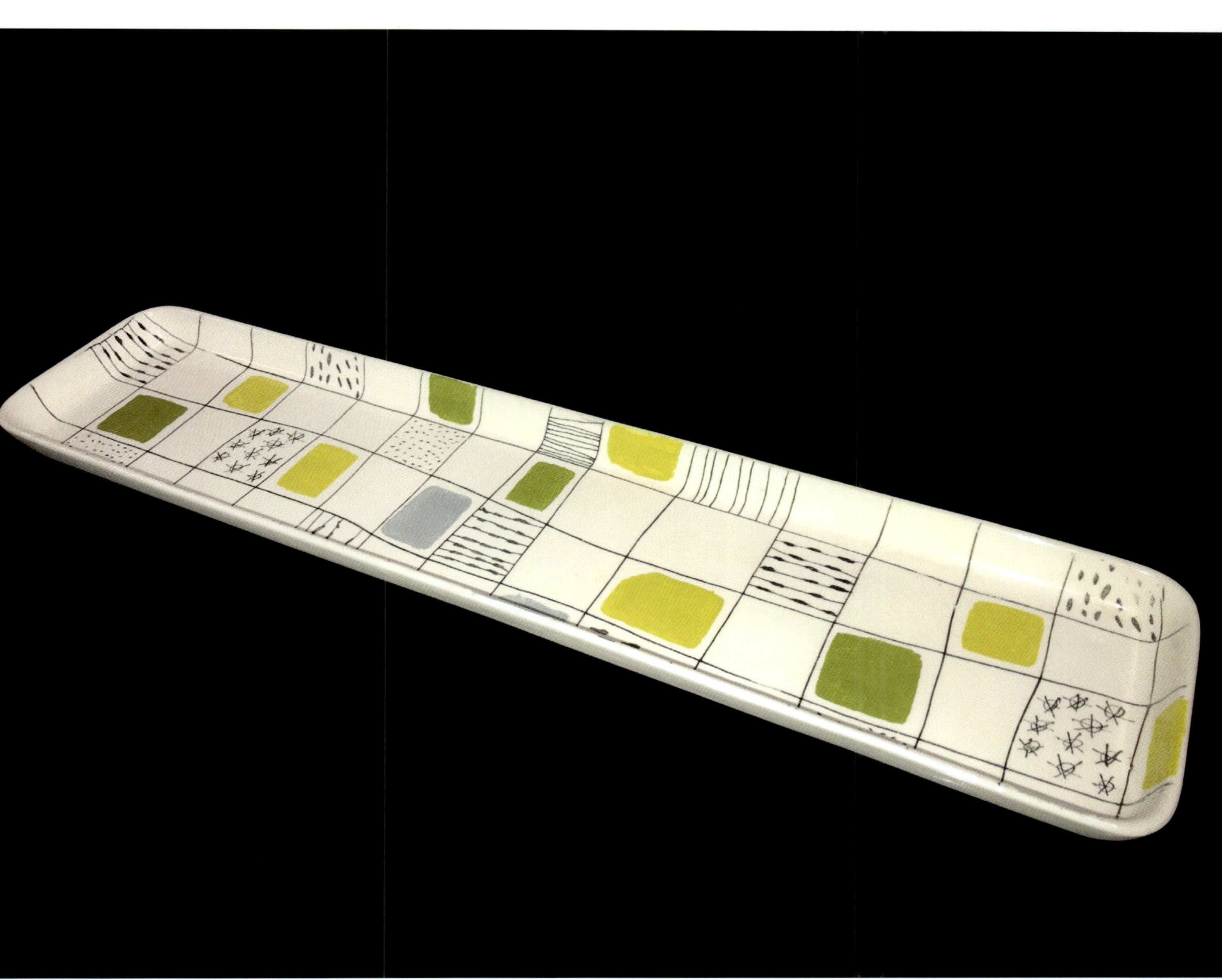

A 'Long Tom' hors d'oeuvres tray, decorated with the 'Chequers' pattern. Terence Conran for W.R. Midwinter Ltd, 1957.

Opposite: Textile, 'Chequers', designed by Terence Conran for David Whitehead Ltd. Roller-printed rayon, 1950. One of several textiles produced by Whitehead's that Conran had designed whilst still studying at the Central School.

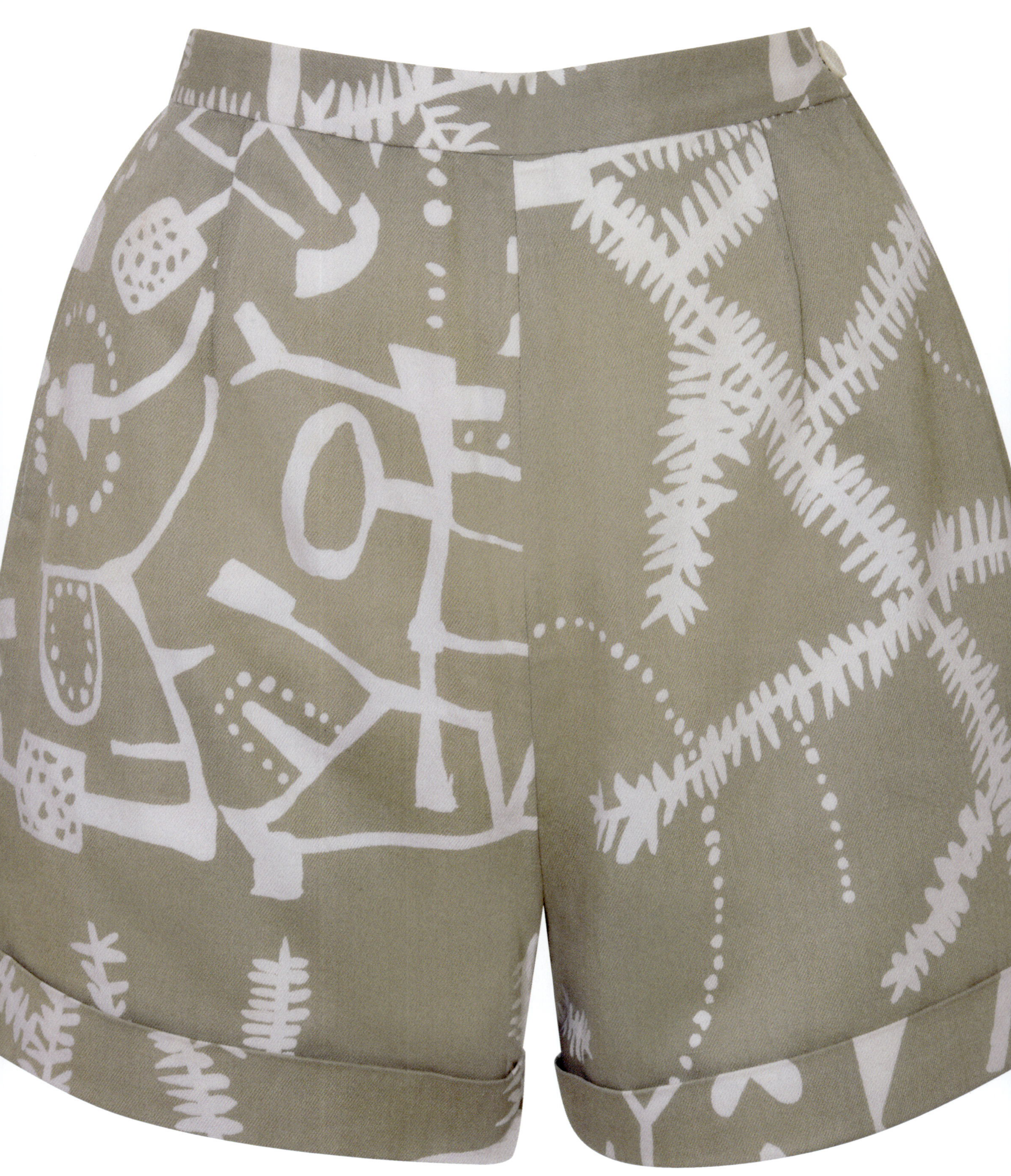

A pair of women's shorts in denim printed with Conran's 'Mani' pattern. Textile designed by Terence Conran for David Whitehead Ltd. 1952. The shorts were manufactured by Renda, part of The Teenage Fashion Group, 1952. Whitehead's decided not to market this range of printed denim, considering it too advanced at that time.

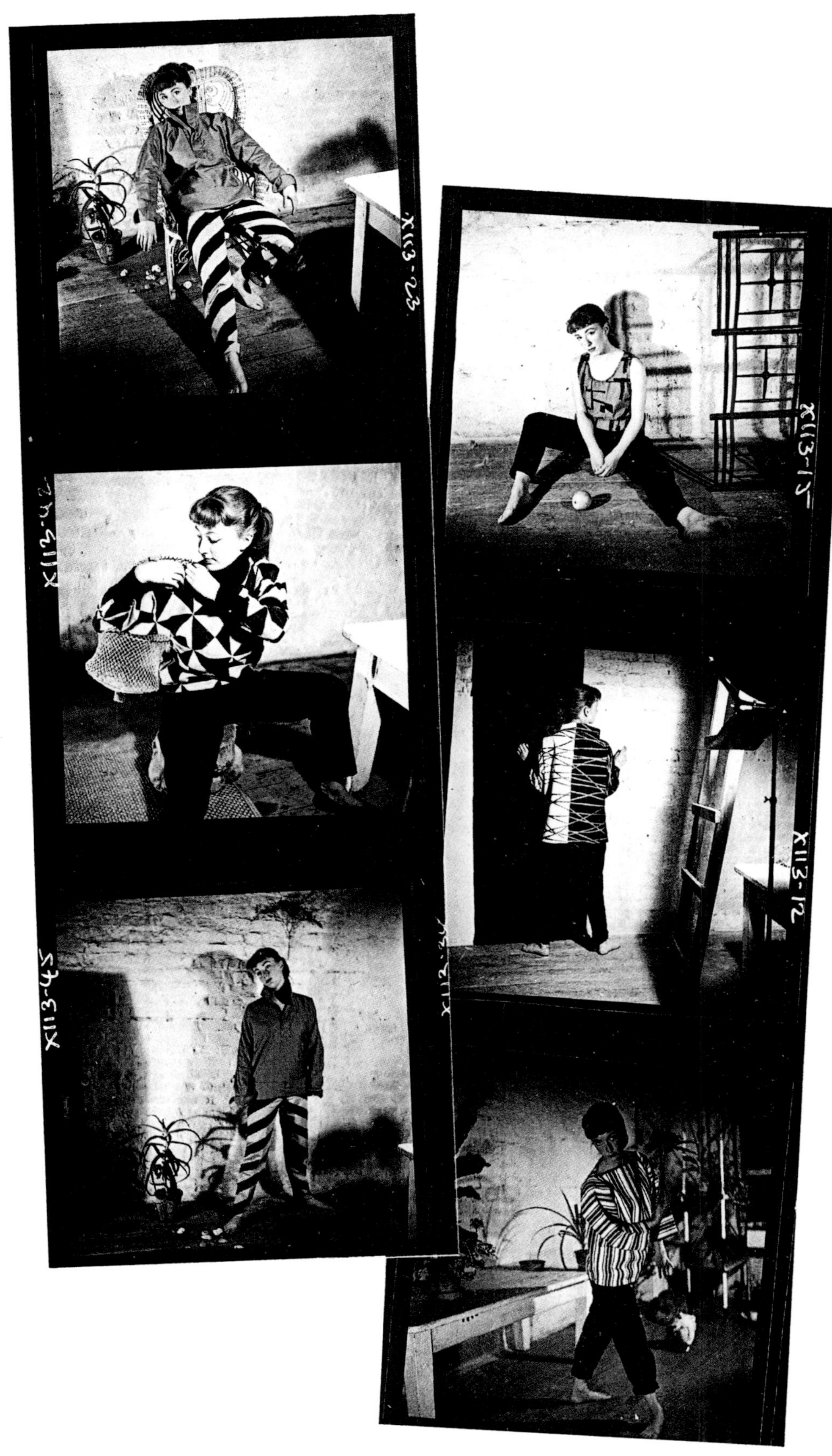

Contact strips of models wearing clothing made in Whitehead's range of printed denim,
designed by Terence Conran, 1952. Photographed by Michael Wickham.

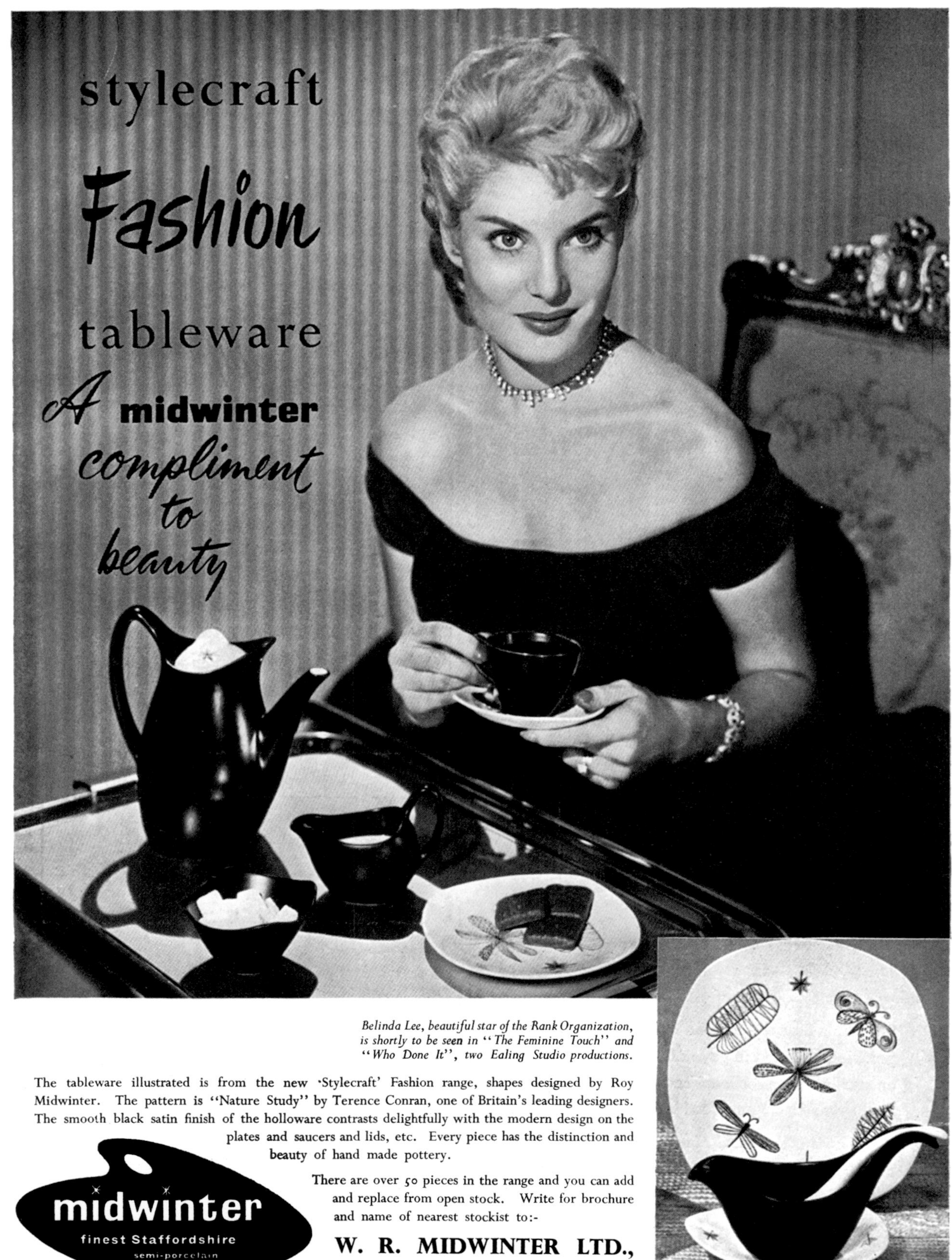

Advertisement for W.R. Midwinter's range of tableware in Conran's 'Nature Study' pattern, 1956.

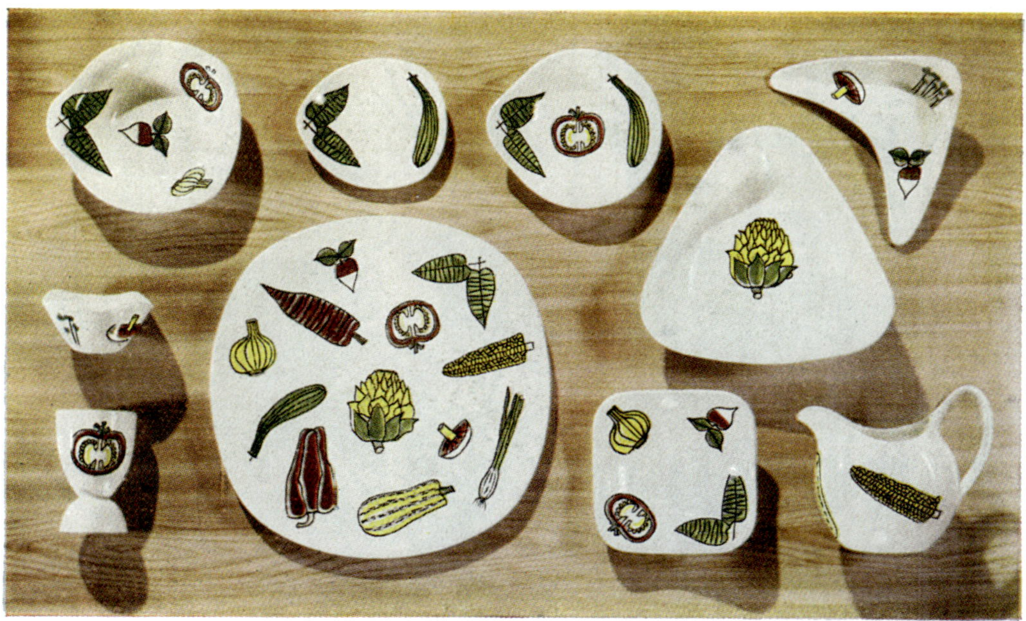

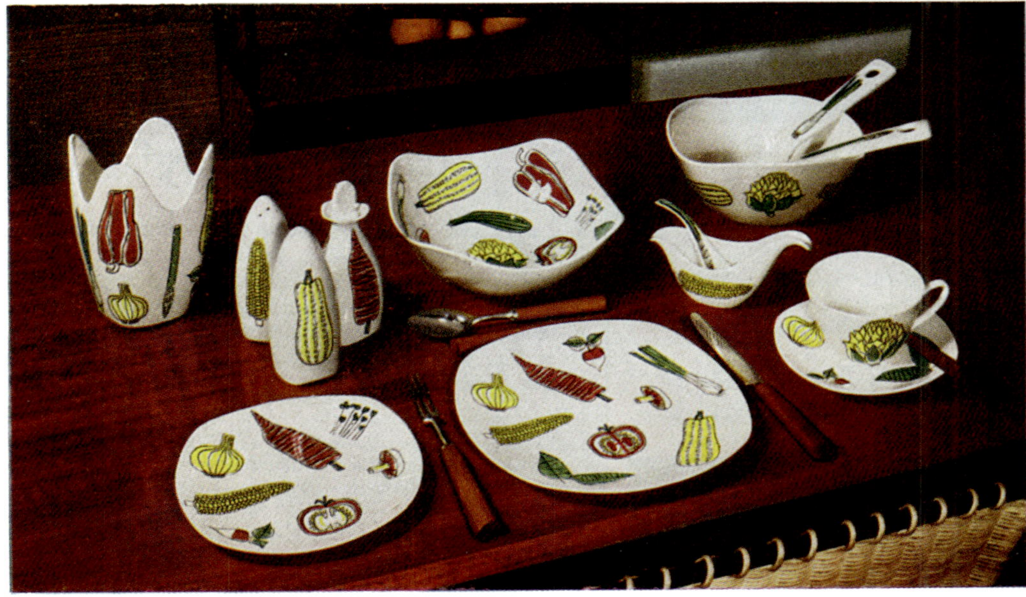

stylecraft *Fashion* SHAPE BY

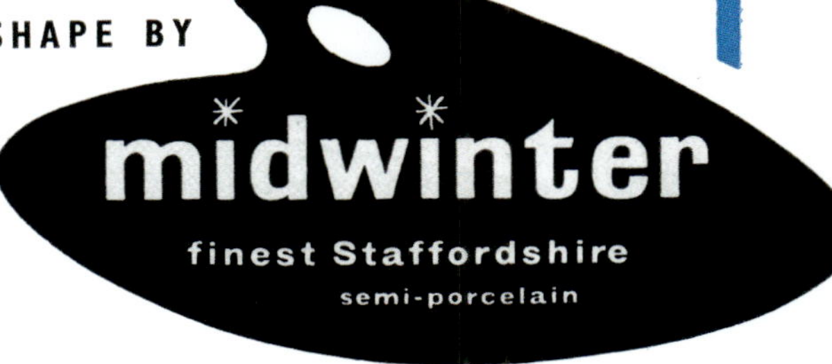

Salad Ware combines the grace and beauty of Roy Midwinter's shape designs with the strikingly sympathetic Terence Conran drawings reproduced in bold striking colours. Decoration is underglaze and unaffected by the weak acids and juices normally associated with salads. The lovely new shapes include such interesting pieces that make up the condiment set.

Colour brochures and price list now available.

W. R. MIDWINTER LTD. (Dept. H.U.G.7.) BURSLEM, STOKE-ON-TRENT

Advertisement for Midwinter ceramics with Conran's new 'Saladware' pattern, 1956.

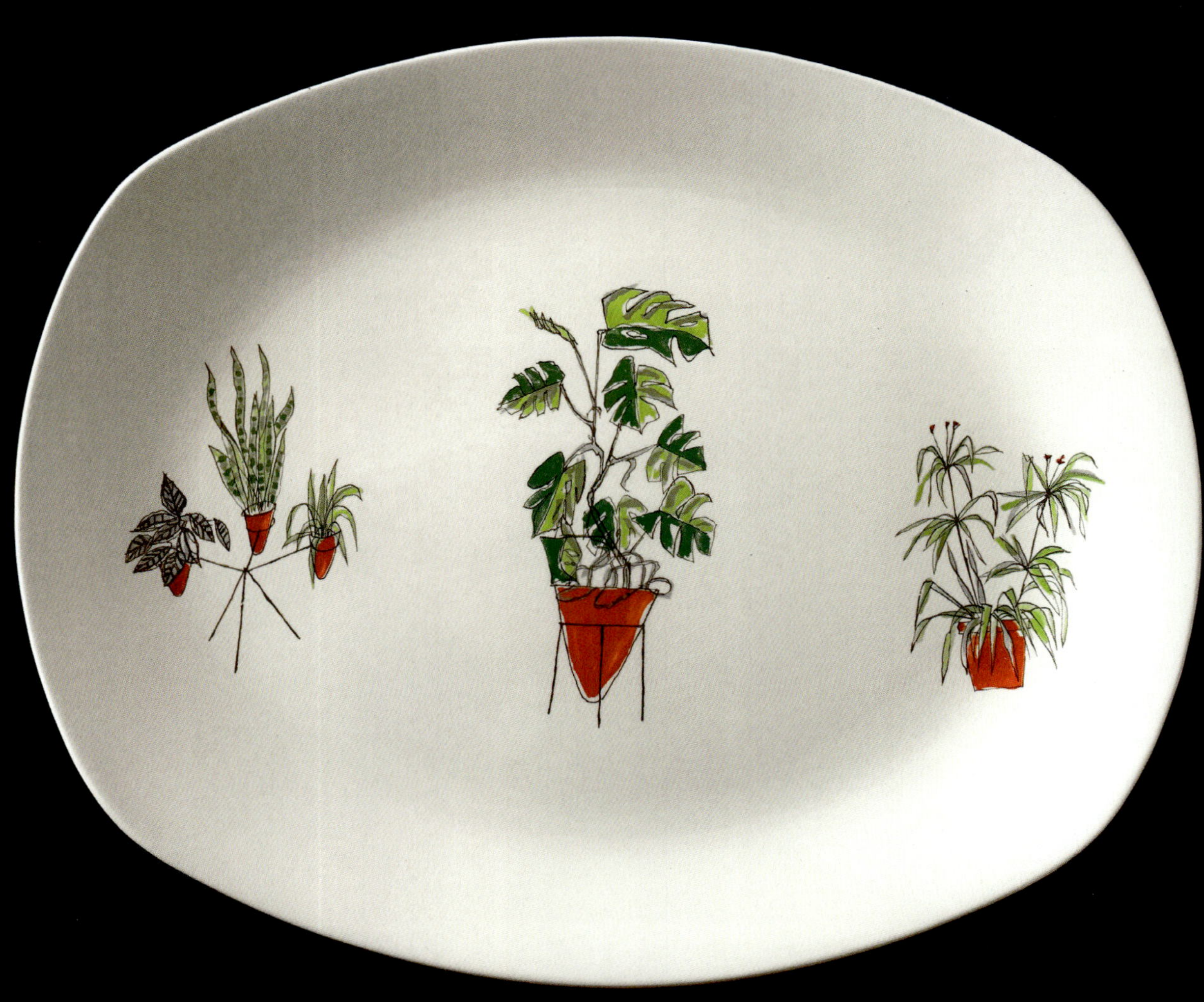

A large serving plate with Conran's 'Plant Life' design for Midwinter, c.1956.

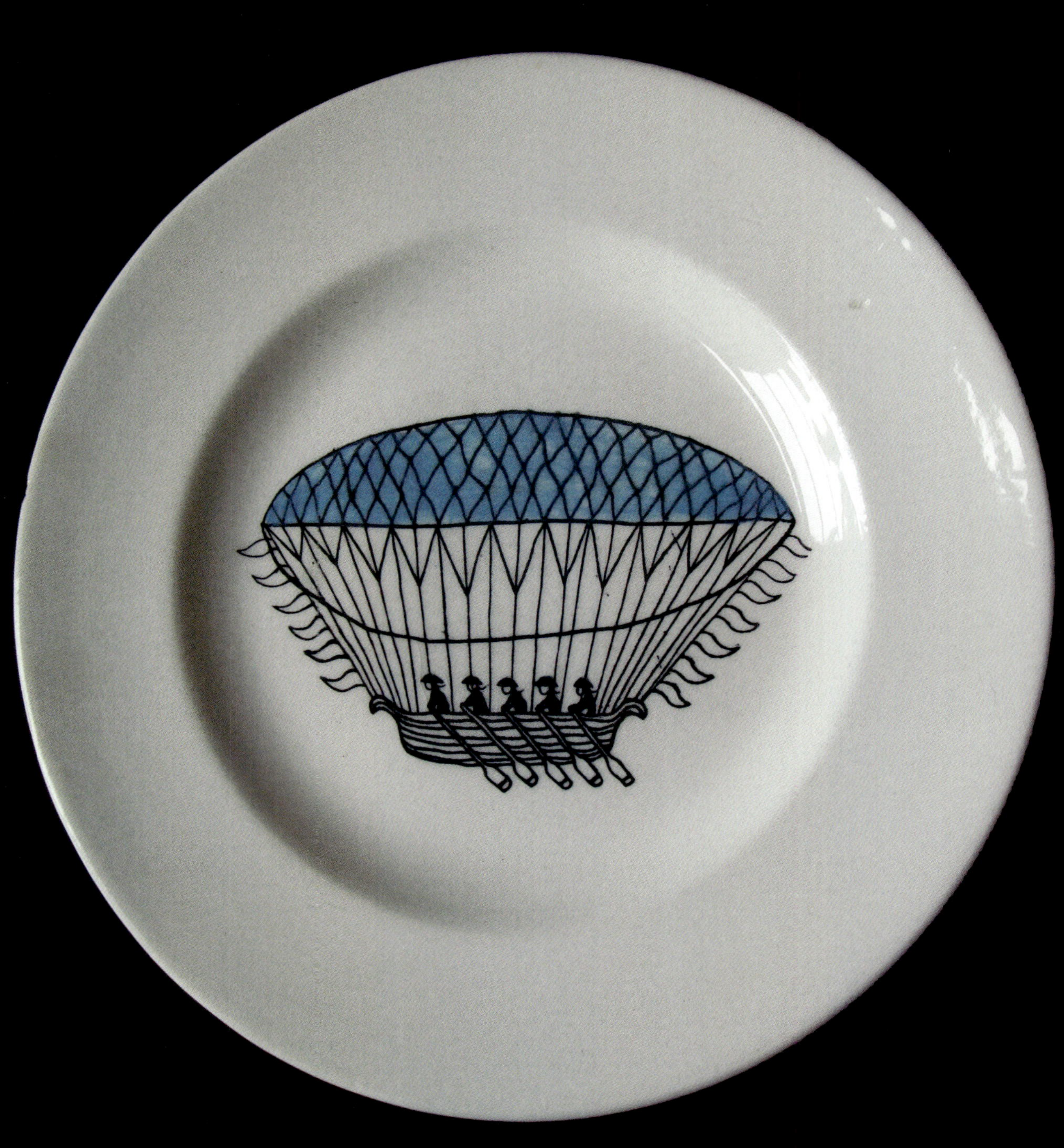

A rare example of 'Balloonware', c.1955. This plate was probably manufactured by Midwinter for retailing by Conran & Co.

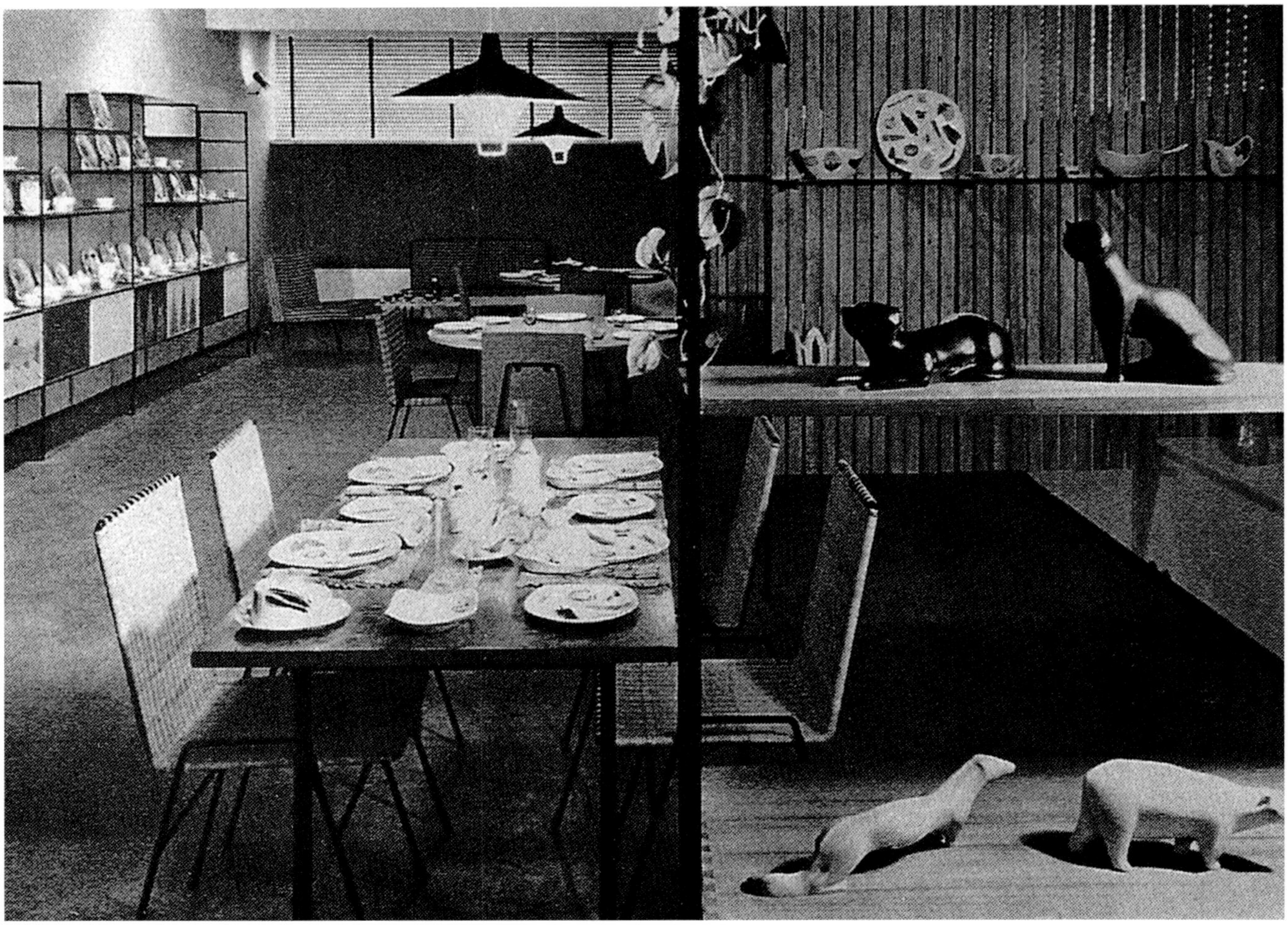

The interior of the new Midwinter showroom, 1956. Commissioned from Conran
by his friend and patron Roy Midwinter.

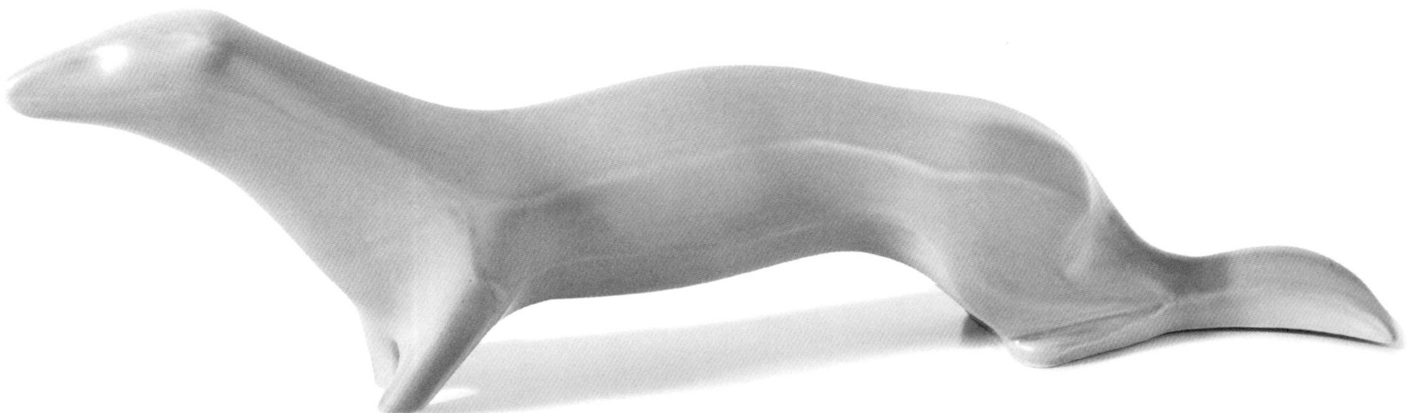

Ceramic scuplture of a stoat by Colin Melbourne, 1956. From the range of
ceramic animalia Melbourne created for W.R. Midwinter Ltd.

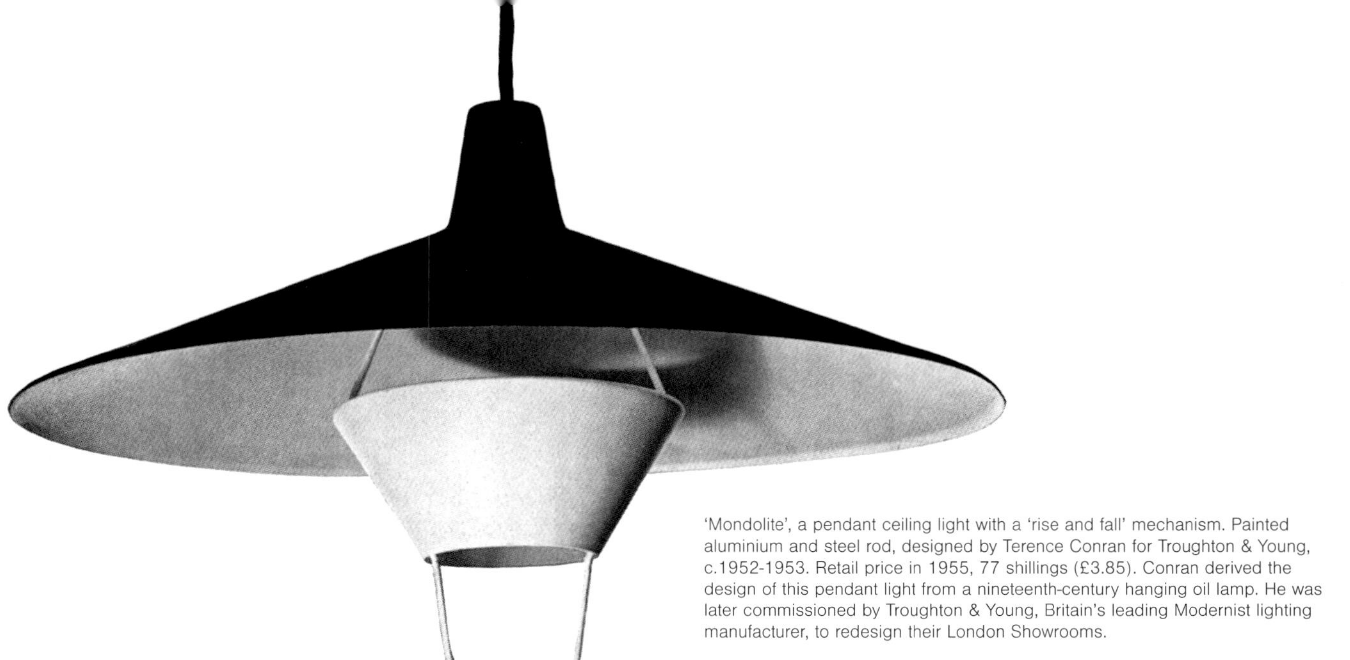

'Mondolite', a pendant ceiling light with a 'rise and fall' mechanism. Painted aluminium and steel rod, designed by Terence Conran for Troughton & Young, c.1952-1953. Retail price in 1955, 77 shillings (£3.85). Conran derived the design of this pendant light from a nineteenth-century hanging oil lamp. He was later commissioned by Troughton & Young, Britain's leading Modernist lighting manufacturer, to redesign their London Showrooms.

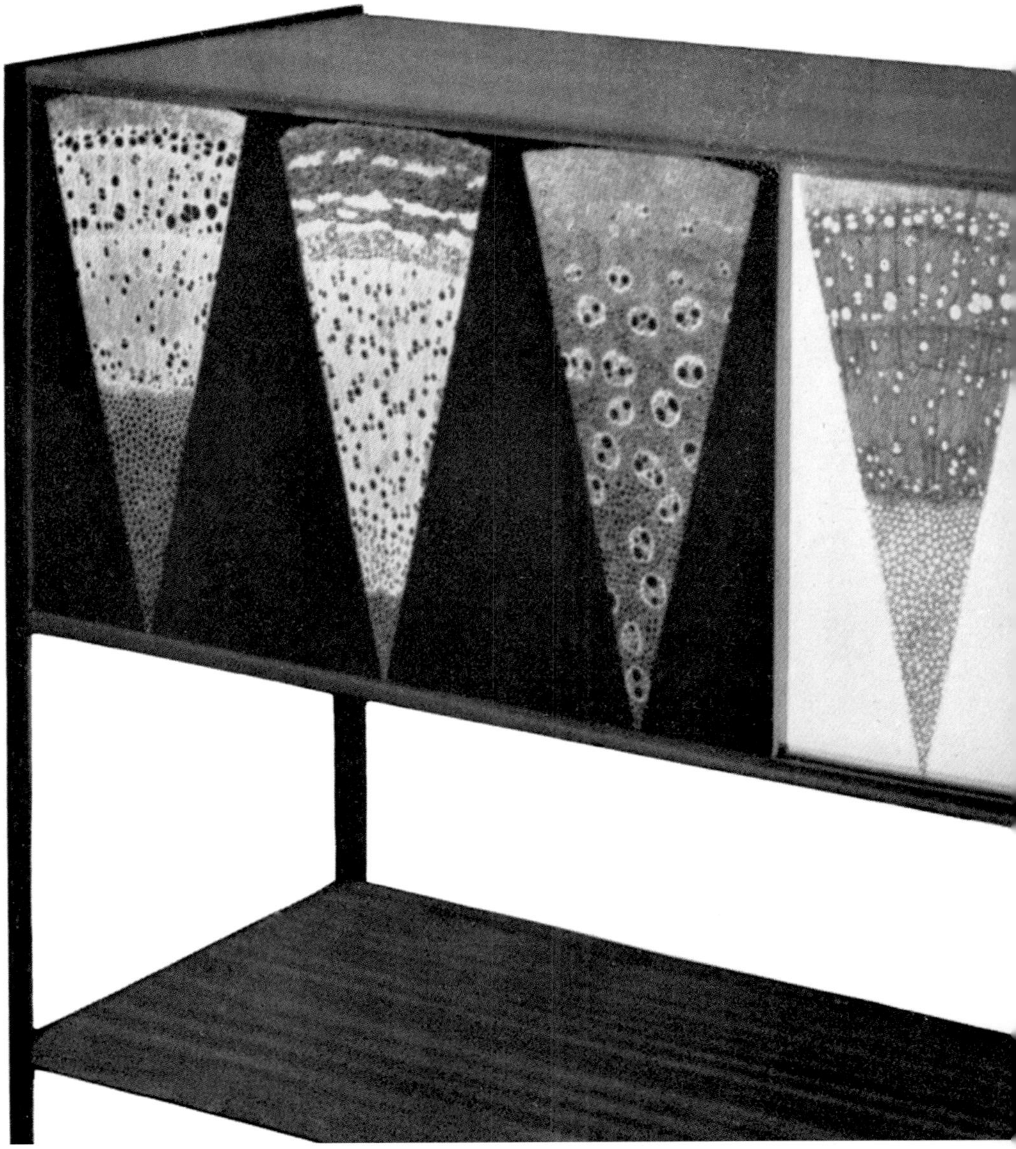

Conran's S.3a cabinet, a smaller version of the S.3 (shown on page 103), was also available with its doors and panels decorated with a black and white 'photo print' of an eighteenth-century tree section. This particular form of decoration was also used on table tops. Other versions of the cabinets were available with photo prints of fireworks or fish, even a tiger on a version used as a child's play cupboard.

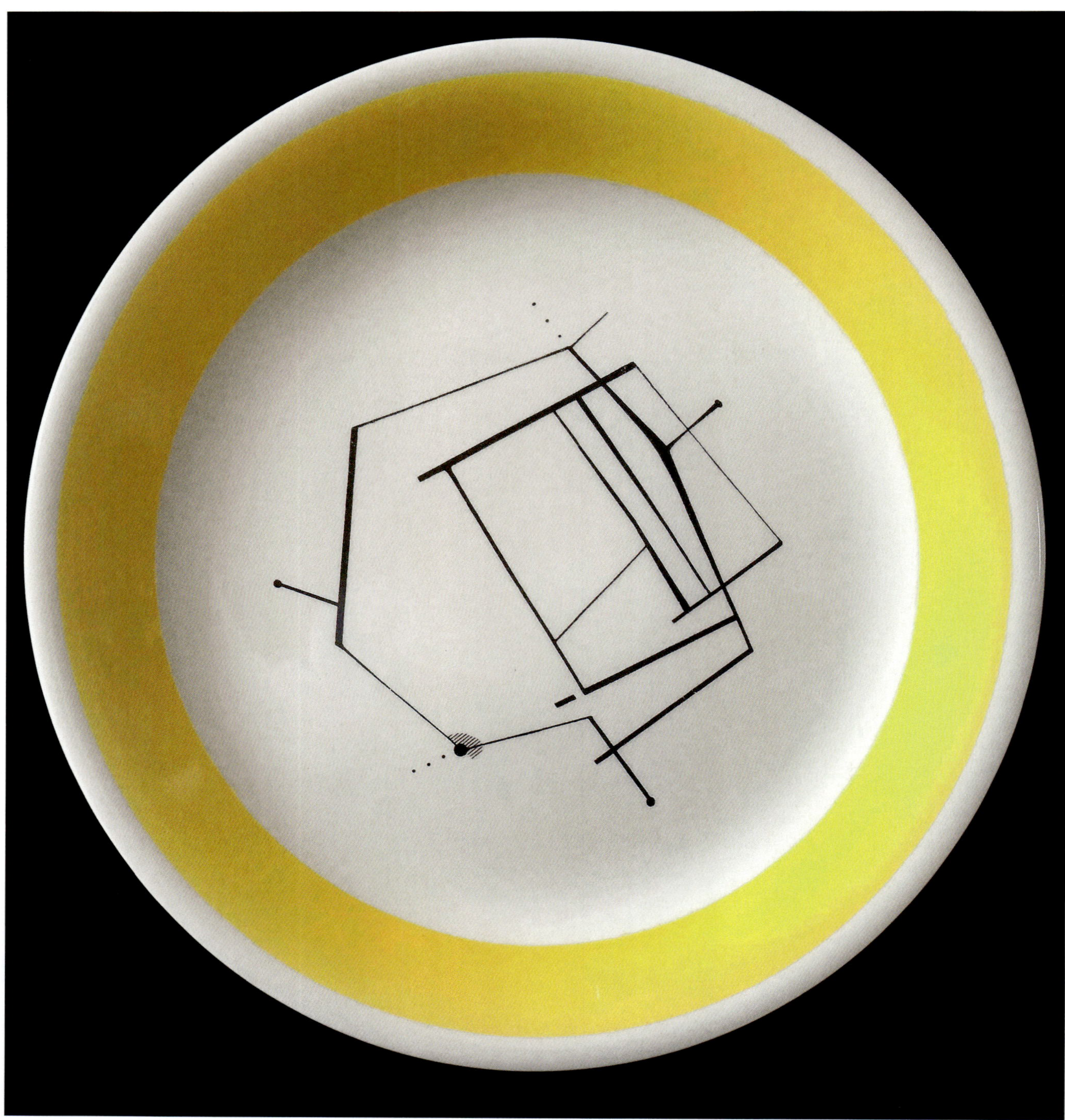

Plate from a service designed by David, Marquess of Queensberry, and Colin Melbourne for their design consultancy, Drumlanrig Melbourne, 1954. David Queensberry was later Professor of Ceramics at the Royal College of Art. A good friend of Terence Conran, it was through Queensberry that Conran met his second wife, the textile designer and author, Shirley Conran.

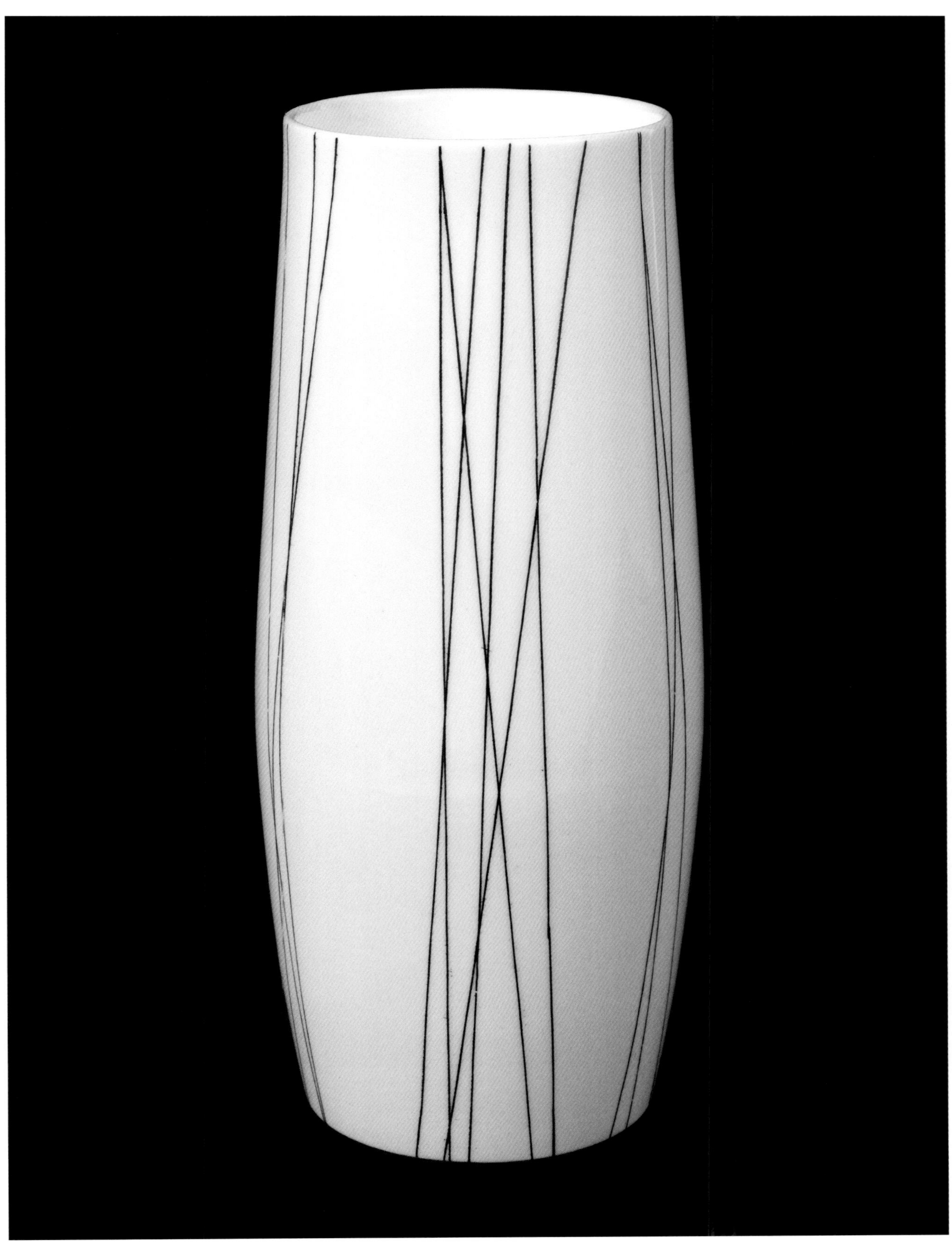

A bone china vase from the 'Lines in Space' series, 1957. Designed by David Queensberry for Crown Staffordshire.
Queensberry later had a major part in designing W.R. Midwinter's new ceramic ranges in the 1960s.

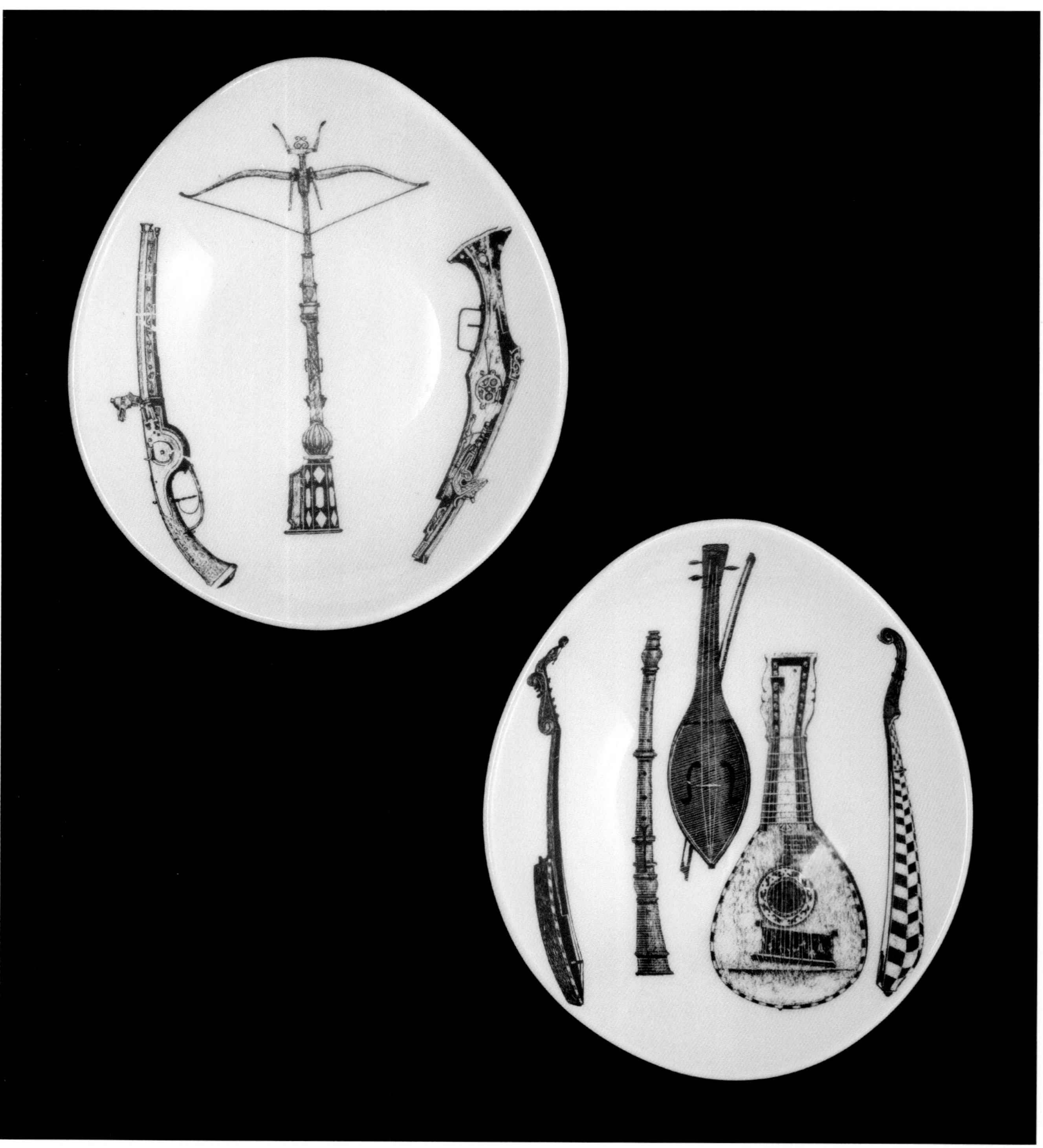

Two bone china dishes from a range by David Queensberry, in collaboration with Tom Taylor, for Crown Staffordshire, c.1956. The decoration of these dishes owes a great deal to the influence of Piero Fornasetti.

Opposite: Textile, 'Black Goblet', roller-printed rayon. Terence Conran for David Whitehead Ltd, c.1952.

Overleaf left: Abstract textile, on screen-printed cotton boucle, Terence Conran for David Whitehead Ltd, c.1952. This textile is strongly influenced by Paolozzi's work, particularly his sculpture of 1949, *Forms on a Bow*.

Overleaf right: Abstract textile by Terence Conran for David Whitehead Ltd, c.1952. Screen-printed on cotton boucle, it sold for twice the price of the company's roller-printed rayons.

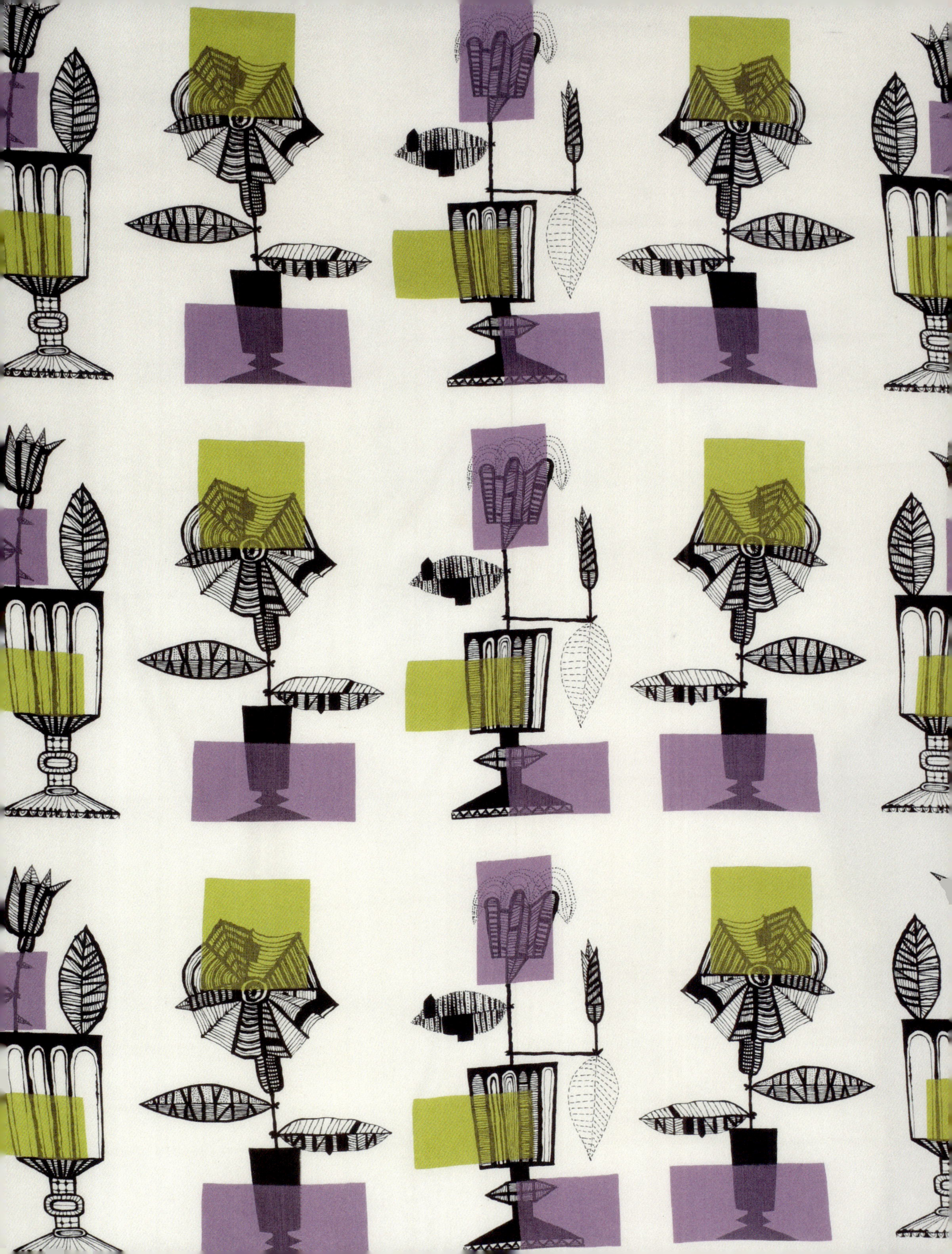

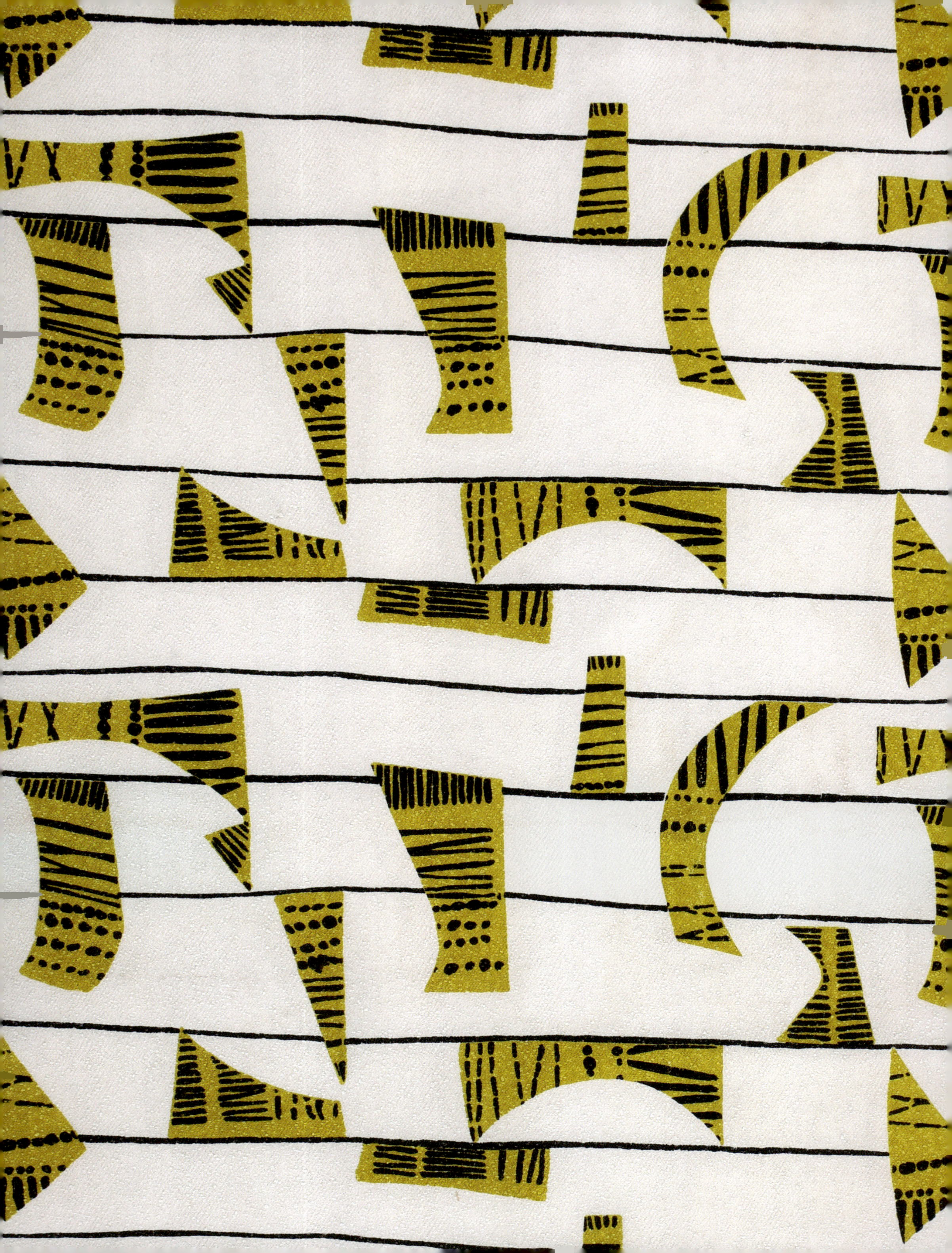

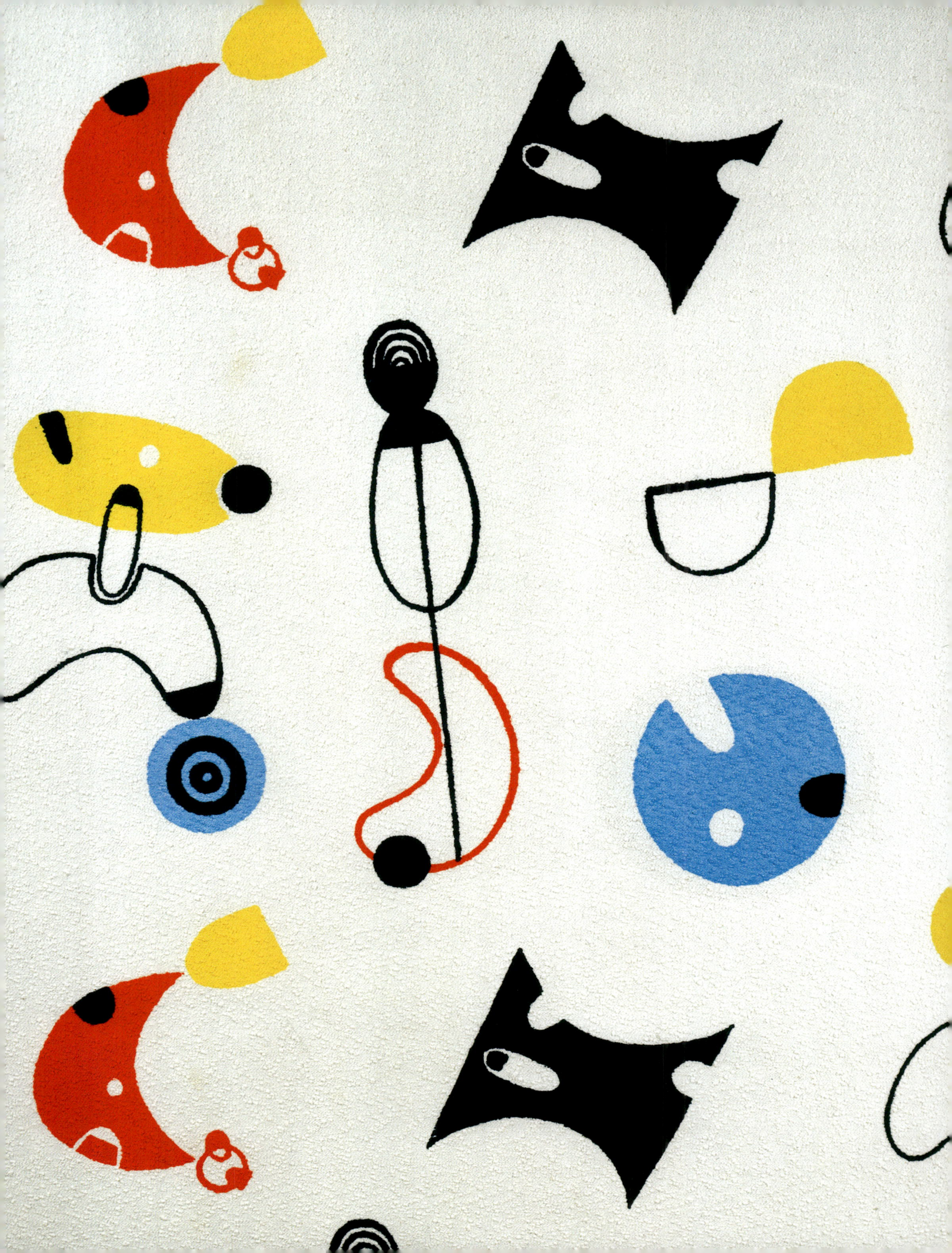

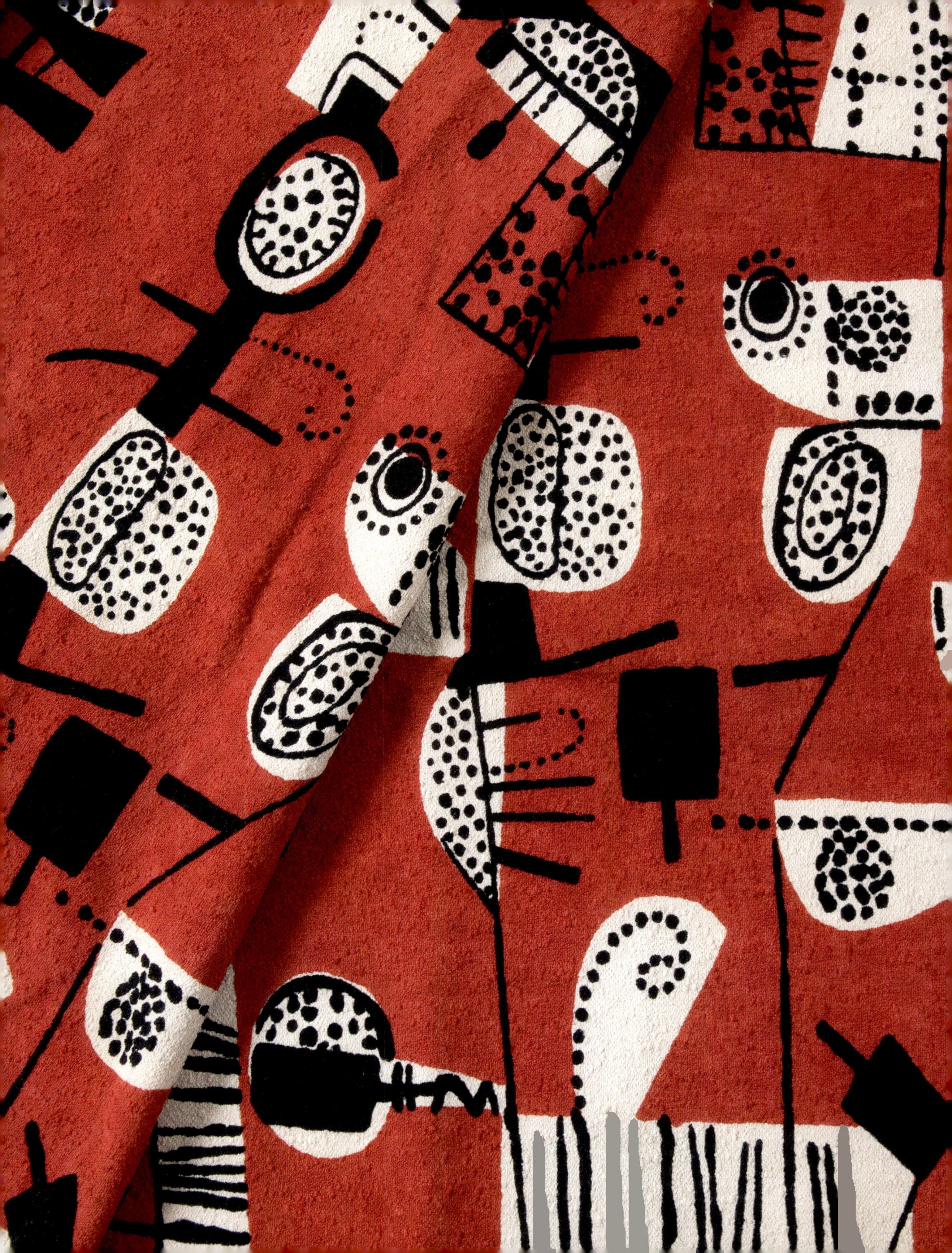

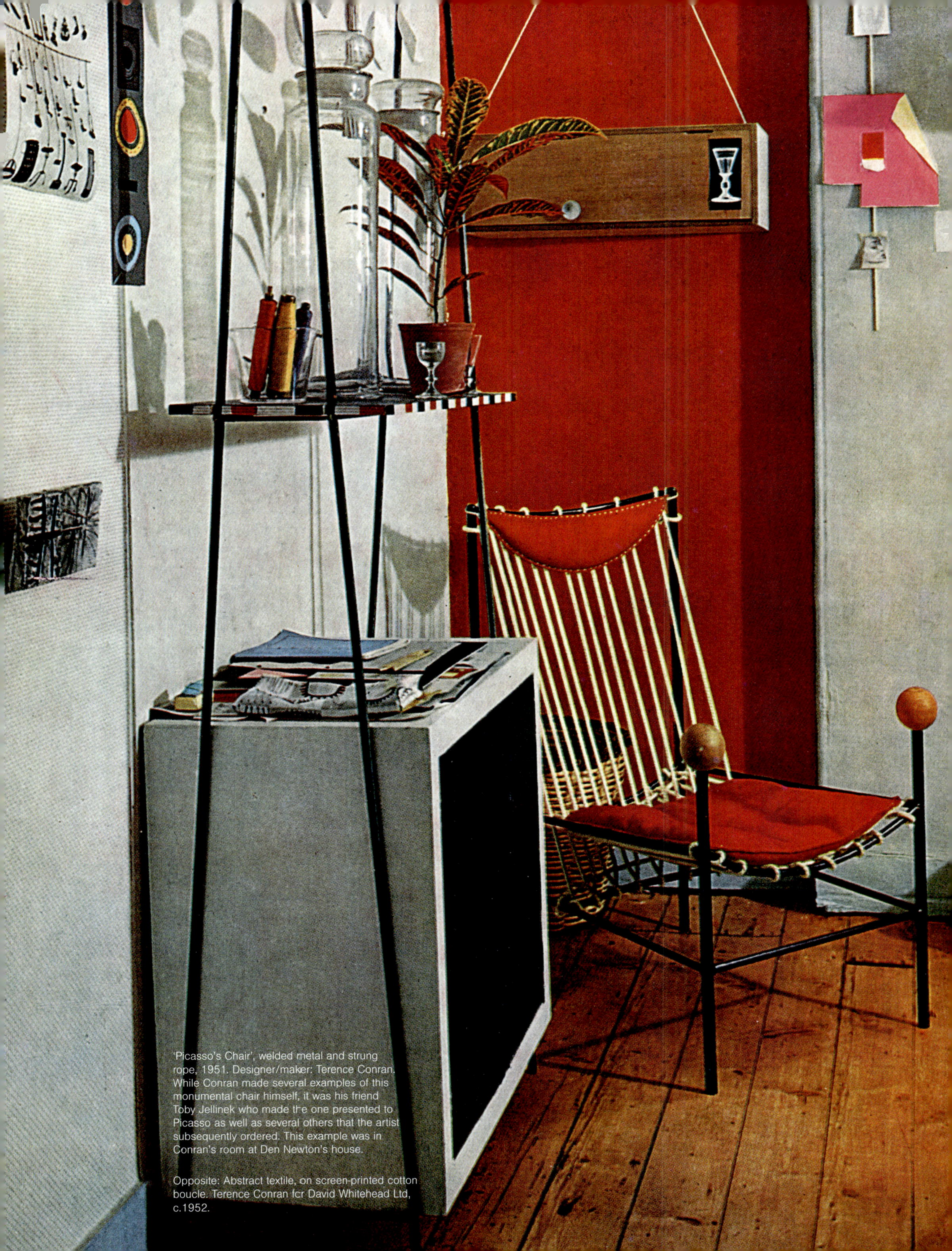

'Picasso's Chair', welded metal and strung rope, 1951. Designer/maker: Terence Conran. While Conran made several examples of this monumental chair himself, it was his friend Toby Jellinek who made the one presented to Picasso as well as several others that the artist subsequently ordered. This example was in Conran's room at Den Newton's house.

Opposite: Abstract textile, on screen-printed cotton boucle. Terence Conran for David Whitehead Ltd, c.1952.

CONRAN FURNITURE

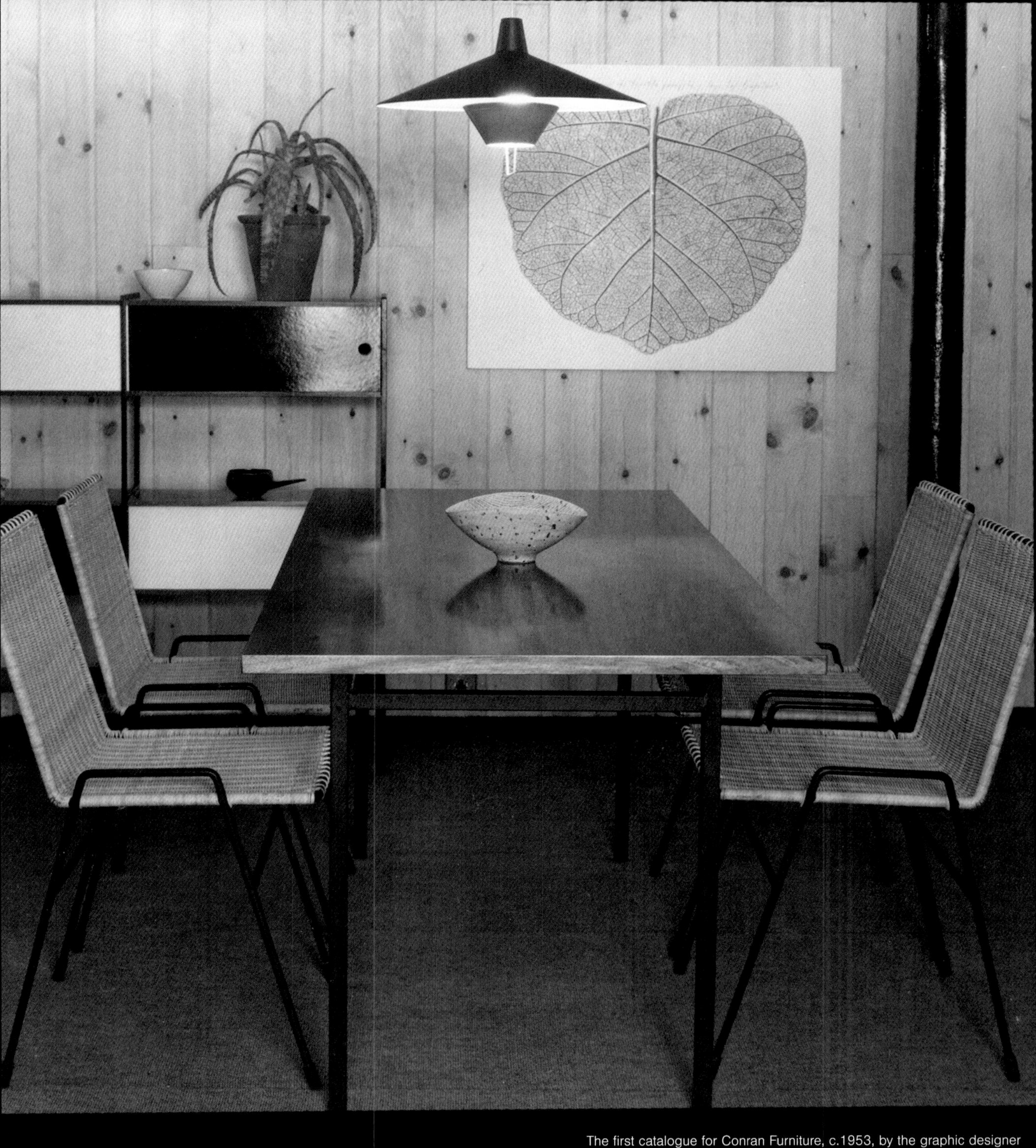

The first catalogue for Conran Furniture, c.1953, by the graphic designer and typographer Ian Bradbery. A former lecturer at the Central School of Arts and Crafts, it was Bradbery who initially convinced Conran to form a design practice catering for all aspects of interior and exhibition design.

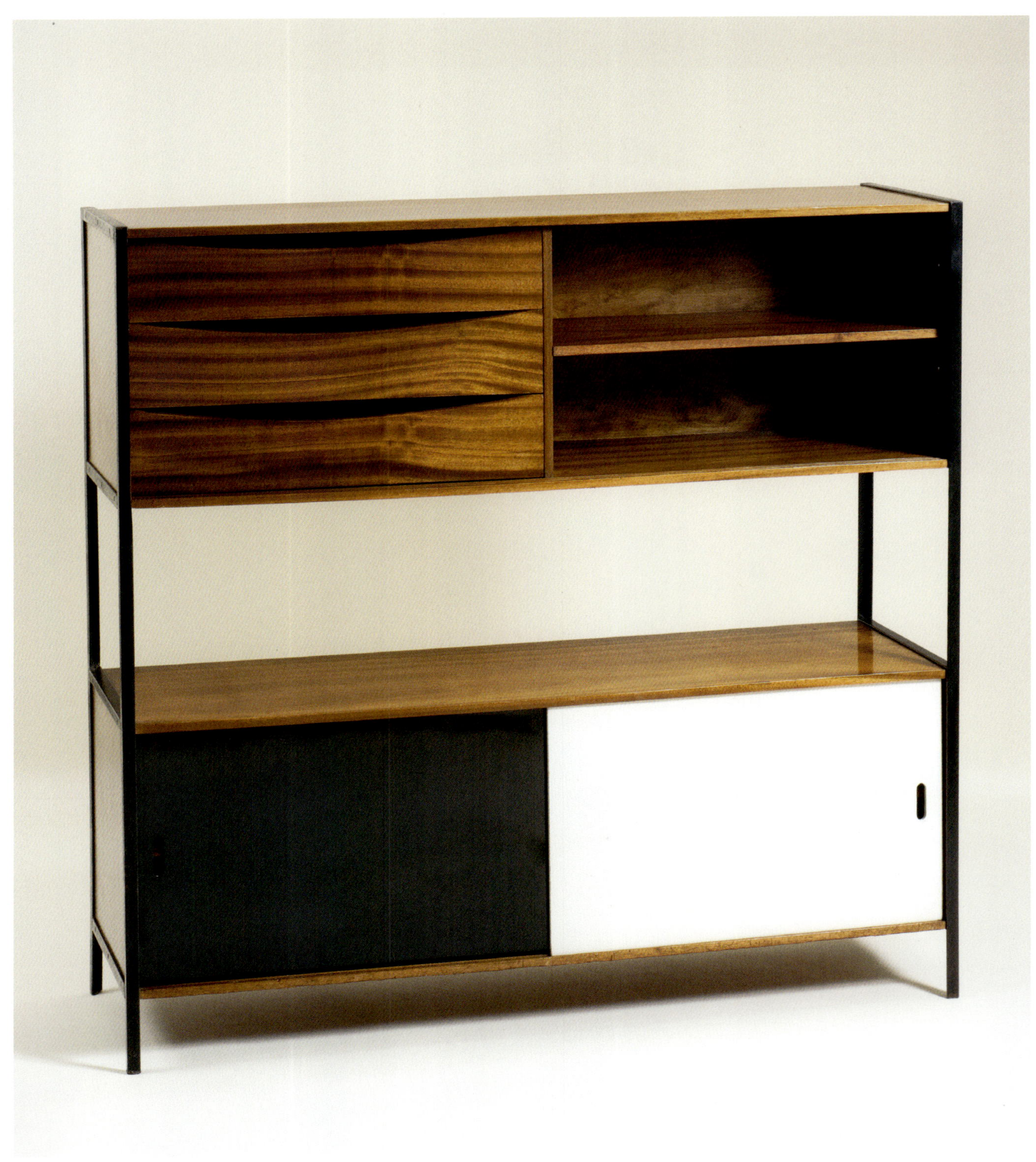

The S.3 cabinet, c.1954. By 1955 the S.1 cabinet was no longer available. In the catalogue; it was superseded by the larger and more versatile S.3.

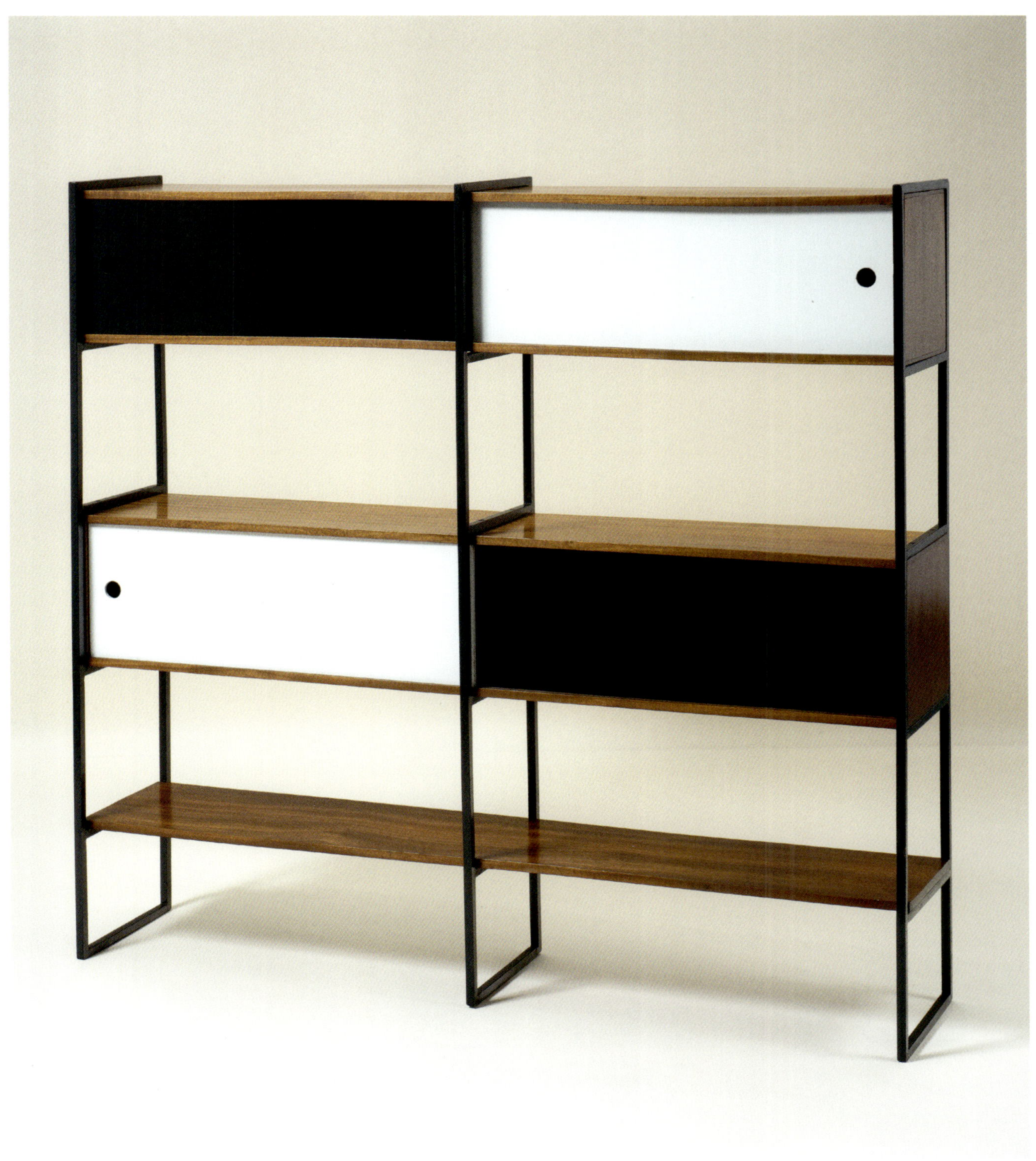

The S.1 cabinet, 1952. As far as is known, the S.1 was the first piece of case furniture from Conran's initial independent range of furniture to be commercially available. At that early period he was still personally making the furniture with the much valued assistance of Eric O'Leary, a former technician with the sculptor Henry Moore.

TERENCE CONRAN: EARLY MEDIA INTEREST

IN 1951, Den Newton, who had an interest in 'primitive art' and owned a small collection of Paolozzi's African-inspired sculptures, arranged for the design editor of *House & Garden*, Cynthia Blackburn, to photograph them for a feature she was writing on sculpture in the home. She came accompanied by her future husband, the painter and photographer Michael Wickham, who subsequently became one of the most influential of Conran's mentors. While looking around, they were so impressed by the 'boho' ambiance of the house in general and of Conran's rooms in particular, that Wickham decided to take a suitably moody 'arty' photograph of Newtown, Conran and Turnbull 'moving in', which was later published in the 'Roundabout' section of *House & Garden*'s January 1952 issue. The accompanying article also promised readers a more extensive follow-up story on the subject. From then on, *House & Garden* regularly supported Conran's work and ideas well into the 1960s and the Habitat years. In many ways *House & Garden* fulfilled for Conran and his friends and associates much the same role as the Council of Industrial Design's monthly publication *Design* did for the design establishment, but with a much wider, commercially orientated remit.

IN THE EARLY 1950s the magazine also supported Paolozzi's and Turnbull's excursions into the applied arts. Paolozzi's approach to interior design is probably best seen in his and Nigel Henderson's work, on which they'd collaborated with the husband and wife team of architects, Jane Drew and Maxwell Fry. A photograph by Wickham of a room in Drew's own home, not only shows an armchair covered in a textile commissioned from Paolozzi, but also a collage by him and a large sculpture by Turnbull, with lighting by the sculptor Bernard Schottlander. Examples of Schottlander's lighting were also used in the Hampstead flat of Colin St John Wilson, later architect of the British Library, in the forecourt of which stands Paolozzi's well-known sculpture of Sir Isaac Newton. Wickham's photographs of St John Wilson's flat, in *House & Garden*'s July 1952 issue, also show furniture by Conran, a sculpture by Turnbull and a painting by the artist and architect Jon Catleugh, who later, between 1961 and 1962, was Conran's director of design. A feature in the 'News in Print' section of *House & Garden*'s February 1952 issue illustrates textiles by both Paolozzi and Conran, one of which, by Conran, was used for curtaining by the Institute of Contemporary Arts.

House & Garden's great interest at this time in both Contemporary design and Modern art was largely the result of the impact made by the Festival of Britain the previous year. This interest, however, was not confined solely to the magazine. The June 1951 'Festival' edition of *Furnishings from Britain*, a quarterly magazine for the export trade, has a feature on the interiors and furnishings of the Institute of Contemporary Arts, then recently established in London's Dover Street, which the article directly compares with MoMA, New York's Museum of Modern Art. One of the illustrations is of an extraordinary sculptural concrete table, the joint work of Paolozzi and Conran, which stood in the entrance hall of the ICA. Conran's work received a particularly significant boost when the architect Phillip Johnson, the influential doyen of American Modernism and Director of the Department of Architecture at MoMa, bought a chair from him. Even more importantly, Ian MacCallum, editor of the prestigious *Architectural Review*, personally commissioned Conran to design furniture for both his home and office. Earlier, in 1952, the *Review* had featured a significant article on Conran's first solo exhibition, held at Simpsons of Piccadilly, 'Ideas and Objects for the Home'.

Opposite: A moody, artistic photograph by Michael Wickham of Terence Conran, the sculptor William Turnbull and their friend and landlord, the writer and poet Douglas Newton, moving into the Newtons' newly bought house in Chelsea, January 1952.

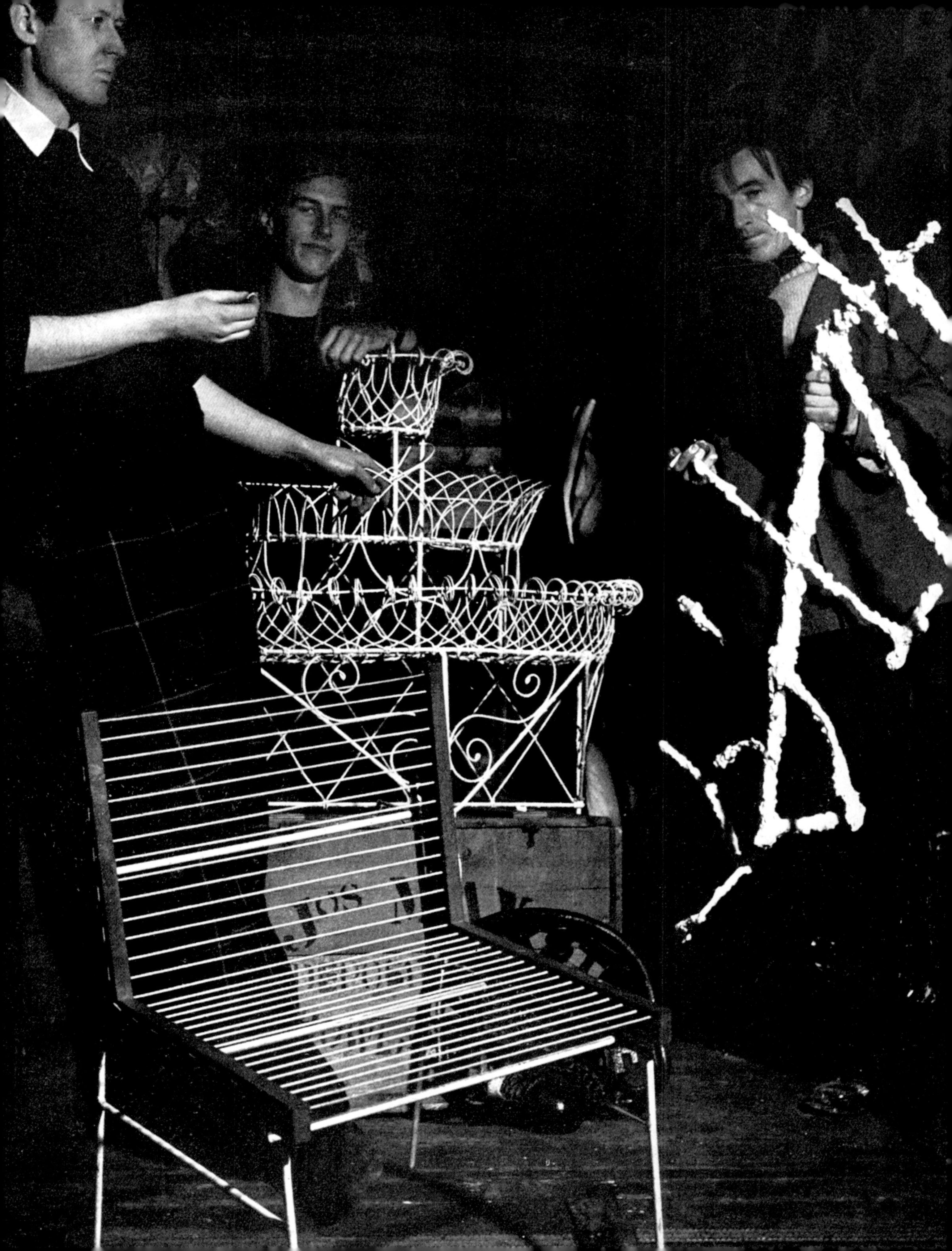

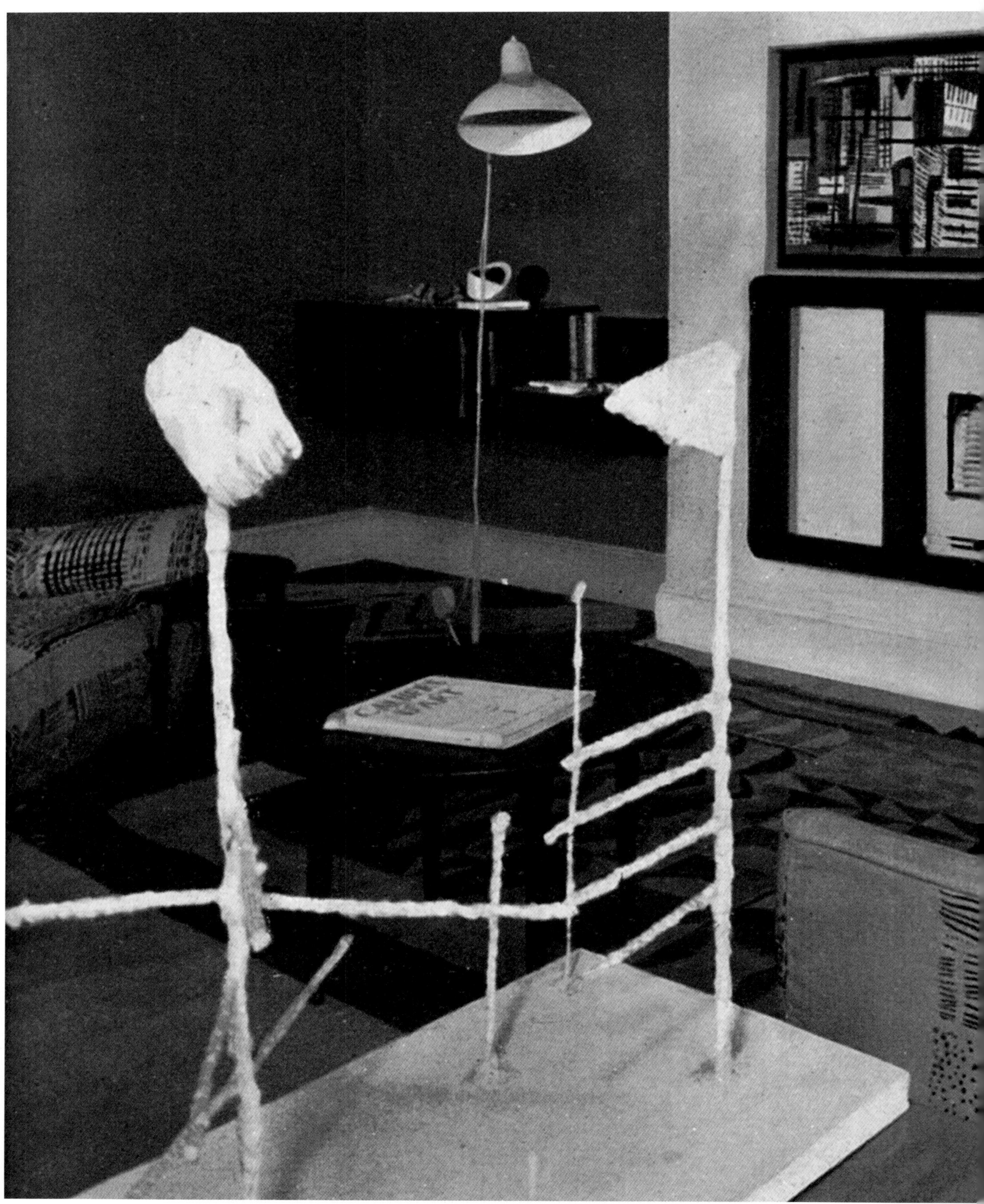

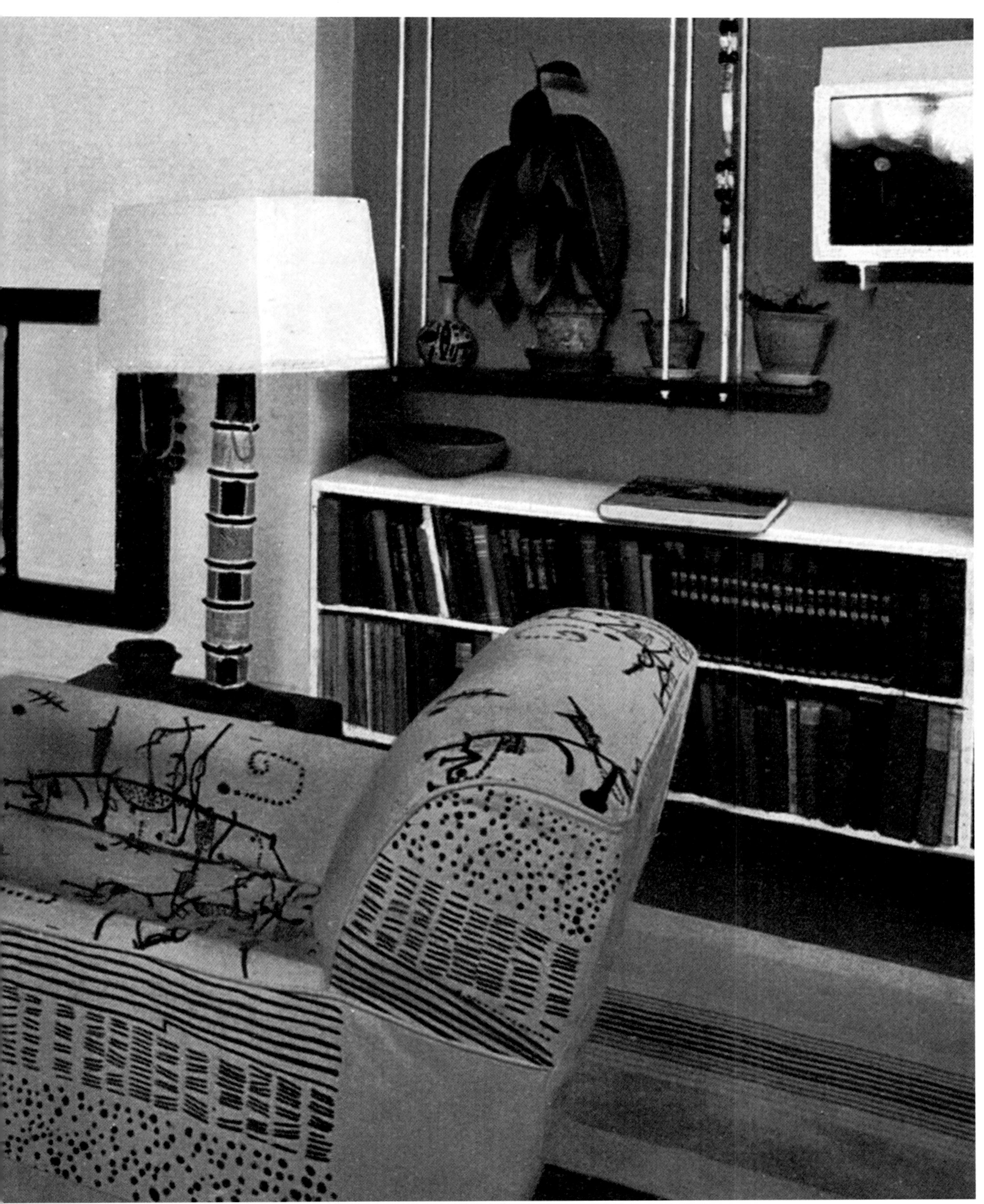

The living room of the architect Jane Drew, wife of the Modernist architect Maxwell Fry, 1952. Hand screen-printed textiles by Paolozzi cover the chairs, a sculpture by William Turnbull stands nearby and a 'Mantis' floor-standing light by Bernard Schottlander Illuminates the scene.

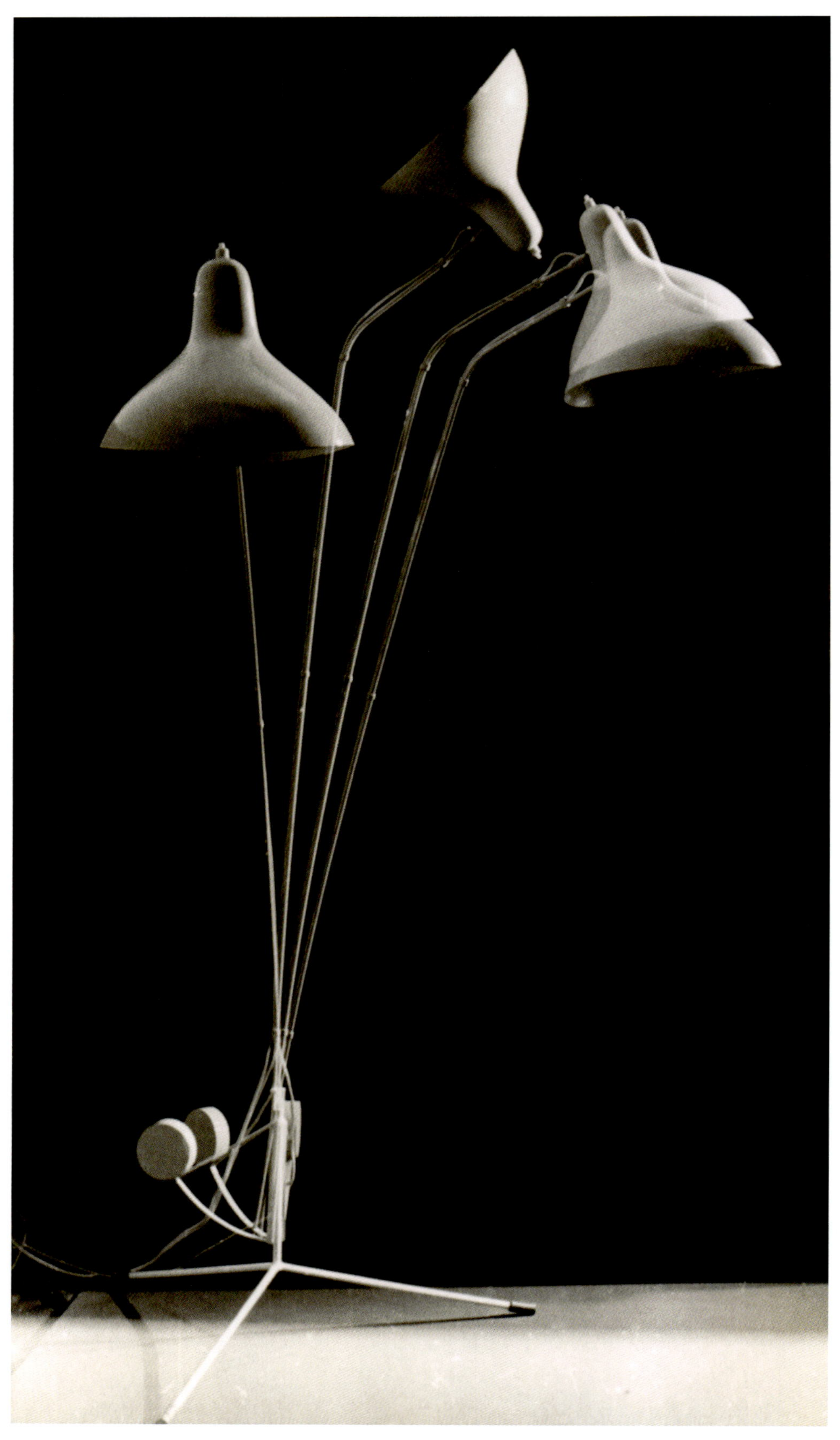

A publicity photograph from 1951 of Schottlander's 'Mantis' light, displaying its flexibility and kinetic qualities in a series of multiple exposures.

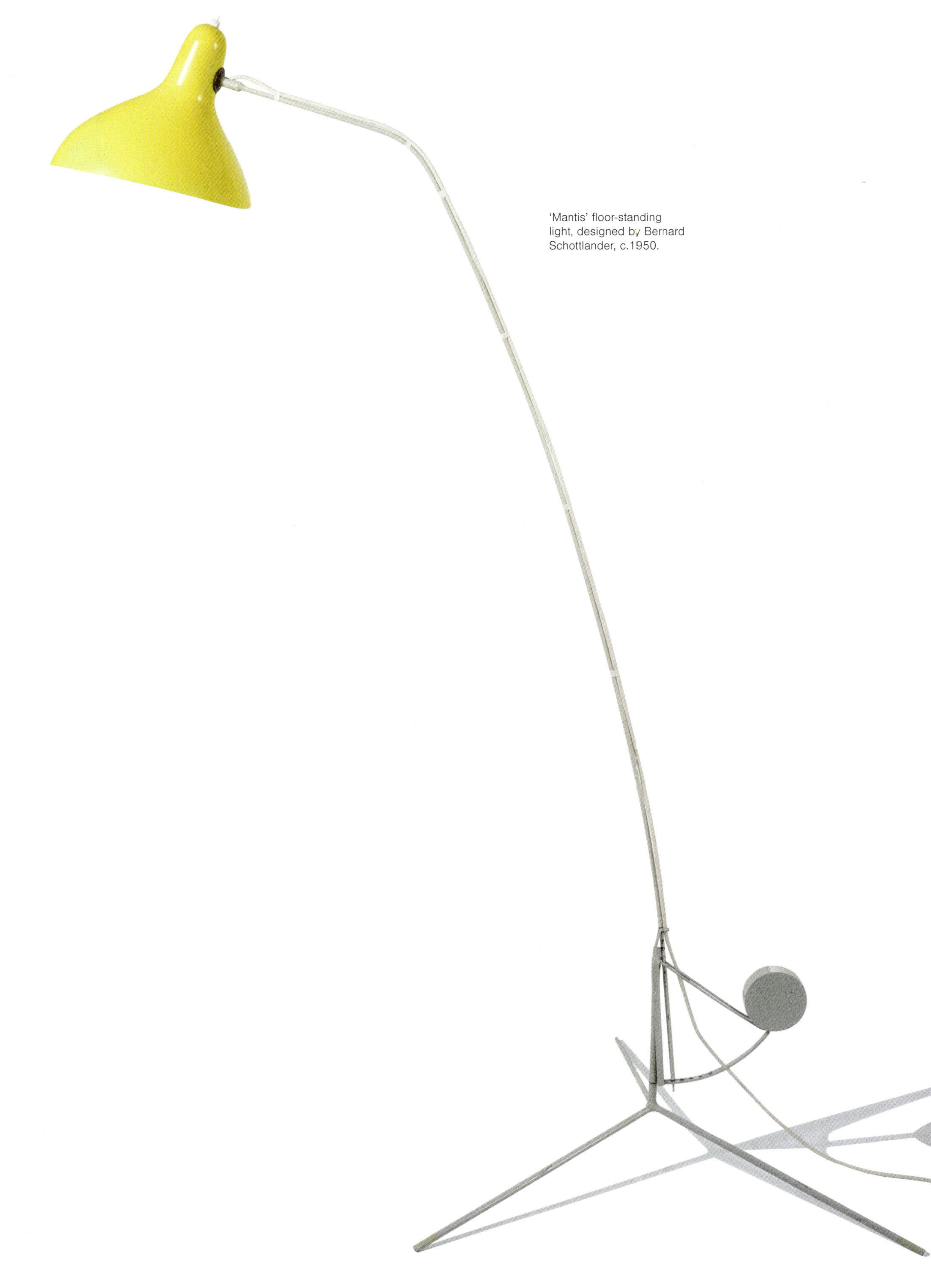

'Mantis' floor-standing light, designed by Bernard Schottlander, c.1950.

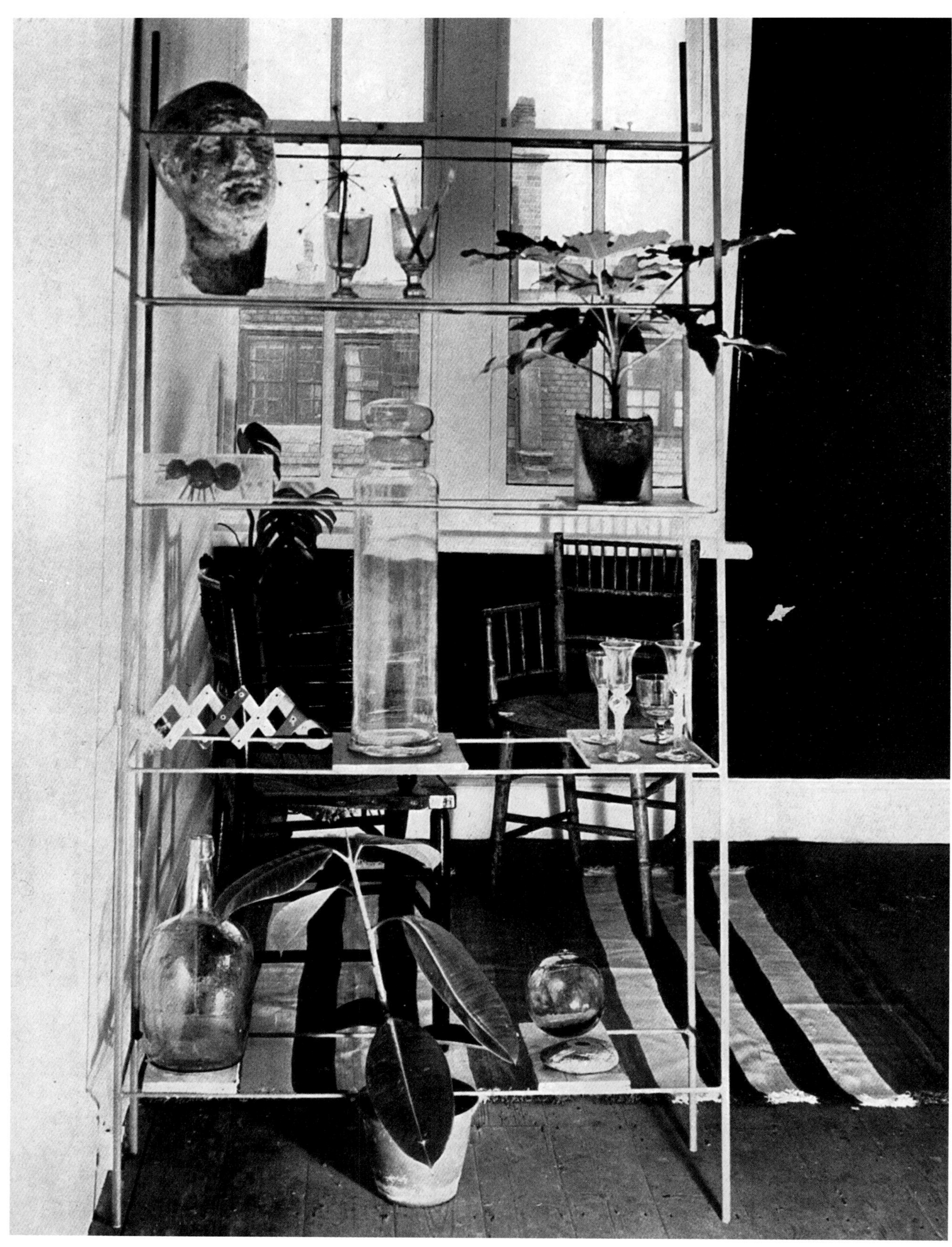

Douglas Newton's personal 'museum' of ephemera, 1952. Many of the pieces subsequently turned up in interiors by Conran. An early proto Pop object, 'Bug in a Box', by Christopher Wetherbee, stands in pride of place on a Conran shelving unit.

Opposite: The flat of Colin St John Wilson, architect of the British Library, 1952, with furniture by Terence Conran.

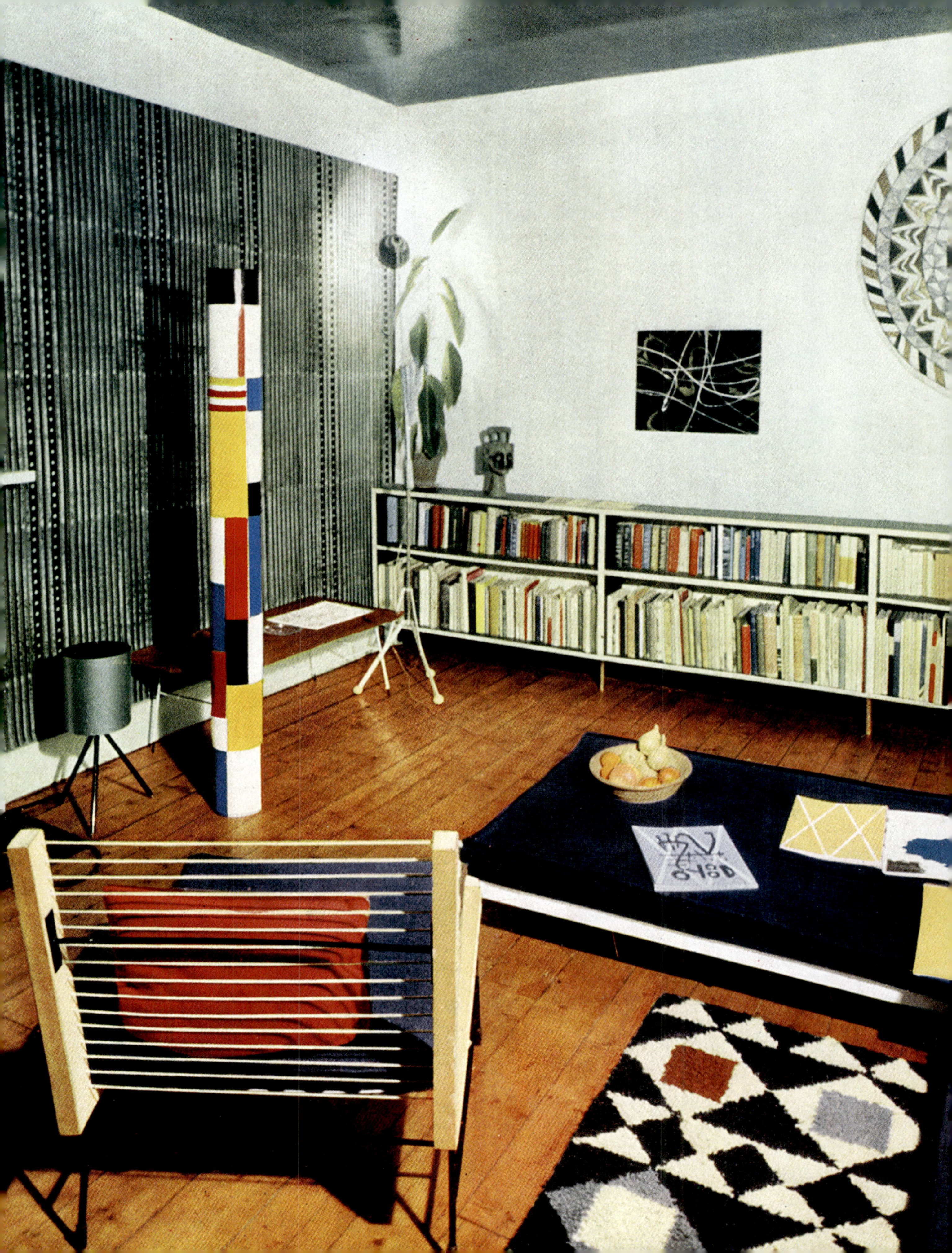

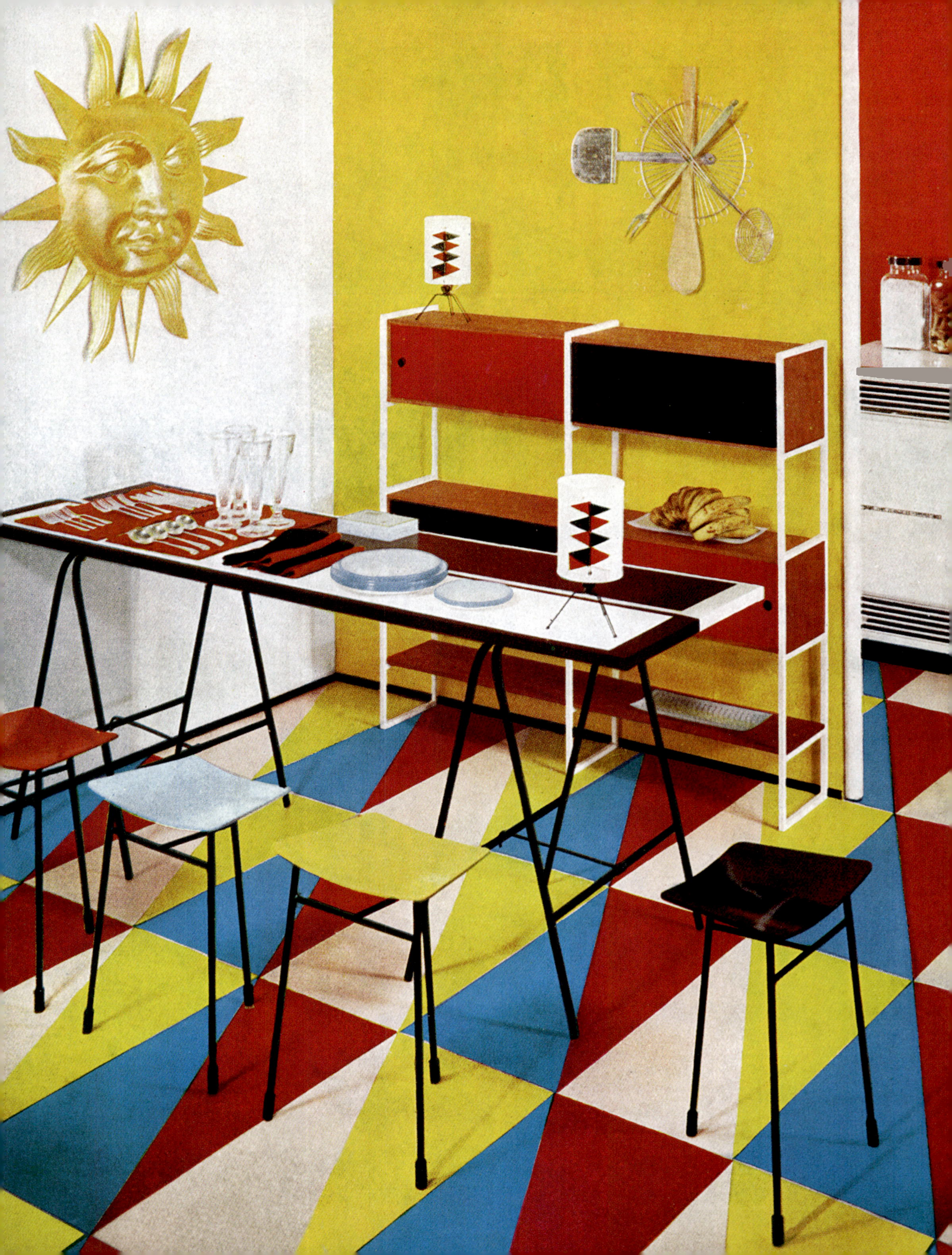

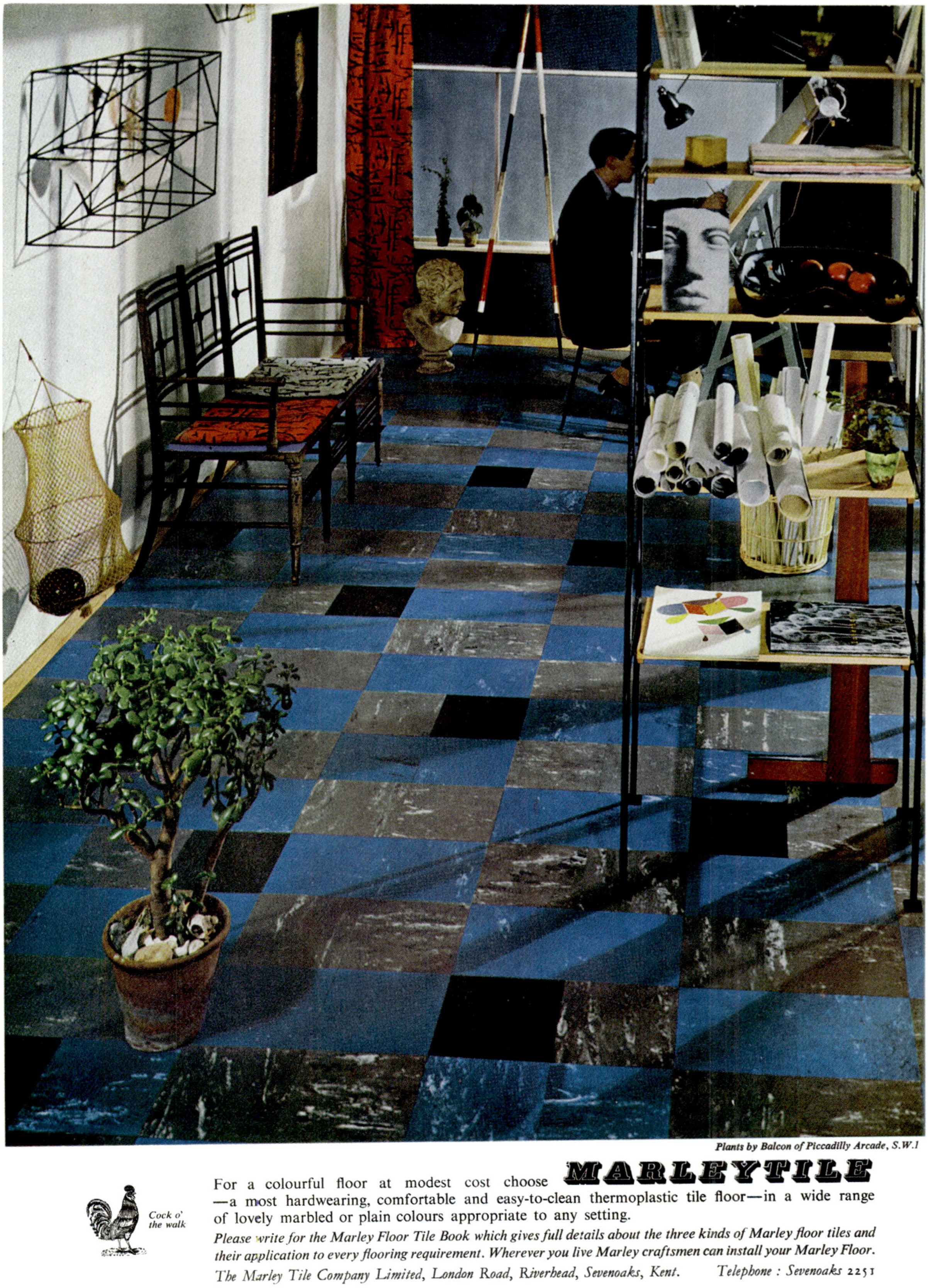

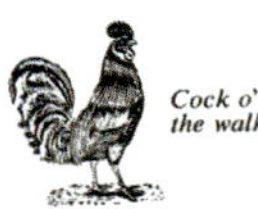

Advertisement for Marley Floor Tiles, 1953. The set appears to be Conran's top-floor accommodation at Den Newton's House. Dressed with Conran's own furniture, textiles and personal objects, and with himself sitting at the drawing board. It also features his three-seater version of William Morris's 'Sussex' chair, designed by the painter Ford Madox Brown.

Opposite: Room set photographed by Anthony Denny in 1953, featuring Conran's C.1 and a set of stools he'd designed, made by Else Lennon.

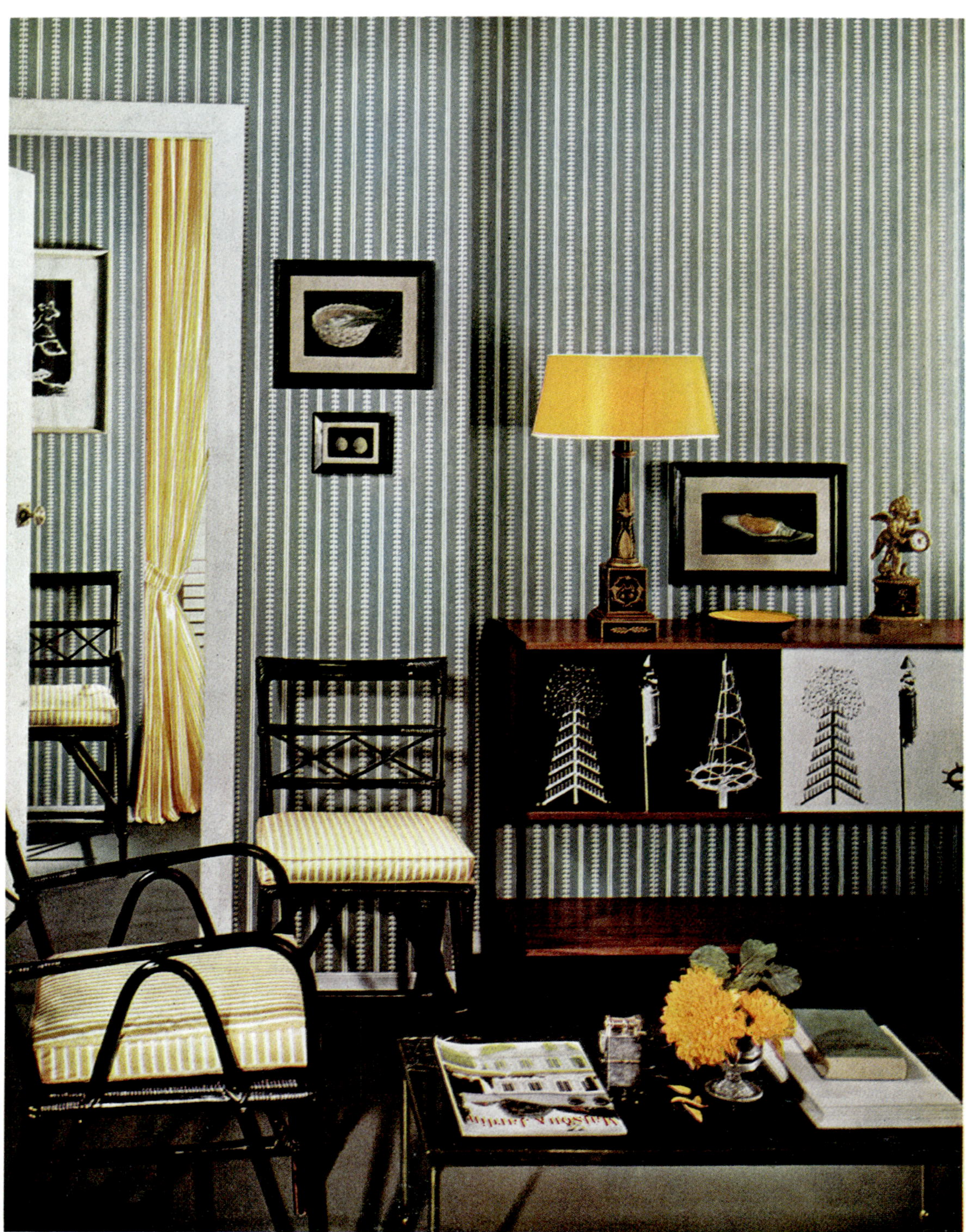

Advertisement for Crown Wallpapers. Featuring an example of Conran's C.3a cabinet decorated with black and white 'photo-prints' of fireworks. Very suitable for an upmarket 'Belgravia' interior.

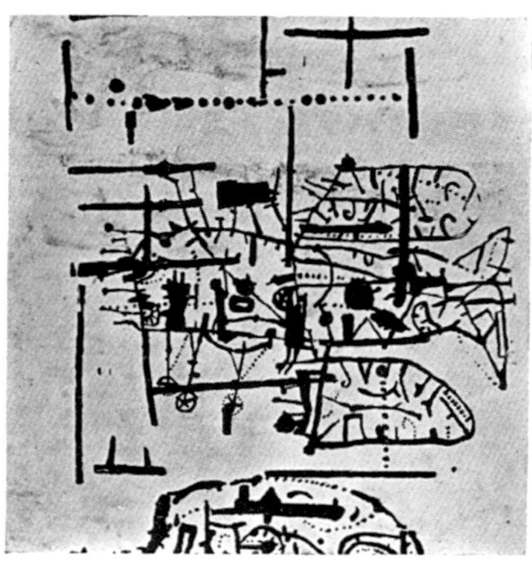

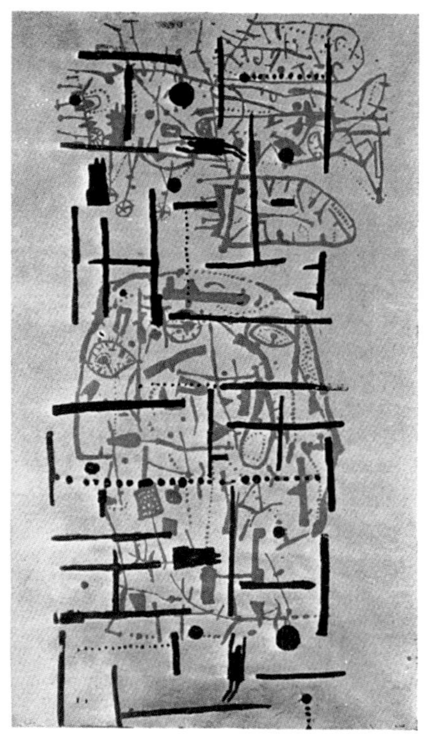

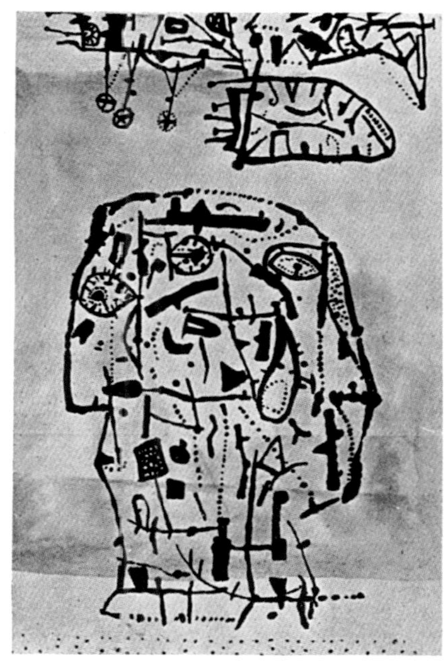

Textile designs by Paolozzi and Conran, 1952. While Paolozzi's designs, achieved by super-imposing one design on top of another, were only available directly from the artist, Conran's were available on a more commercial basis from Dunn's of Bromley and Liberty of London.

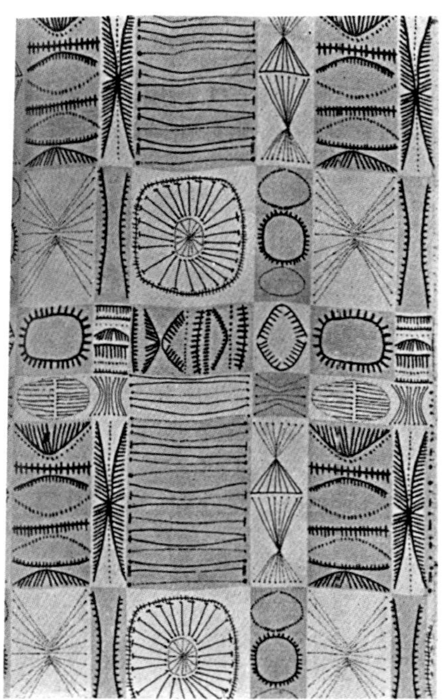

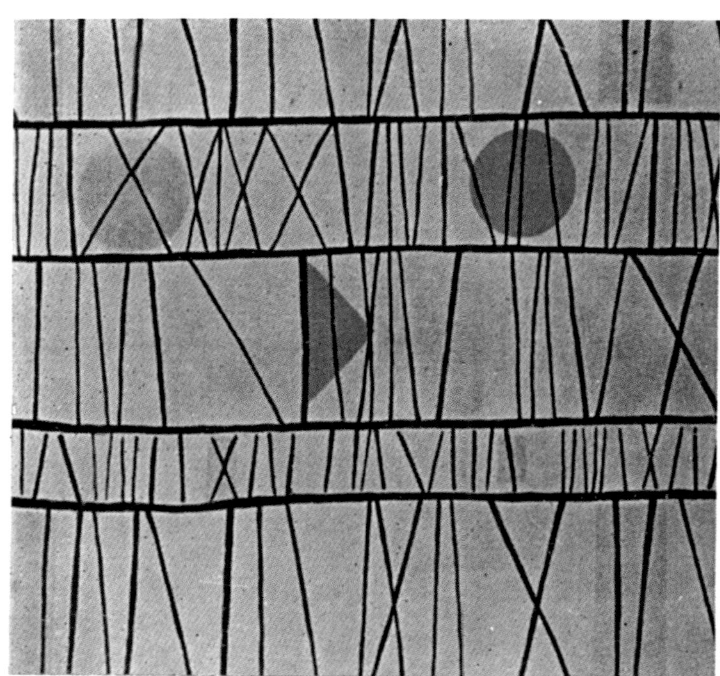

TERENCE CONRAN: EARLY EXHIBITIONS AND INITIAL RECOGNITION

FROM SCHOOL ONWARDS, Conran appears to have been much more involved with the avant-garde art scene in London than the more architecturally related discipline of design, although he did not seem to have any strong artistic aspirations himself. As Charles Handley-Read had perceptively understood, his skills were not in art per se but in the appreciation of pattern, form and colour. Conran's close personal friendships with outstanding artists among the avant-garde of the day were similar to those between William Morris and members of the Pre-Raphaelite Brotherhood.

THIS BECAME VERY apparent in 1953, when a group of leading British Constructivist and Abstract artists held the last in a series of joint exhibitions of their work – the 'Weekend Exhibitions' – at 22 Fitzroy Street, W1, the London studio of the Abstract painter Adrian Heath. [37] Like Conran, Heath had been a pupil at Bryanston School, but from an earlier generation. Several celebrated teachers and former students of the Central School of Arts and Crafts exhibited, among them Paolozzi and Nigel Henderson, the sculptor Robert Adams and the artist Victor Pasmore. Other 'leading lights' of the British avant-garde who took part were Ben Nicholson, Kenneth and Mary Martin, Terry Frost, Roger Hilton and William Scott. The Constructivist artist Anthony Hill, another school friend of Conran's from Bryanston and a fellow student of his at the Central School also exhibited and, almost as a matter of course, Conran was invited to show pieces of his furniture. While the exhibition was not necessarily a triumph for him, neither was it particularly so for any of the other participants and after its third staging was deemed to have run its course.

HOWEVER, CONRAN'S DESIGNS and ideas had already received much wider exposure and critical acclaim when, in 1952, he had been given an exhibition of his work at Simpsons, a prestigious department store in Piccadilly in London's West End. From its inception in 1936, Simpsons had a long association with Modernism, and Conran's exhibition was largely due to the patronage and enthusiasm of Natasha Kroll, the store's art director, who had spent some time at the Bauhaus in Berlin in the early 1930s. She first encountered Conran's work through his boss, the architect Dennis Lennon. A friend of Kroll's, Lennon had shown her some chairs Conran had designed for the Rayon Design Centre. She later recalled: 'I saw Terence's work and I thought it fresh. It was a student's work, but in the days when student work was exciting.' [38]

THE EXHIBITION WAS reviewed for the formidable academic journal *The Architectural Review* by Conran's landlord, friend and mentor, Den Newton, who stated that: 'Conran's work represents the same break with conventional craftsmanship in furniture that Turnbull's and Paolozzi's does with the tradition of stone cutting in sculpture.' [39] He concluded: 'Conran's strict economy has an elegance which prevents it becoming arid, particularly since it is often combined with bright gloss colours.' Newton's review was suitably illustrated with artistically expressive photography by Nigel Henderson, Paolozzi's friend and close associate from the Independent Group.

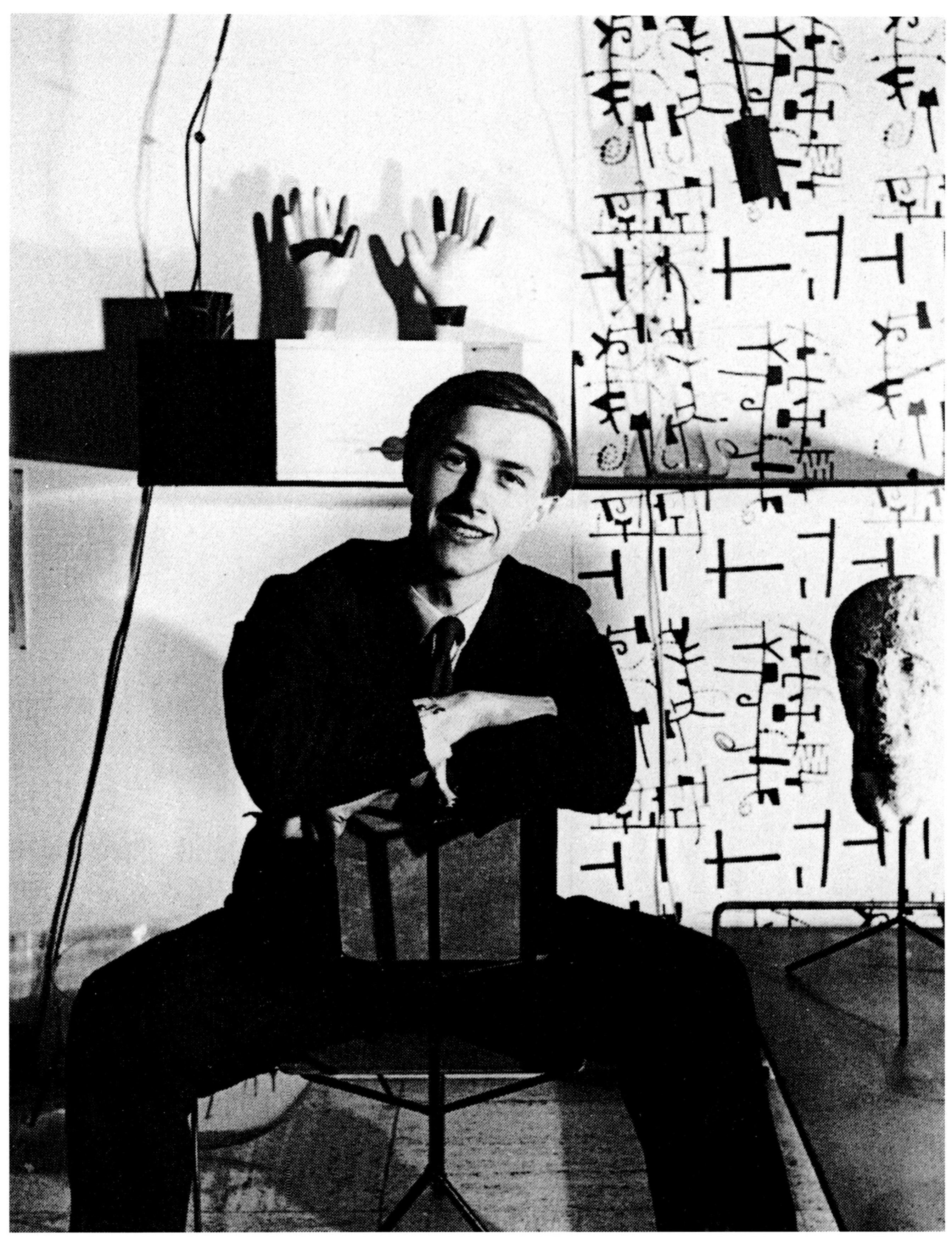

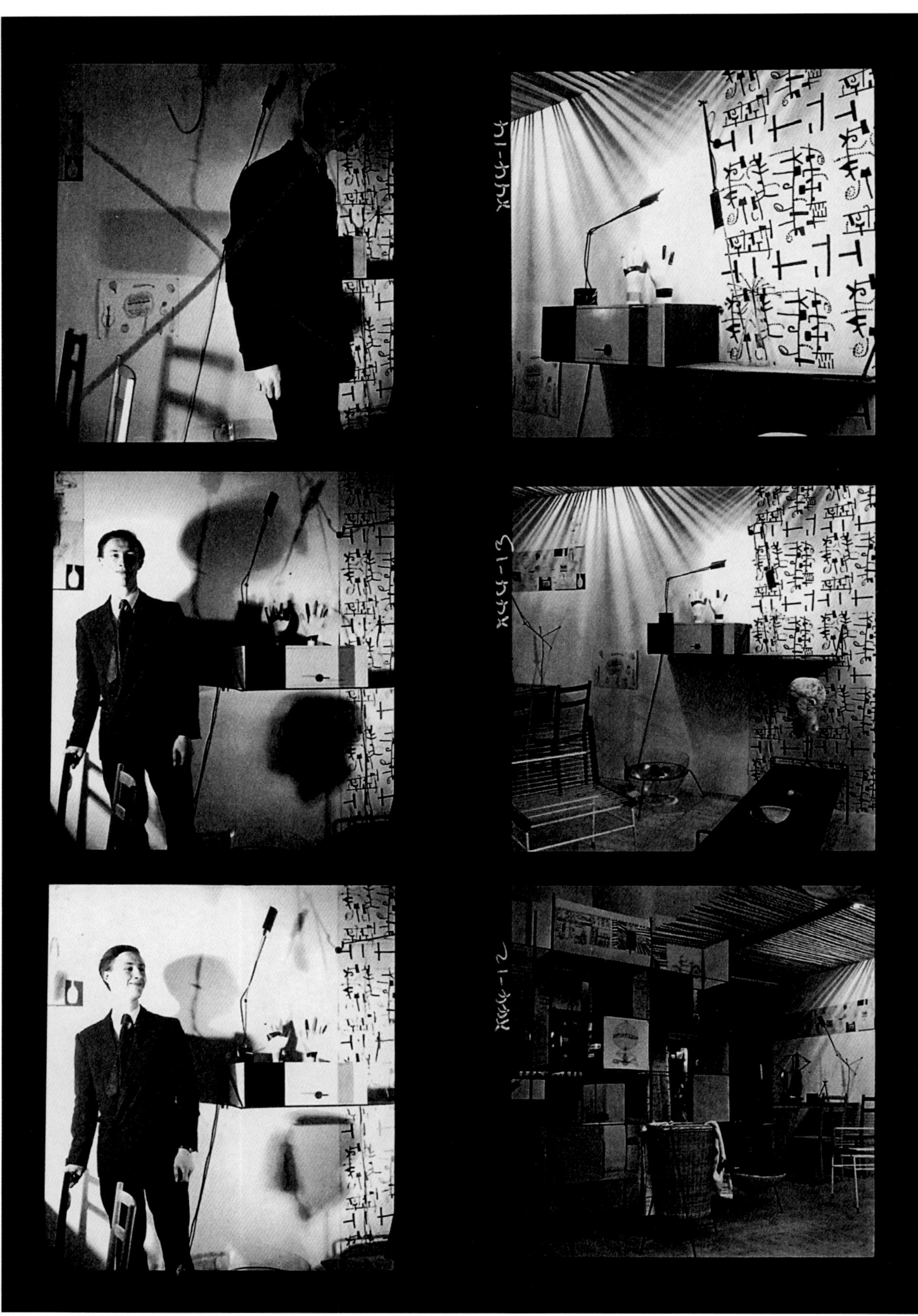

Michael Wickham's contact sheets of the Simpsons exhibition.

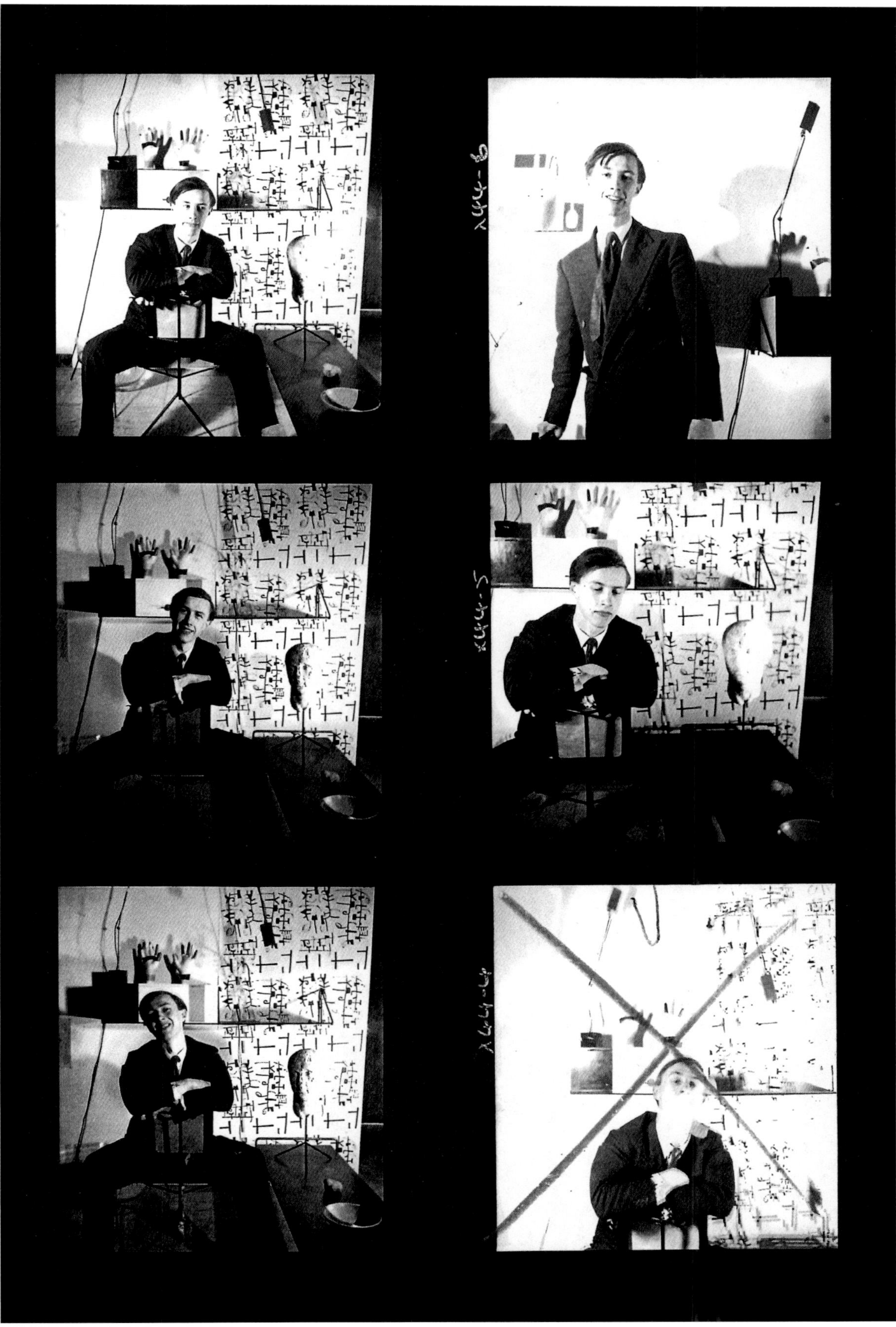

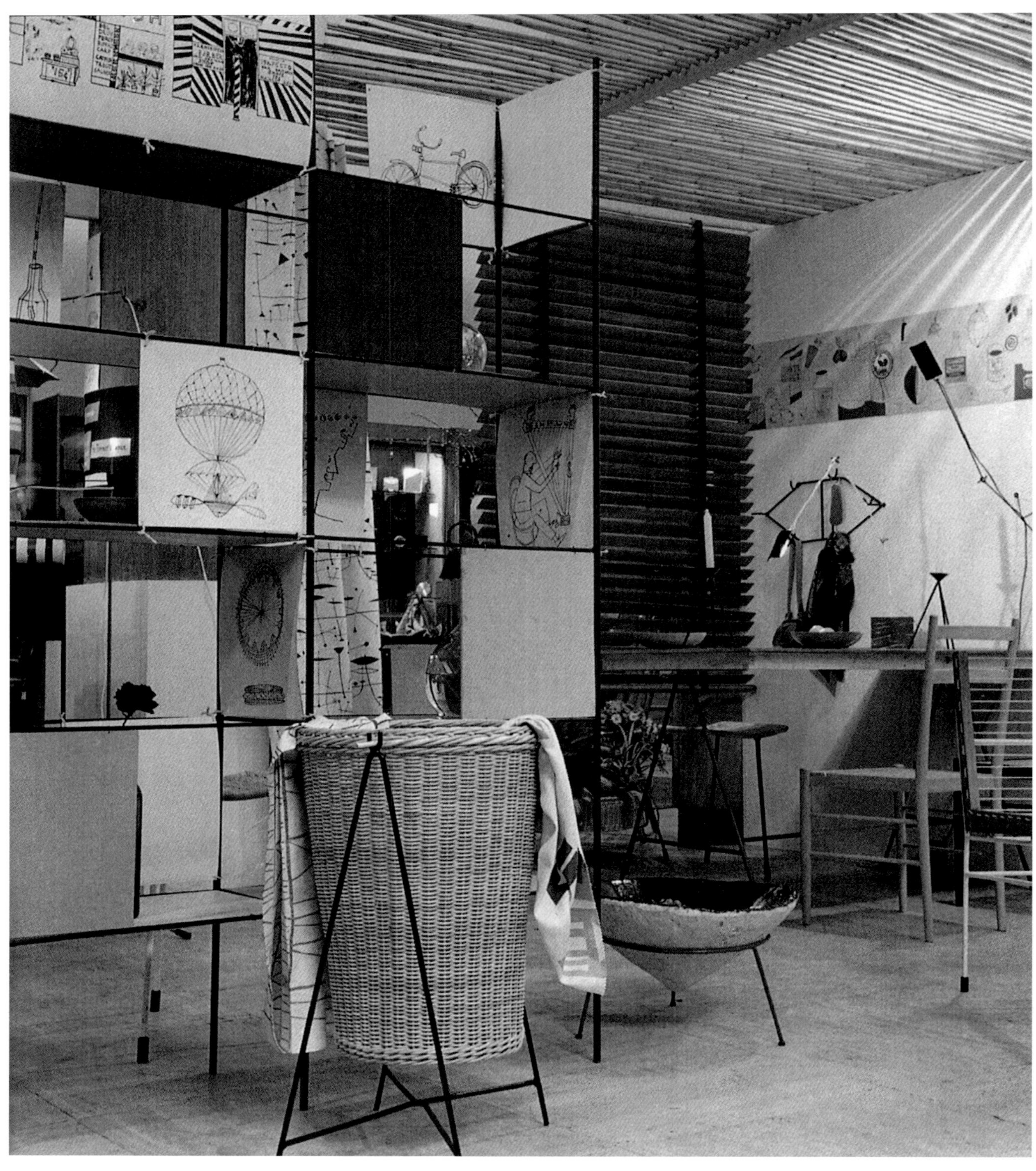

Conran's exhibition display at Simpsons. In order to complete the furniture for the exhibition's opening, Conran was obliged to employ Pegrams to fabricate some of the metalwork and Tisserands to weave the cane onto the metal frames.

TERENCE CONRAN: BASKETWEAVE AND OTHER PROJECTS

F ROM 1952 ONWARDS, life and work continued successfully for the young Conran in a whirlwind of exhibitions, commissions, patrons, marriages and children, ever onwards and upwards. However, the velocity of this rather frantic progress was occasionally interrupted by short-lived detours, such as the Basketweave project in 1954, which he carried out in partnership with, amongst others, the writer Wolf Markowitz. The idea had been to import and retail a range of inexpensive 'Contemporary' style wicker furnishings made in Madeira to Conran's designs. The project though was short-lived, as the Board of Trade unexpectedly imposed quotas on the import of wicker basket ware, which brought Conran's plan to a rather abrupt halt. However, one particularly successful item in the Basketweave range, the Cone chair, had a long life far beyond that of the original project and has since become one of the better known pieces of popular British design from the 1950s. Another Conran product, which like the Basketweave project is also popularly associated with 1950s design, was a range of terracotta plant pots with welded metal stands, which were, perhaps surprisingly, originally commissioned from him for *The Architectural Review*.[40] He subsequently immortalised these pots in 1957 in his well known design 'Plant Life' for Midwinter's Stylecraft range of table ware.

SHORTLY AFTER HIS second marriage in 1955, Conran returned to his original interest, textile design, and with his new wife Shirley set up Conran Fabrics, which shortly after became her responsibility. A little later, with his encouragement, she took a course in textile design at his old alma mater, the Central School of Arts and Crafts, where she proved extremely talented. Initially, Conran – soon to teach textile design himself at the Royal College of Art – tutored her, but she also received some extra tuition and advice from Laura Ashley's husband Bernard, an old acquaintance of Conran's, who had first met him at the opening of the Soup Kitchen in 1953.

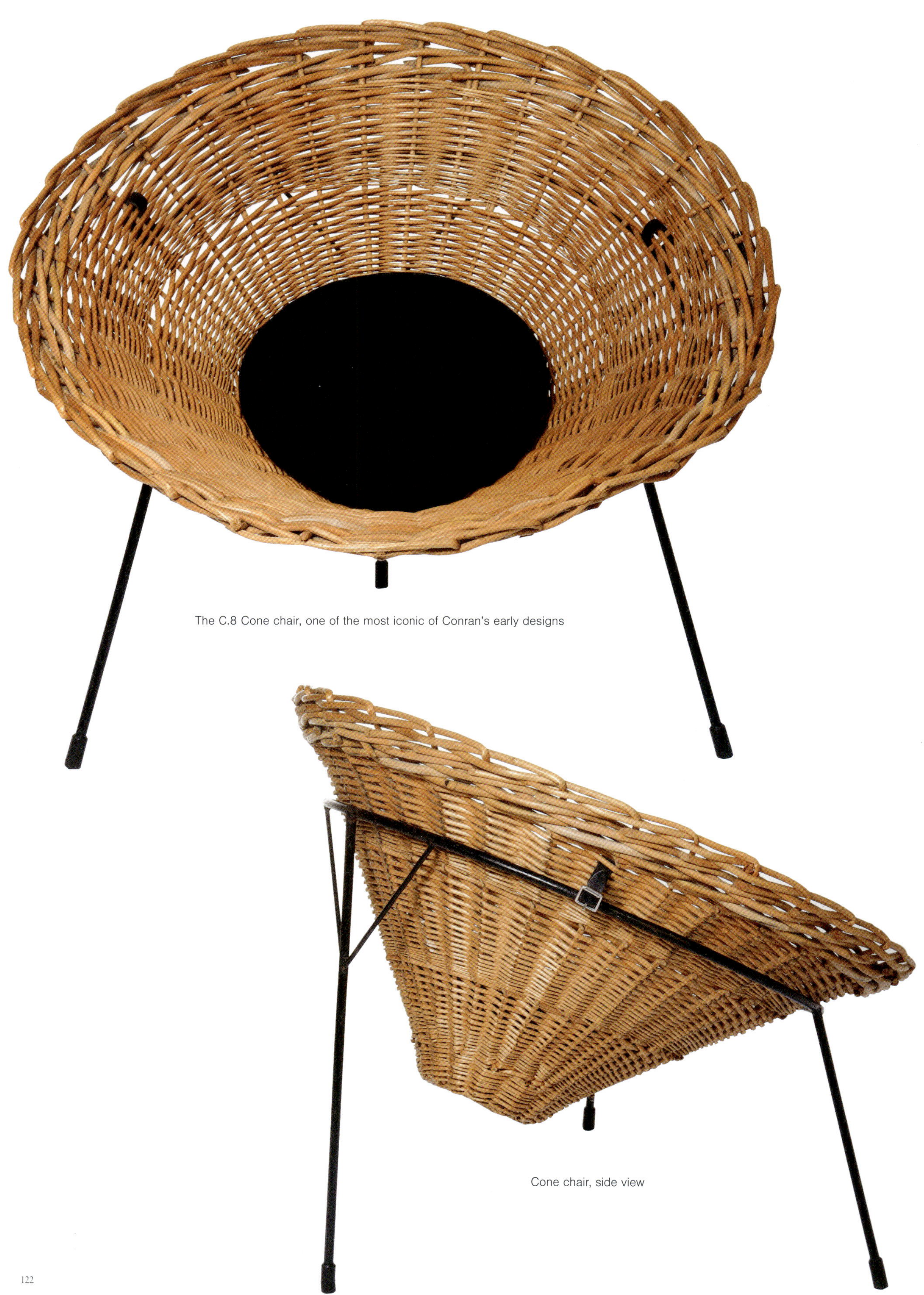

The C.8 Cone chair, one of the most iconic of Conran's early designs

Cone chair, side view

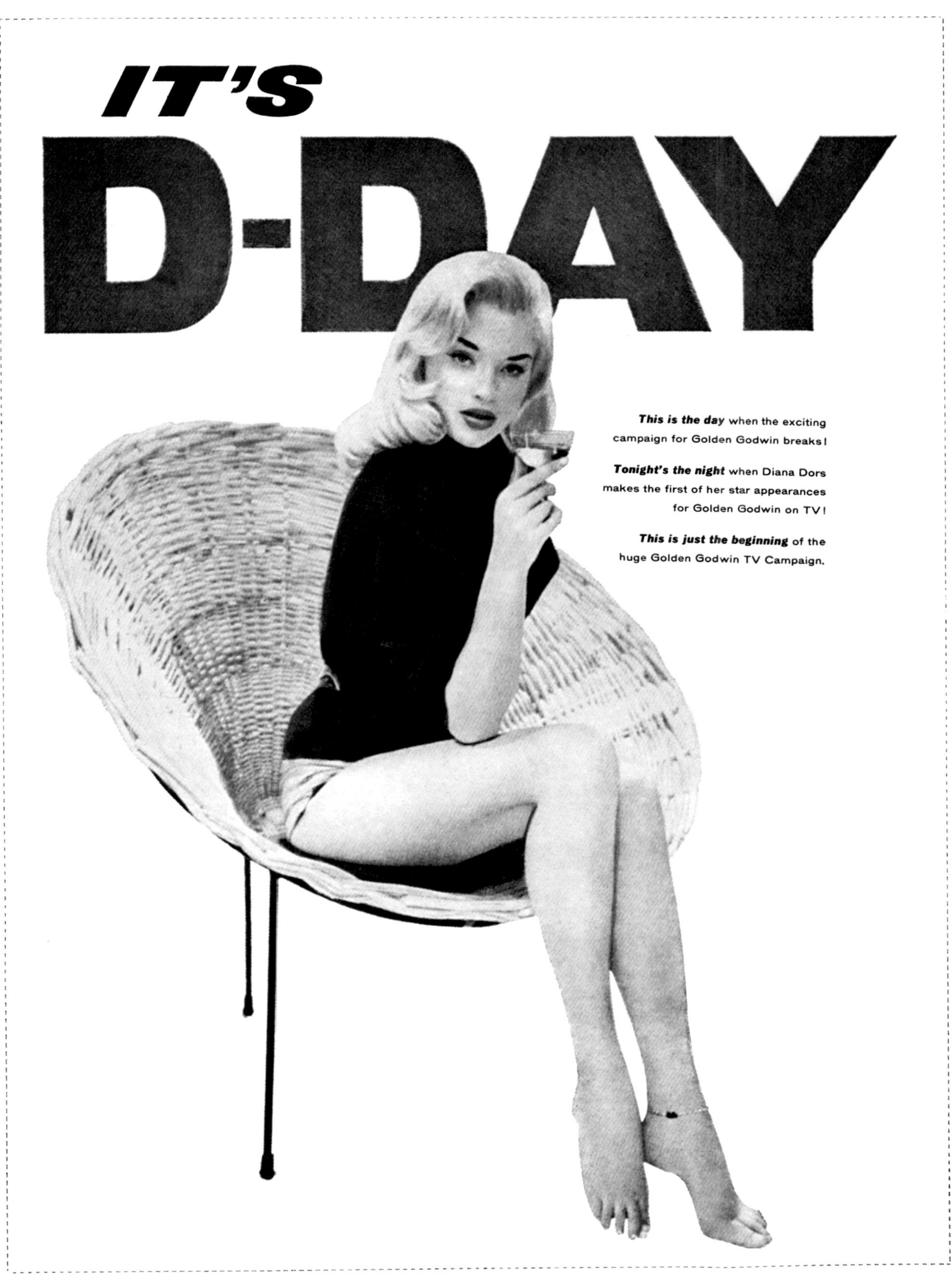

The film star Diana Dors posing in a Cone chair to publicise
Bulmers Cider's new drink, Golden Godwin, c.1955.

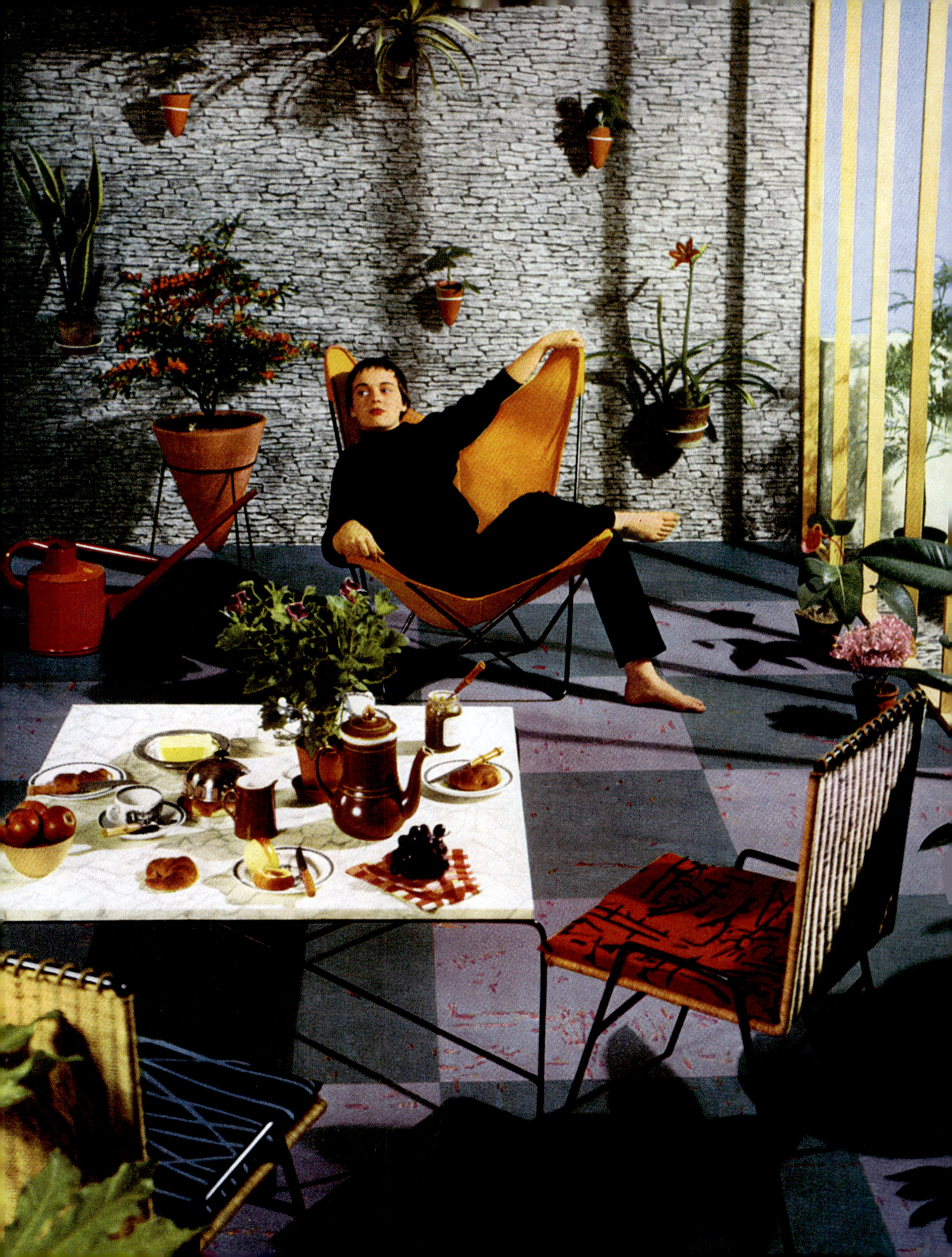

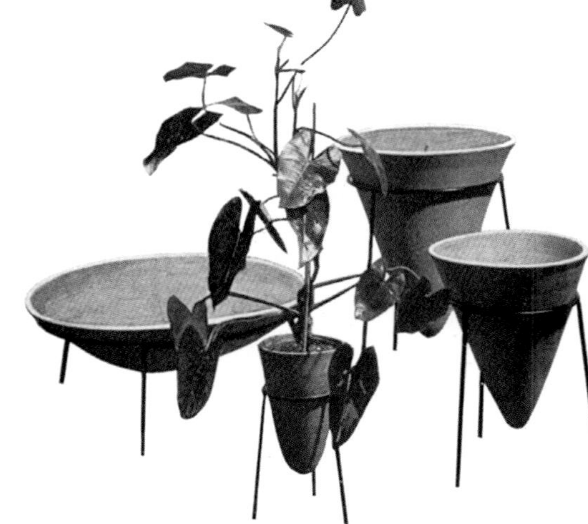

Advertisement for Conran Furniture, showing examples of his range of terracotta planters with welded metal stands, the inspiration for his design 'Plant Life'.

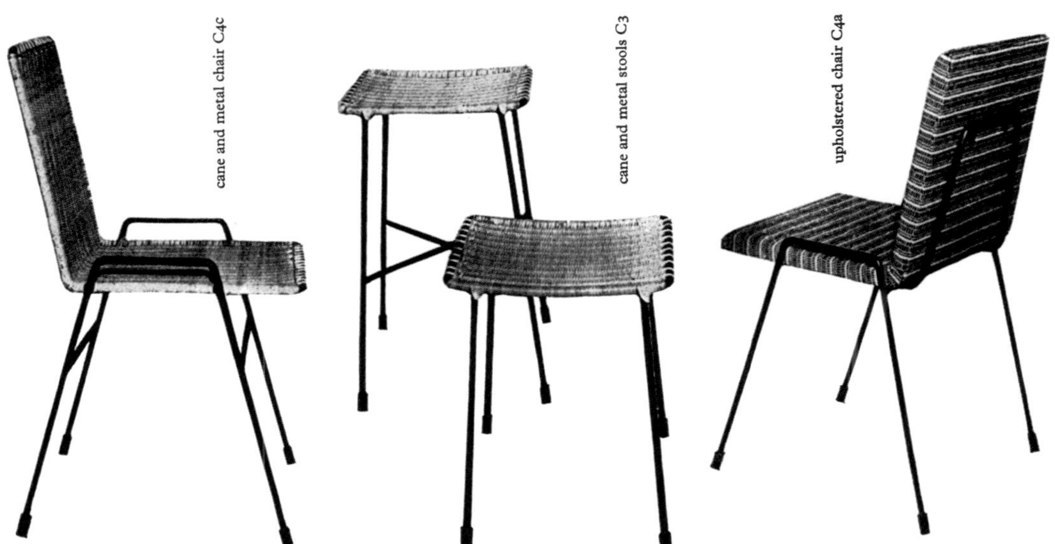

Conran Furniture advertisement for the C.4 chair, 1955. The architect Phillip Johnson, doyen of American Modernism, was sufficiently impressed that he ordered a C.4 for his personal use.

Opposite: Advertisement for Marley Floor Tiles, 1953. A Conran interior with examples of his furniture and textiles, including one of his terracotta plant holders with its tripod stand and several of his C.4 woven cane and steel-framed chairs. After the Basketweave project ended, the C.4 and the Cone chair continued to be sold as part of Conran Furniture's standard ranges of domestic and contract furniture.

BERNARD AND LAURA ASHLEY: URBAN RURALISM

I N THE EARLY 1950s, Bernard and Laura Ashley had originally set up a small silk-screen printing operation, literally working on the kitchen table in their small flat in Pimlico, which was situated close to Chelsea and the King's Road. Here they first produced headscarves, neckerchiefs, tablemats and other such furbelows, very much on a handmade Arts and Crafts cottage industry basis, which Bernard – always extremely self confident and competitive – successfully marketed with great aplomb to prestigious London department stores such as Heal's and John Lewis. In order to capitalise on this initial success they were soon obliged to move off the kitchen table to a succession of ever larger rented spaces, until they were eventually able to produce up to three hundred yards of fabric a week. These early Ashley Mountney Fabrics, as the operation was then known, bore no relationship to the romanticised ruralisim of the style now usually associated with the Laura Ashley name.

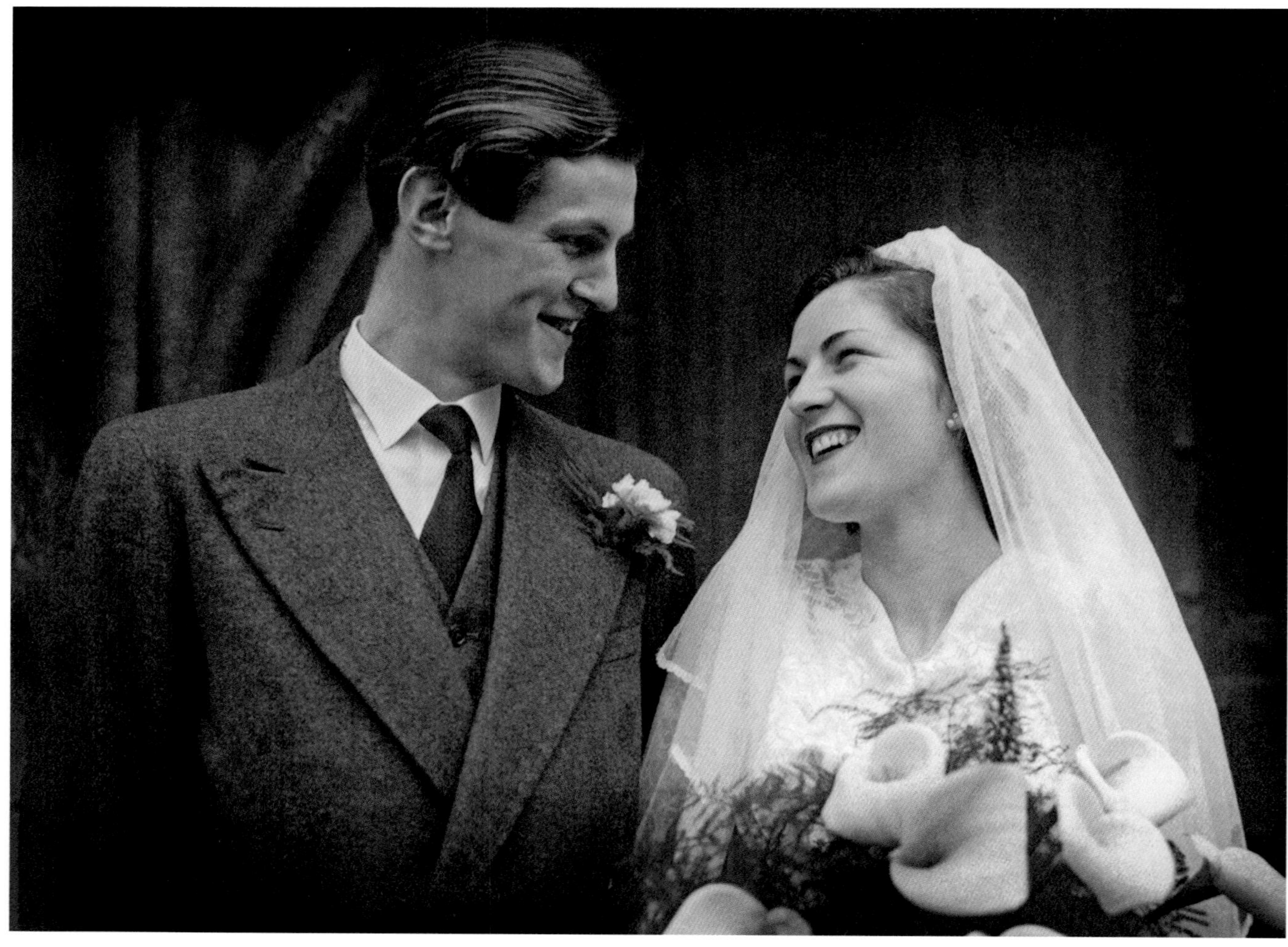

Rather, the designs were boldly modern; some, like 'Patio', the work of Bernard, while others, in an uncompromisingly avant-garde style, such as 'Plaza' and 'Circuit', were commissioned from Bernard's friend, the architect John Sayers. Although these textiles were originally intended for the contract market, the first mention of them in the press was May 1955 in *House & Garden*, where they were promoted as high-end home furnishings. Conran himself sometimes required a limited amount of a textile he'd designed for a particular one-off commission, which he would have printed by Bernard, who was able to produce short runs of a design quickly, with little fuss and at not too great a cost.[41]

ONE OF ASHLEY MOUNTNEY'S most important clients for their contract textiles was the P&O shipping line. It was specifically for use in the ballrooms on the company's liners that Bernard created 'Jazz Players', probably his first example of a Pop textile. The design is an unexpectedly sophisticated Pop Art collage of black and white photographic images, by the photographer Peter Keen, of Humphrey Lyttelton's Jazz Band. With the rapid expansion of the contract side of the business, by 1955 the company was again in need of even larger premises. Bernard and Laura's answer was to move to an old coach house located just outside London at Brasted in Kent. It was here they first produced what are probably some of the earliest examples of commercial Pop design – a range of tea towels printed with witty and ironic images taken mainly from Victorian and Edwardian advertising. Fornasetti's influence may be discerned in this often surreal and humorous use of antique engravings, even more so than that of Paolozzis' and Henderson's Hammer Prints workshop. A popular seller, the success of the range was international, available in leading department stores throughout Europe, Australasia and America. However, it was the marketing of these that brought about the change of the company's name from 'Ashley Mountney' to 'Laura Ashley'. Although the tea towels later proved a great commercial success, Bernard at first thought producing them 'very degrading' and decided to use 'Laura's name on the label instead of his own'.[42] Well, well, well, one lives and learns!!

LAURA, RECOLLECTING FAMILY reminiscences of the various types of utilitarian aprons worn by her grandmother and great aunts when in service in the late Victorian and Edwardian eras, was inspired in 1959 to add to the tea towels a series of large practical aprons, made in a strong cotton drill printed with the same ironic Victorian graphic designs. Shortly after, a range of gardening smocks was also produced in the same cotton drill, but printed with a variety of stripes devised by Bernard. These were clearly derived from the hard-wearing navy blue twill smocks traditionally worn by French artisans, particularly fishermen, which were already popular in Britain among bohemian 'arty' types such as the studio potter Lucie Rie, sculptors like Barbara Hepworth and art school students in general. The Ashleys' more upmarket version for lady gardeners also looked well when worn with jeans or the various types of trews, pedal pushers, capri pants and ski pants, increasingly popular as casual wear with cool young women in the early 1960s.

THE RANGE OF SMOCKS and aprons was extended soon after the Ashleys' move to Wales in 1961, with the addition of Laura's first commercially produced dress design. Originally conceived as a maternity smock, it became known as the Basic Dress, and was literally put together in ten minutes from four simple panels. It was first made in a cotton drill, either printed with a combination of Bernard's subtly coloured stripes or one of Laura's neat, small scale patterns, the earliest of which, 'Daisy Print no. D94', she had designed in 1959. Inexpensive, versatile, easy to wear and maintain, the popularity of the Basic Dress ensured that it remained in production for some years, although it was later produced in a variety of more luxurious fabrics than the original cotton drill.

BERNARD, WHO – on his passport, for instance – always described himself as an engineer and print technician, felt strongly that 'experimental printing is of the utmost importance to the fabric designer.'[43] The often apparent immediacy of the Ashleys' early hand silk-screen printing on tough workhorse textiles, combined with the ultra efficiency and simplicity of these early dresses and smocks, is surprisingly more in sync with revolutionary textile design and fashion in Soviet Russia in the 1920s, than the romanticised retro-ruralism usually associated with the Laura Ashley label in the later 1960s and 1970s. More importantly, it was the introduction of the smocks and the Basic Dress which marked the beginning of the Ashleys' metamorphosis from small-time textile printers to major international fashion entrepreneurs.

Opposite: Bernard and Laura Ashley on their wedding day, 22 February 1949.

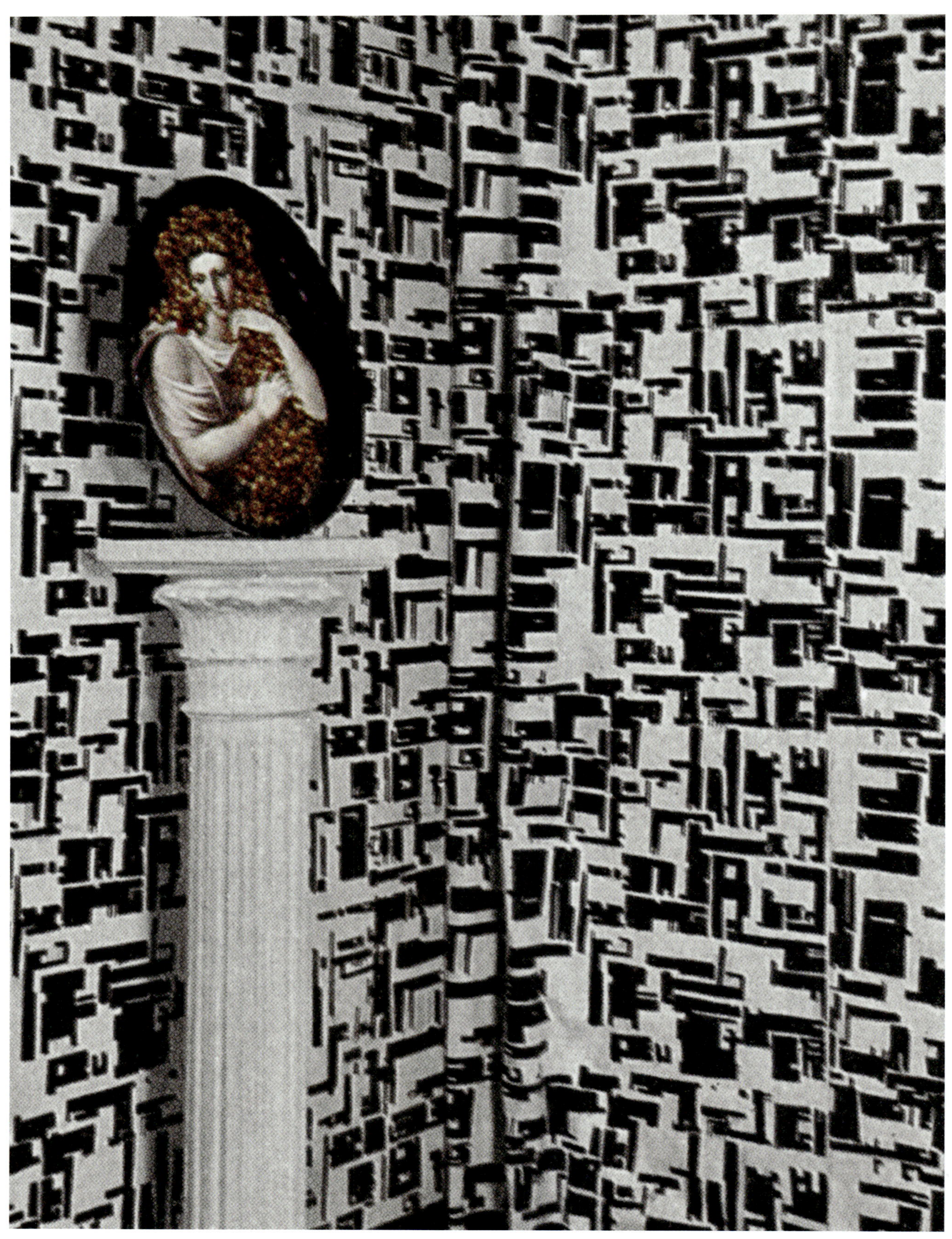

Advertisement for 'Plaza', a coordinated textile and wallpaper by Ashley Mountney, 1955. The company's original name
was an amalgamation of Laura's and Bernard's surnames. A tray by Fornasetti is displayed on the column.

Opposite: Textile, 'Plaza,' screen-printed cotton, designed by the architect John Sayers and printed by Bernard Ashley
for Ashley Mountney, c.1955.

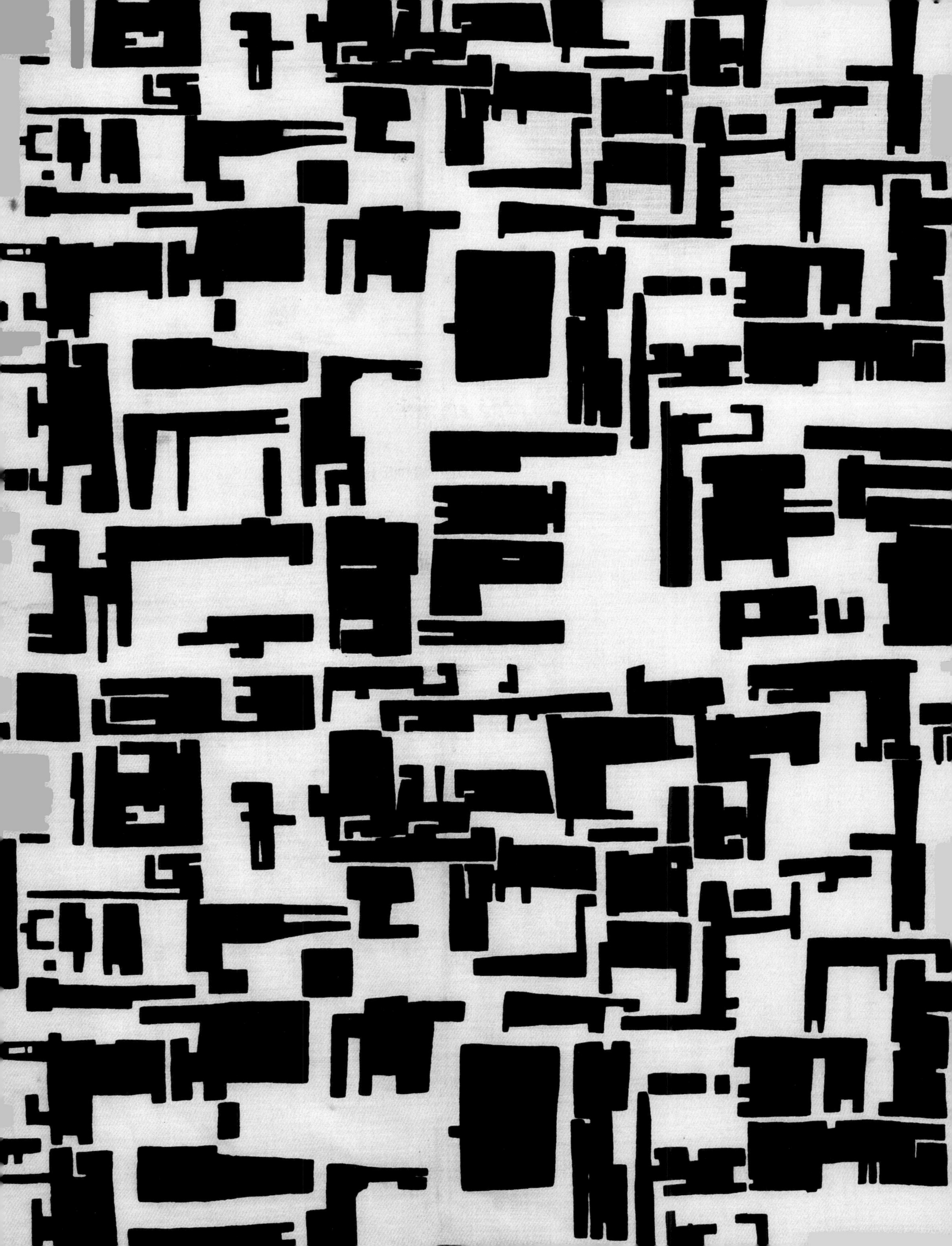

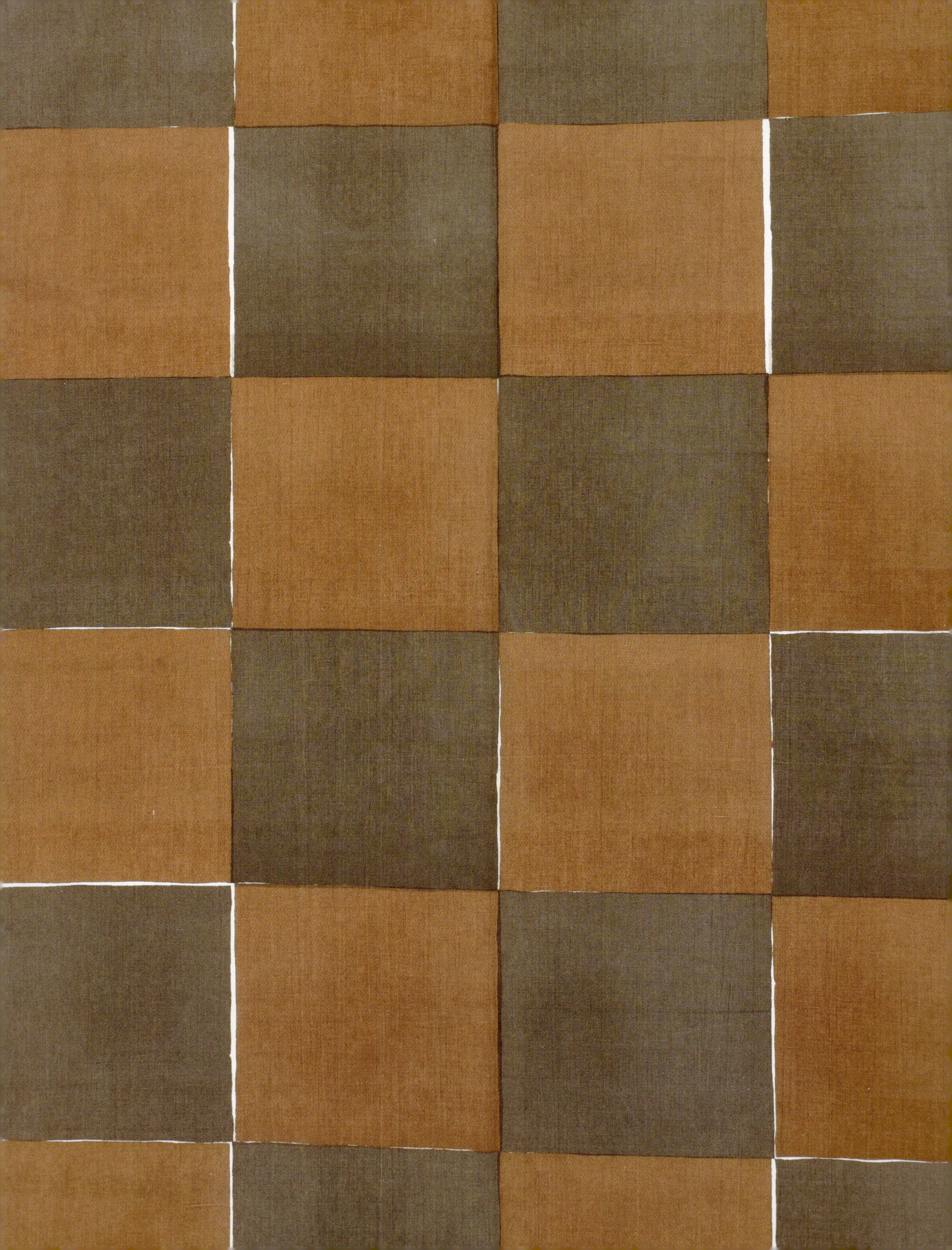

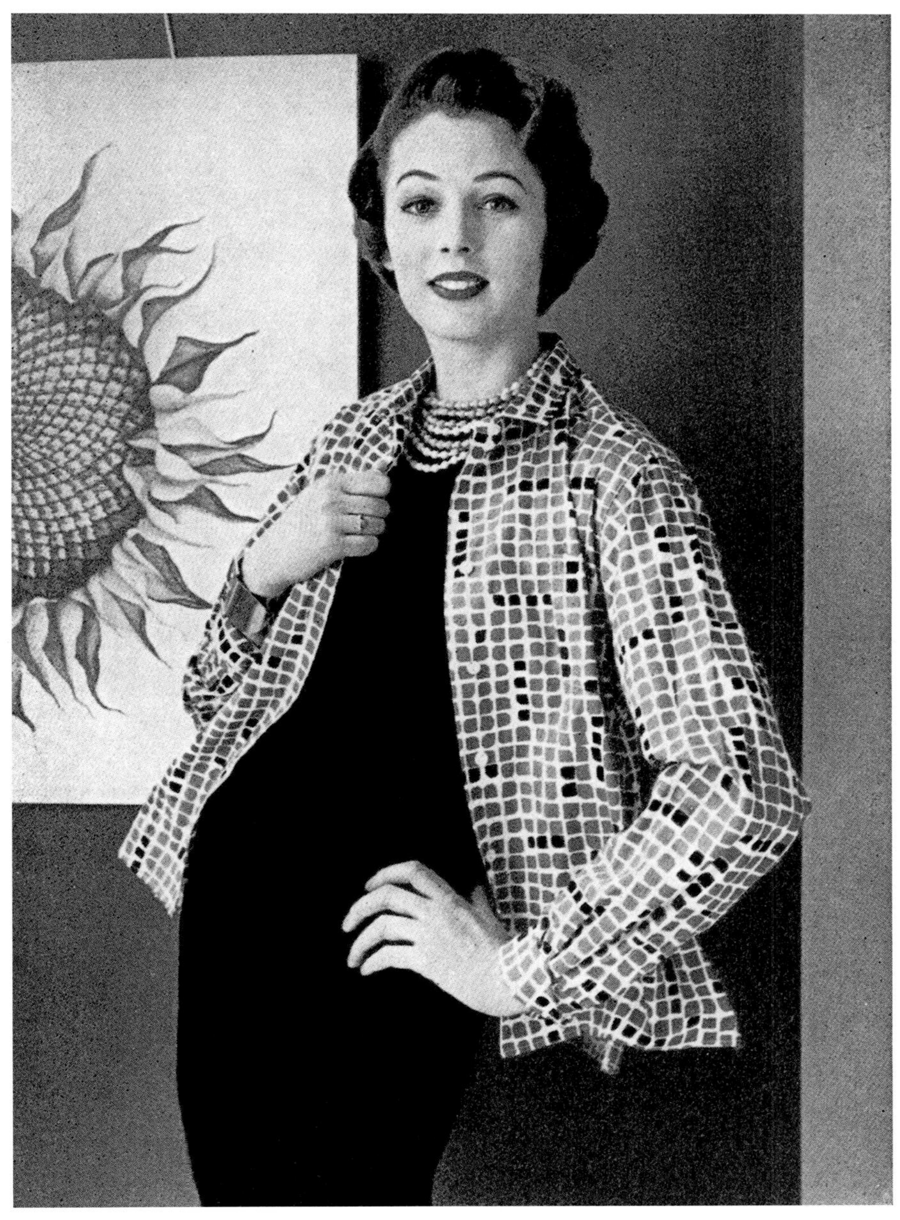

Silk jacket by Ashley Mountney, c.1955-1956. Illustrated in Terence Conran's book *Printed Textile Design*. A Conran 'Photo Print' of an enlarged eighteenth-century engraving of a sunflower hangs on the wall. Photograph by Conran's sister, Priscilla Conran.

Opposite: Textile, 'Patio', screen-printed cotton, designed and printed by Bernard Ashley for Ashley Mountney, c.1955.

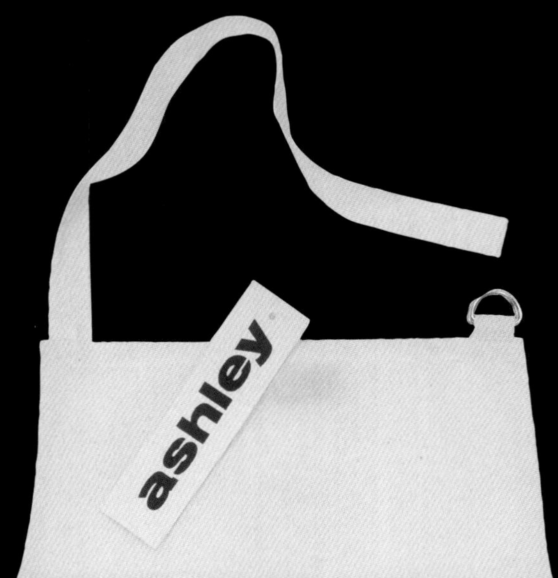

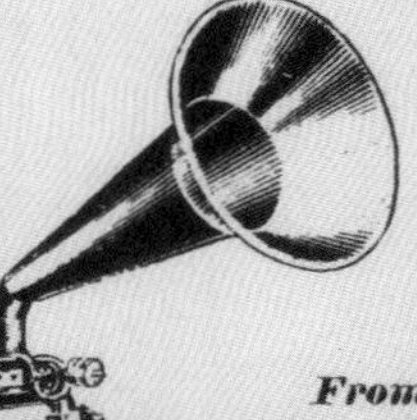

It was Laura who added aprons to the range of tea towels, based on those her grandmother wore in the Edwardian period. Ironically, it was the tea towels which brought about the change of the company's name from Ashley Mountney to Laura Ashley, as Bernard was, at first, too embarrassed to market them under the Ashley Mountney name.

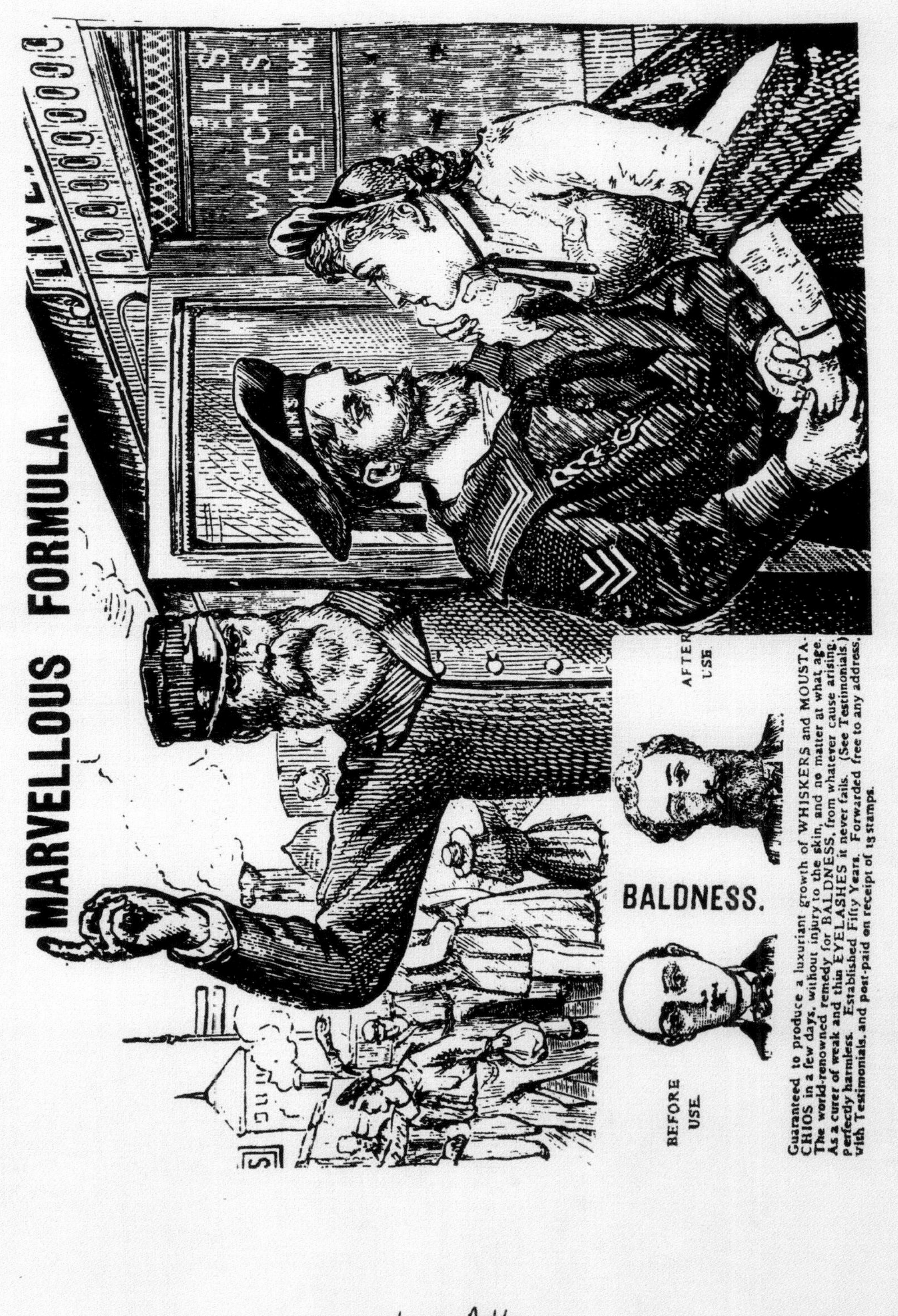

Tea towel, 'Beards', c.1957-1958. The Ashleys' remarkable and internationally successful range of tea towels, wittily decorated with prints of nineteenth-century advertisements, an early example of the Pop aesthetic.

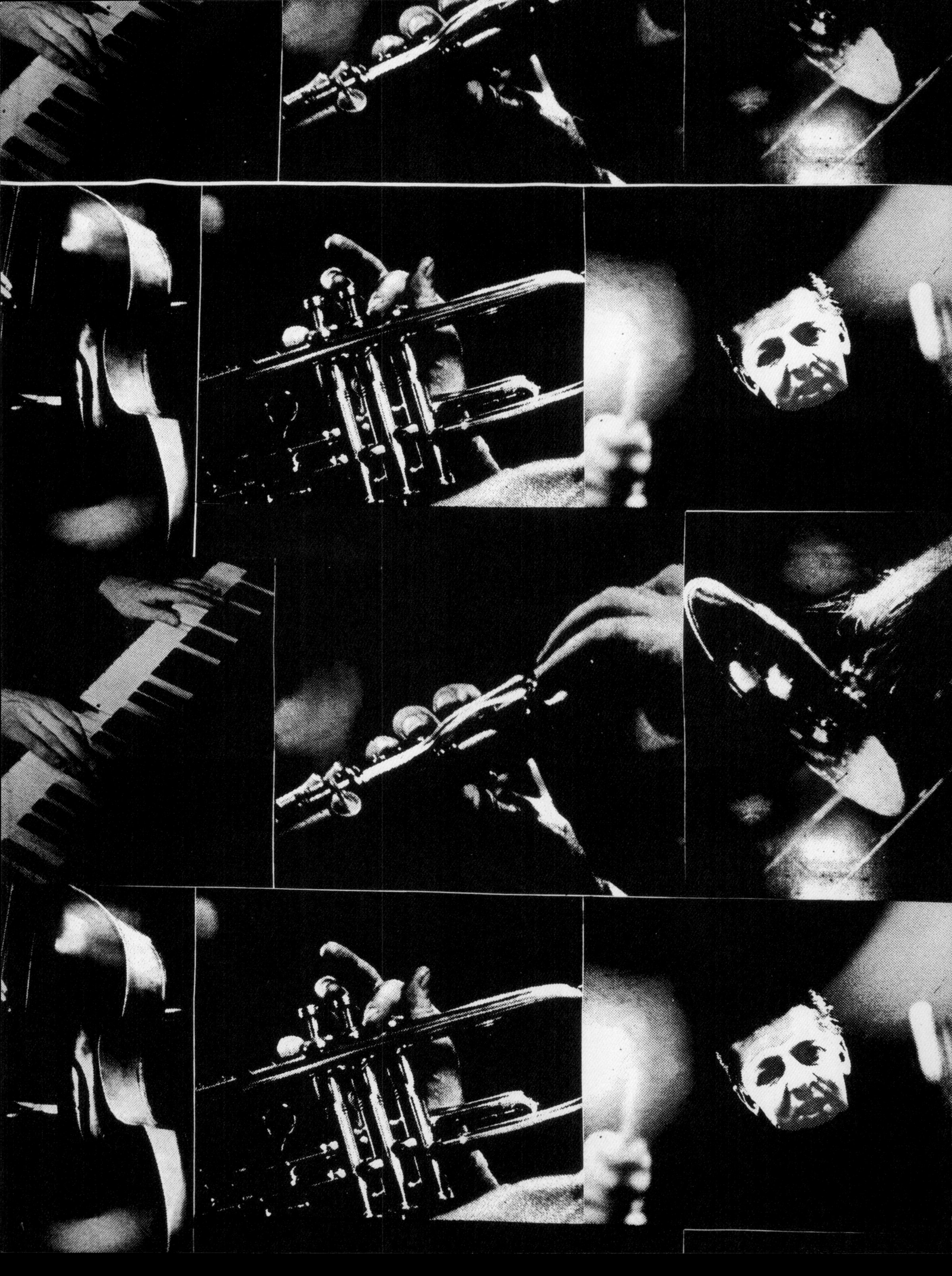

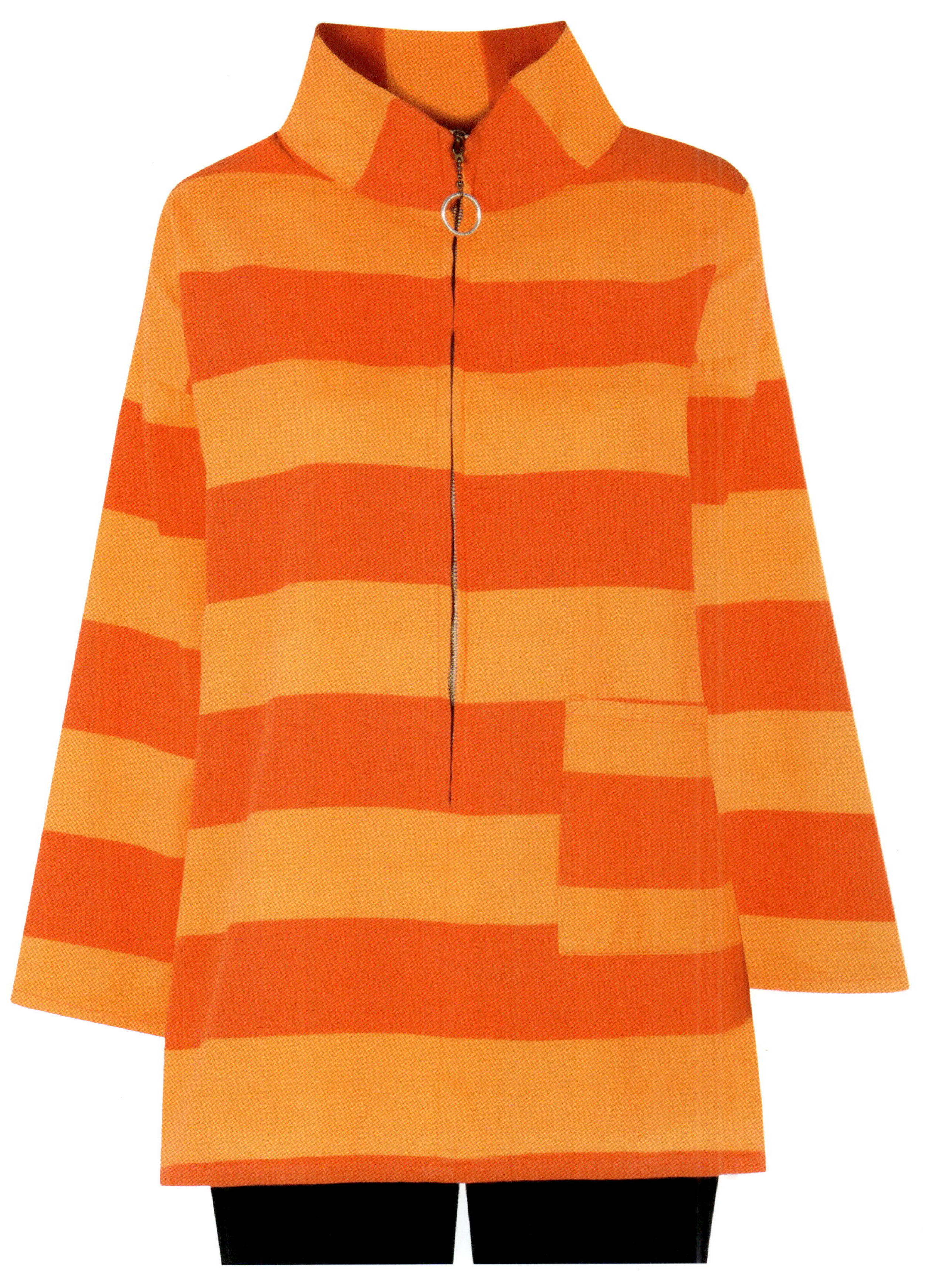

The first items of clothing Bernard and Laura sold commercially, were a range of 'gardening' smocks c.1959-1960. They were made in a strong cotton duck, printed with a variety of stripes devised by Bernard. The smocks proved very popular with fashionable young women, who wore them as casual wear with trews, pedal pushers and ski pants.

Opposite: Textile, 'Jazz Players', screen-printed cotton. The design is a collage of photographs by Peter Keen of Humphrey Lyttelton's jazz band. Designed and printed by Bernard Ashley, c.1958. This textile was commissioned by the F&O shipping line for use in the ballrooms on liners such as the Oriana.

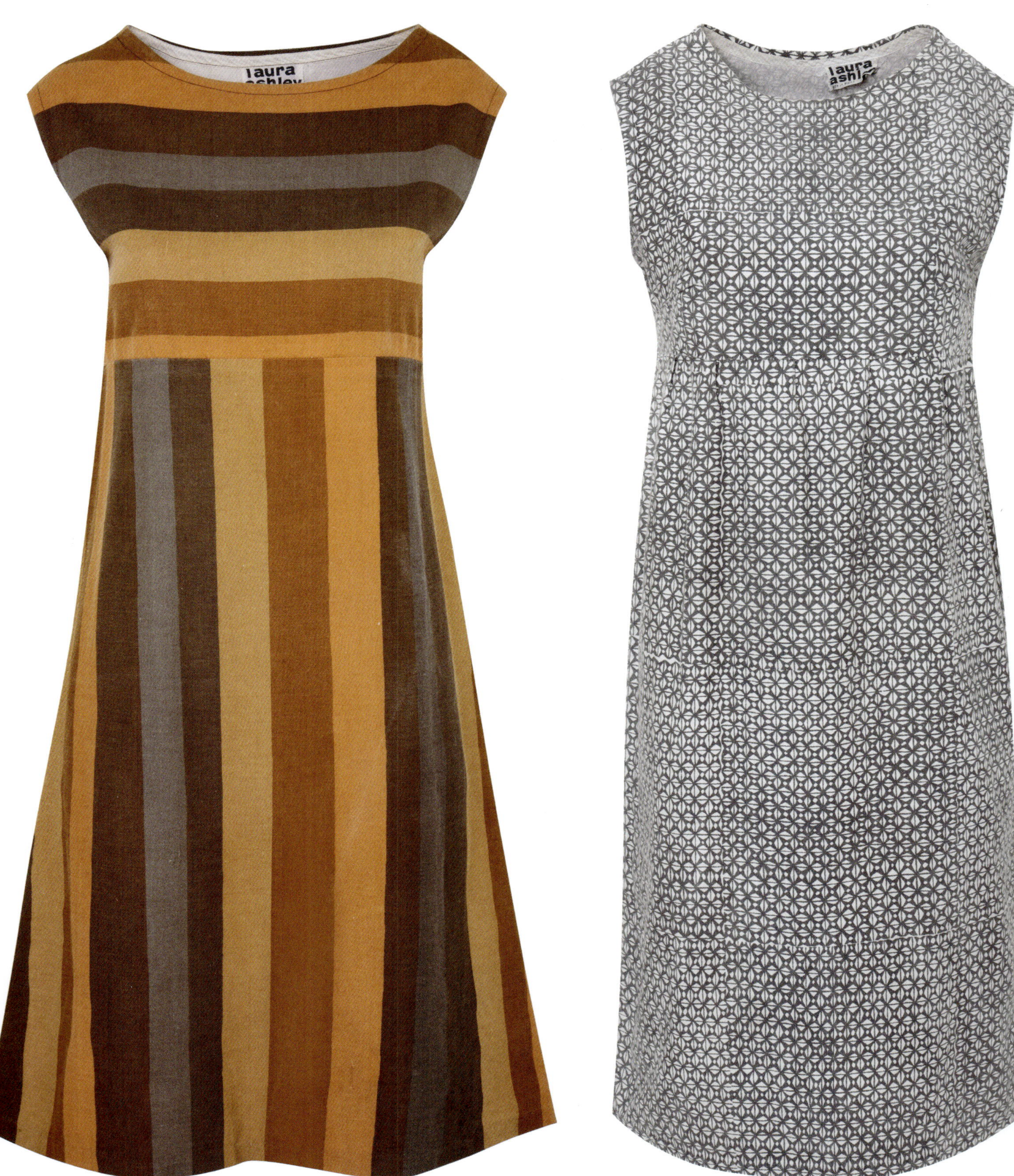

The Basic Dress c.1961, is the first dress sold under the Laura Ashley label. Made at their newly acquired premises in Wales, the dress was jointly devised by Bernard and Laura. Originally intended as a maternity smock, it was extremely functional but attractive in its simplicity. Made from only four pieces of cloth, it could be assembled in some ten to fifteen minutes. This example is realised in Bernard's striped cotton drill.

Basic Dress, c.1961. This early version is in a cotton drill printed with one of Laura's first simple patterns.

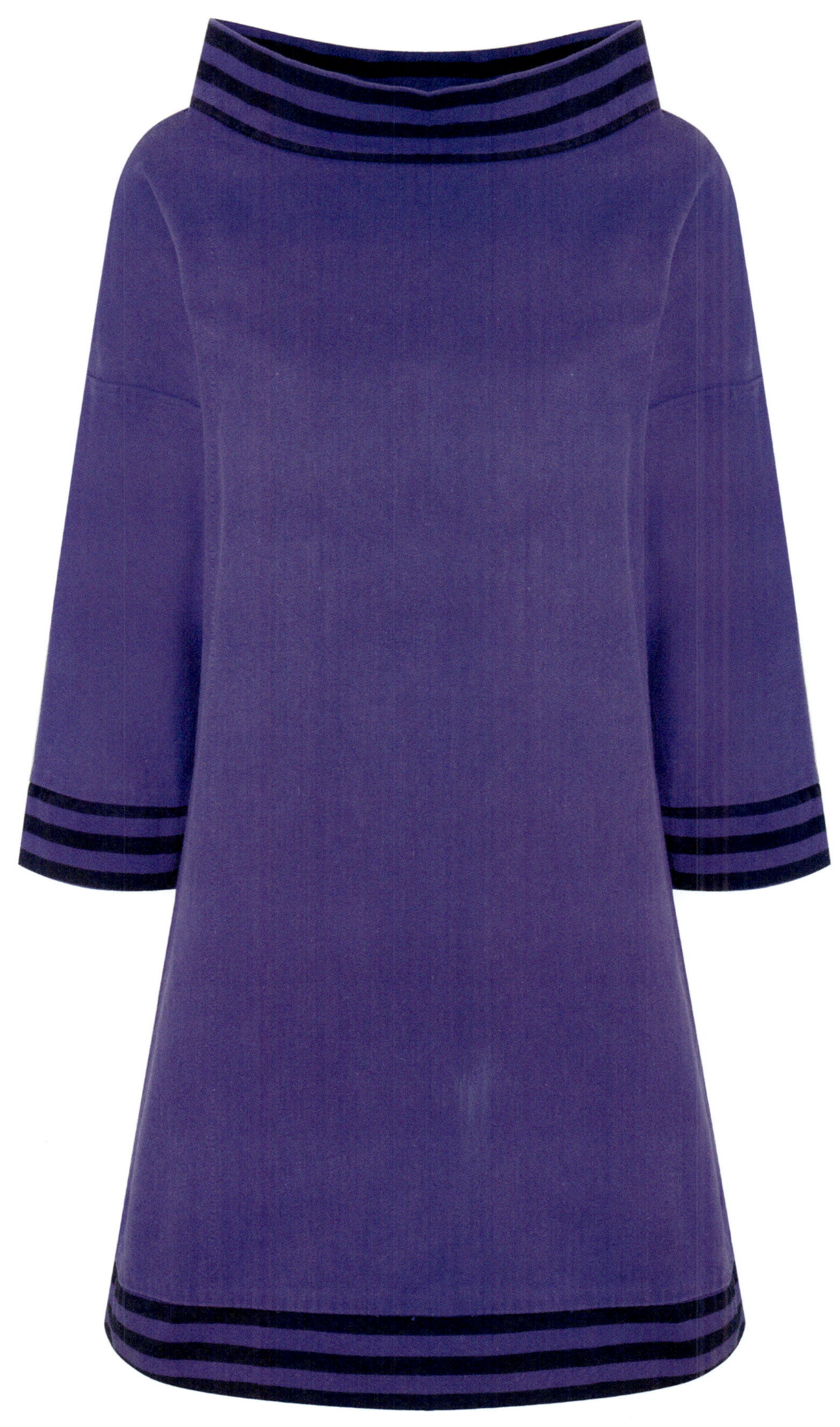

Smock Dress c.1964-1965. A development of the Basic Dress, smocks like this, worn with coloured tights, were a central part of the Ashleys' fashion range in the mid 1960s. The striped fabric of the boat neck collar and borders were printed separately.

MARY QUANT: EMPIRE 1961–1970

IN 1960, WITH a new decade ahead and Bazaar No. 2 successfully under their belts, Quant and Plunket Greene began to seek fresh fields to conquer. The first in a series of momentous developments came in 1961, when they registered a wholesale company trading as Mary Quant Limited. From then on her designs, no longer exclusive to the Bazaar boutiques, were available in more than 20 upmarket department stores throughout the country. The Bazaar name was then dropped from the label, to read instead, 'Designed by Mary Quant London', although this was very soon abbreviated to 'Mary Quant London'. She subsequently said the decision to launch this first tentative sortie into the mass market was one of the most important the company ever took.

THAT SAME YEAR, 1961, she and Plunket Greene also made a reconnaissance trip to New York to discover what opportunities there might be of gaining an entree into the potentially lucrative American fashion market. Yet, despite attracting much interest from enthusiastic New York fashion editors and journalists, who had plans for features in magazines like *Life* or *Seventeen*, backed up by a promotion of Quant's clothes in Saks of Fifth Avenue, no solid orders or business propositions were forthcoming. However, shortly after a somewhat crestfallen return to London, they received a unexpected phone call from a Mr Paul Young, a representative of J.C. Penney, the biggest chain of department stores in America. It was a call with far reaching consequences; Quant later wrote that it changed:

> 'The whole course of our business lives ... to establish us in the fashion trade in America and in other parts of the world; and to mushroom, eventually into a multi-million-dollar deal.'[44]

FOUNDED IN 1902, by the early 1960s the J.C. Penney stores were generally seen as somewhat stolid but trustworthy purveyors of rather dull fashions to an equally dull, lower middle class, middle-aged clientele, and sales were dwindling. Attempting to reverse their somewhat out-moded image, the company had originally sent Paul Young on a mission to Europe to seek out the work of adventurous young fashion designers in France, Italy, Britain and Scandinavia, in the hope of commissioning collections from them. In the event, however, Young's great appreciation of Quant's designs and his instant personal rapport with her, led him to successfully convince the J.C. Penney executive they need look no further for a designer than Quant and to authorise him to conclude a sole contract with her. With more than 1,700 of Penney's stores spread across the States, this was the mass market with a vengeance and, as ever confident, Quant and Plunket Greene firmly grasped the opportunity with both hands. Her first collection for Penney's, designed expressly for the youth market, was launched in early 1962, amid great acclaim and much American razzmatazz, at the British embassy in Washington, D.C. Quant continued to carefully cultivate her relationship with the company throughout the 1960s, particularly with James Cash Penney himself, and successfully designed several collections each year for them, until 'old man' Penney's death in 1971.

FOR THE REMAINDER of the 1960s Quant was one of the most sought after fashion designers in the United States, seen as part of the 'British Invasion' with a status similar to that of The Beatles and The Rolling Stones. Eventually, her clothes from both the more exclusive Mary Quant London range and the Ginger Group were sold across the full American retail spectrum, from the mass market catered for by the J.C. Penney stores, to the rarefied exclusivity of Neiman Marcus in Dallas and upmarket Manhattan department stores such as Lord and Taylor and Bergdorf Goodman. As in Britain, Quant's new informal boutique style of fashion retailing spread quickly across the States. Among the first to successfully emulate the full Quant experience was the New York boutique Paraphernalia. When set up late in 1965, with Betsy Johnson as principal designer, Paraphernalia's debt to Quant and Bazaar was openly acknowledged and the company's publicity boasted of selling clothes from her ranges, alongside the designs of other 'fab' young British fashion designers, such as Marian Foale and Sally Tuffin. Paraphernalia was also closely associated with Betsy Johnson's good friend Andy Warhol. Betsy was then married to John Cale, a member of Warhol's pop music group, the Velvet Underground, while Edie Sedgwick and 'Baby' Jane Holzer, the superstars of Warhol's Silver Factory films, often modelled Paraphernalia's clothes. Quant's enormous popularity in the United States endorsed her fame worldwide and her Mod fashions have since become icons of the era, an inextricable part of the popular image of the 1960s.

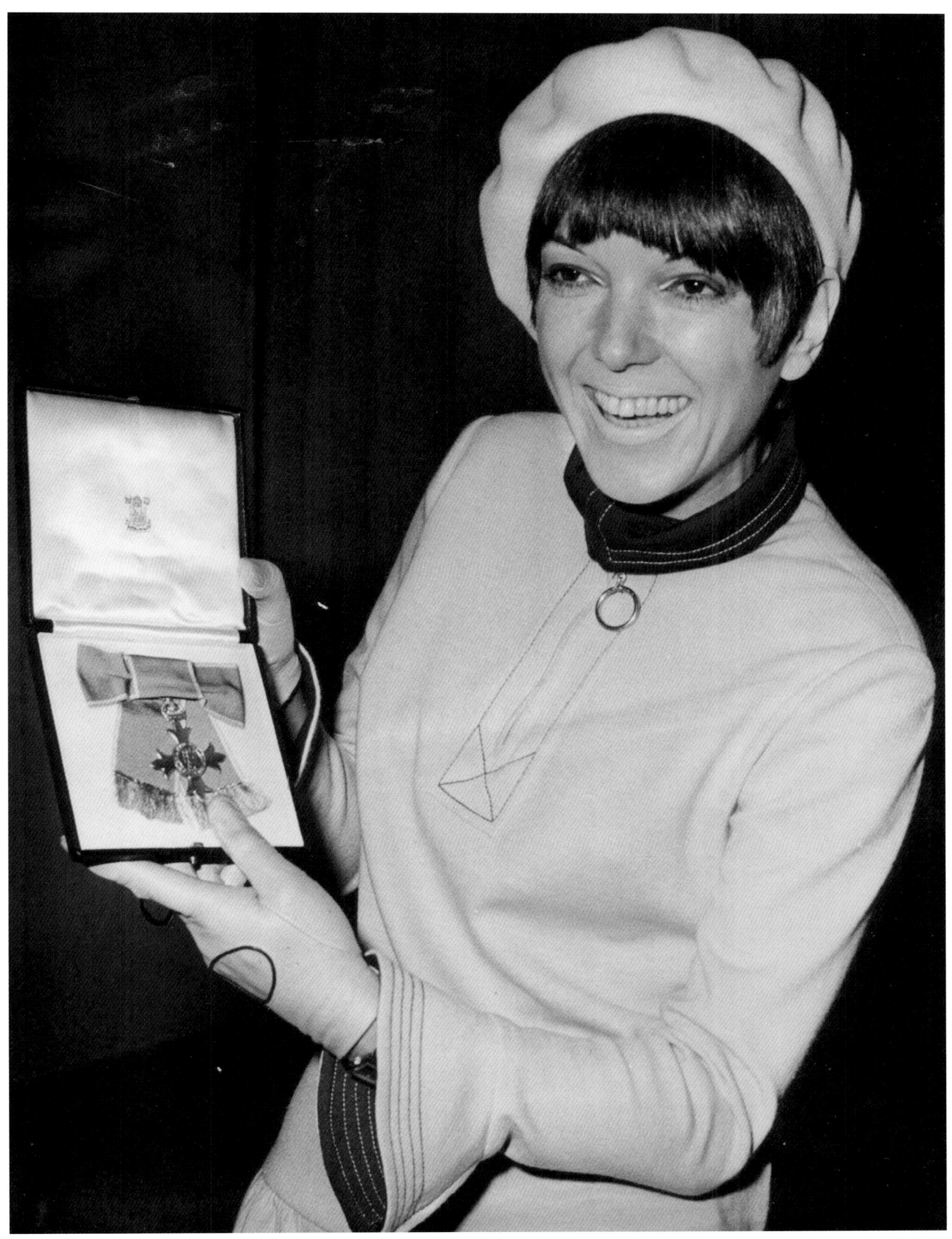

Mary Quant was awarded the Order of the British Empire (O.B.E) in 1966.

EARLIER IN HER CAREER, Quant had sometimes expressed a wish to make her clothes available to the widest possible market at prices affordable by most. She was at last able to realize this dream when she launched the Ginger Group, the diffusion range for which she is now best known. To achieve this she was served well by the experience she gained designing for J.C. Penney and the American mass market. Prior to this, clothes with the Bazaar or Mary Quant London labels had been relatively expensive and exclusive, her largely London-based clientele being mainly drawn from her own social milieu, the Chelsea Set, and other well-heeled fellow travellers. A little later in the 1960s, the cockney fashion model Twiggy was emphatic that 'Bazaar was for rich girls'.[45] When faced in 1961 with the dilemma of her work becoming further allied with elite fashion, a version of French couture or part of the mass market, she had made a tentative move towards the latter. In 1963 she decided to go the whole hog and became the founder-director of the Mary Quant Ginger Group Wholesale Clothing Design and Manufacturing Company. It was then that the '60s finally got underway. 1963 not only saw the launch of Quant's Ginger Group, but also the advent of British Beat music and what were to become the global phenomena of The Beatles and The Rolling Stones. After a long incubation, Swinging London had at last arrived.

Mary's Great Ideas: 1964–1967

'MINI SKIRTS, PLASTIC COATS AND SHOES, COSMETICS, TIGHTS AND BODY STOCKINGS, PAPER PATTERNS FOR THE HOME DRESSMAKER, AND TO CROWN IT ALL, AN OBE.'

EVIDENTLY ENERGISED BY the ever-growing scale of her achievement, Quant worked throughout the remainder of the 1960s in an extraordinary bout of creativity. As early as 1963 she had shown great interest in the new plastics, seen as the fabrics of the future, the Space Age. She particularly liked the properties of the plastic Polyvinyl Chloride, better known as PVC [46] and after somewhat unsatisfactory initial attempts to use it, she successfully created for the Alligator company in 1965, an acclaimed collection of rain- and shower-proof wear, much of which was in black and white PVC. Inspired by Op Art, the designs were intended, in part, to create kinetic illusions, the result of the effects caused by the optical patterns working in tandem with the wearer's movements.

BY THE END of 1966 the popularity of Op Art and Space Age fashion began to fade and the somewhat related visual effects of psychedelic patterns, apparently inspired by the experience of 'acid trips' induced by the hallucinogenic drug LSD, began to take their place. The whiplash curlicues and generally over-heated delirium of Art Nouveau design was also absorbed into the psychedelic aesthetic and Quant, with her uncanny ability to anticipate the zeitgeist, appears to have foreseen the vogue for Psychedelia as early as 1965, when she designed a group of clothes using the 'Lotus' range of Art Nouveau influenced textiles by Liberty of London. One of these, a jacket with a vividly coloured design of writhing poppies, was worn by the actress Jane Asher on the set of the now iconic film *Alfie*.

A LITTLE LATER she began another venture in a most unlikely partnership with the work-boot manufacturer G.B. Britton of Bristol and together they mass produced inexpensive extruded moulded plastic footwear, the Quant Afoot range. Although variations of the basic Shoe Boot were also available, such as the Mule Boot or the Daddy Long Legs, the project had an unfortunately short life, largely due to a rather hesitant response from a somewhat unconvinced public. Among common complaints were the shoes' coldness in winter and the uncomfortable sweatiness generated in warm weather.

ALTHOUGH QUANT is usually thought of as the creator of the miniskirt, in neither of her autobiographies does she directly say she was. Other fashion designers, such as the French couturier André Courrèges or the British fashion designer John Bates, have claimed to be its originator, but the reality was never so straightforward. In the UK for instance, since at least the mid 1950s skirts had been worn at least on the knee, if not an inch or two above, by more adventurous teenage girls and young women, particularly art students and jazz and Rock 'n' Roll fans. Quant would have been well aware of this popular street trend and, from at least 1964, began to enthusiastically take skirt lengths ever higher until they reached the extreme of the 'micro minis' of the late 1960s.

1966 WAS A particularly important year in the expansion of the Quant Empire. It was the year her extraordinary achievement was officially recognised when she was awarded an OBE for her services to the fashion industry. It was also the year in which she finally drew the many threads of her varied interests together. In 1965 she wrote:

> 'What a great many people still don't realise is that the Look isn't just the garments you wear. It's the way you put your make-up on, the way you do your hair, the sort of stockings you choose, the way you walk and stand... All these are part of the same feeling.' [47]

BETWEEN 1964 AND 1966 she had concentrated on realising the total Quant Look, launching ranges of tights, pantyhose and body stockings, ostensibly to counteract the more adverse aspects of wearing ever shorter skirts, to which she soon after added her new range of unstructured underwear. In 1964 she collaborated with the hairdresser Vidal Sassoon when he recreated the classic 1920s 'bob' as the 'five point' cut, an elegant close-cut geometric 'wash and go' hairstyle which potentially freed women from the drudge of elaborate perms, hair rollers and spray-on lacquer. But probably the most adventurous of her excursions to the further reaches of the fashion universe was the launch in 1966 of the Mary Quant range of cosmetics.

> 'I wanted to design a complete look from head to toe. We had the miniskirts and mini-dresses. We had the tights to match the skinny-rib sweaters, in great colours like Coleman's mustard yellow, plum, ginger and black. We had Vidal Sassoon. Everything looked right except the make-up.' [48]

DERIVED ESSENTIALLY FROM the large kits of cosmetics that fashion models toted around to fashion shows and photo shoots, an association emphasised in the marketing, it took eighteen months to develop the full range of cosmetics. It was then retailed with high sophistication in elegant white, black and silver packaging, prominently emblazoned with Quant's recently evolved daisy logo. The numerous items could either be bought singly or in various permutations in the type of 'kit boxes' favoured by models, such as the Overnighter. Each item was given its own wryly amusing, slightly risqué name by Alexander Plunket Greene – a speciality of his – for instance Starkers foundation. It also seems probable that Quant illustrated the various jokey leaflets accompanying the range in what appears to be her own inimitable hand. The extreme razzmatazz of the champagne launch of the cosmetics on 28 March 1966, at the height of the Swinging London phenomenon, was supported by a suitably high octane poster campaign featuring advertisements for such necessities as Cry, Baby waterproof mascara and Bring Back the Lash! false eye lashes.

POSSIBLY QUANT'S ULTIMATE encounter with the mass market was through the sale of paper patterns to the home dressmaker by the Butterick Company, a worldwide operation without boundaries and with enormous potential. In the earliest days of Bazaar, Quant had herself sometimes utilised Butterick paper patterns to create her own designs, 'cutting out pieces' where she didn't want them and adding more paper where she did. Ebenezer Butterick, a bespoke tailor from Sterling, Massachusetts, founded the Butterick Paper Pattern Company in 1863 as a result of his wife's problems with the crude hit-and-miss sizes of the clumsy card templates for home dressmaking then available to a rapidly expanding American middle class. His answer was the printed tissue paper pattern in graduated multiple standard sizes, a revolution which allowed the less well-off to be fashionably, but inexpensively, dressed in the latest styles each season. In 1964 Quant signed a contract with the company to create a number of exclusive designs for them each year. Her work proved extremely successful. A big seller then for Butterick was 30,000 patterns worldwide, but the sales of Quant's designs often topped 70,000. As with J.C. Penney, she continued to design for Butterick until the early 1970s.

DESIGNS FOR THE AMERICAN MARKET:
J.C. Penney and Butterick Paper Patterns

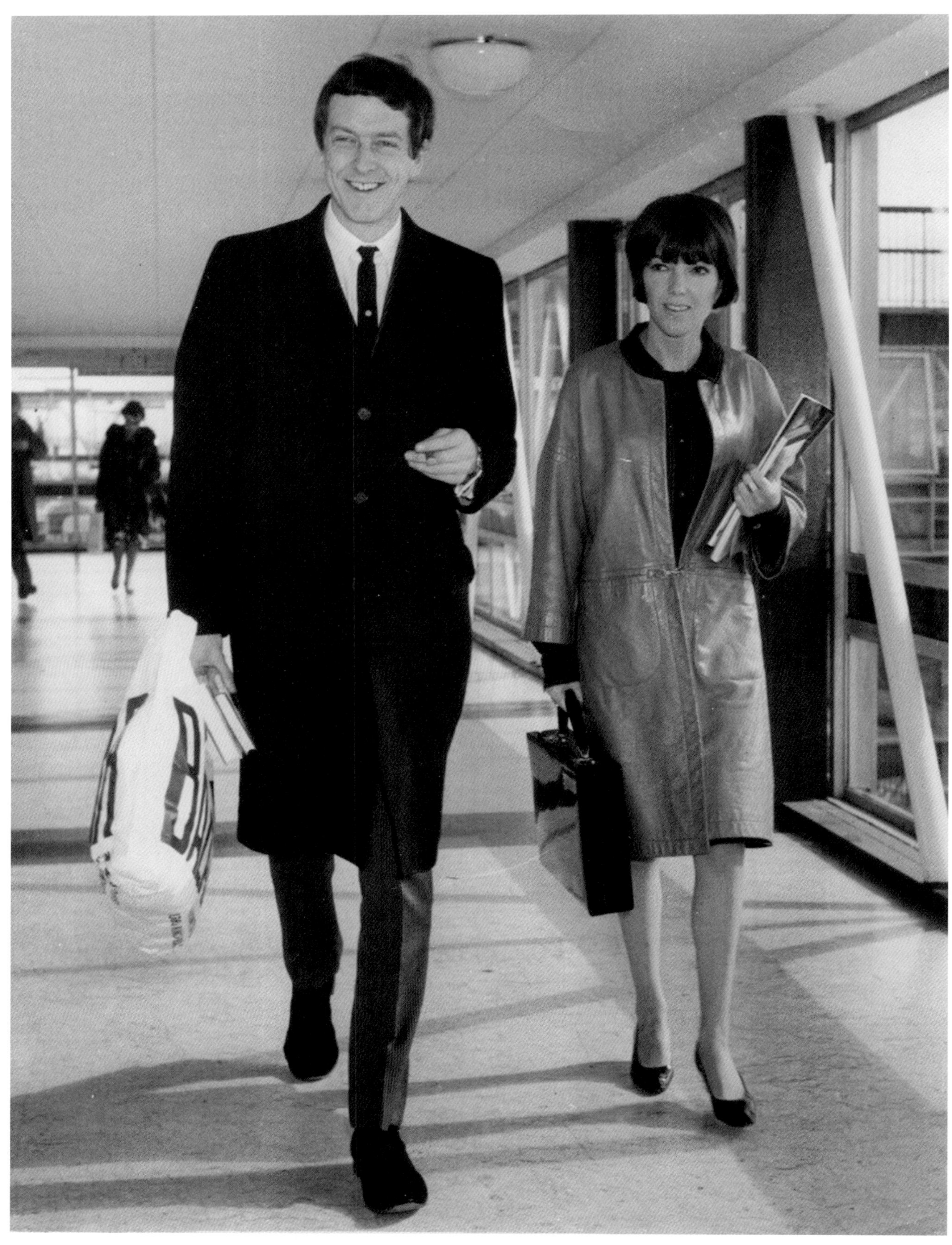

Mary Quant and Alexander Plunket Greene on their way to the United States, 1964.

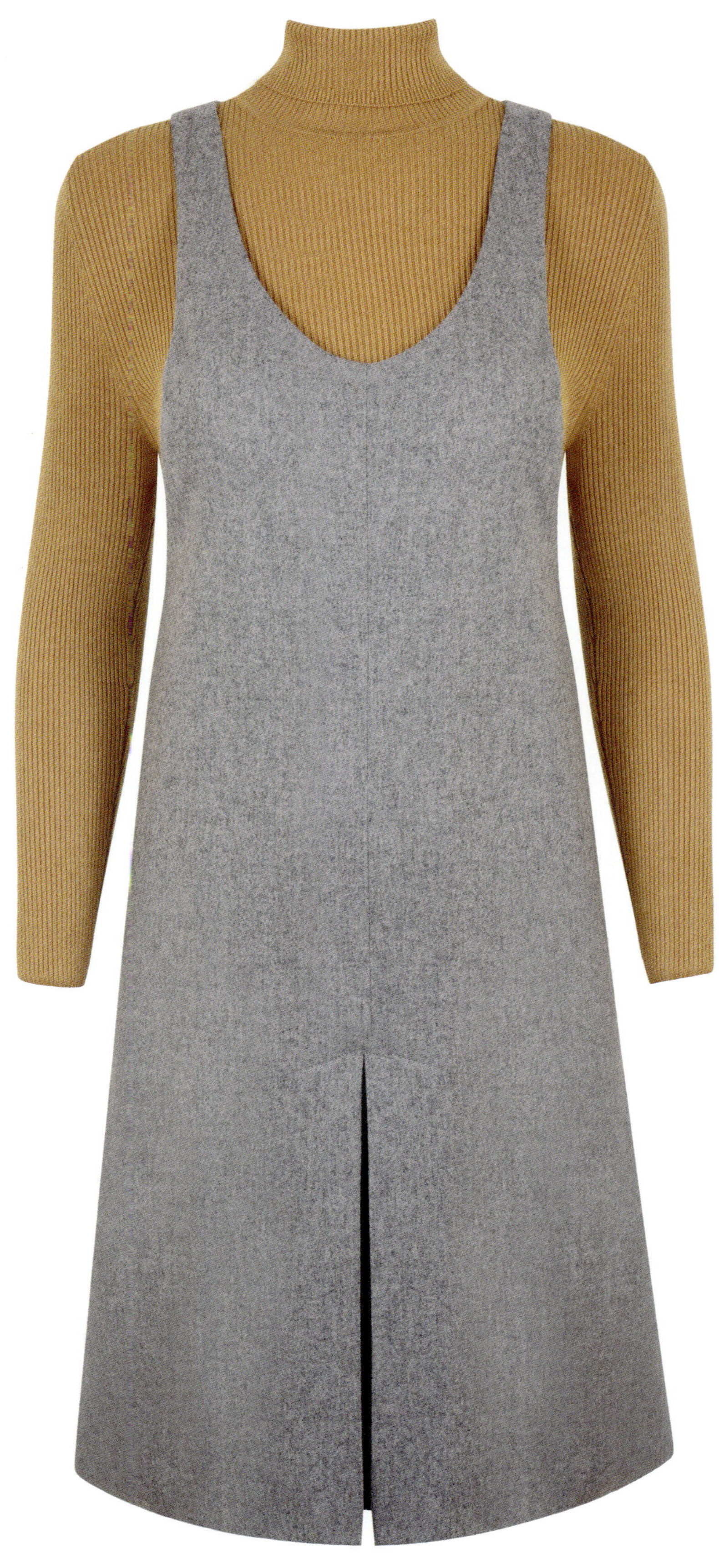

Pinafore dress in grey flannel for J.C. Penney, 1962; one of Quant's first designs for the company.

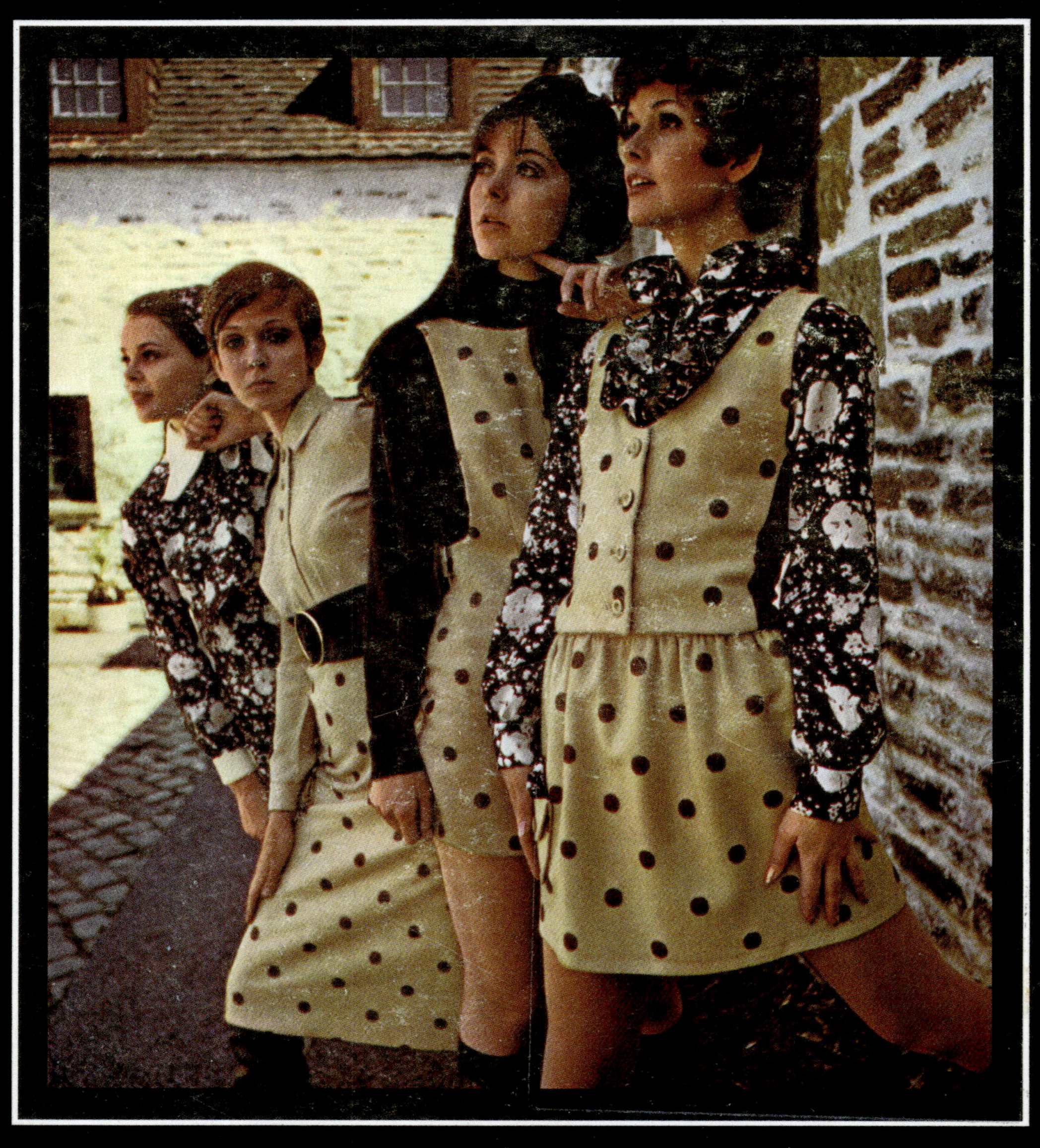

An illustration of the suit on the cover of J.C. Penney's catalogue, Fall 1968.

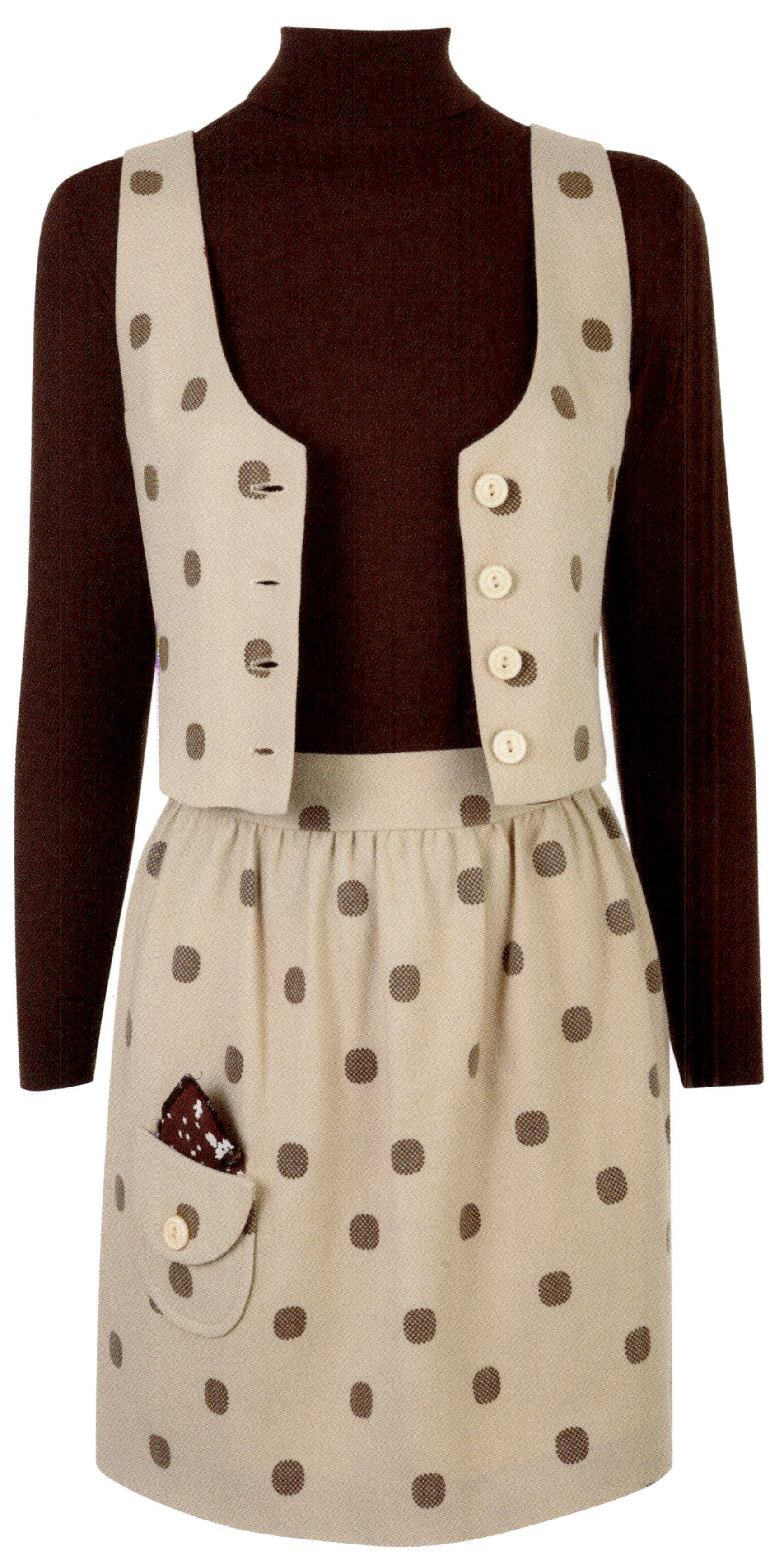

Two-piece suit in a beige wool fabric for J.C. Penney, 1968.

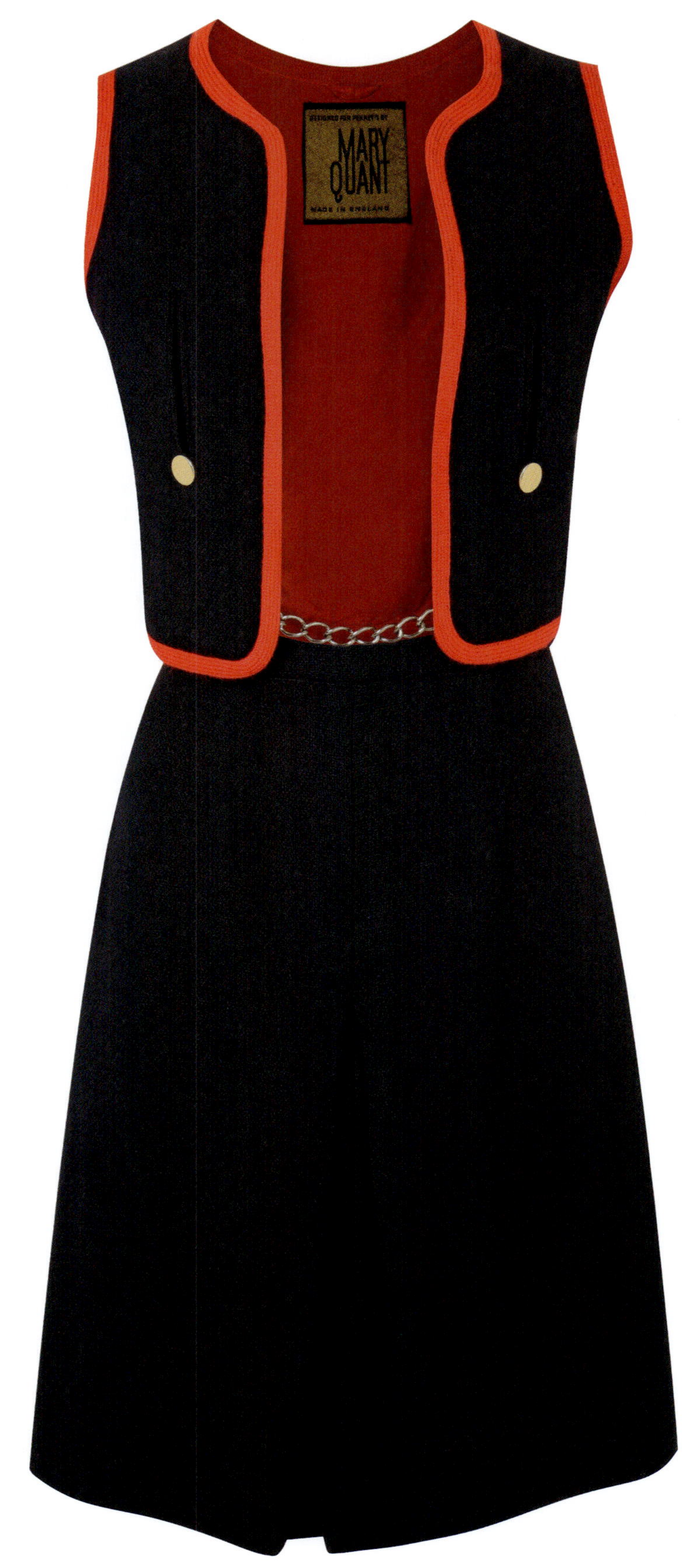

Coal Heaver, a suit in black wool with red trimming for J.C. Penney, 1962. Coal Heaver was also available in England in the autumn of 1962.

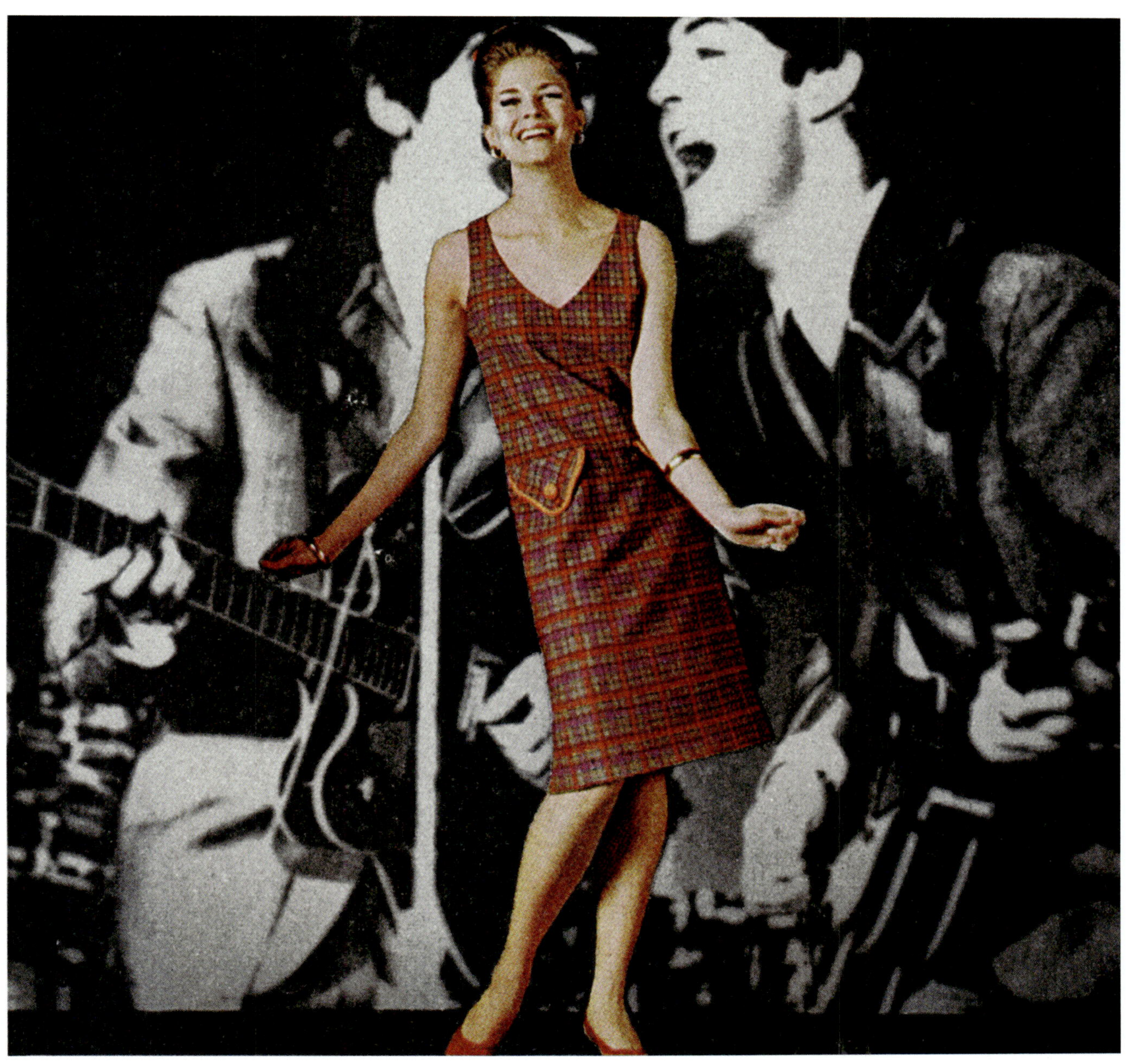

Model in a Quant dress set against a photograph of The Beatles. From an advertising feature in *Ladies' Home Journal* launching Quant's first designs for Butterick Paper Patterns, August 1964. In company with The Beatles, Quant was considered very much part of the 'British Invasion' that year.

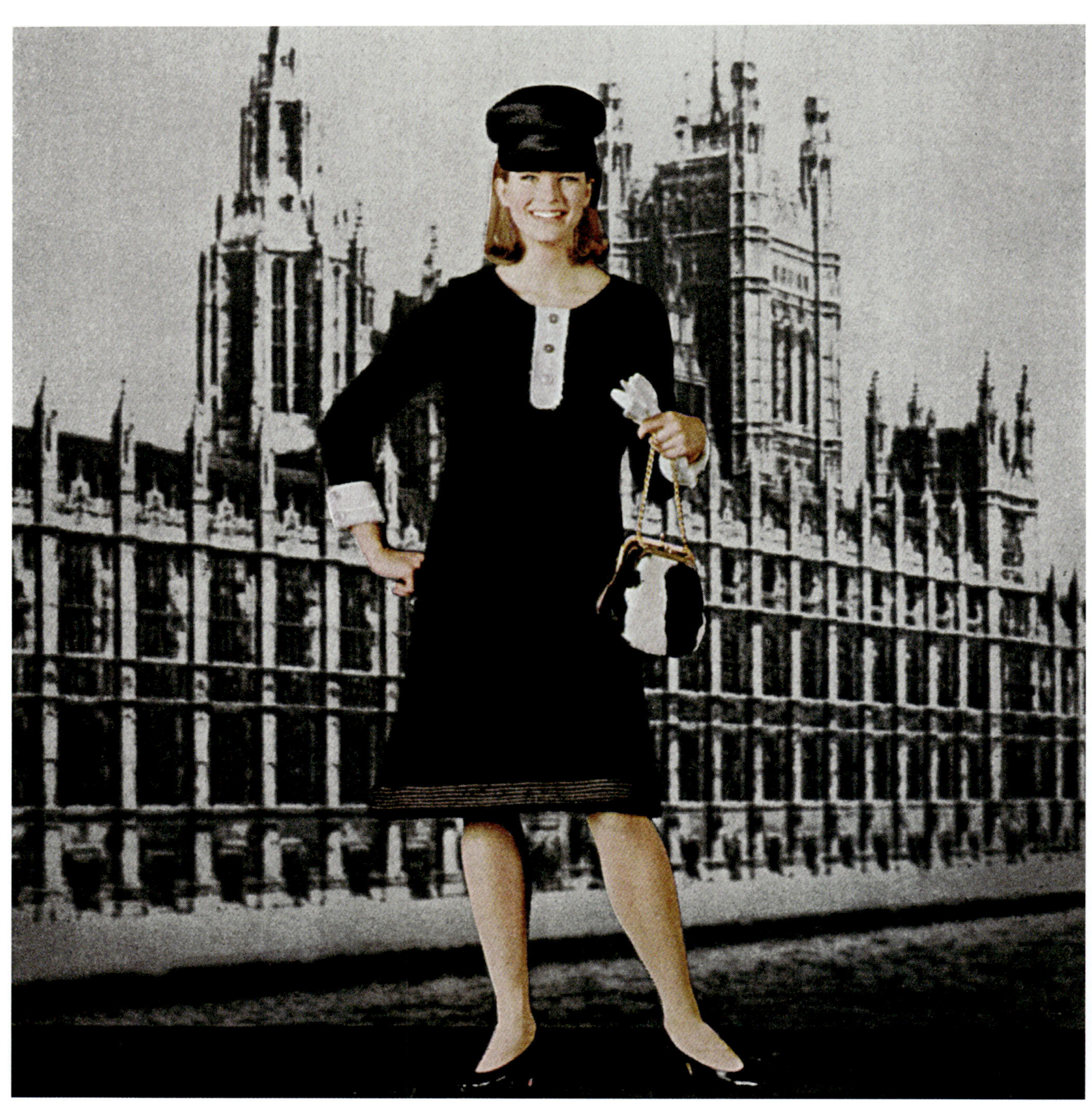

Model wearing Pattern No. 3288, set against the Houses of Parliament. Taken from an advertising feature in *Ladies' Home Journal* announcing the launch of Quant's designs for Butterick Paper Patterns, August 1964.

BUTTERICK

3288

75¢
Canada 85¢

size **10**

bust **31**

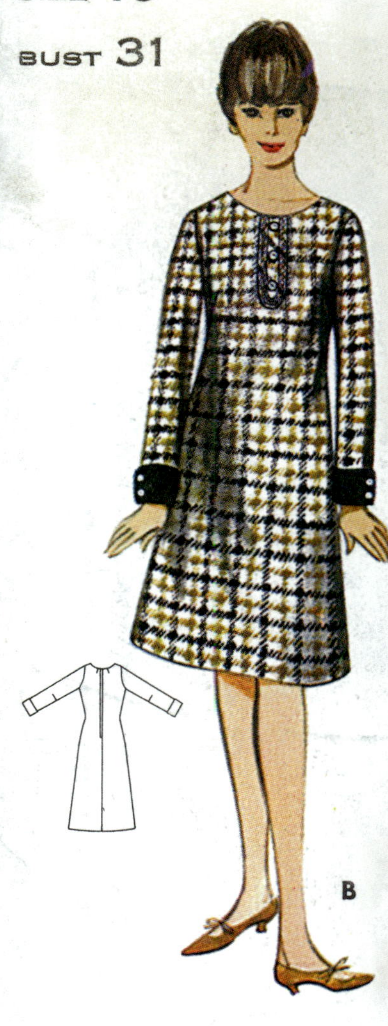

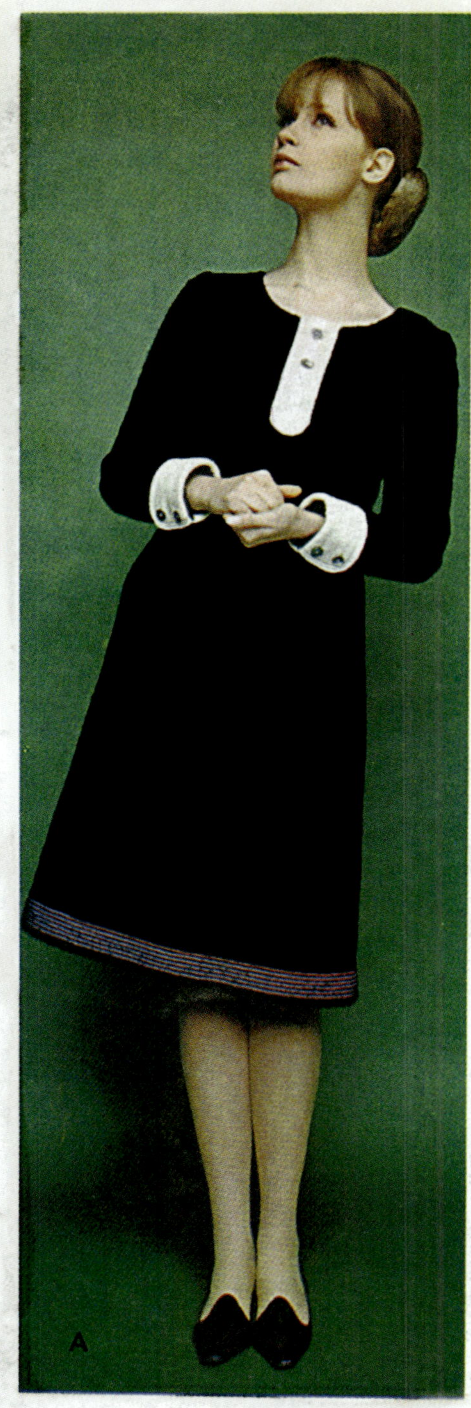

LONDON:

A **MARY QUANT**
——————— DESIGN

JUNIOR   MISSES

9 11 13 | 10 12 14 16

Quant paper pattern for Butterick No. 3288, 1964.

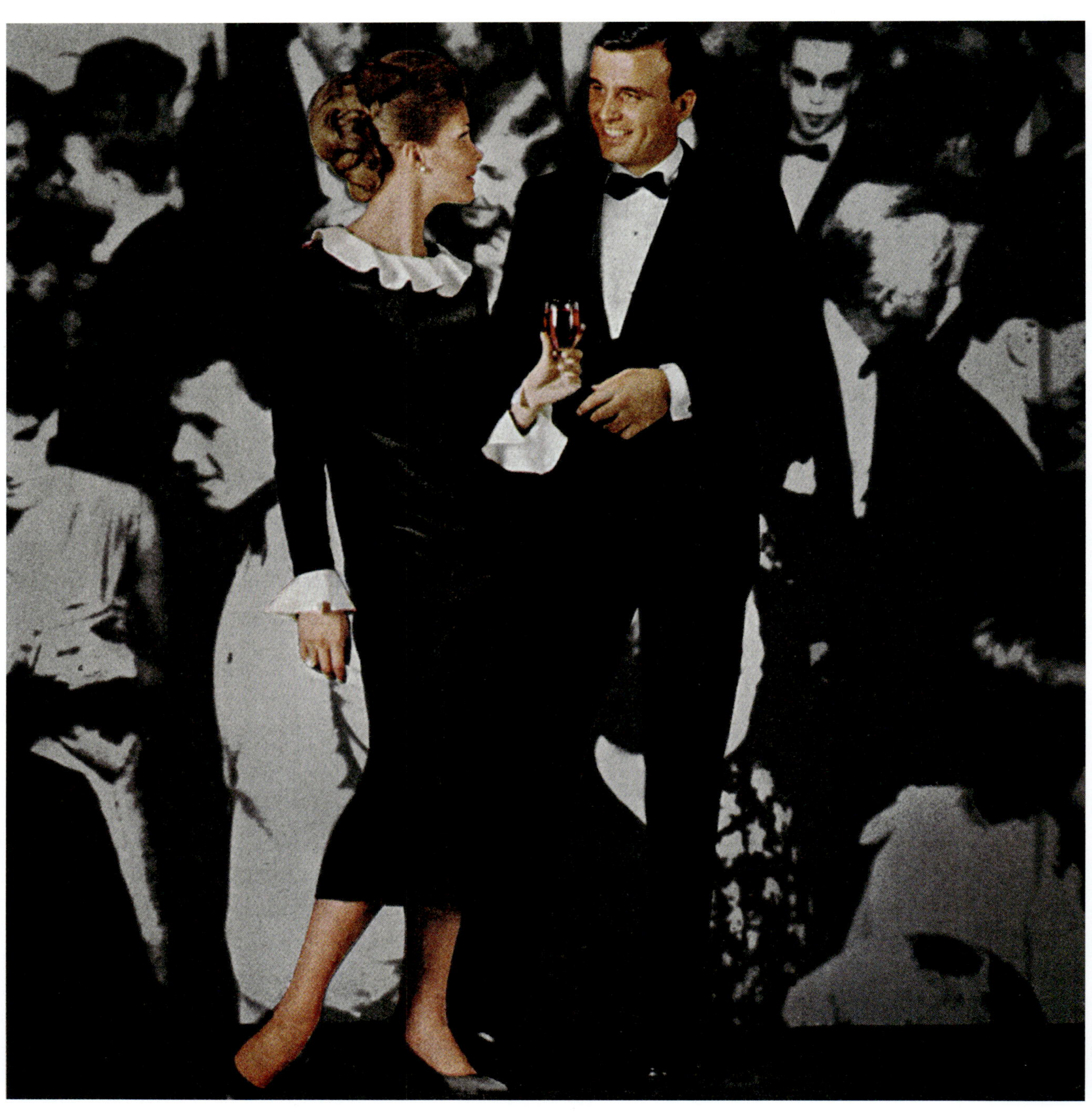

James Bond lookalike with a model wearing Pattern No. 3287 from the Butterick patterns feature, 1964. Taken from an advertising feature in *Ladies' Home Journal*.

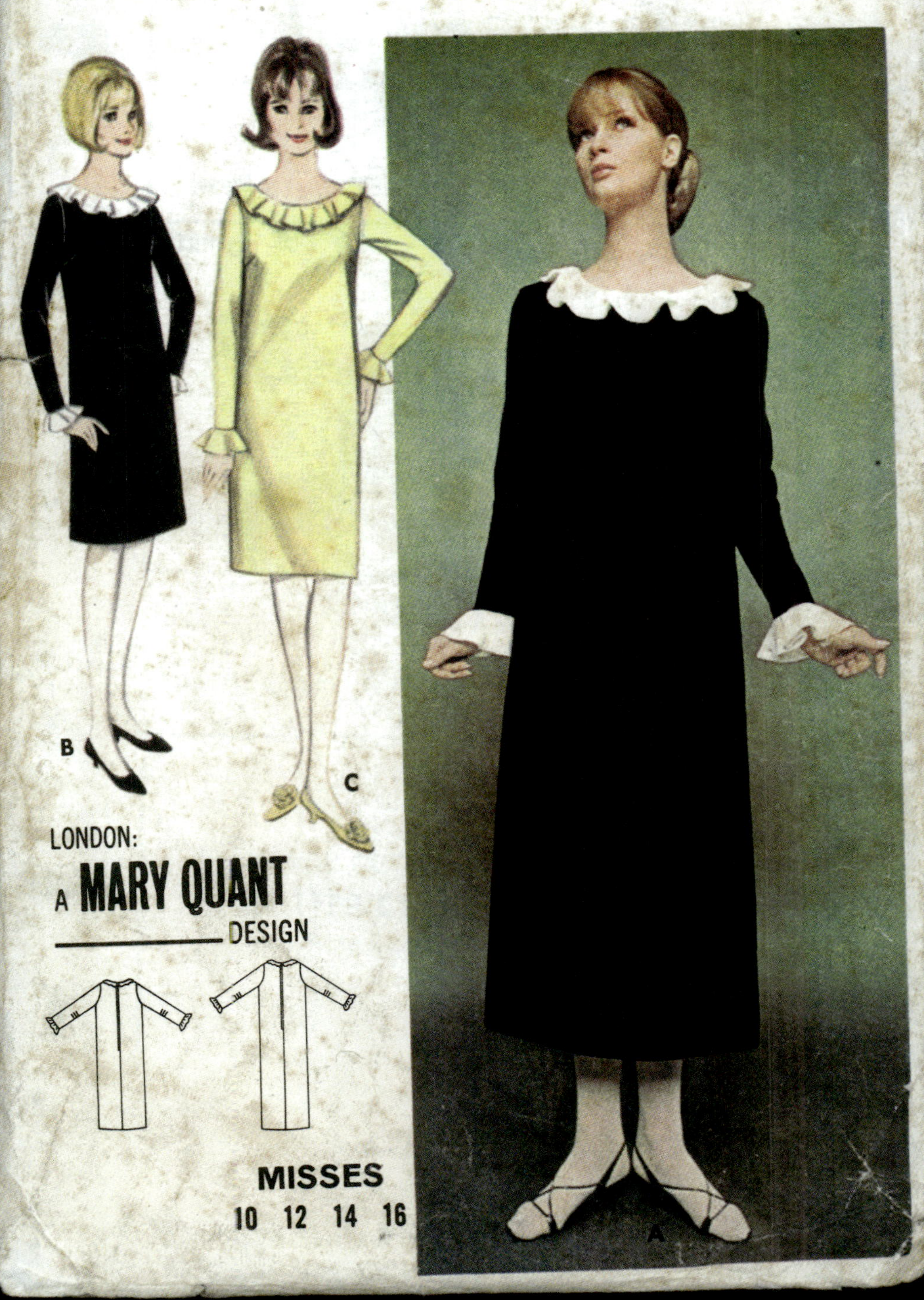

Quant's pattern for Butterick, No. 3287, 1964.

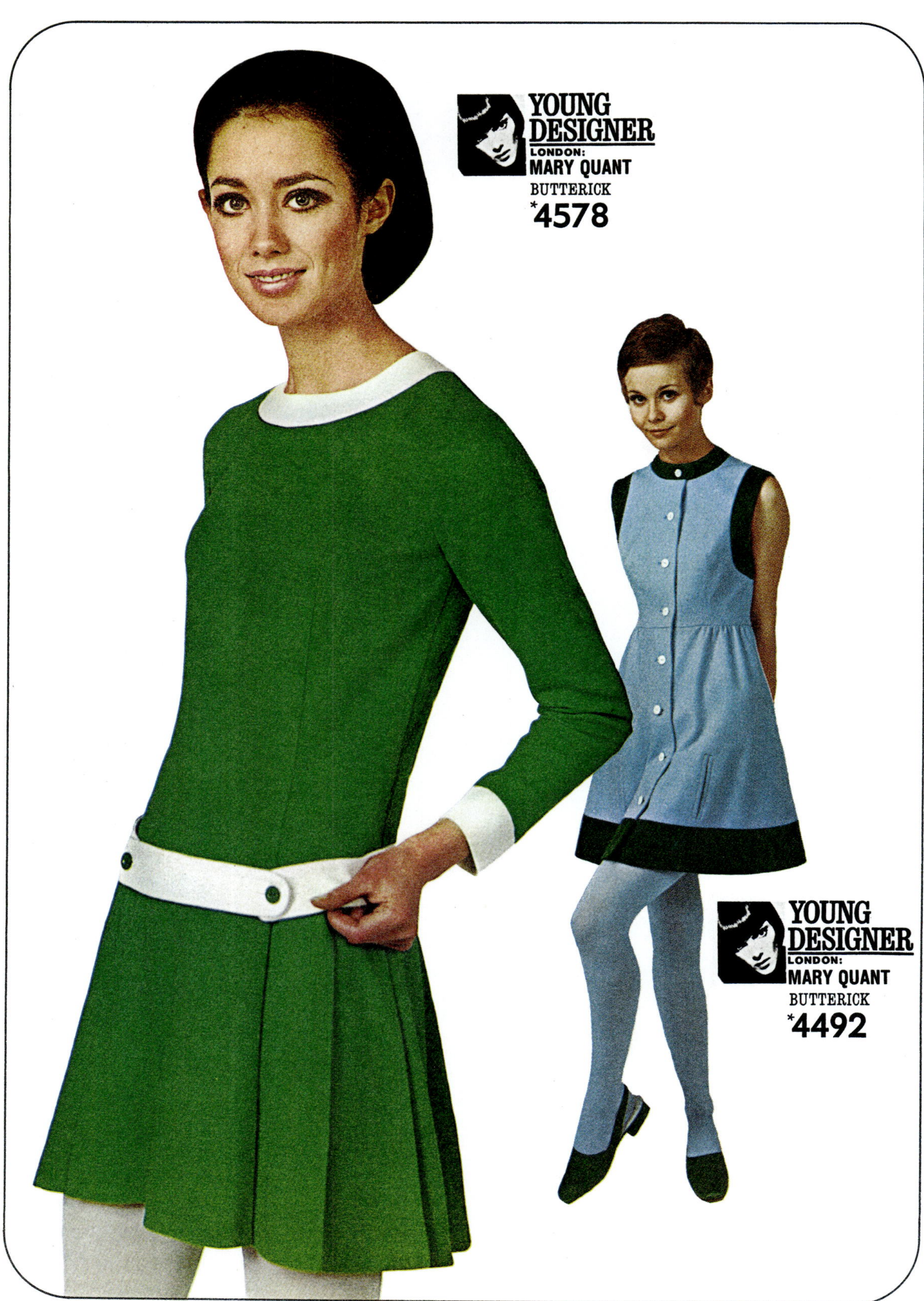

Models wearing Quant's patterns, Nos. 4492 and 4493. Young Designer section of Butterick's Home Catalogue, Fall 1967.

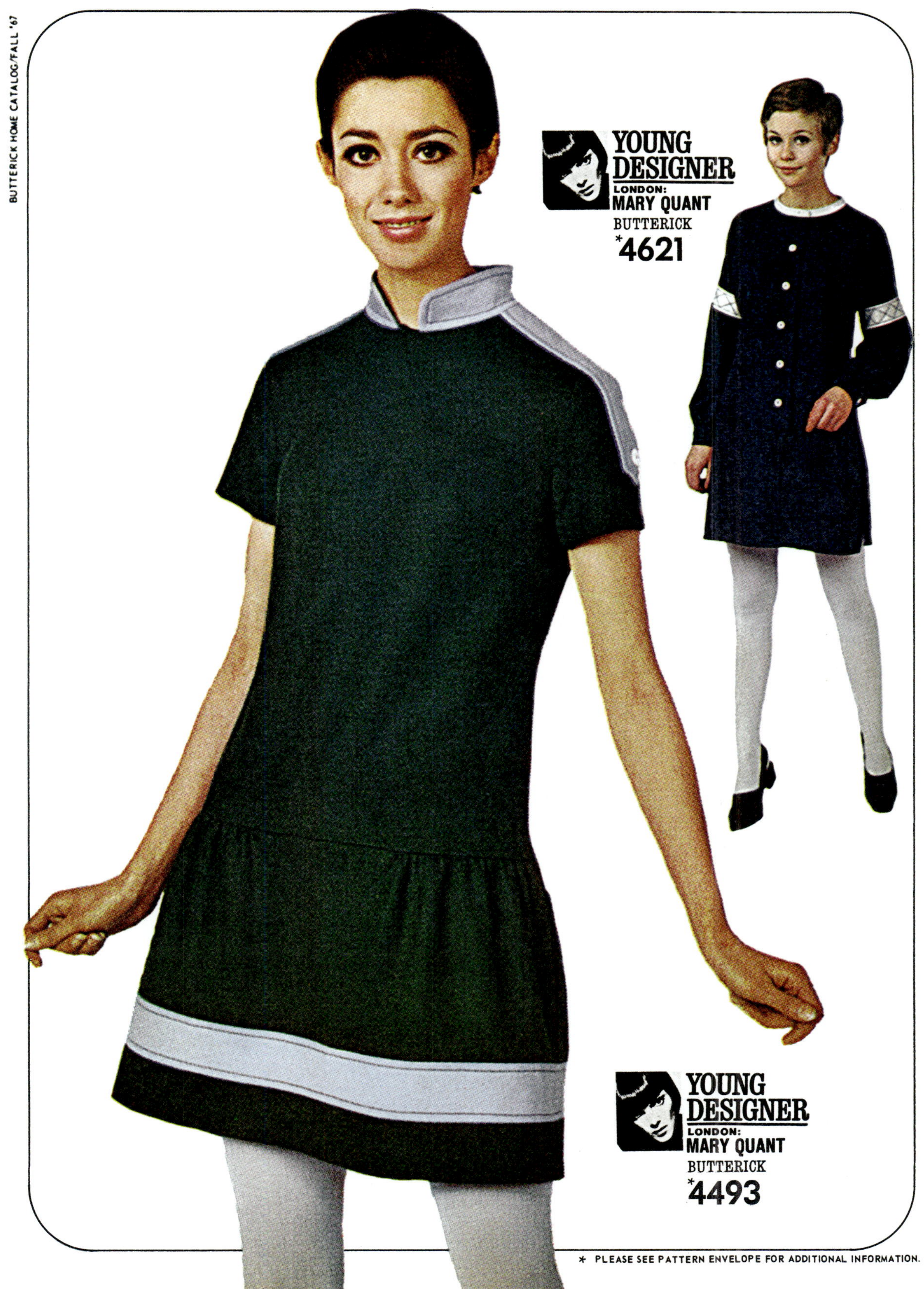
YOUNG
DESIGNER
LONDON:
MARY QUANT
BUTTERICK
*4621

YOUNG
DESIGNER
LONDON:
MARY QUANT
BUTTERICK
*4493

* PLEASE SEE PATTERN ENVELOPE FOR ADDITIONAL INFORMATION.

QUANT FOR ALLIGATOR RAINWEAR:
Op Art and the Space Age

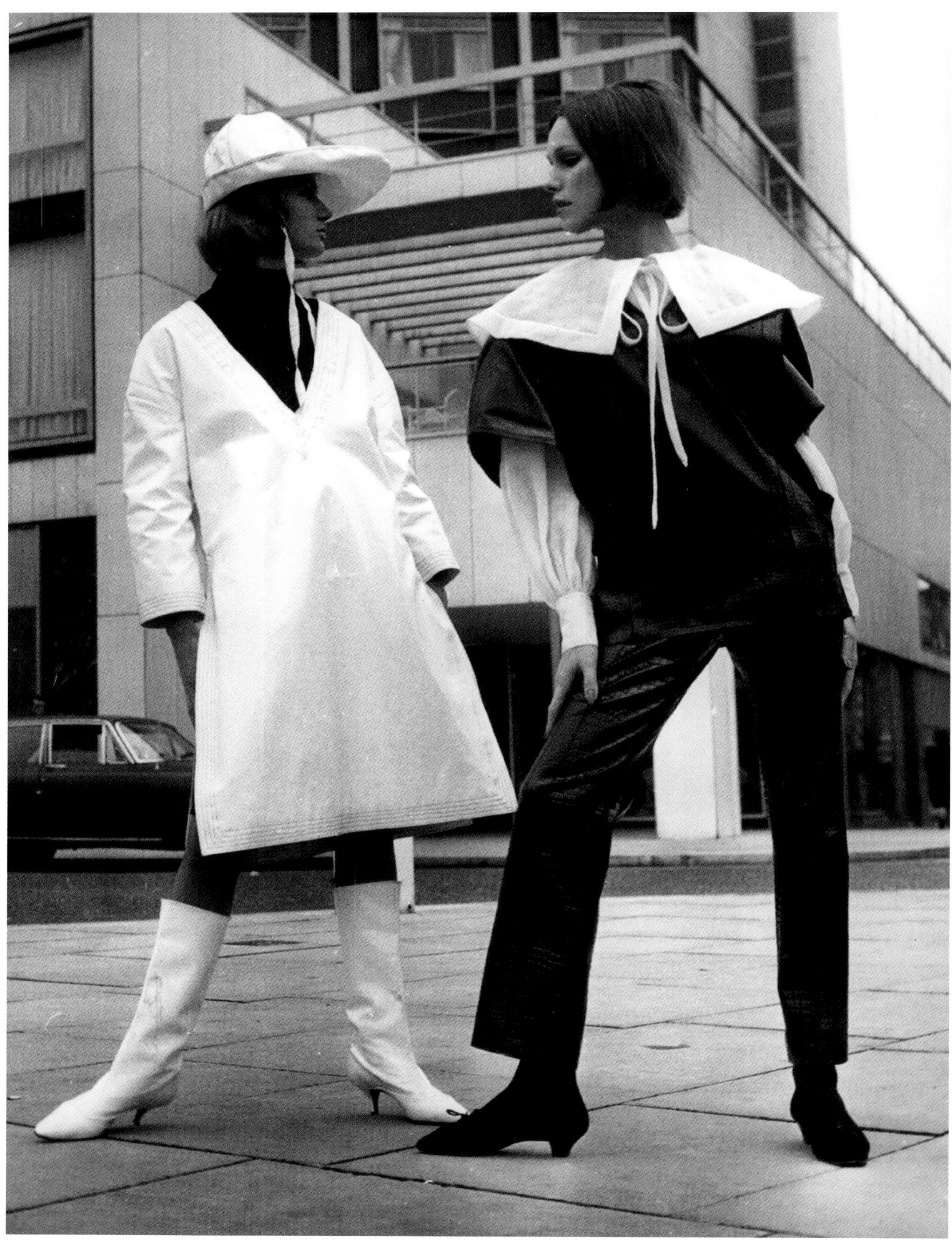

Two designs from Quant's Wet Weather collection, using PVC, 1963;
Quant's first attempt working with this man-made material.

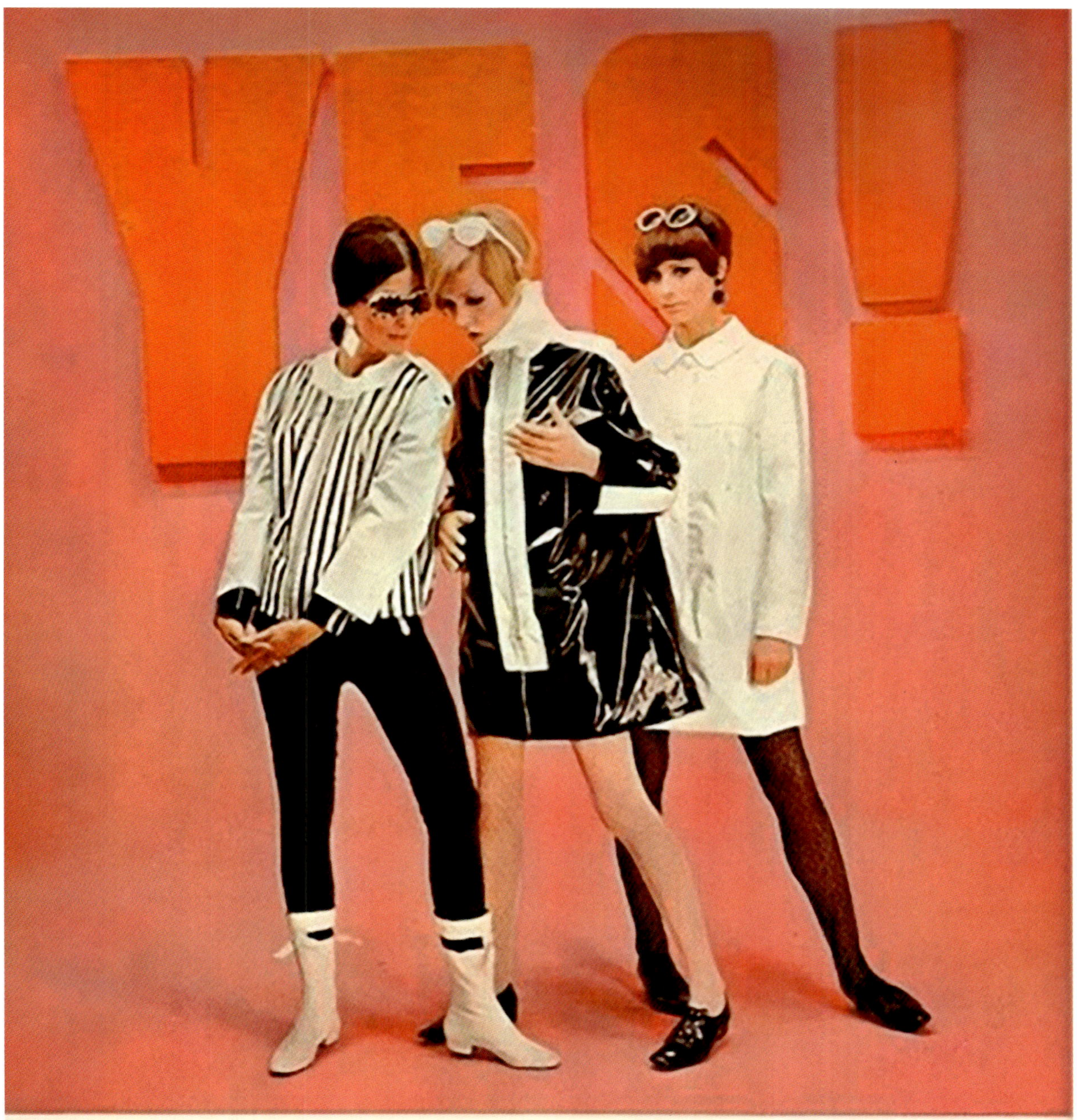

Advertisement for Alligator Rainwear, c.1965-1966. It was for Alligator that Quant designed her iconic range of black and white Op Art PVC clothing.

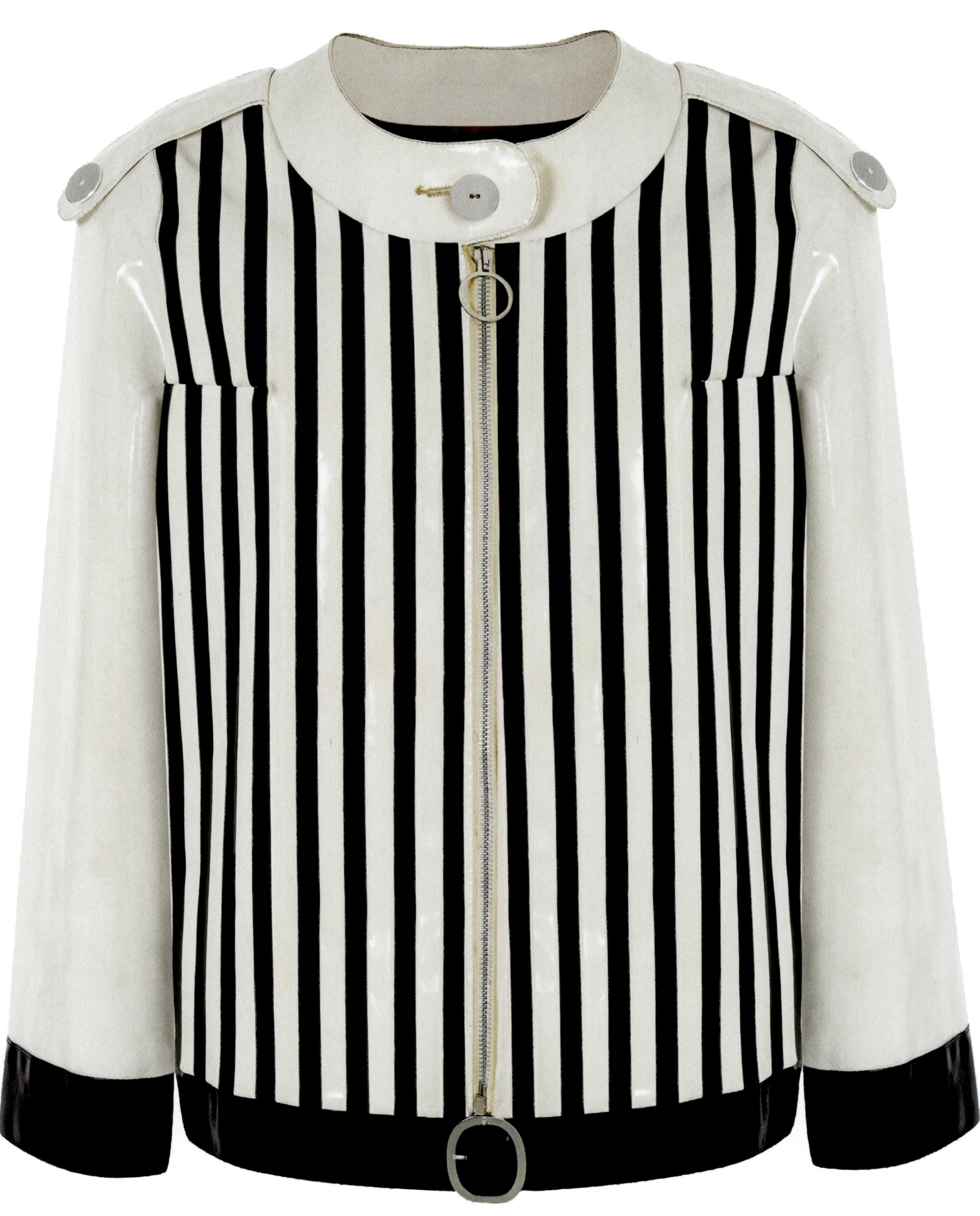

Marquee, a jacket in black and white PVC inspired by Op Art, for Alligator, 1965.

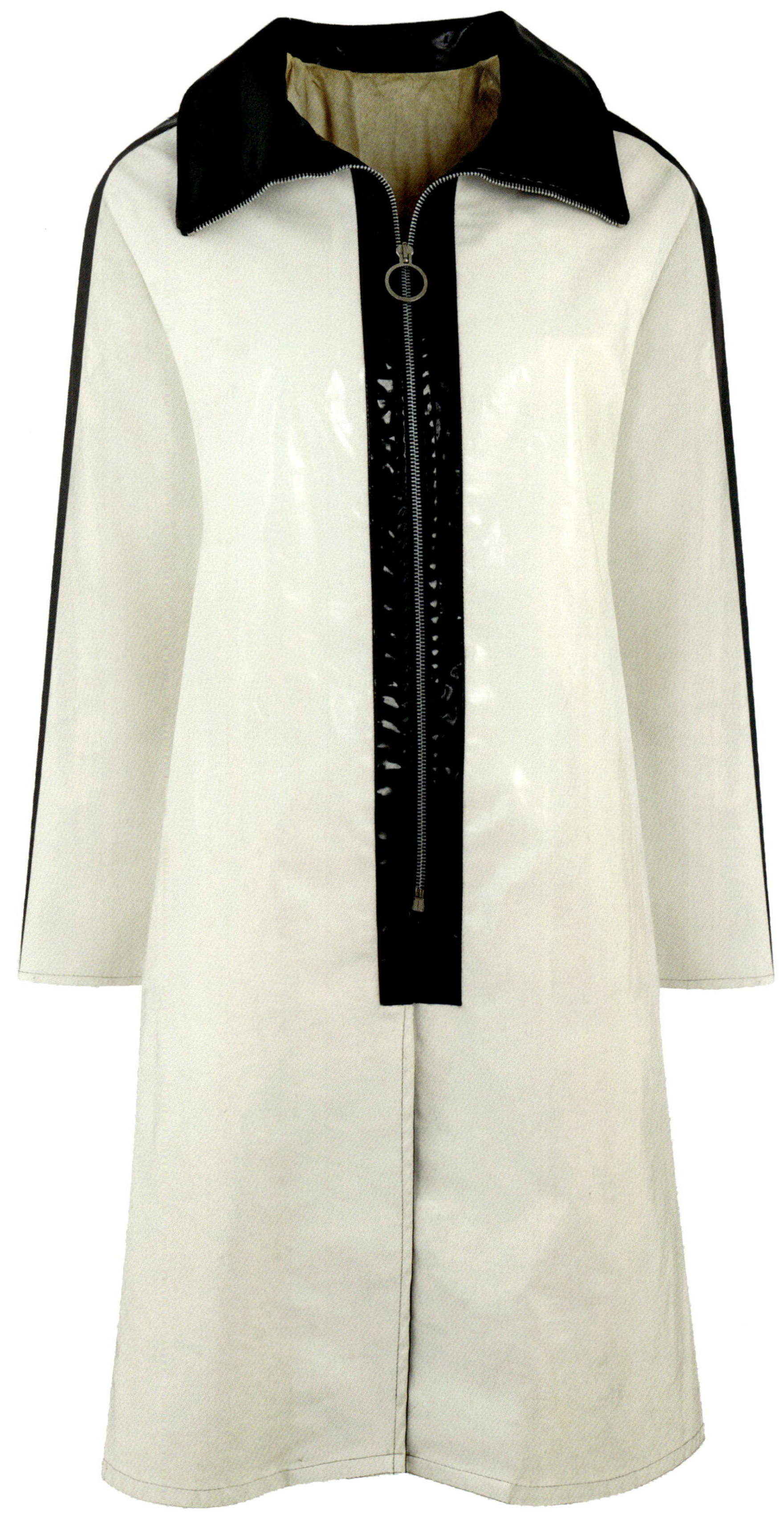

Mood, an Op Art coat in black and white PVC, for Alligator, 1965.

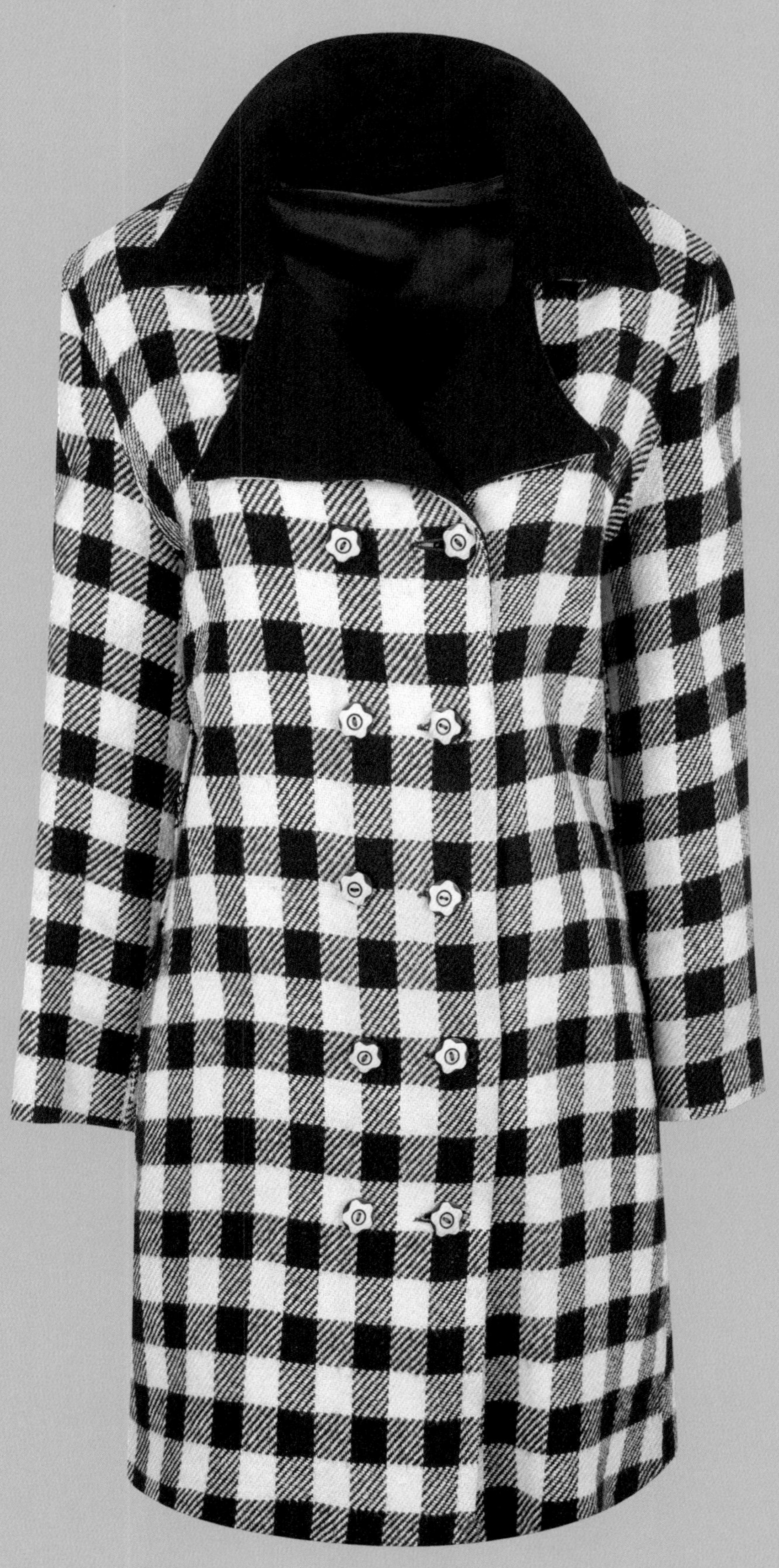

Black and white plasticised wool coat with daisy-shaped buttons, for Alligator, 1965. The buttons represent an early stage in the development of Quant's iconic Daisy logo.

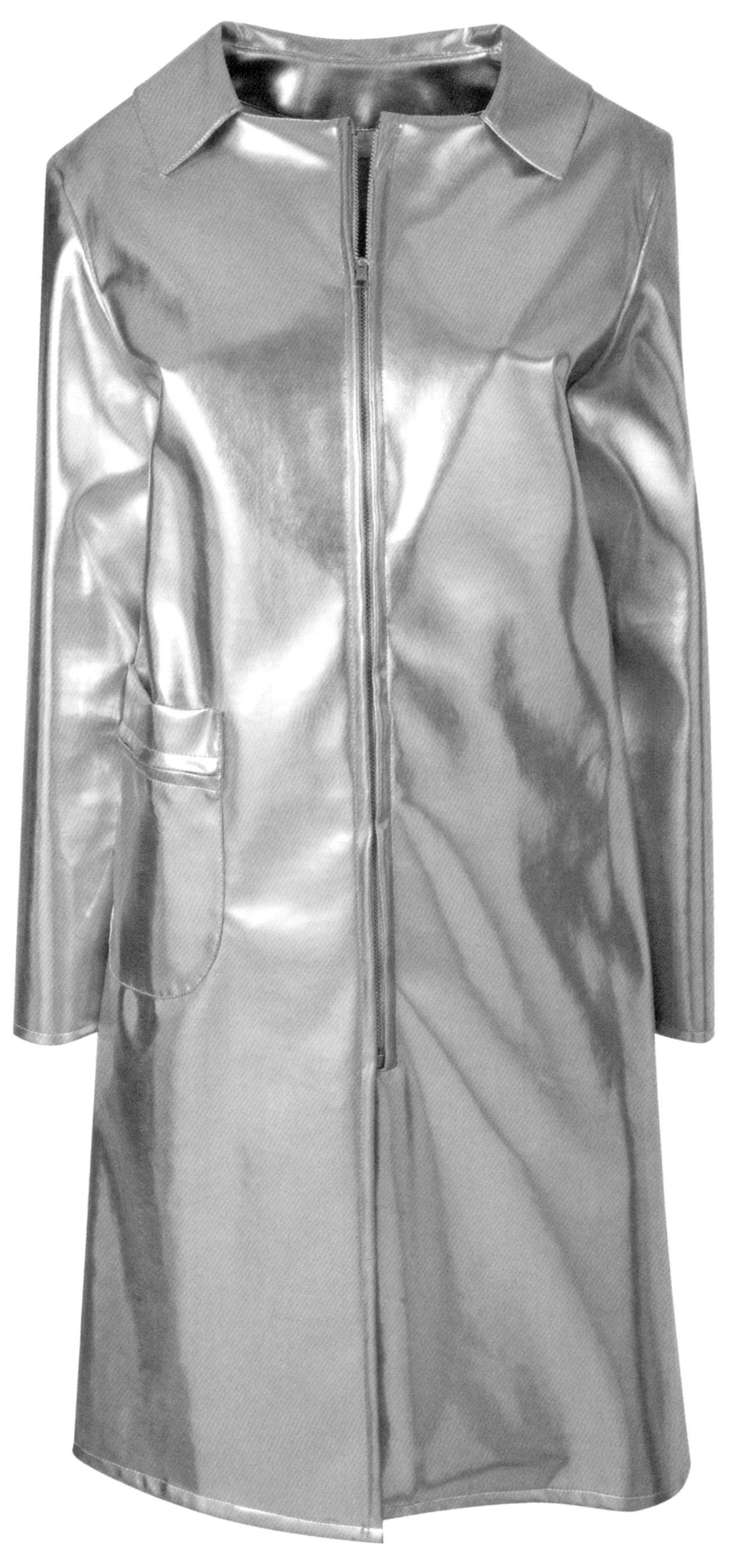

Space-age coat, silver PVC, for Alligator, 1966. Space was another overarching theme of the mid 1960s, which reached its zenith in the 1968 Sci-Fi film *2001: A Space Odyssey*.

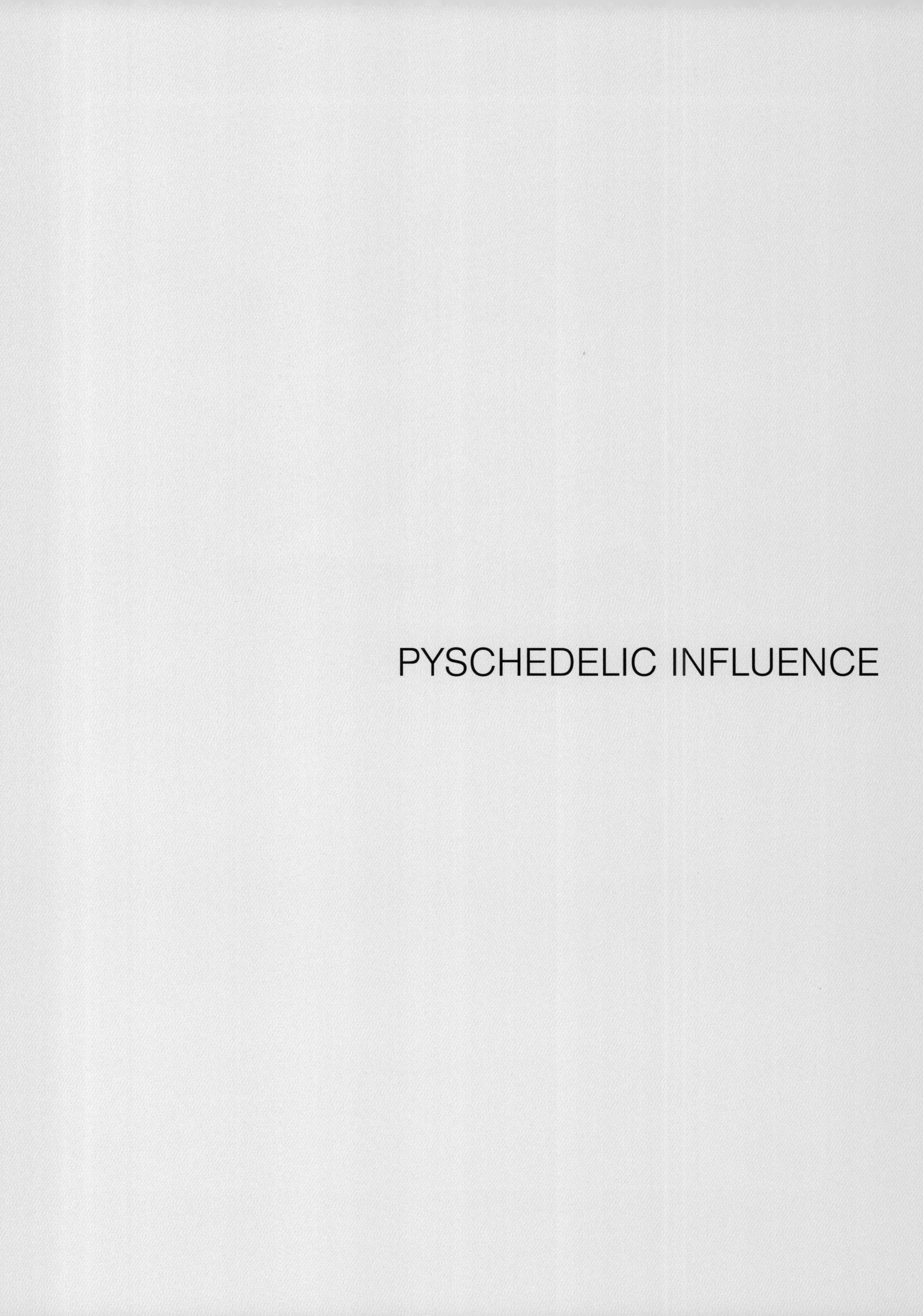

PYSCHEDELIC INFLUENCE

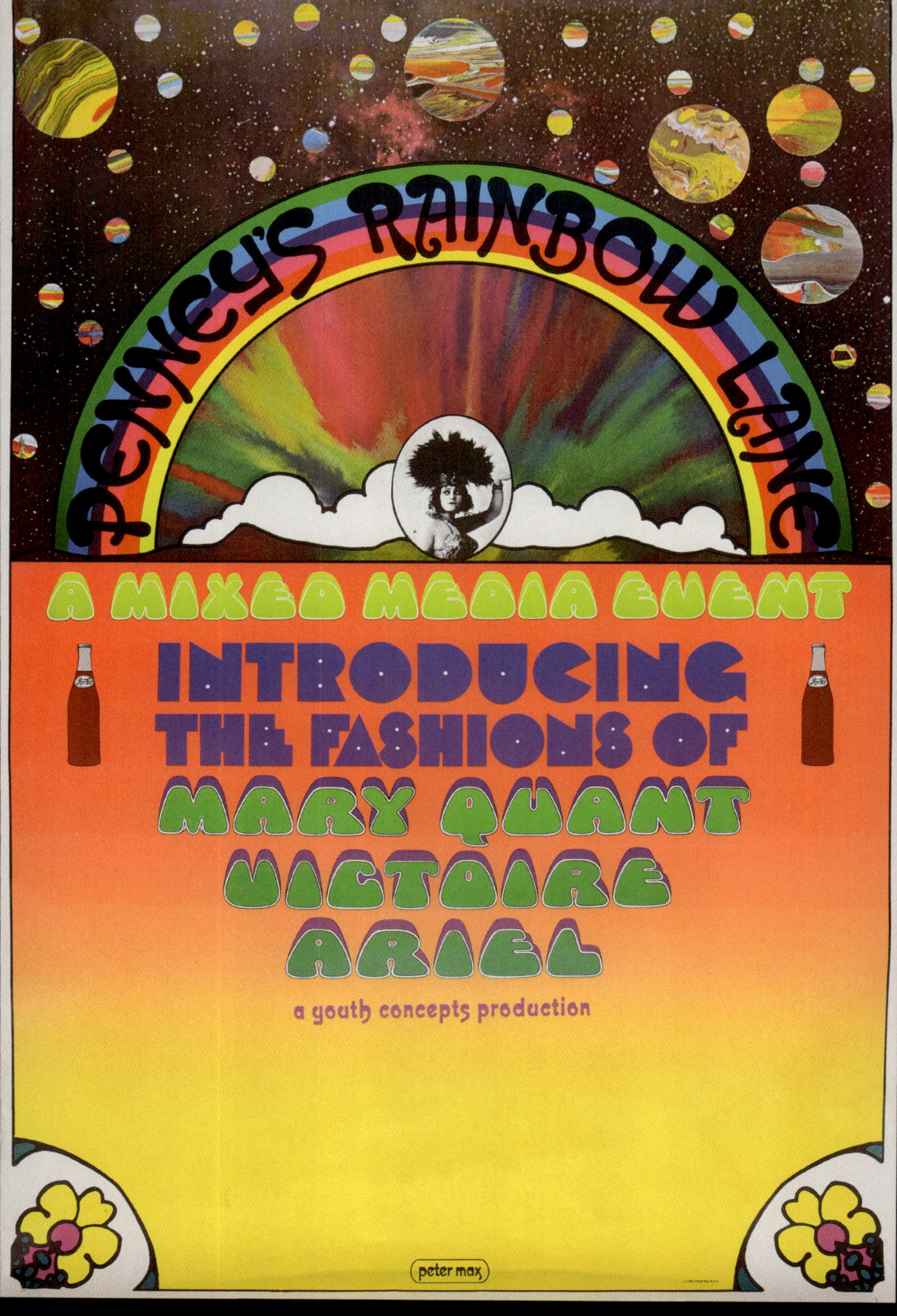

Psychedelic poster by Peter Max, 1968. Advertising J.C. Penney's Rainbow Lane, a mixed media event featuring fashions by Mary Quant, Victoire and Ariel.

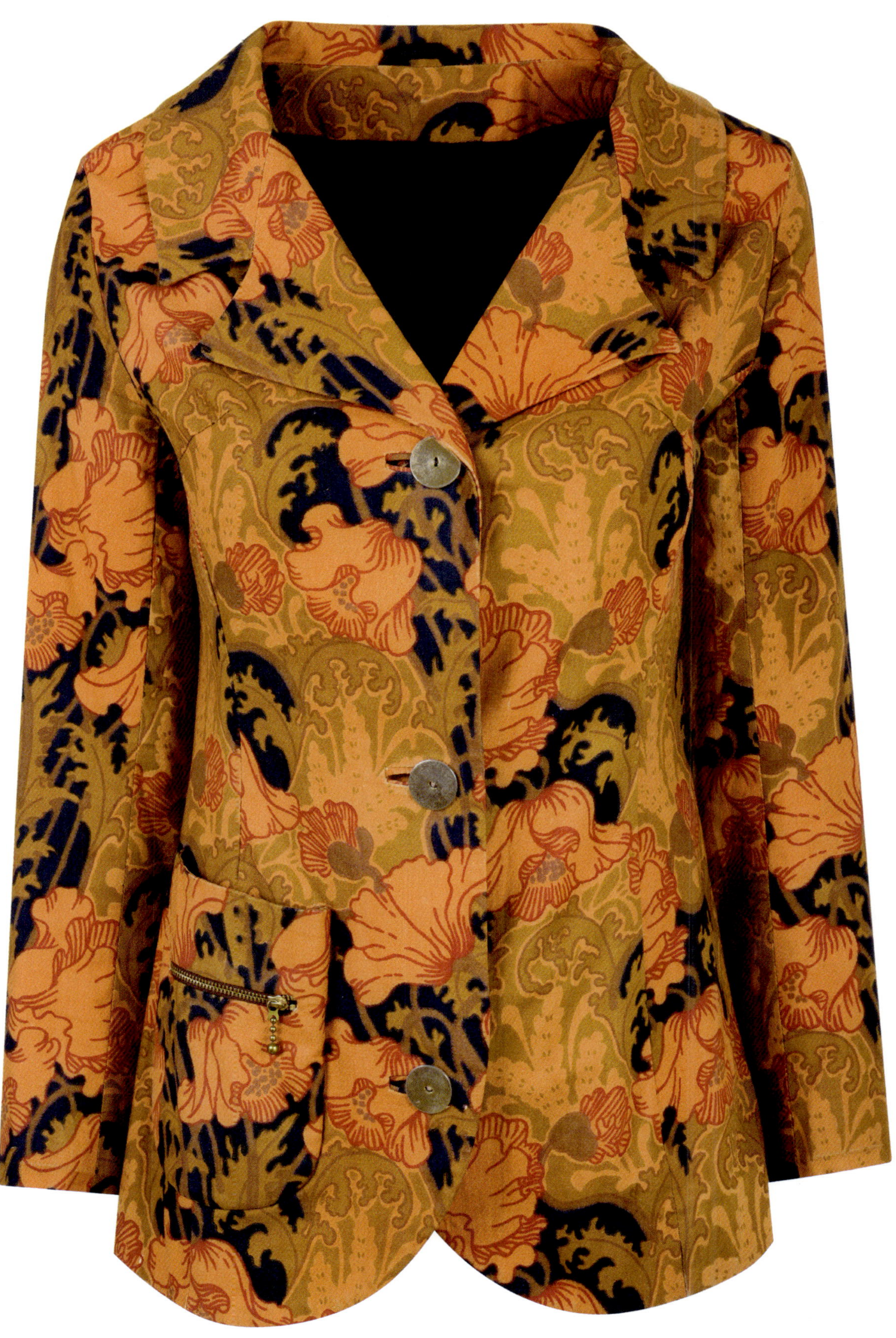

Psychedelic-style jacket by Quant for the Ginger Group, 1965. It is realised in a textile with an Art Nouveau design by Liberty of London. Originally an early twentieth-century block-printed fabric, which Liberty converted to a screen-print and issued as part of their 'Lotus' collection in 1959.

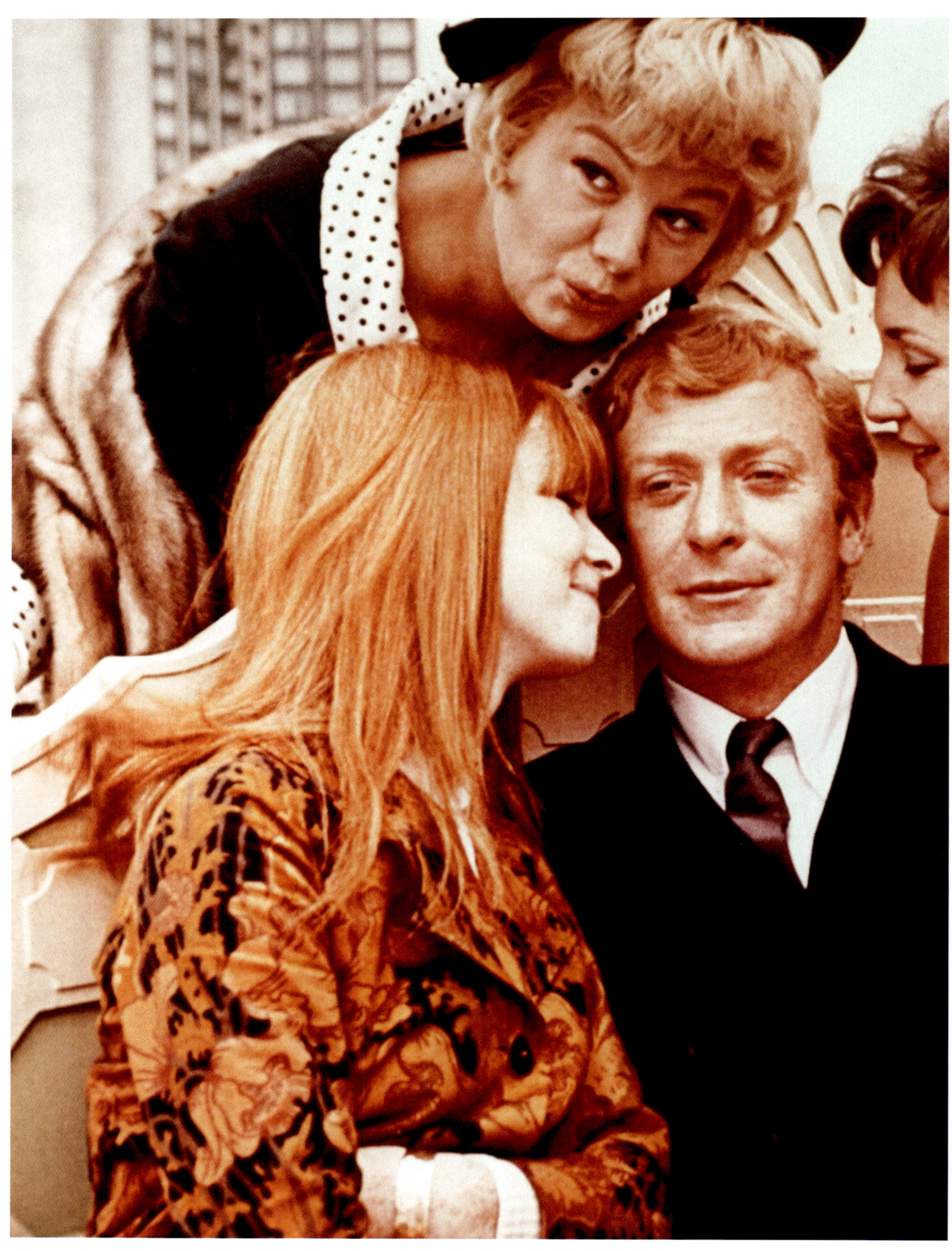

Paul McCartney's then girlfriend, actor Jane Asher wearing Quant's Psychedelic jacket on the set of the film *Alfie* in July 1965. She is pictured with the film's other stars, Michael Caine, Shelley Winters and Harold Pinter's first wife, the actor Vivien Merchant.

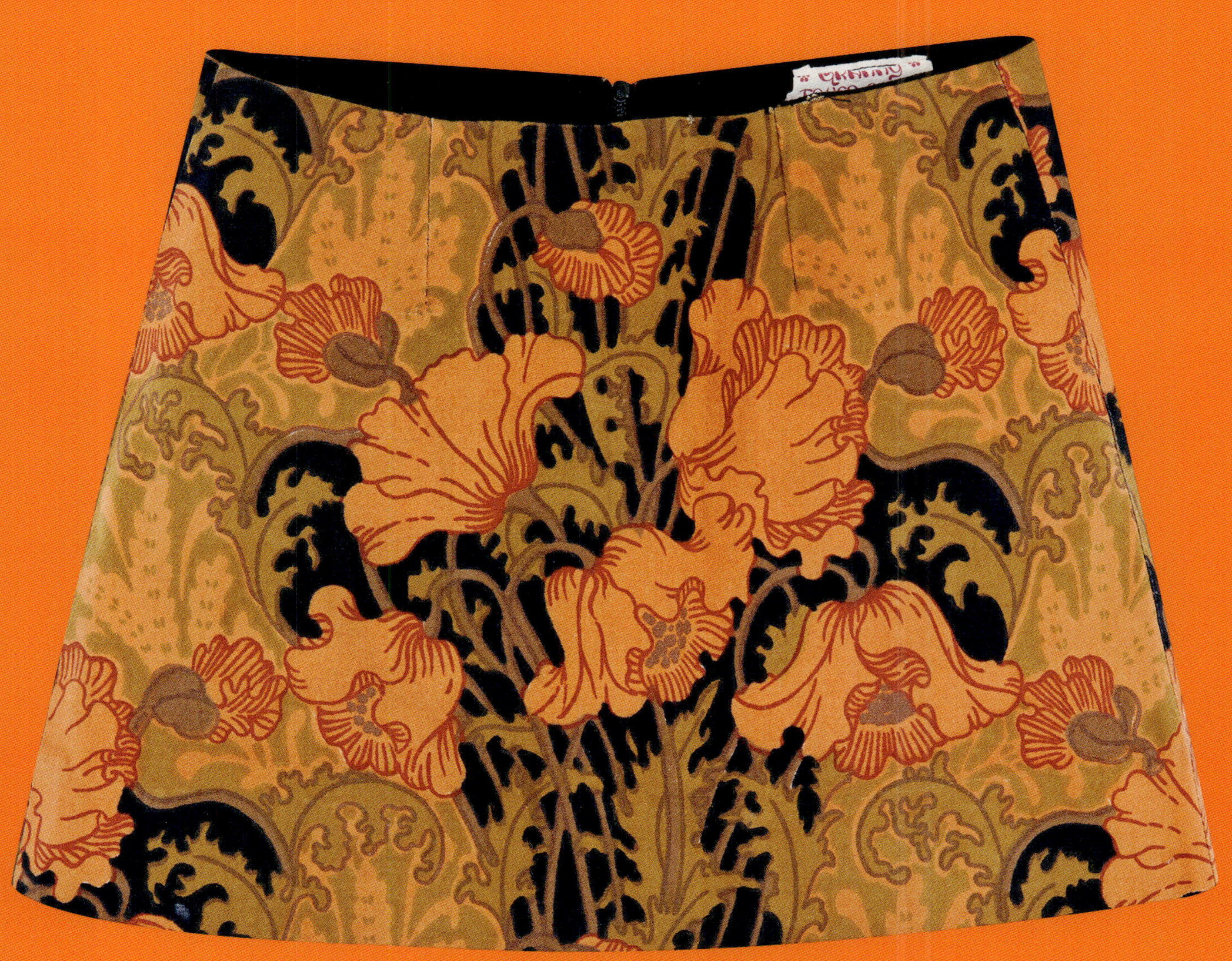

Miniskirt, 1967, in the same Liberty fabric as Quant's Psychedelic Jacket. The skirt is by London's leading Pop boutique, Granny Takes a Trip. Quant's early anticipation of the Psychedelic mood is remarkable.

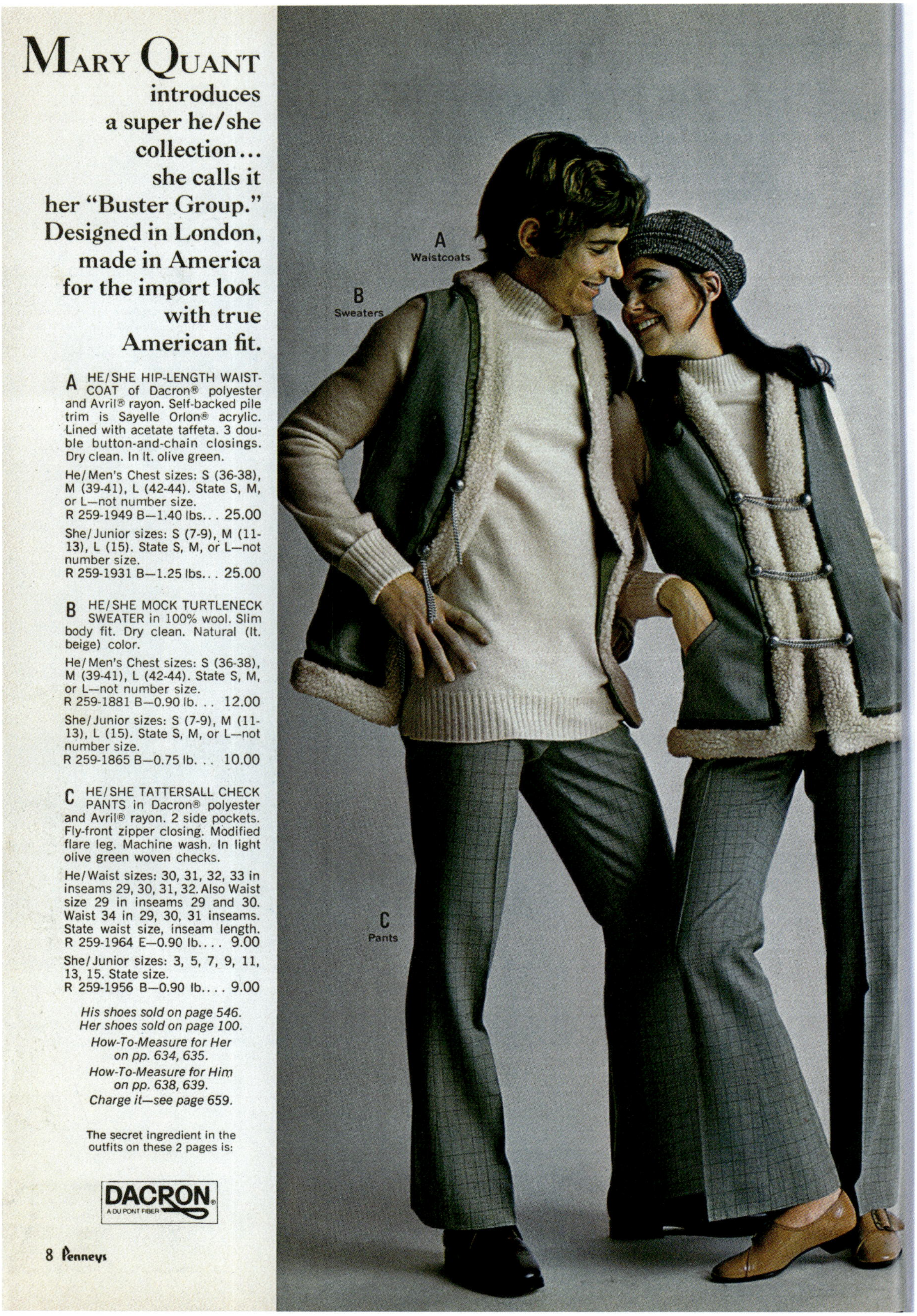

Mary Quant

introduces a super he/she collection… she calls it her "Buster Group." Designed in London, made in America for the import look with true American fit.

A HE/SHE HIP-LENGTH WAIST-COAT of Dacron® polyester and Avril® rayon. Self-backed pile trim is Sayelle Orlon® acrylic. Lined with acetate taffeta. 3 double button-and-chain closings. Dry clean. In lt. olive green.

He/Men's Chest sizes: S (36-38), M (39-41), L (42-44). State S, M, or L—not number size.
R 259-1949 B—1.40 lbs. . . 25.00

She/Junior sizes: S (7-9), M (11-13), L (15). State S, M, or L—not number size.
R 259-1931 B—1.25 lbs. . . 25.00

B HE/SHE MOCK TURTLENECK SWEATER in 100% wool. Slim body fit. Dry clean. Natural (lt. beige) color.

He/Men's Chest sizes: S (36-38), M (39-41), L (42-44). State S, M, or L—not number size.
R 259-1881 B—0.90 lb. . . 12.00

She/Junior sizes: S (7-9), M (11-13), L (15). State S, M, or L—not number size.
R 259-1865 B—0.75 lb. . . 10.00

C HE/SHE TATTERSALL CHECK PANTS in Dacron® polyester and Avril® rayon. 2 side pockets. Fly-front zipper closing. Modified flare leg. Machine wash. In light olive green woven checks.

He/Waist sizes: 30, 31, 32, 33 in inseams 29, 30, 31, 32. Also Waist size 29 in inseams 29 and 30. Waist 34 in 29, 30, 31 inseams. State waist size, inseam length.
R 259-1964 E—0.90 lb. . . . 9.00

She/Junior sizes: 3, 5, 7, 9, 11, 13, 15. State size.
R 259-1956 B—0.90 lb. 9.00

His shoes sold on page 546.
Her shoes sold on page 100.

How-To-Measure for Her on pp. 634, 635.
How-To-Measure for Him on pp. 638, 639.
Charge it—see page 659.

The secret ingredient in the outfits on these 2 pages is:

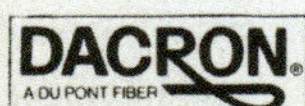

Buster jerkin illustrated in J.C. Penney's Catalogue, 1969.

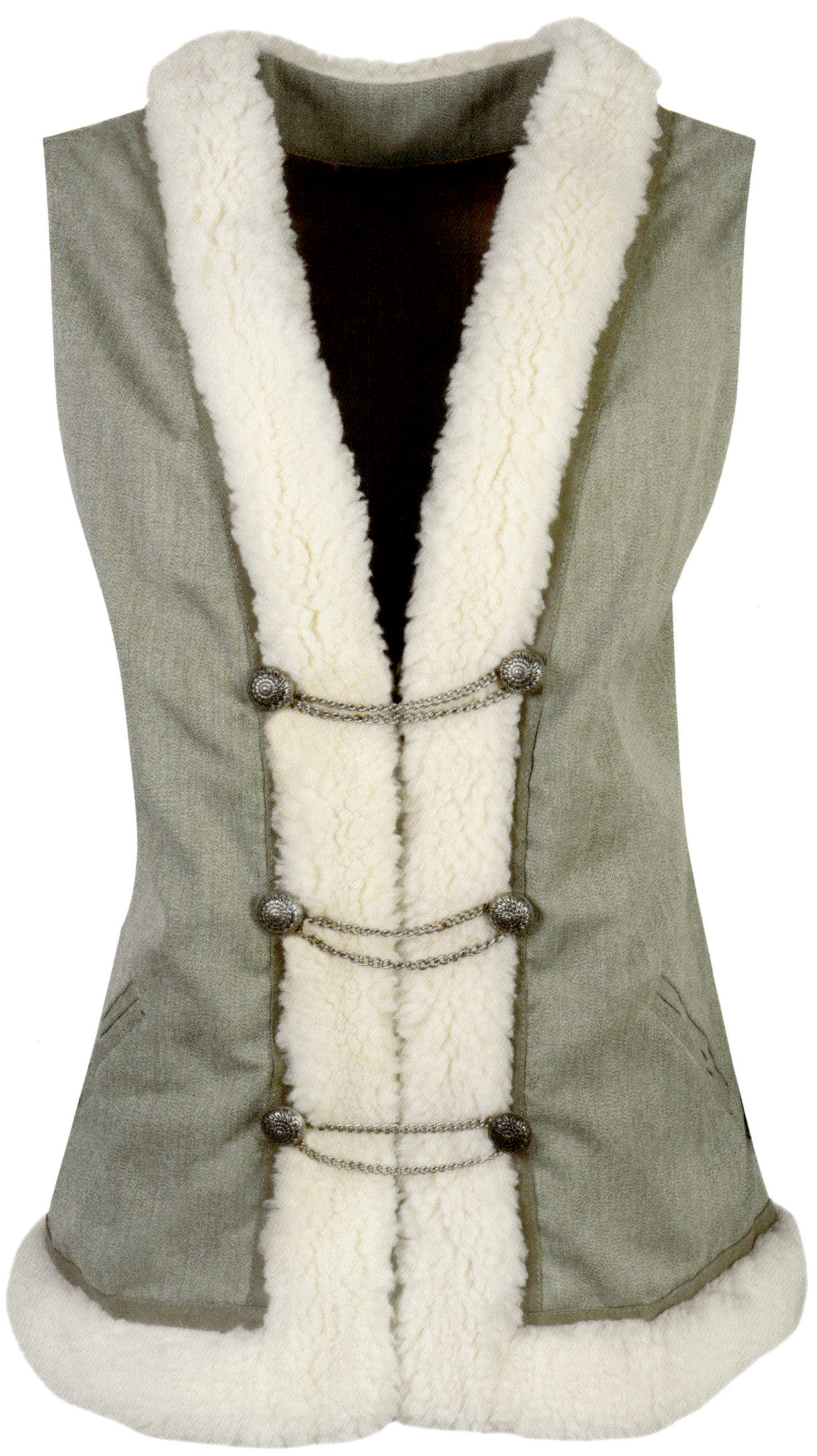

Jerkin in The Beatles' 'Sgt Pepper' style, from Quant's Buster range, a unisex group of clothing for J.C. Penney, 1969.

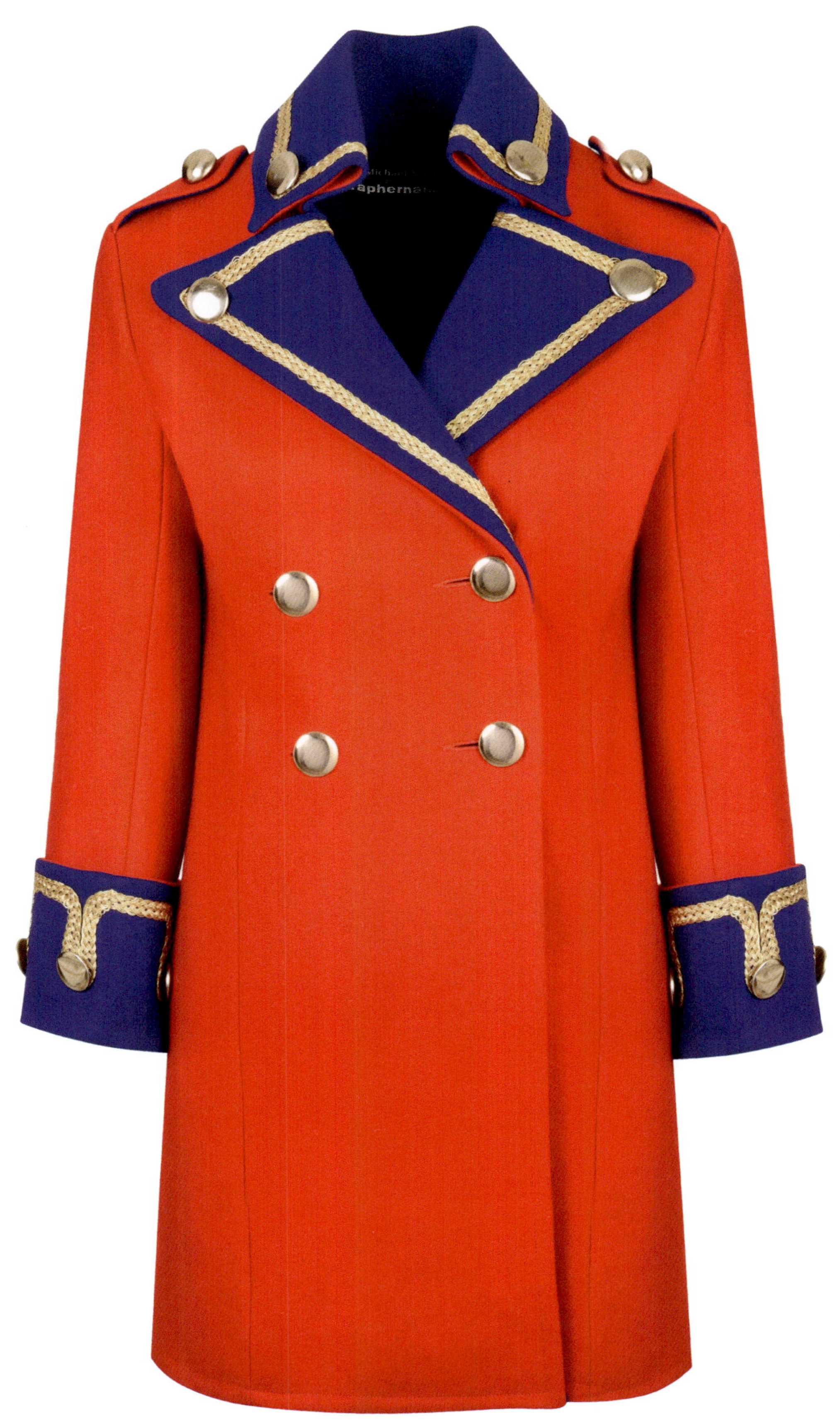

'Sgt Pepper' military-style Frock Coat by the designer Michael Mott for Paraphernalia, 1967-1968. Paraphernalia, New York's leading boutique, openly acknowledged its debt to Mary Quant and her boutique, Bazaar.

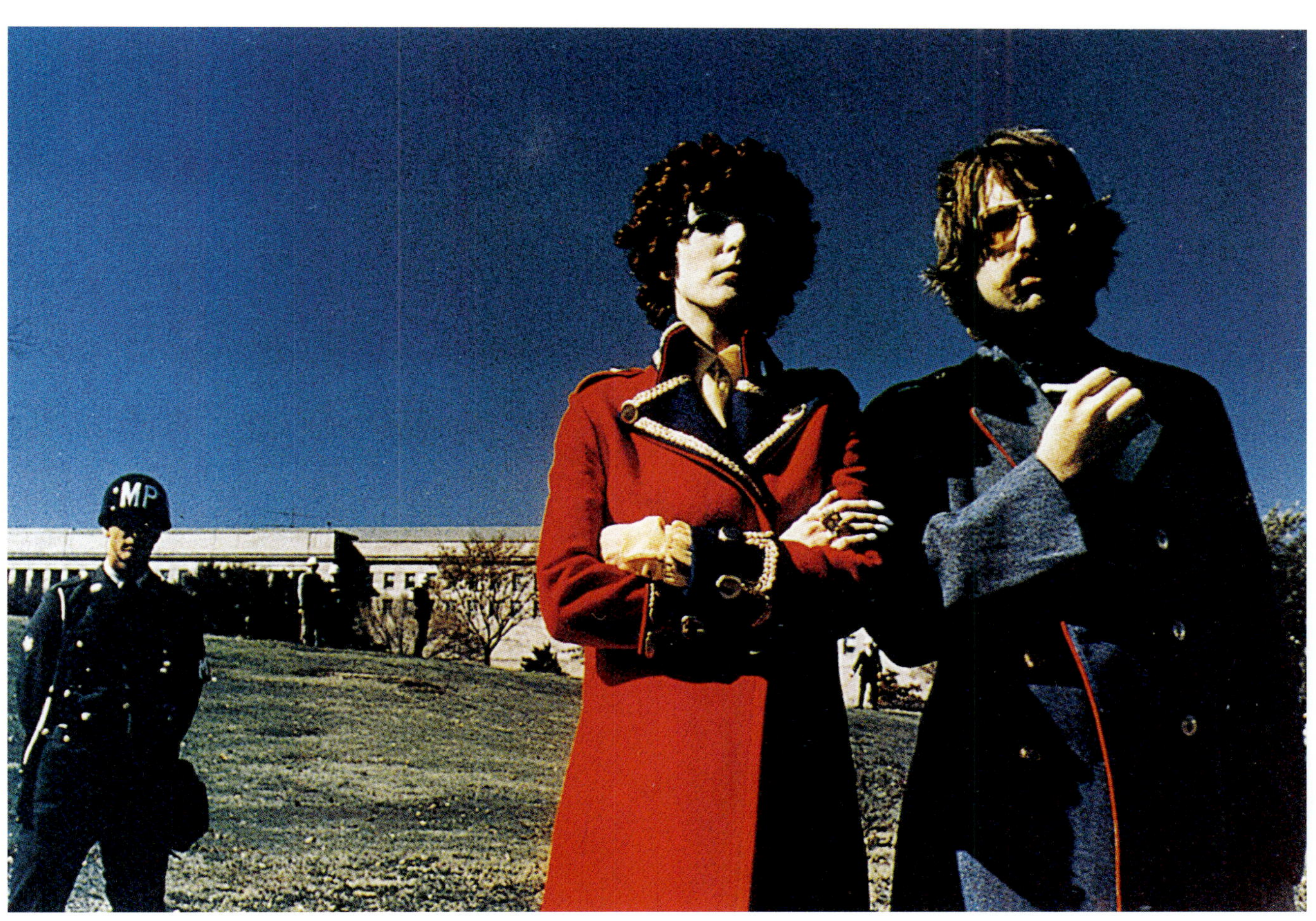

Michael Mott and his wife Barbara, wearing 'Sgt Pepper'style military coats at an anti
Vietnam war demonstration outside the Pentagon, Washington D.C., c.1968.

THE GINGER GROUP 1963–1971

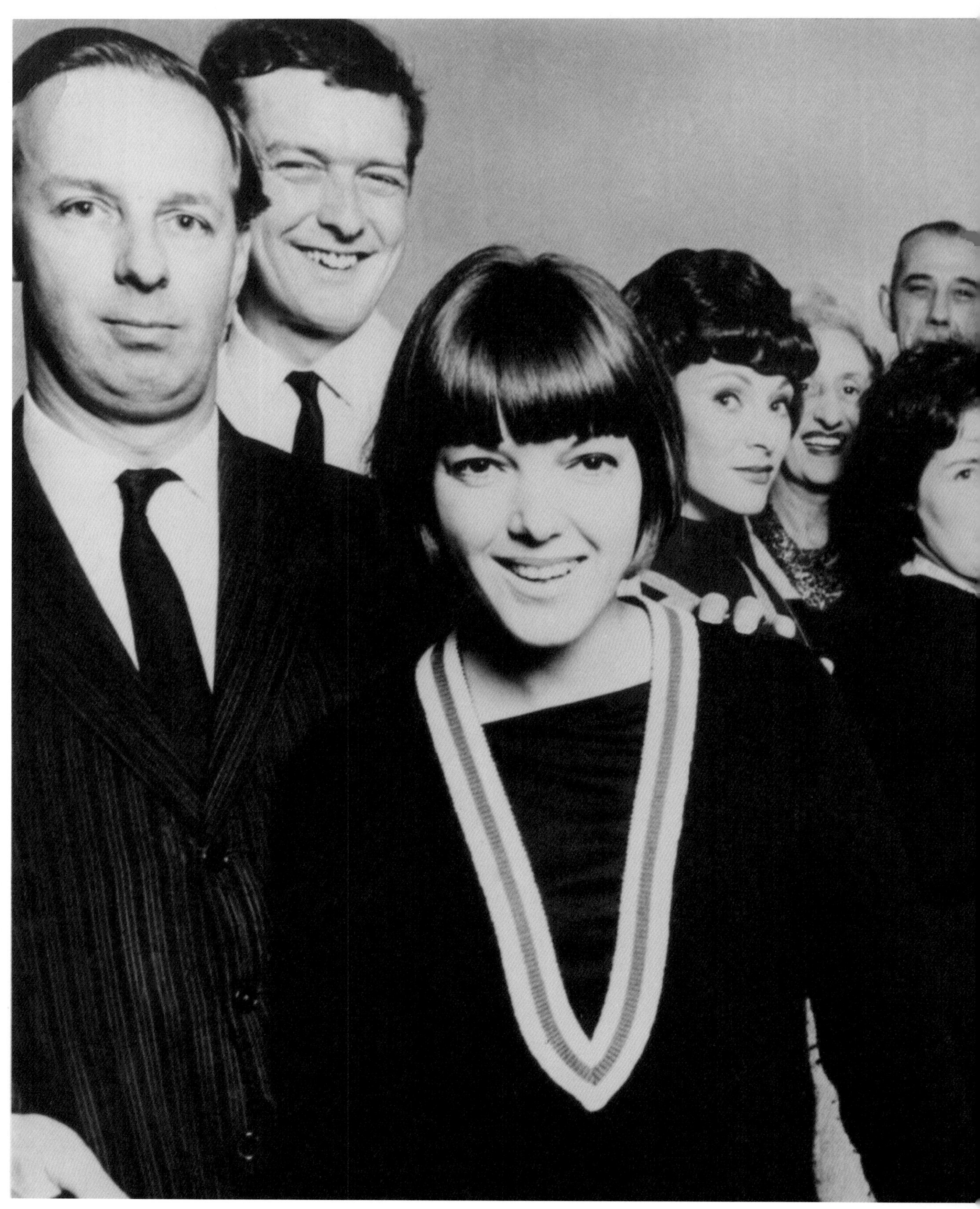

Mary Quant's team, 1963. On the extreme left of Mary is Bazaar's chairman and founder, Archie McNair; behind him stands Mary's husband and fellow founder, Alexander Plunket Greene. Tottman, the company's delivery man is on the far right.

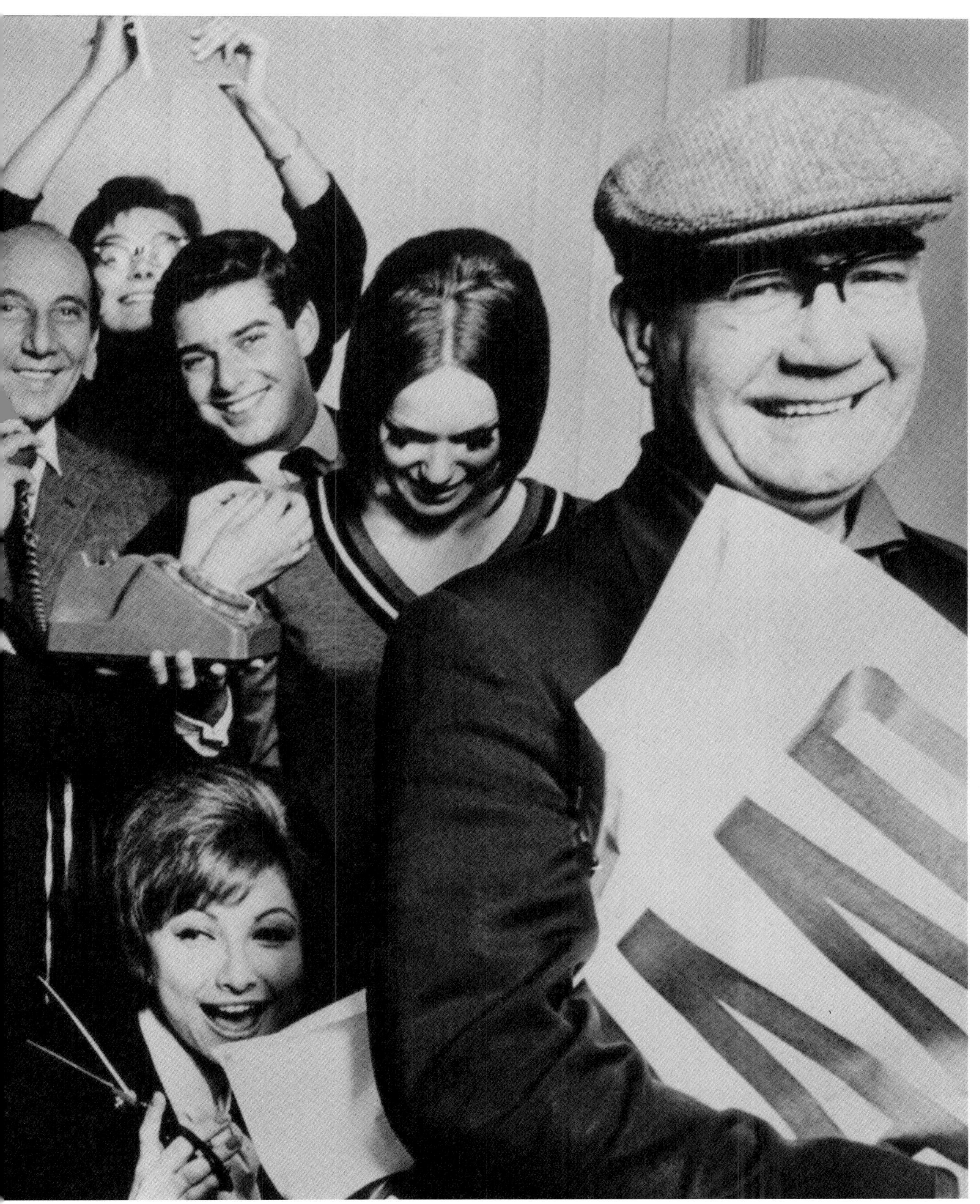

Overleaf: British Joys (A Picture of Mary Quant). A collage paying tribute to Mary Quant by the American Pop artist, Jim Dine, 1965.

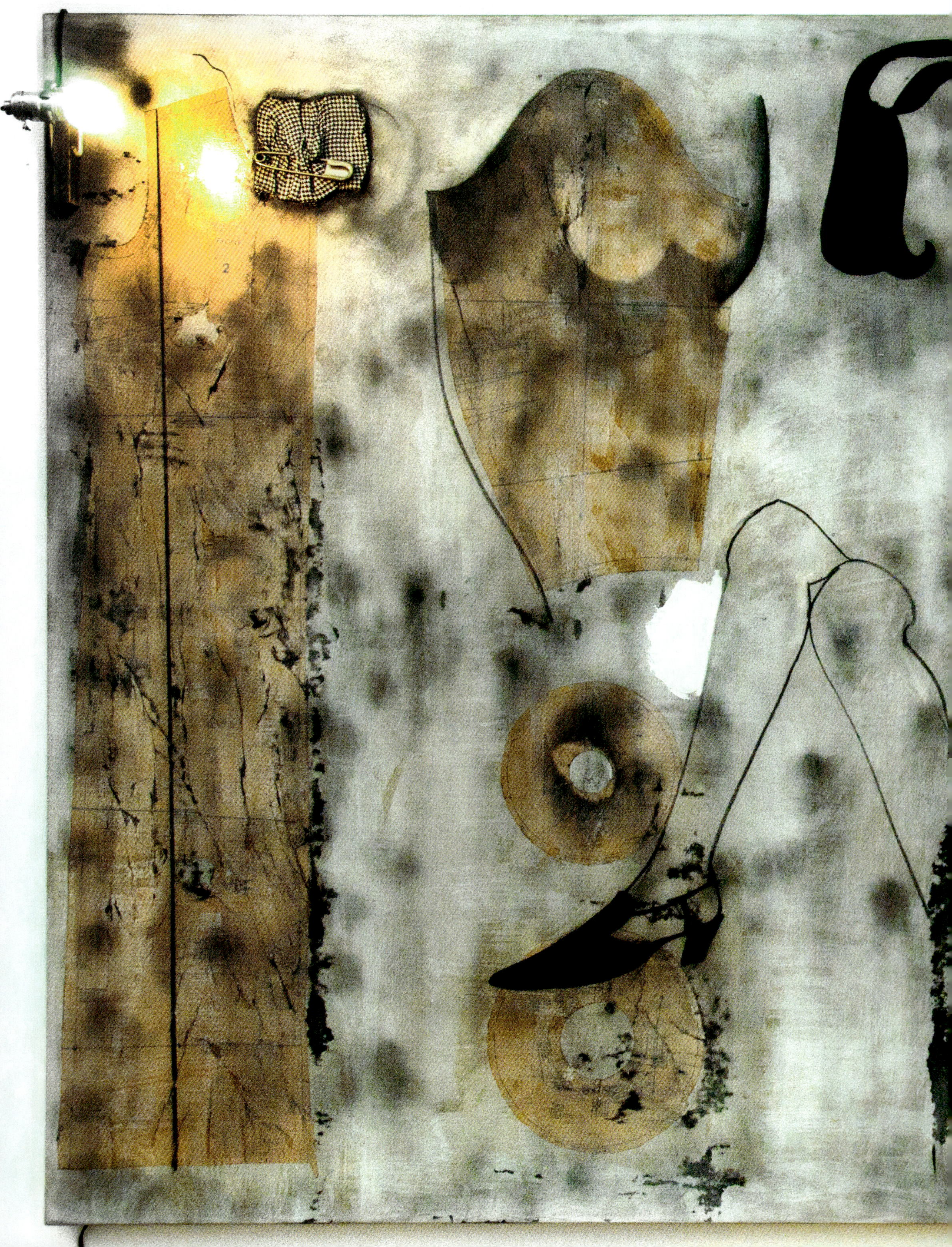

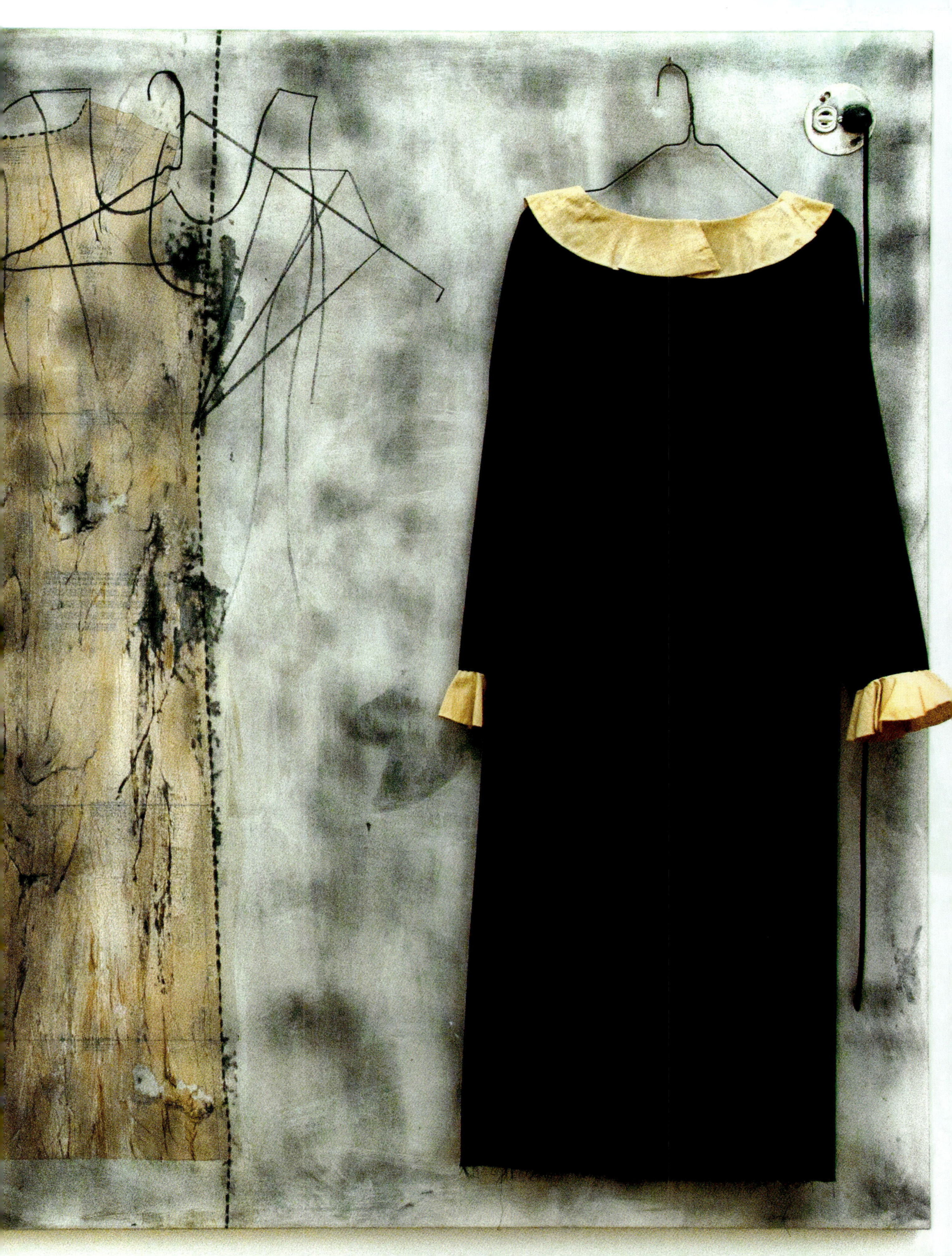

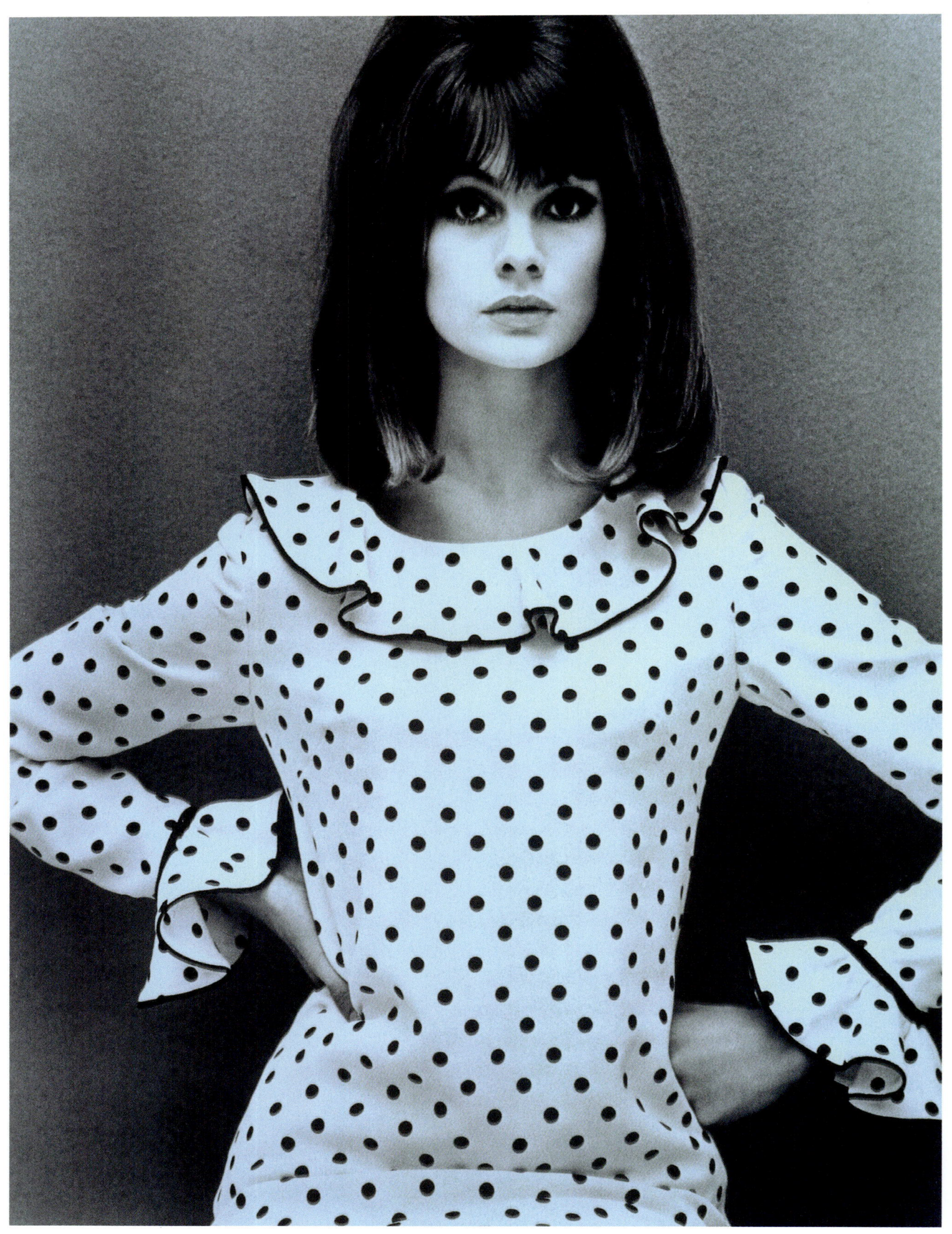

The British supermodel, Jean Shrimpton wearing Daddy's Girl, 1964, one of Quant's most successful dresses from her Ginger Group. It was photographed that year being worn by many celebrities, among them, the Liverpudlian singer Cilla Black.

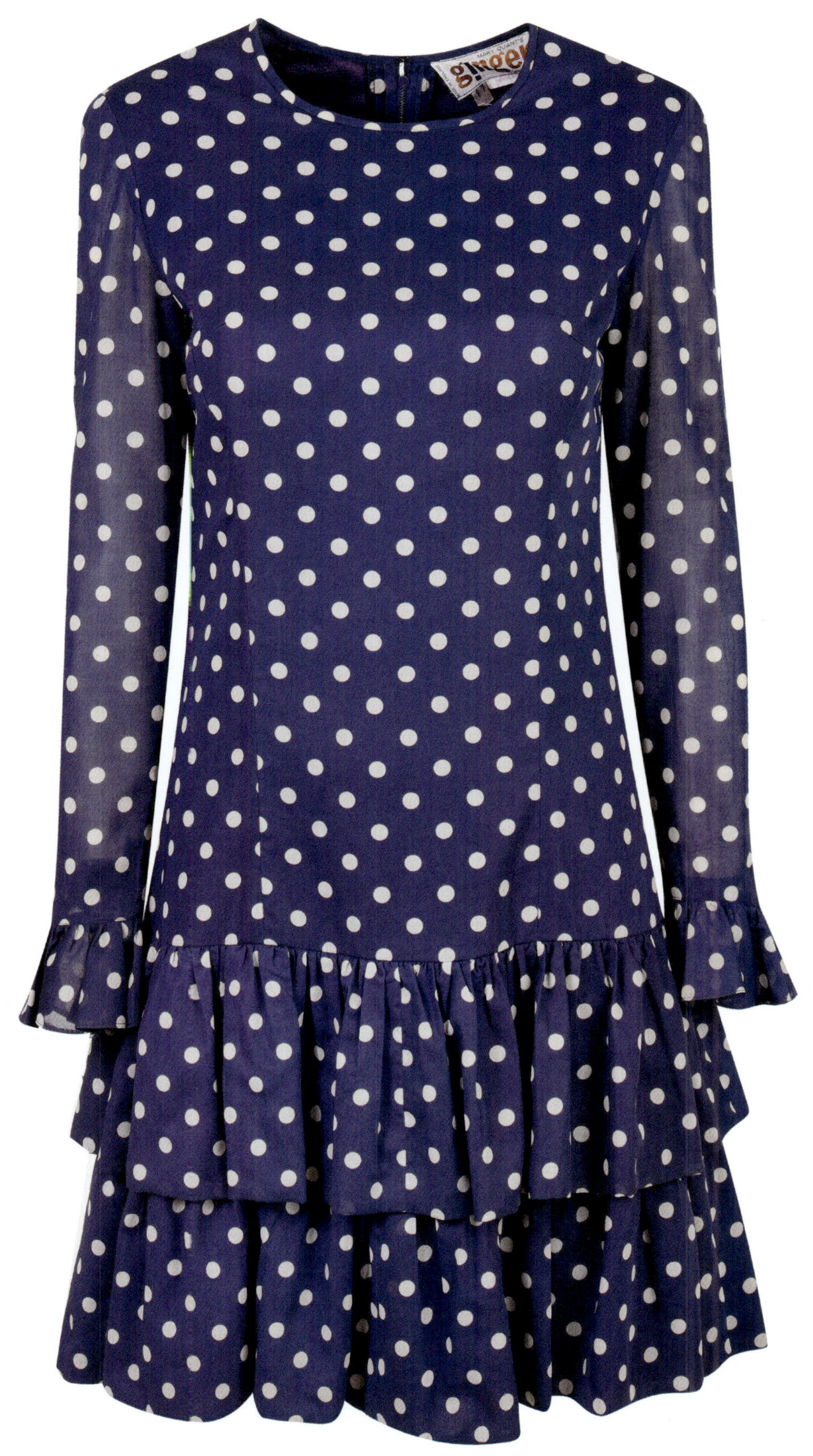

Dress in a dark blue polka dot acetate, a version of Daddy's Girl, c.1964.

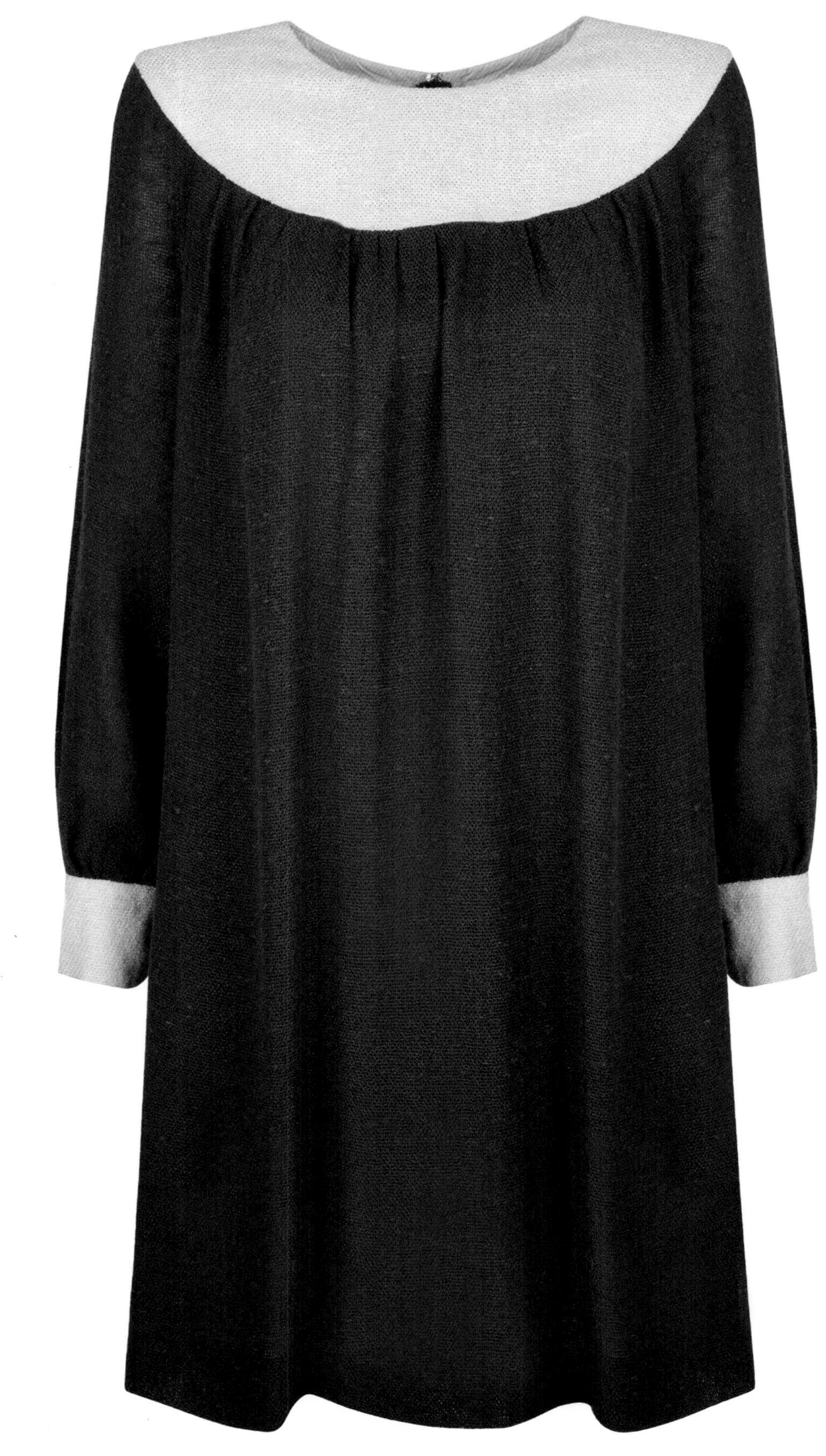

Smock dress in blue and white cotton fabric, c.1964.

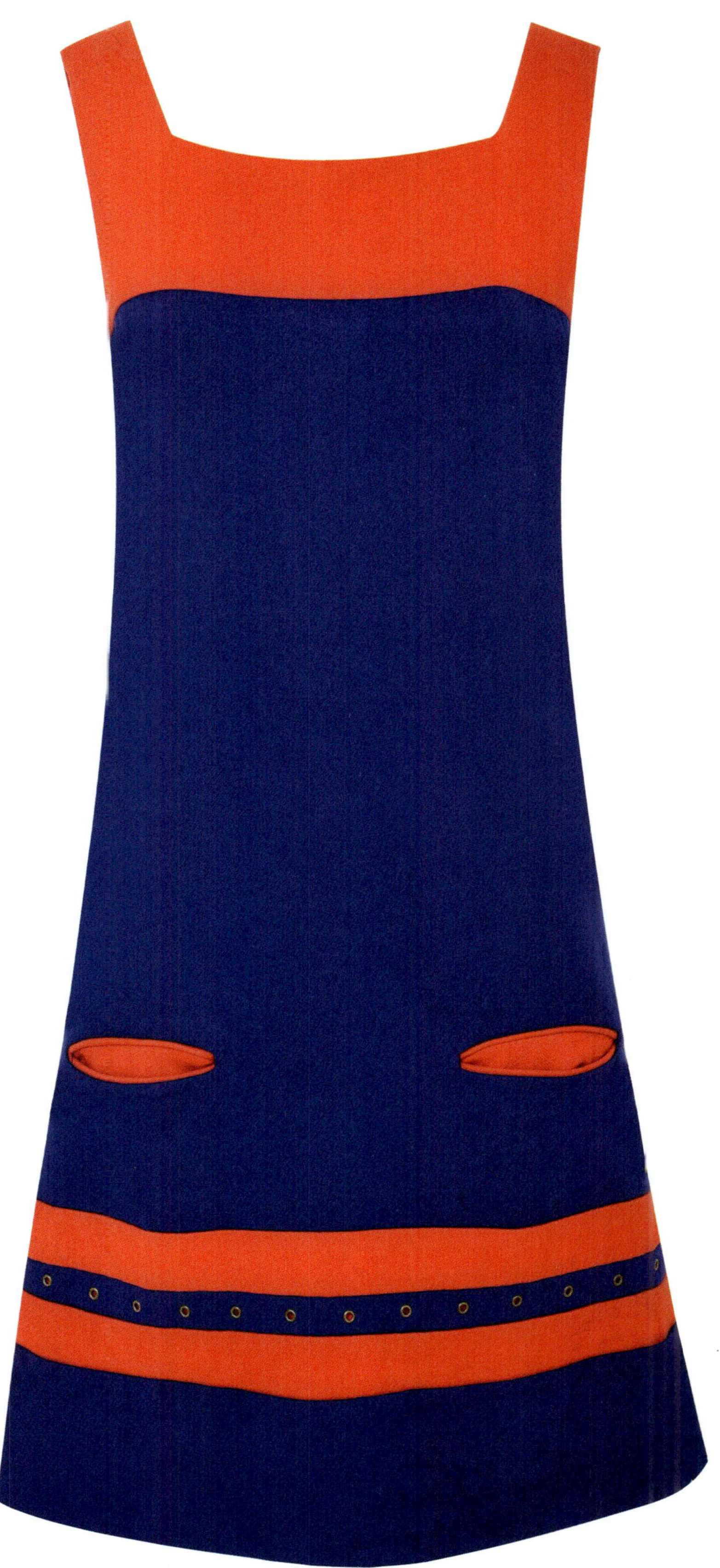

Red and blue woollen dress with Rivet decoration to the hem, c.1965. The supermodel Patti Boyd wore an example in 1965 for a fashion shoot for the magazine *Seventeen*, with the pop group the Merseybeats and the actors David Warner and Tom Courtney. Patti Boyd later married George Harrison and subsequently the 'Guitar God' Eric Clapton.

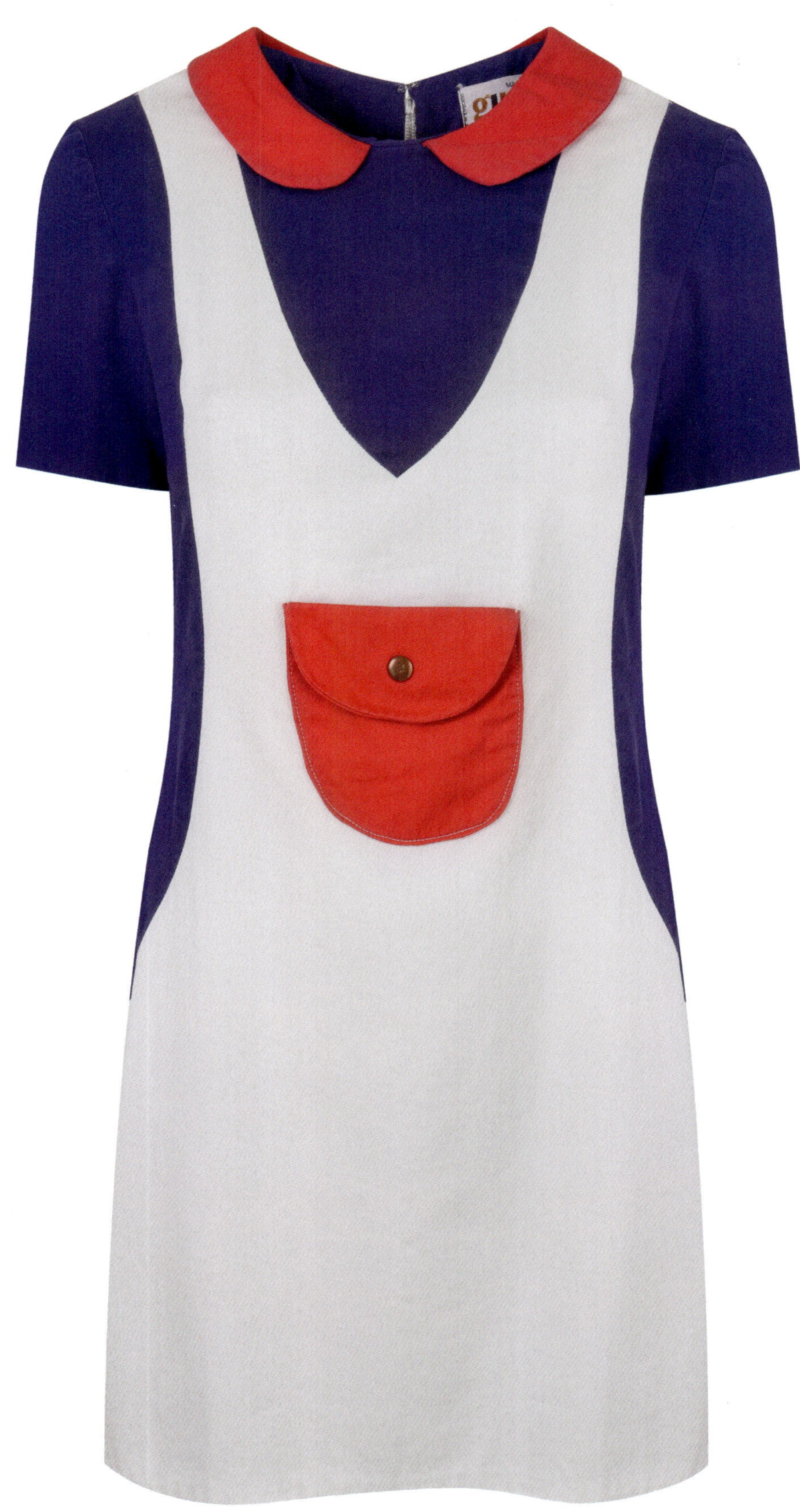

A red, white and blue cotton dress, c.1966. This dress shows the influence of the vogue for clothing made from Union flags, such as those worn by members of The Who pop group.

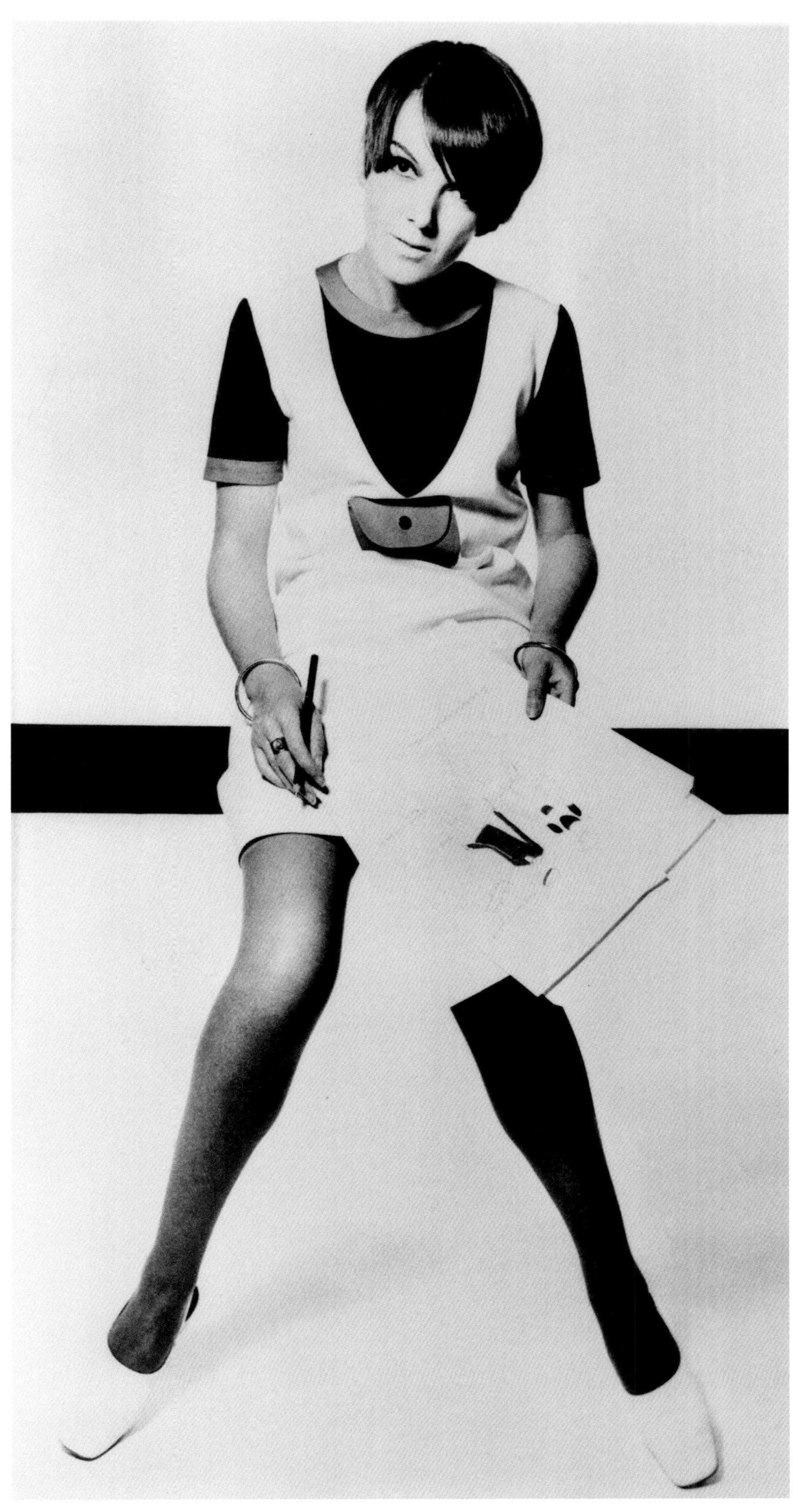

This iconic image of Quant wearing a variation of the red, white and blue
dress was used on the packaging of stockings and tights, c.1966.

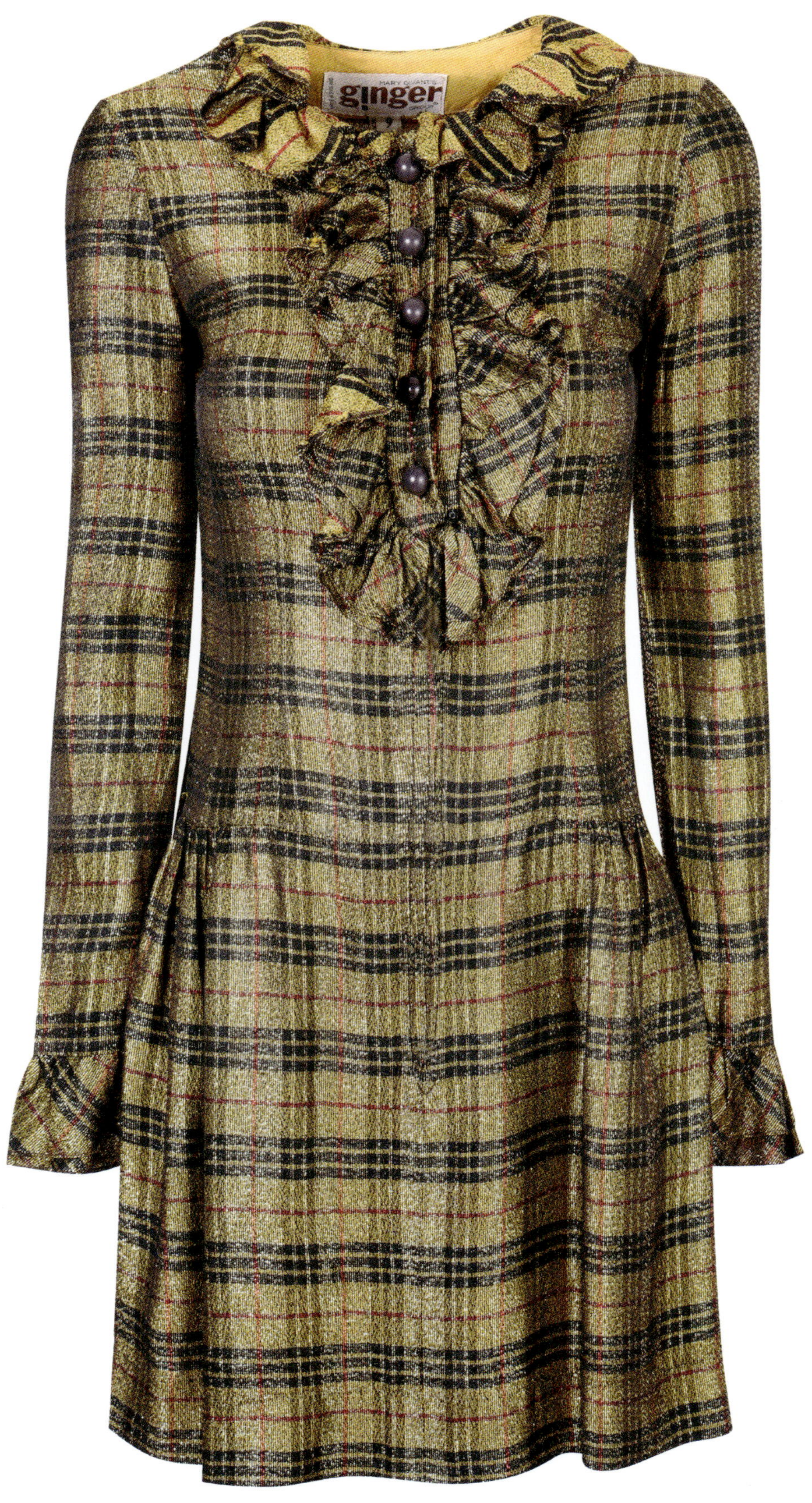

Party dress in gold and brown checked lamé, c.1966-1967.

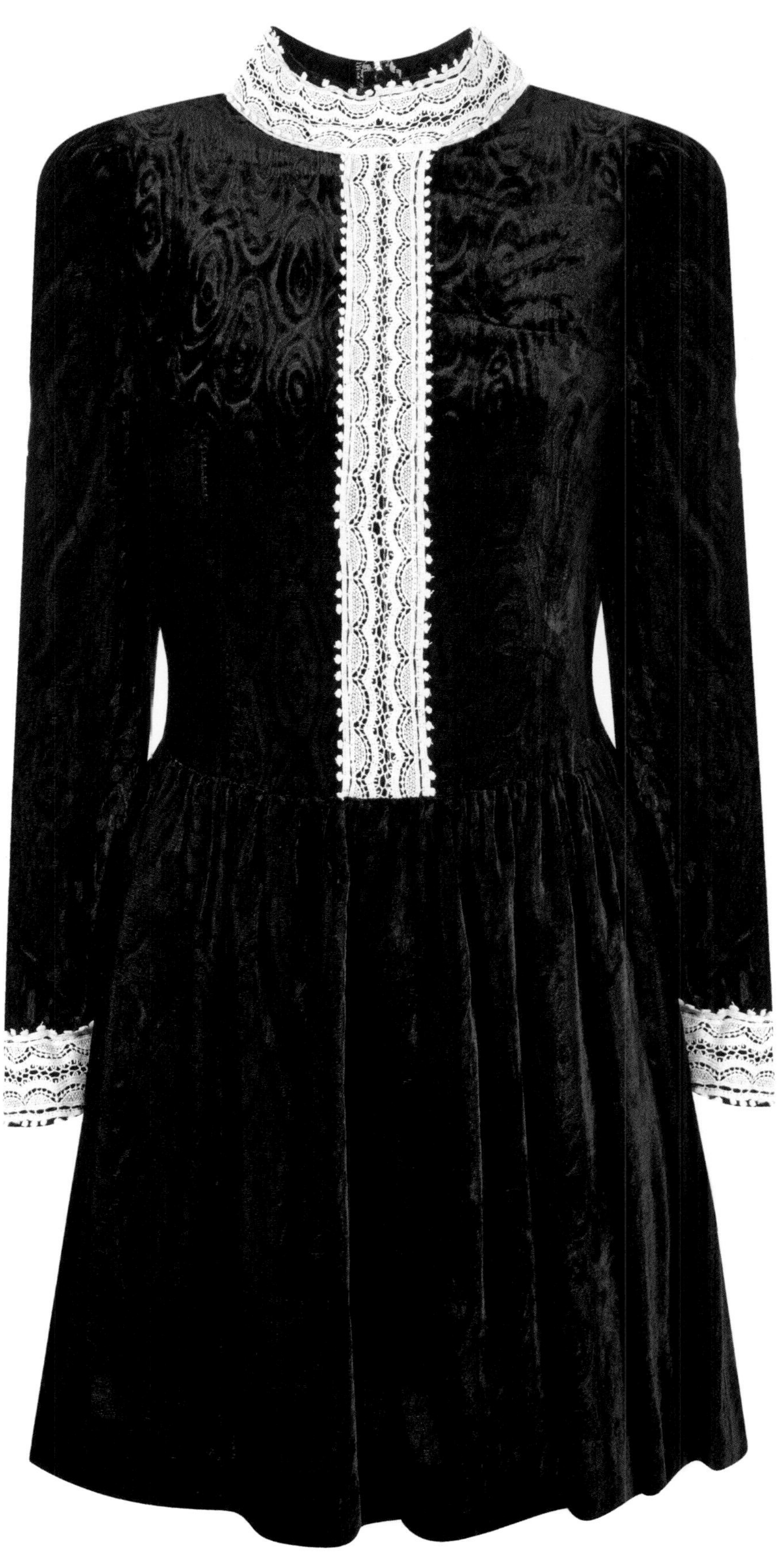

Victorian-style dress in black figured velvet with white lace collar and cuffs, 1967.

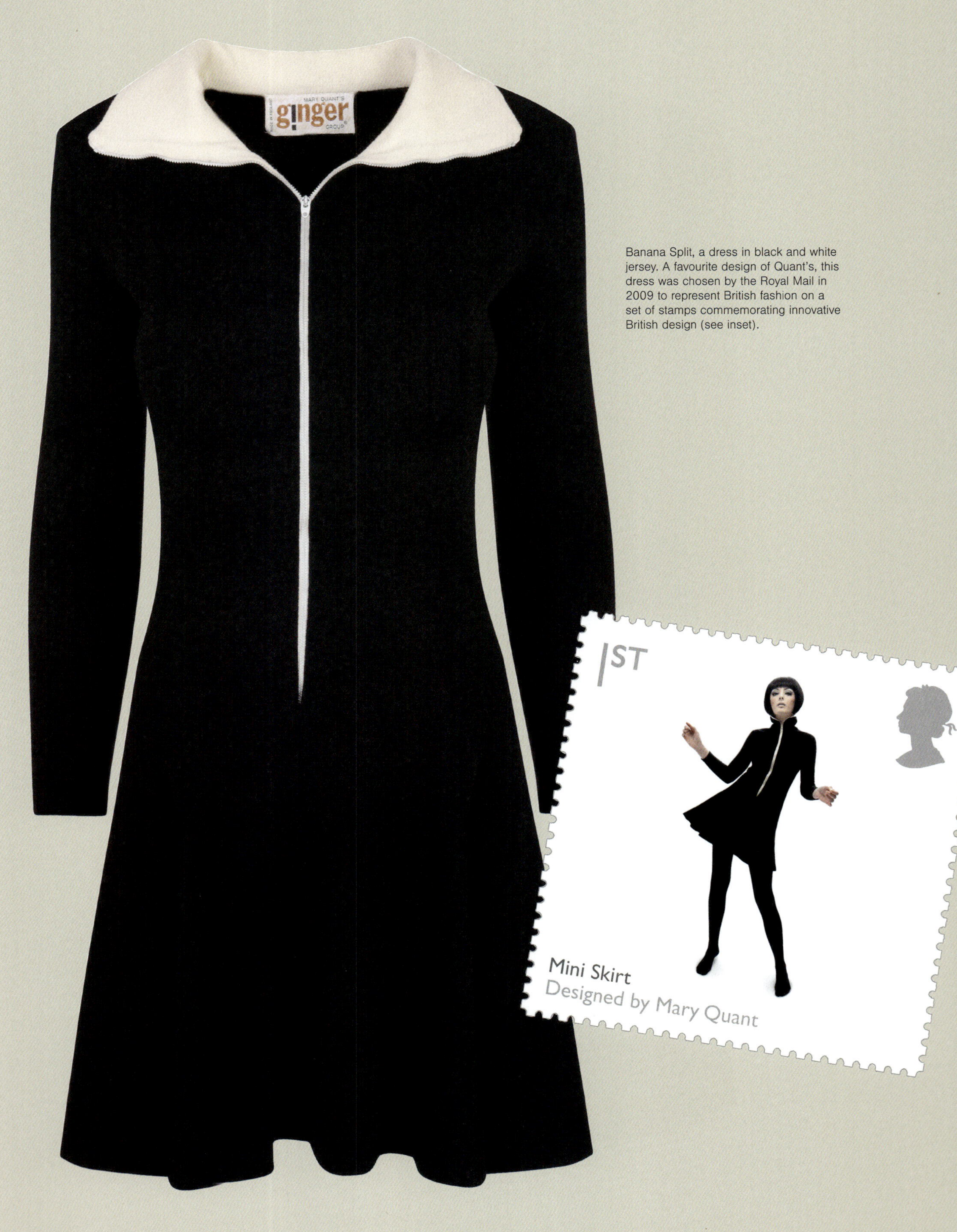

Banana Split, a dress in black and white jersey. A favourite design of Quant's, this dress was chosen by the Royal Mail in 2009 to represent British fashion on a set of stamps commemorating innovative British design (see inset).

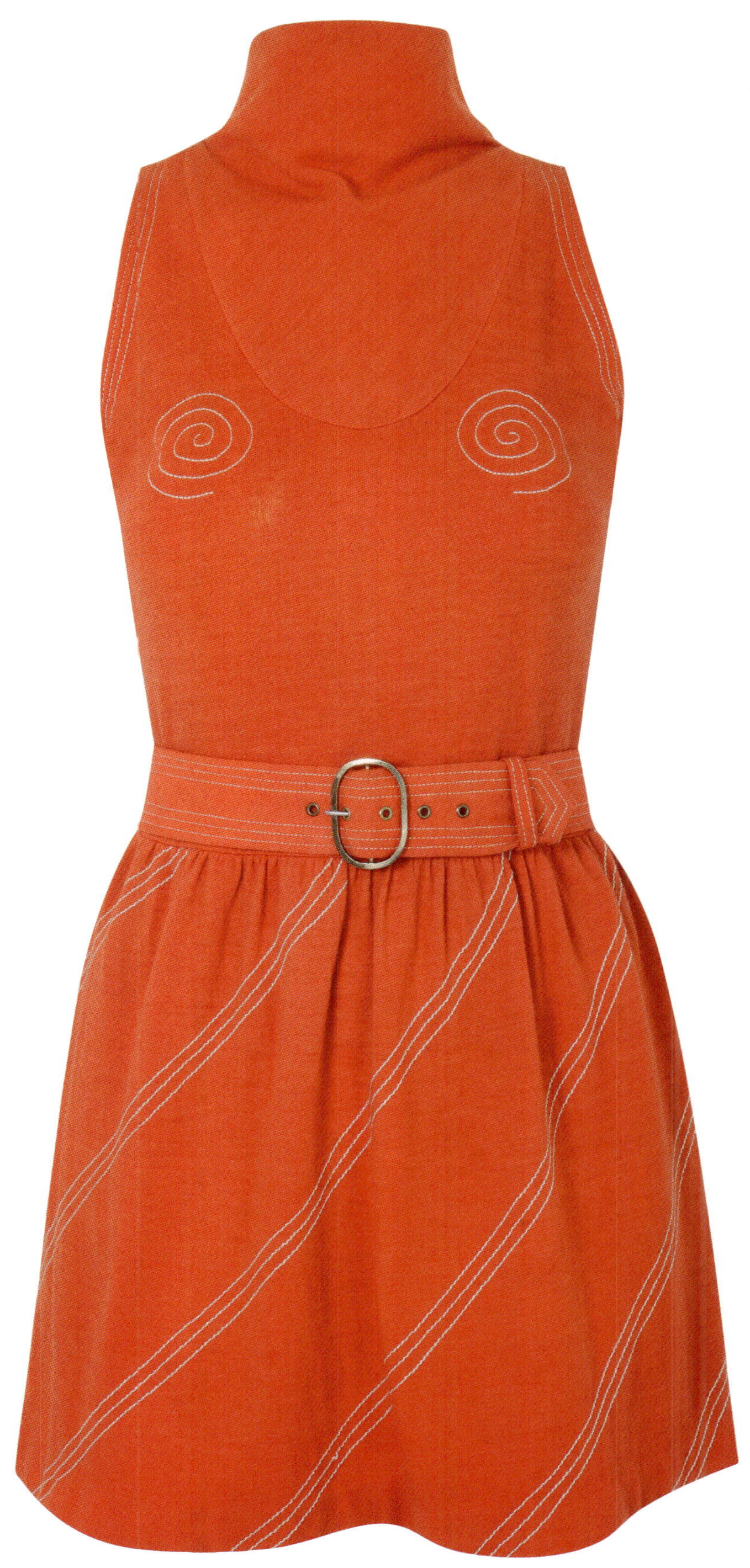

Dress in red cotton jersey with decorative 'jean-style' white stitching, c.1967-1968. The type of stitching commonly found on jeans was often used by Quant for decorative effects.

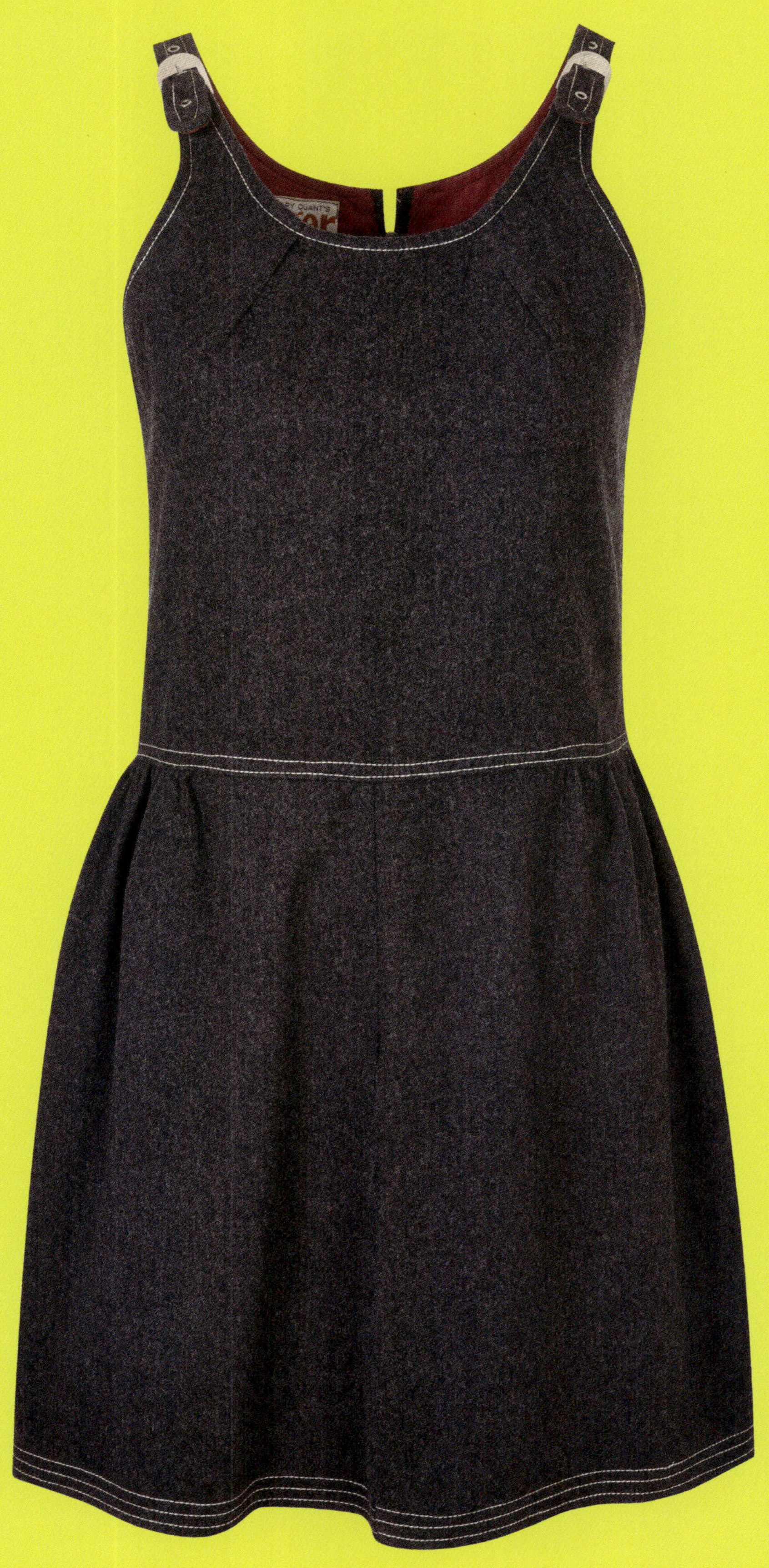

Dress in grey flannel with white 'jean-style' stitching and silver-coloured metal buckles, c.1968. Since the earliest days of Bazaar, grey flannel had been one of Quant's favourite fabrics. A utilitarian cloth associated more with uniforms and work clothes than high fashion, it seems to have been almost a symbol of rebellion for her.

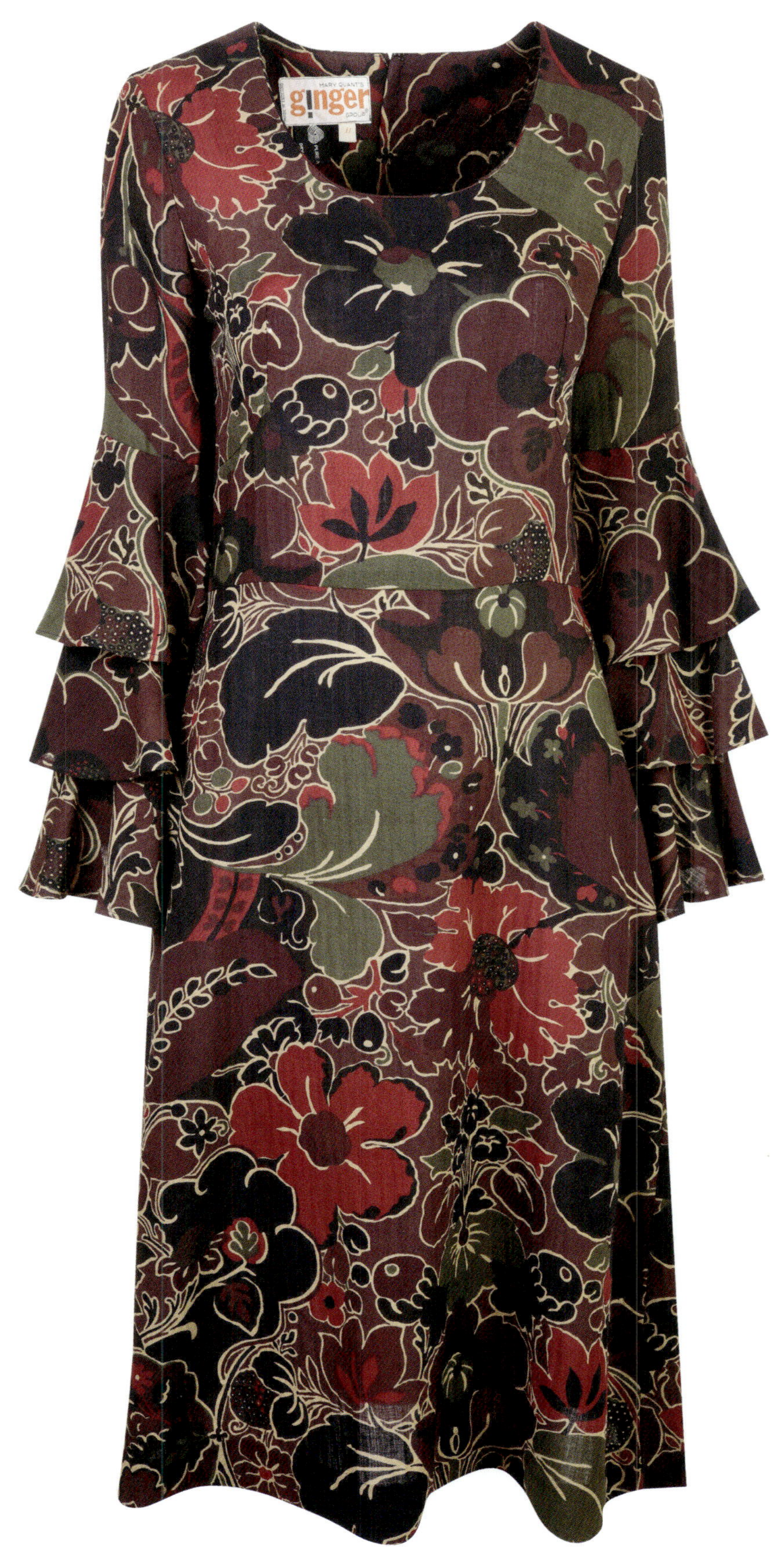

Dress in Medici, a printed Varuna Wool fabric by Liberty of London (the fabric's design is attributed to Bernard Nevill), c.1970-1971. The style of this dress defines a moment when Quant moved away from the radical modernity usually associated with her work, towards the retro romanticism of the 1970s.

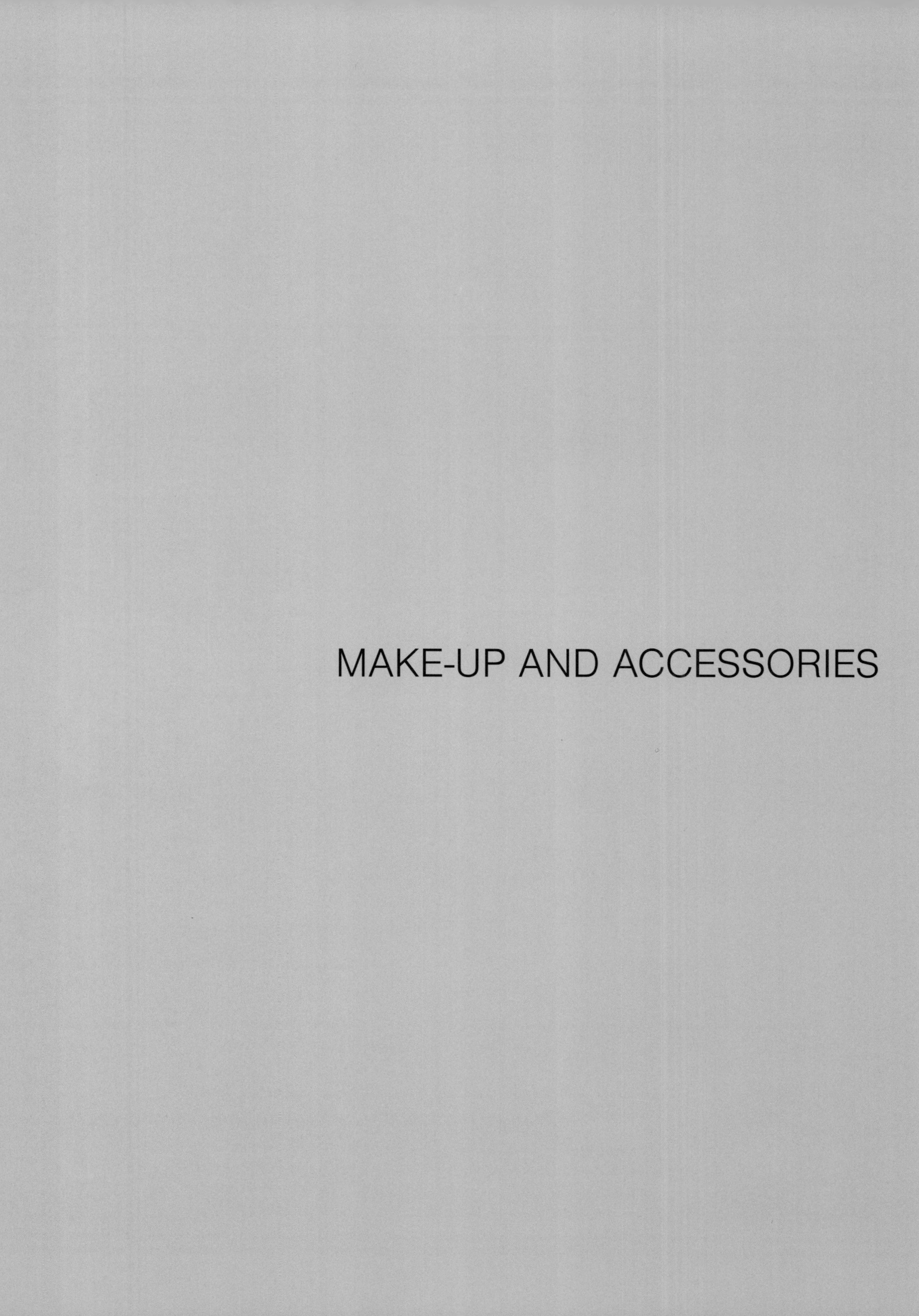

MAKE-UP AND ACCESSORIES

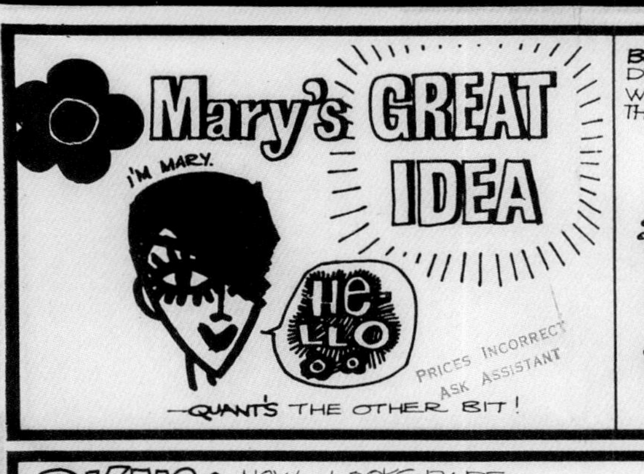

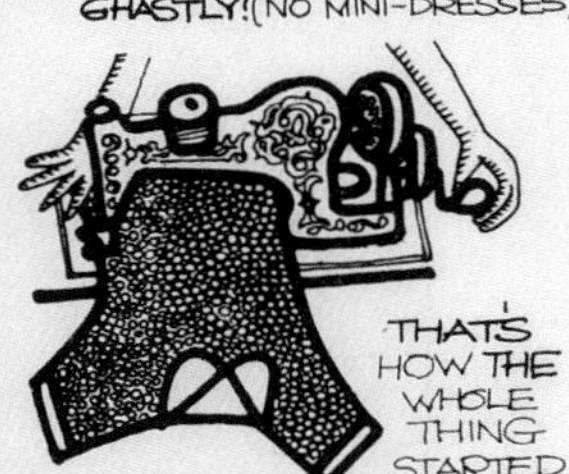

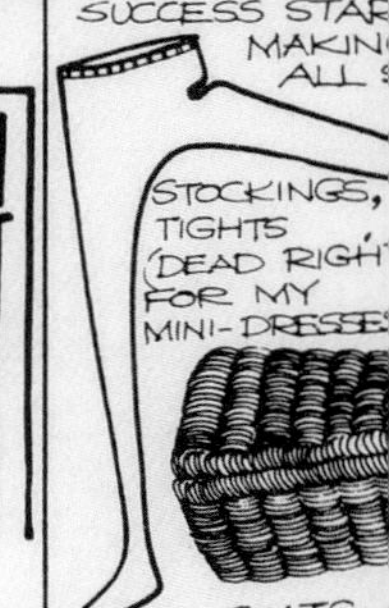

Skin:

NOW — LOOKS BARE. FACES BEAUTIFULLY BONED.

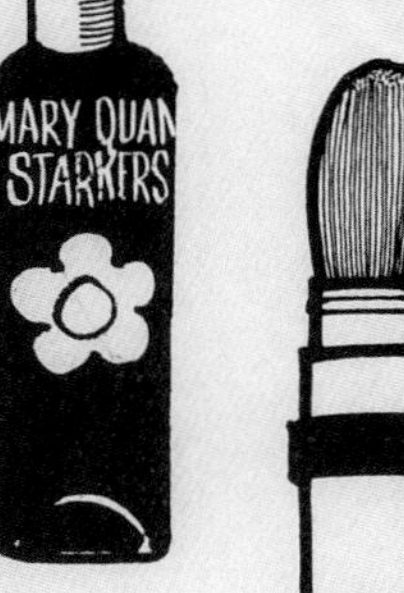

STARKERS
Nude make-up. Like skin but not quite bare. Semi-matte finish. Three tones. 7/9

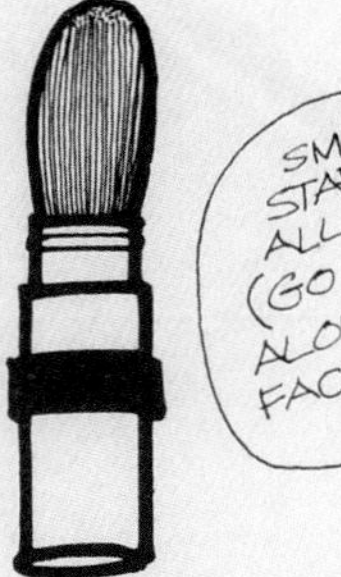

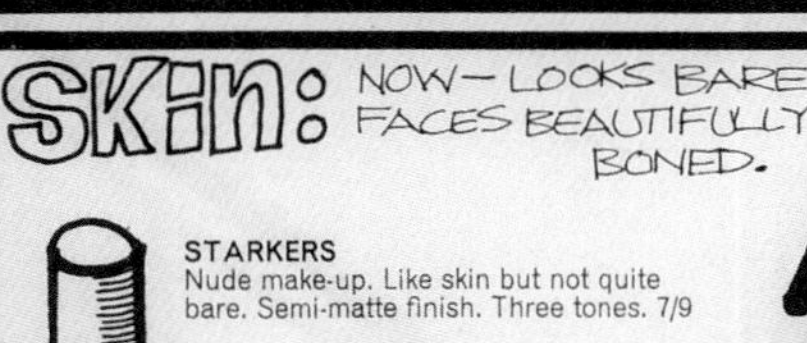

FACE BRUSH
Soft and moppy (for brushing on Face Shapers and Face Final). Slide-up-and-down case protects brush. Clever! 12/9

FACE SHAPERS
Pair of pressed powders coutour face in a new way. Natural shadower and pearl ivory bone highlighter. 12/9

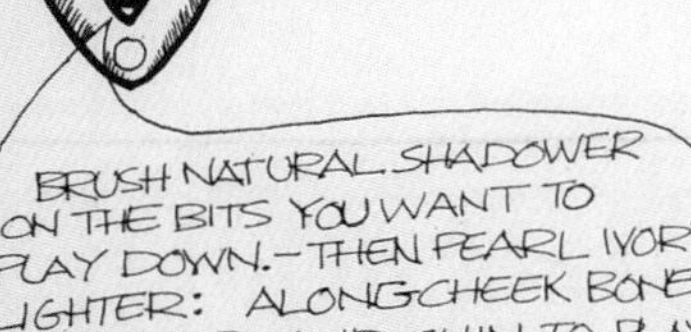

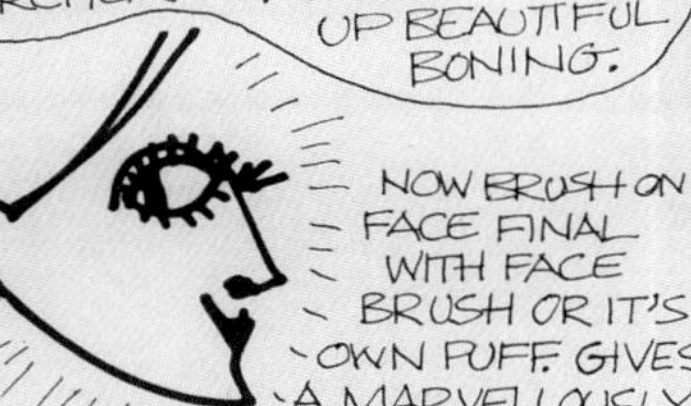

FACE FINAL
Clear matte finish. Almost invisible – transparent. So just one colour (adds bloom to Starkers and Face Shapers). Use with its own puff, or even better, Face Brush. 10/9

NOW EYES: — THE BIG STUNNERS. FORGET ABOUT COLOURING, GO FOR SHAPING.

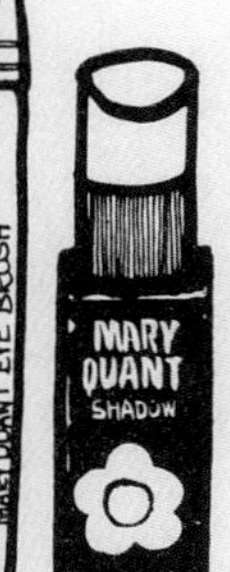

EYE BRUSH
Soft sable chisel. Right for shadowing and lining. 6/9

LIQUID SHADOW
Paints on (shaping comes easy). Dries fast. *Stays matte.* Marvellous smoky-smudge colours. Plus white, silver and gold. (Sable Eye Brush separate). 7/9

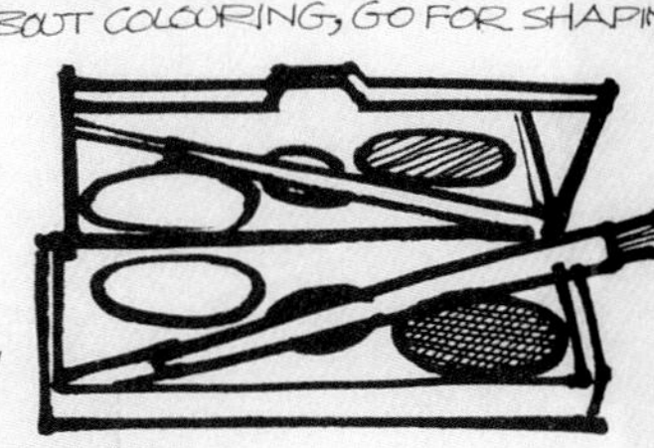

EYE SHAPERS
Crafty. Twin pressed shadows, one always pearl white. Bouncy sable chisel brush just right for shaping. 12/9

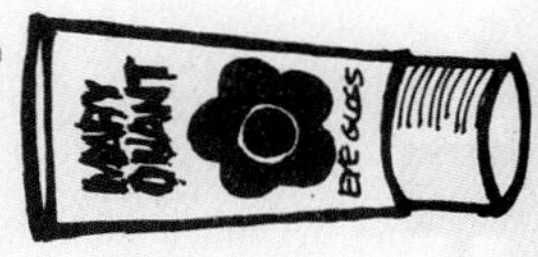

EYE GLOSS
Breakaway highlighter for the new naked-er eye! Transparent. Non-greasy. Lots of pearl. Lots of shine. Drys fast to a high gloss. 7/9

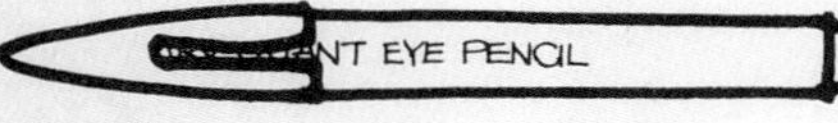

EYE PENCIL
Extra big, extra soft. Silver cap protects its point. 5/9

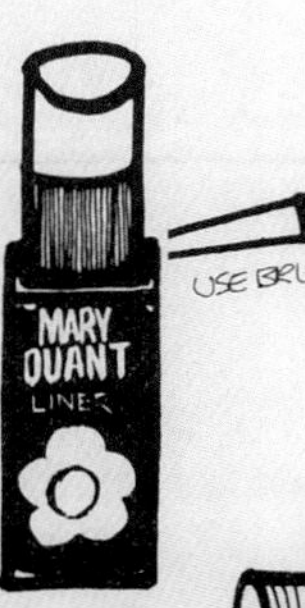

LIQUID LINER
Denser line, heightened effect. (Sable Eye Brush comes separate). 7/9

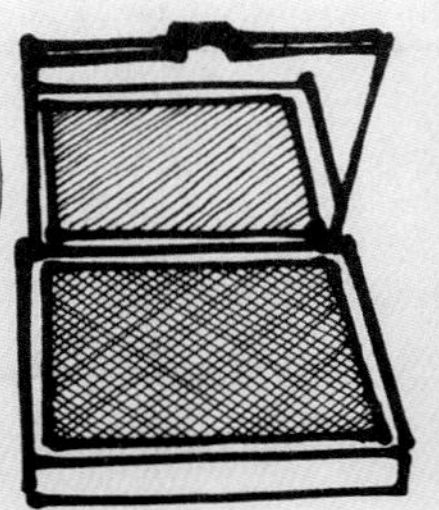

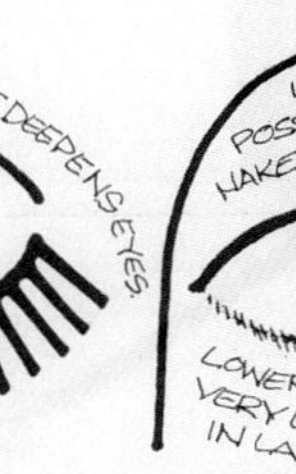

LIQUID MASCARA
Really different. Brush is *the* biggest chunky spiral. Lays on mascara thick and fast (yet separates every lash). Special formula makes double-sure of terrific build-up. 12/9 Refill 7/9

NEW STOR

LASHES:

— LINE UP OF BEAUTIFUL FAKE FLUTTERERS. REAL HAIR WITH SPECIAL QUANT LONG-/SHORT TRIMMING. DIFFERENT, GORGEOUS, BUT INCOGNITO.

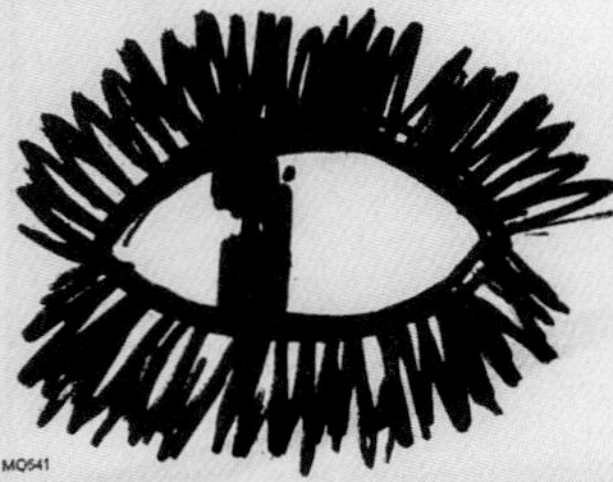

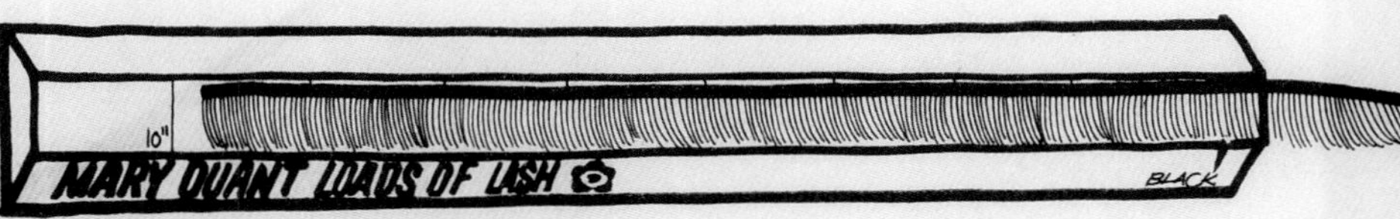

LOADS OF LASH
Self-service lashes! 10″ strip of fine, feathery lash. Snip! Help yourself to just what you want. Wide bits. Mini bits. Little winged bits. Trimmed-down lower lid bits. Or long here-and-there individual hairs. Up to 4 full pairs of lashes on a strip. 42/–

MQ541

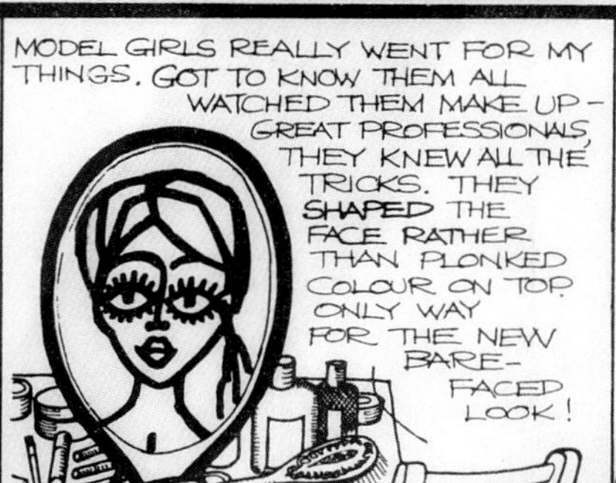

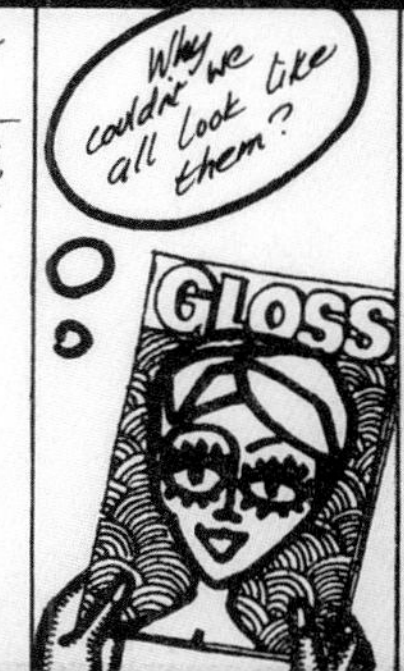

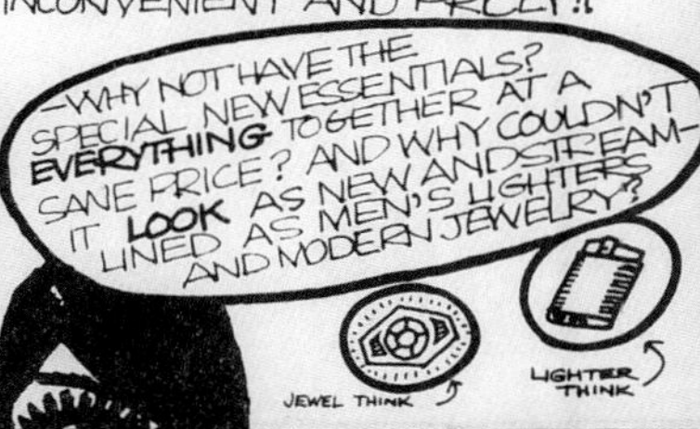

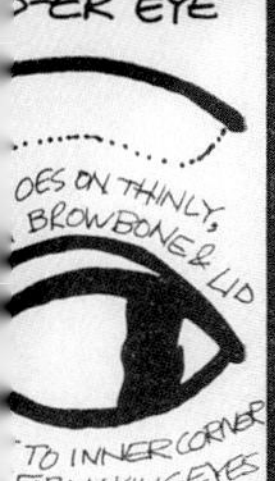

MOUTHS:

GREAT NEW JUST-LICKED LOOK! (MADE FOR THE NEW NAKED-ER EYE.) 2 WAYS TO GO ABOUT IT.

LICK STICK
The shiny-moist, transparent-tinted mouth – first time ever with a *stick!* Previous one-colour efforts never had enough gloss. But Lick Stick is *2-faced:* one side all transparent pearly gloss, the other shiny pearl colour. Very moist – very kind to mouths. Looks lush – glossy, *transparently* brighter. 9/9

BRUSH LIPSTICK
Invented the shiny-moist just-licked look. Softest possible pan of colour. All moistness, glossiness, pearliness. Slicks on thin as can be with own sable chisel brush. 9/9 Refills 5/9

LIPSTICK
New moistness. Just the in-group colours (plains and pearls), quick-changing. 7/9

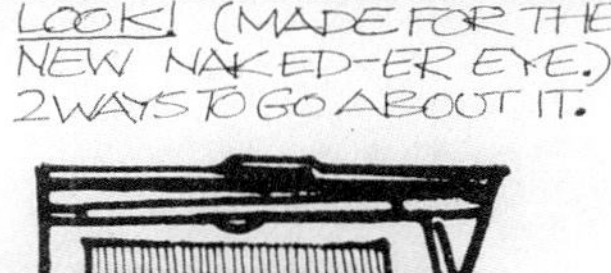

LIP SHAPER PENCIL
Does what it says. Really shapes mouth. BROWN-PINK colour shadows off edge of lips, shapes them, rounds them out sexy. 5/9

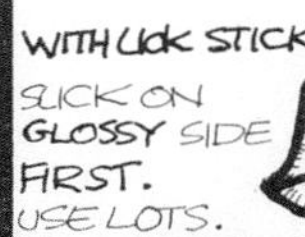

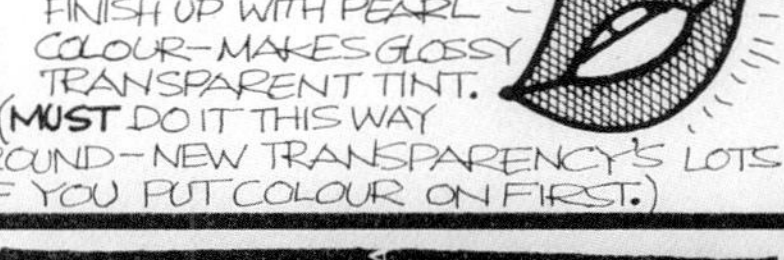

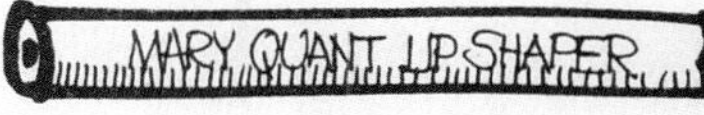
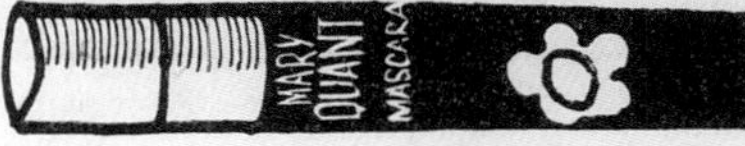

TEARPROOF LIQUID MASCARA
Commonsense special. *Really waterproof* (i.e. tearproof, swimproof, weatherproof!!). Absolutely smudgeproof. Chunky spiral brush and formula for slick separation and big fast build-up. 12/9 Refill 7/9

NAILS:

—UPDATED 30's LOOK. SMART NEW IDEA. ADD ONE THAT'S FABULOUS.

NAIL POLISH
Special non-obvious colours except one flag-waving red. 6 colour basic is range. Some plain, some frosted. 7/9

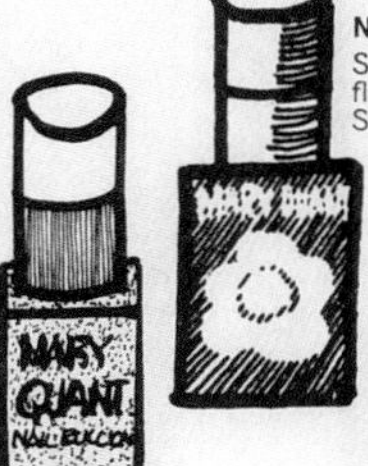

NAIL BULLION
Quant's gold and silver nail loot! Transparent nail polish glittering with 24ct. gold leaf and shiny silver. Wear it solo – 3 coats for something sumptuous. Or 1 or 2 transparent coats over your pet pearl or plain colour for sur-tax dazzle. 9/9

NAIL MAKE-UP
The *new* idea. 2 shades make 1 never-before colour.
Grey + White Pearl = CHROME
White + White Pearl = PVC WHITE
Beige + White Pearl = CAMEL +
9/9

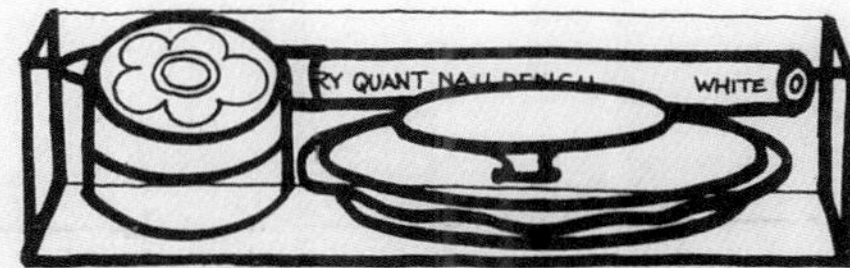

NAILSHINE KIT
Cream and buffer together in 30's style do the big shine-up bit. Moistened nail pencil tips nails pure white. Just massage cream's new conditioners into nail base – where they do most good. Buffing stimulates like mad, builds up natural shine. 17/6

PAINT-BOX

WHOLE FACE IN A MINUTE!

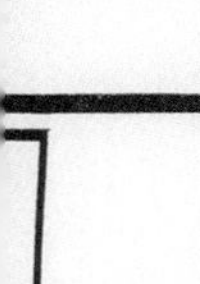
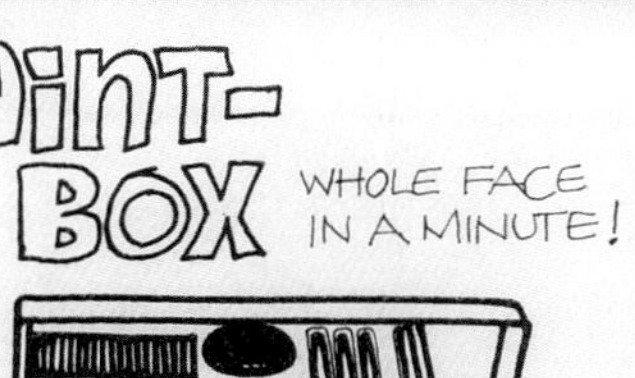
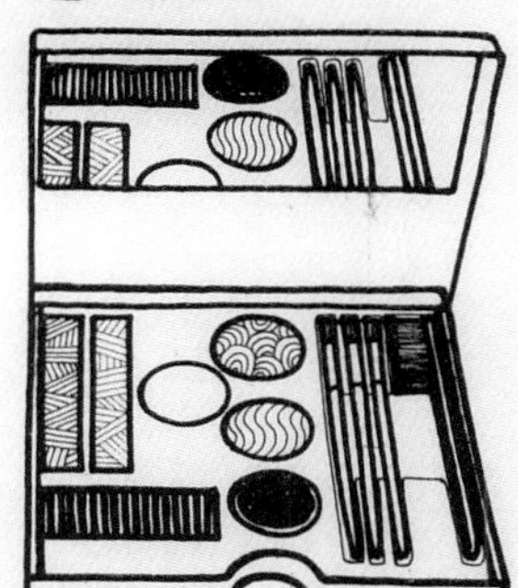

PAINTBOX
An organised this minute face – the complete works! Ready at hand, no fuss. Streamlined. Mirrored. 2 Brush Lipsticks, 3 Eye Shapers, Cake Liner, Block Mascara, all those special brushes. All set and raring to go for a new face *now!* 42/-

KITBAG:

SLICK, ZIPPERED HIDEAWAY FOR ALL YOUR QUANT MAKE-UP!

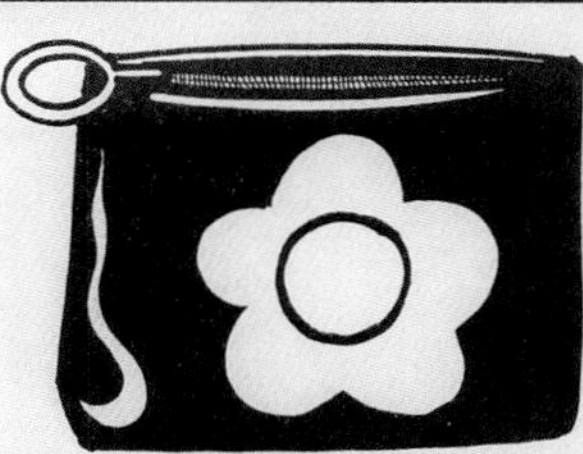

KITBAG
Outsmarts all those frilled and fussy padded satin things. A streamlined make-up kit. Shiny black or white PVC. Practical! Right-size (to hold lots). Washable inside and *out!* And a *huge* zip-ring for quick draw. 12/9

SMELL:

TWO-TIMING MODERN PERFUMES (FROM FRANCE) A.M. & P.M.

Why? There just wasn't a great smell that was really *now*. All the classic French ones and the new arrivals evoked *old* nostalgias, memories that have absolutely no meaning for us – our generation. That's how *A.M.* and *P.M.* happened. Distilled in France. Two moods. For the two sides of *you* – the nice girl-next-door and the red-hot sexpot. *A.M.* blends into *P.M.* – they're complementary.
A.M. – suggests fresh, flirty innocence. Freckles, long grass, marguerites and marigolds.
P.M. – is warm, rich, narcotic, with a come-on sexiness. Suggests wine, summer-night smells, approaching bedtime.
Both are you!

All sorts of perfume ways – but most you can spray! Perfume Cologne. Perfume Spray. Cologne Spray. Perfume Atomiser. Perfume Milk. Talc. (The whole story's in my separate Perfume Leaflet).

MARY QUANT COSMETICS LTD. Chelsea London England

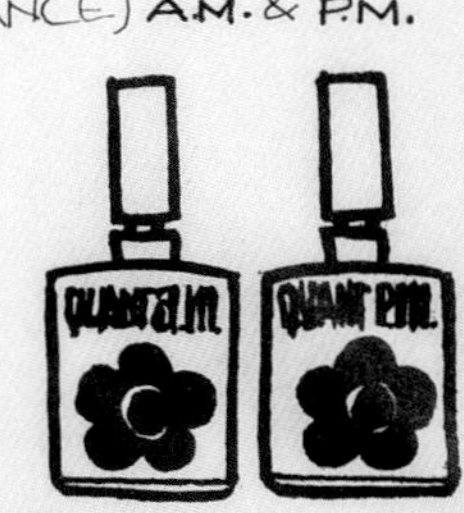

'Mary's Great Idea'. A poster illustrating Quant's ranges of makeup in the late 1960s.

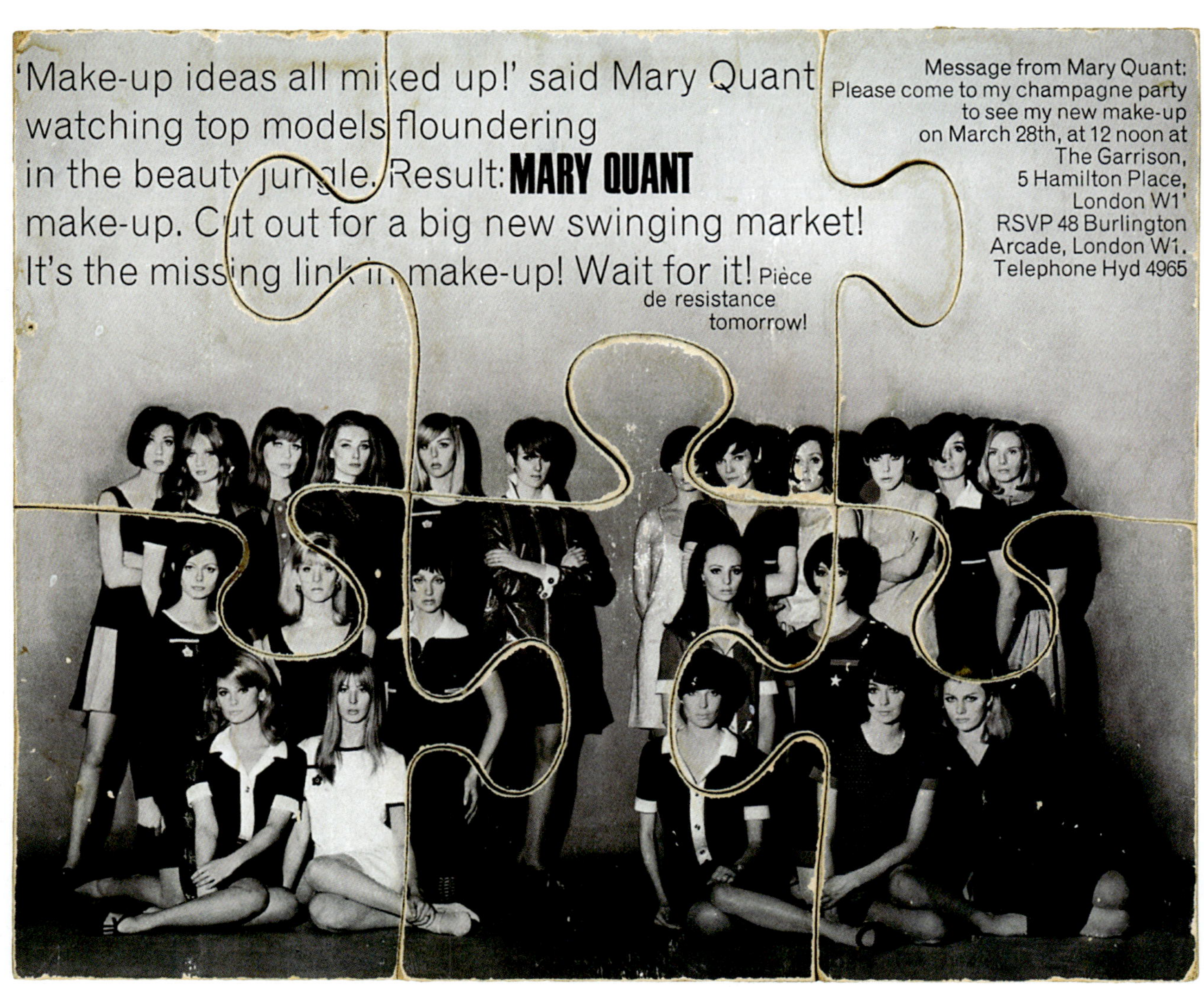

Invitation to the launch of Quant's first range of makeup, 1966.

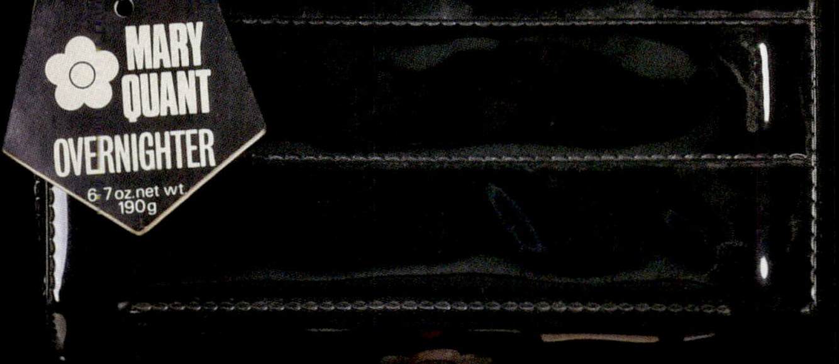

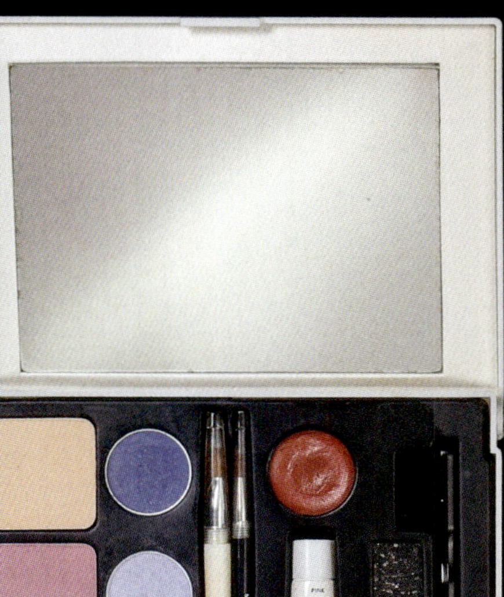

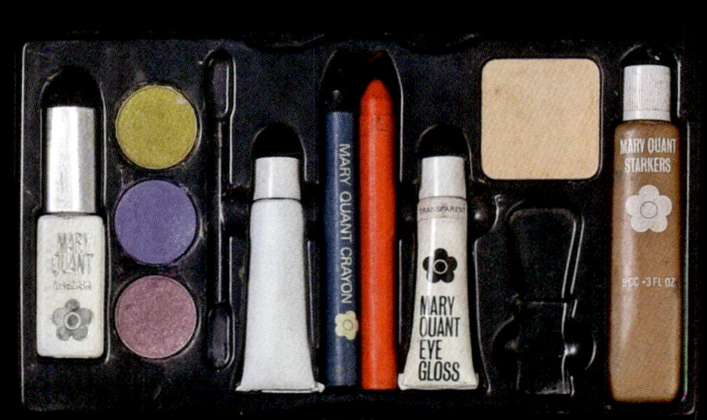

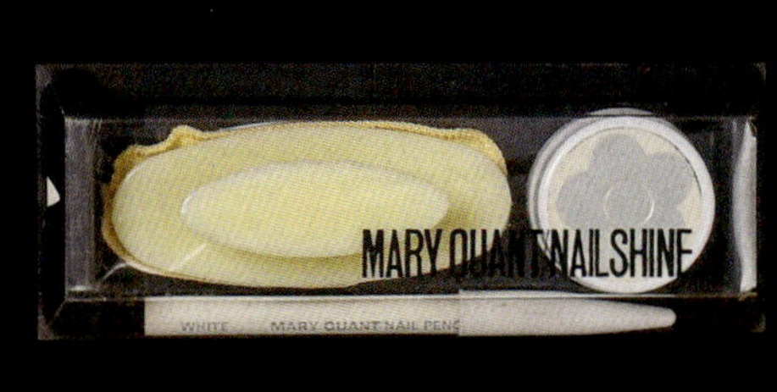

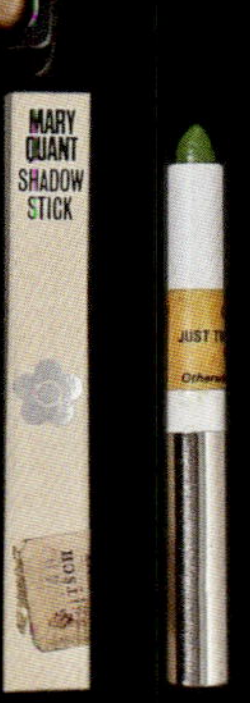

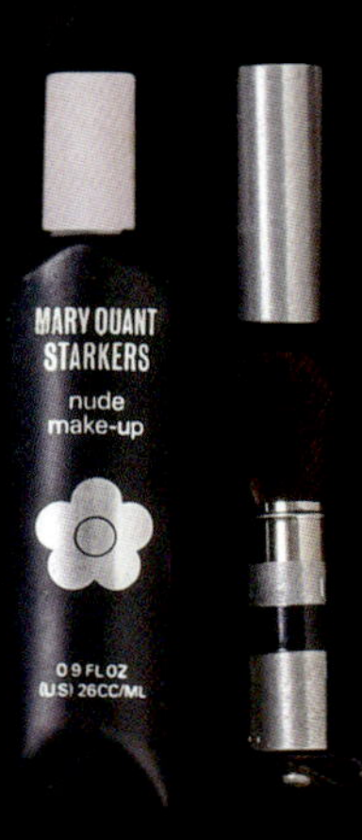

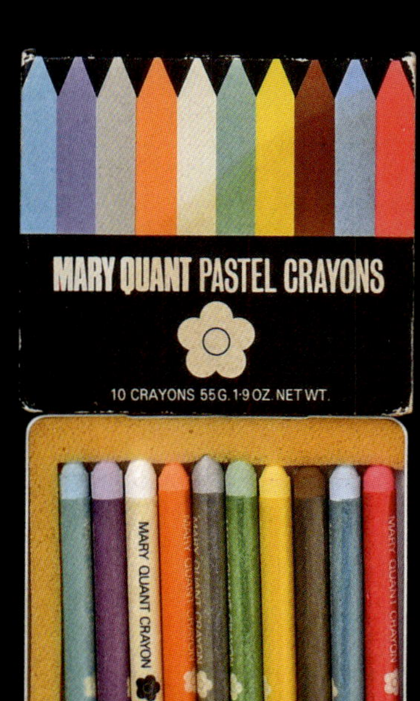

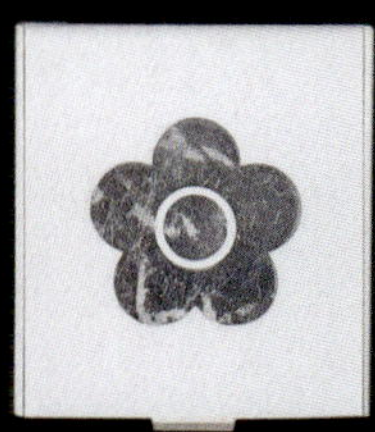

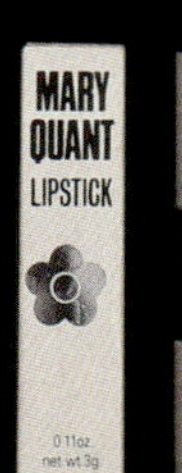

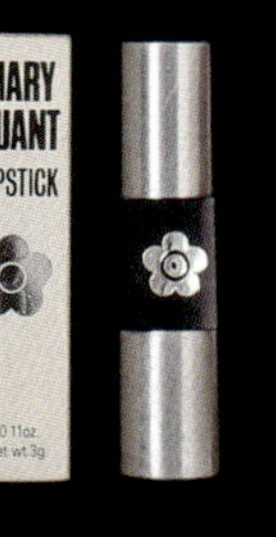

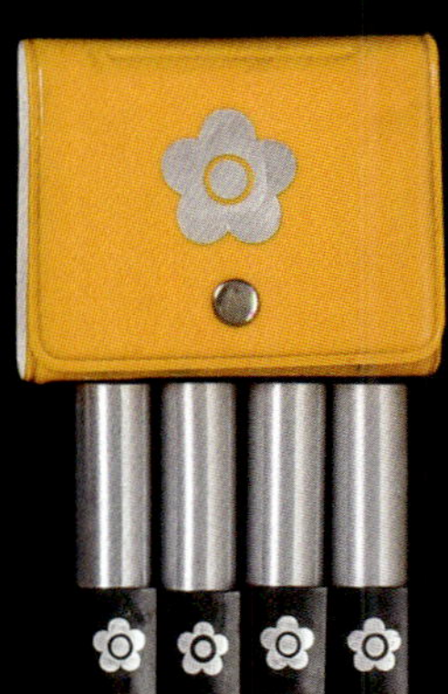

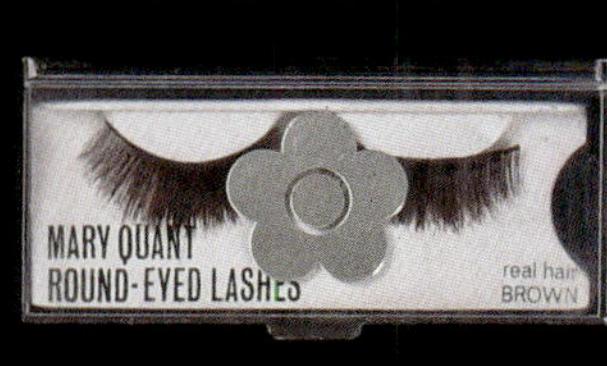

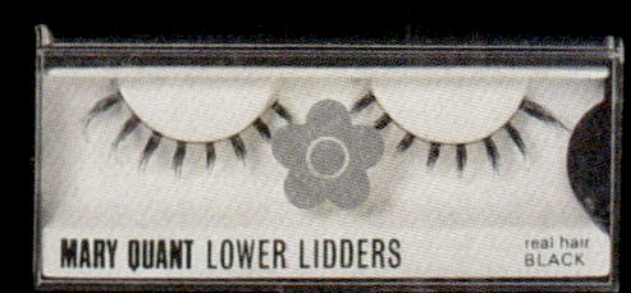

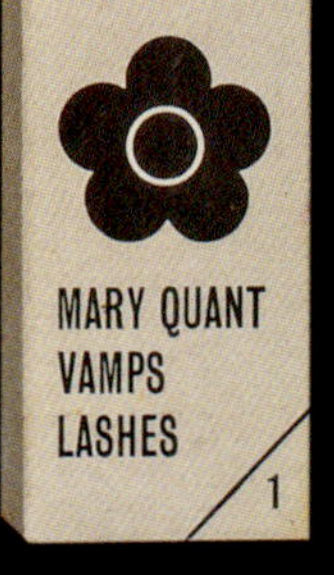

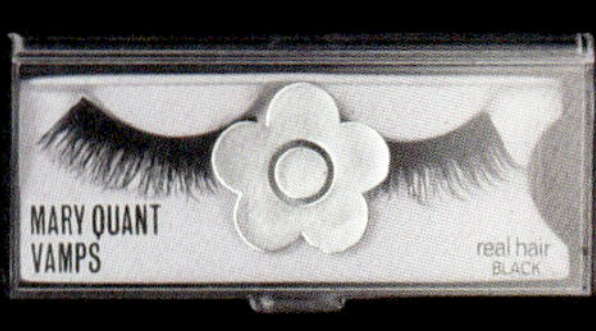

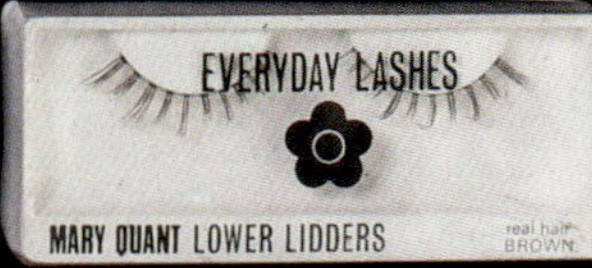

Items from the first makeup range, c.1967.

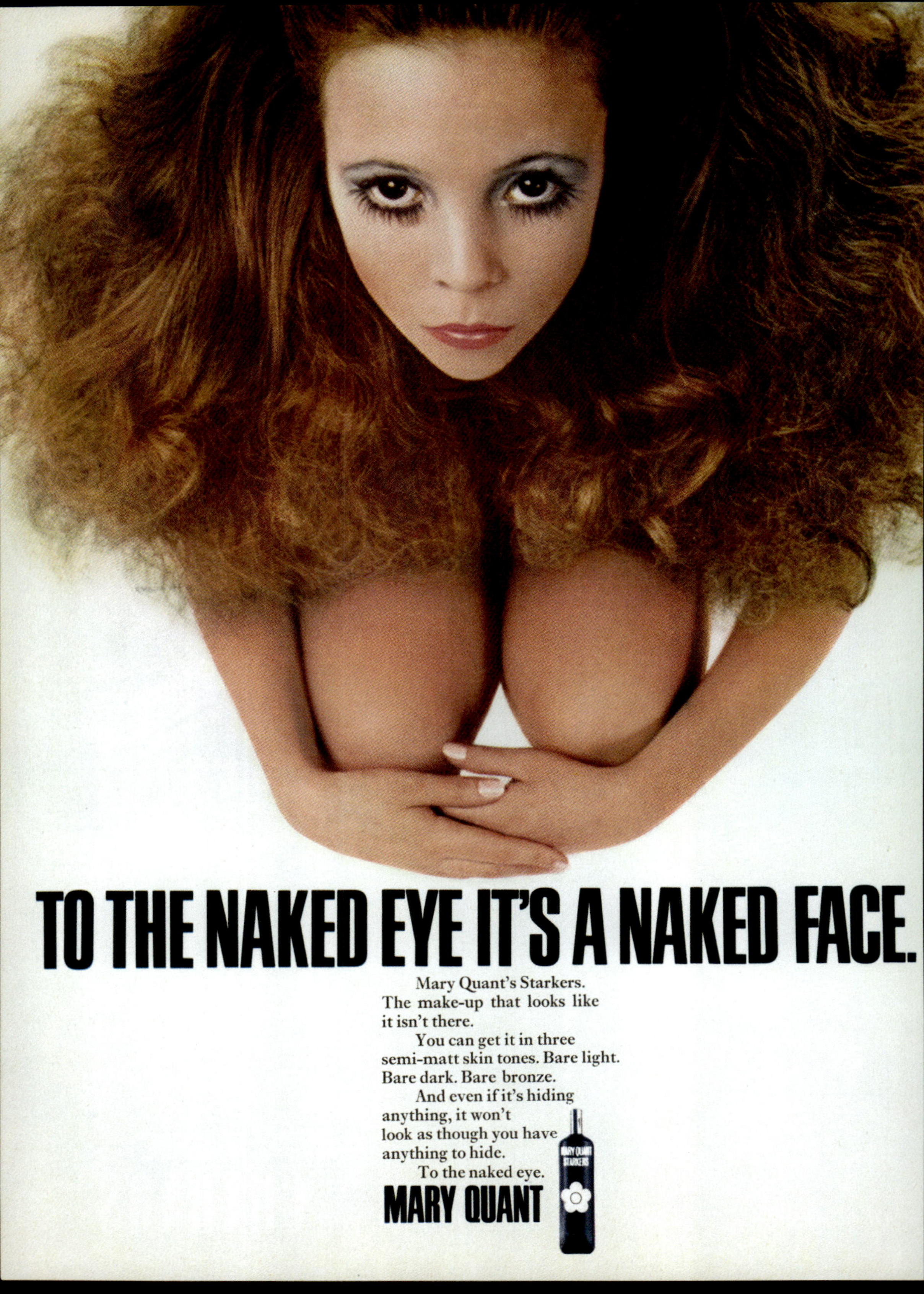

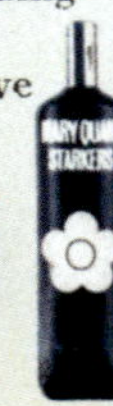

Advertisement for Quant's 'Starkers' foundation, featuring the American supermodel Penelope Tree.

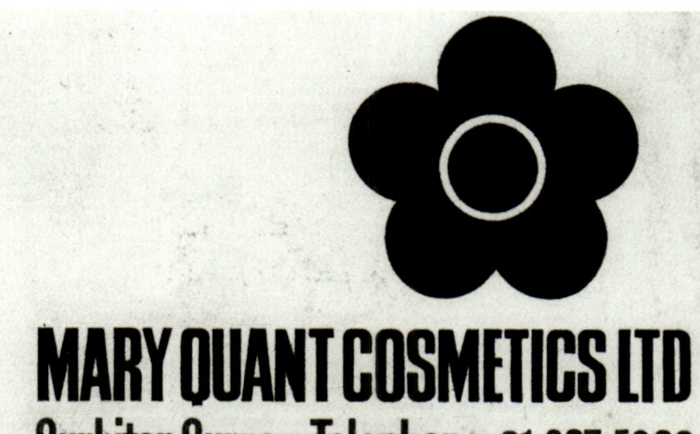


```
NEW  COLOURS  FROM  QUANT

Two for the lips - PLUM JULEP  and COOL CLARET.
Clear, clean colours that give lips that 'just
bitten' look.  Colour that blends into the natural
lip colour, leaving lips looking dark, moist and
shiny.  Great shades to wear with Jeepers Peepers Eyes.

Plum Julep  -  sunburnt plum
Cool Claret - deep bronzed peach
Both  9s.11d.

Six for the nails - great new pearly colours, w th
more colour power than ever before.  Bright, bold
colours - the names say all.

Brazen Bronze      -      pearled-up fudge
Wanton Wine        -      delicious offbeat mauve
Potent Pink        -      pretty powerful pink
Crazy Crimson      -      light spicy red
Provoke Peach      -      powerful, over-ripe
Ripe Red           -      red with a dash of pink


Titch Nail Polish  5s.11d.
```

Directors: Mary Quant, Alexander Plunket Greene, Archie McNair, Stanley Picker (USA), Brian Baldock

Circular announcing the addition of new colours to Quant's range of makeup, c.1968.

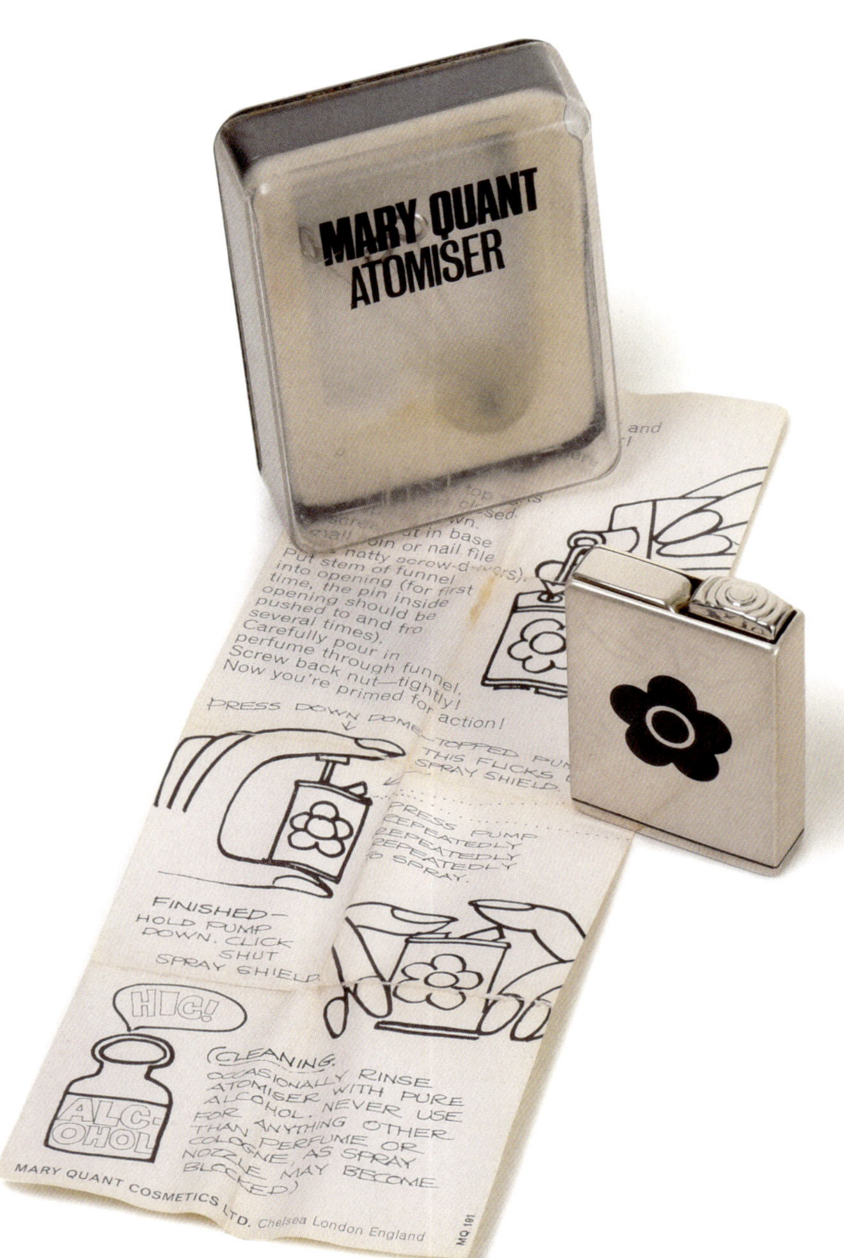

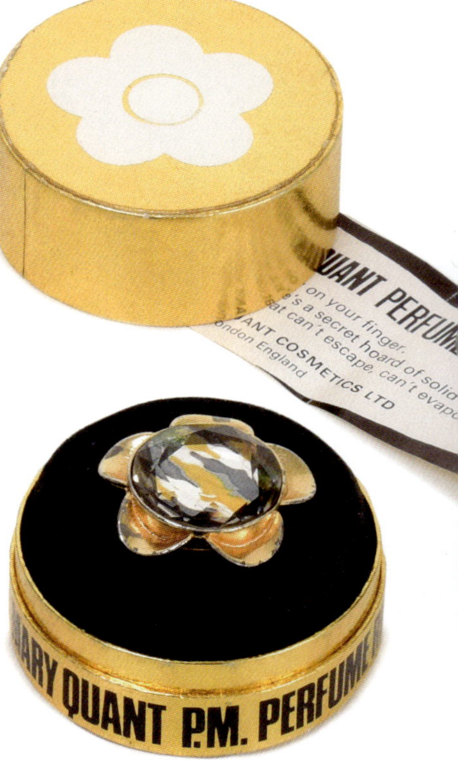

Finger ring containing solid perfume and an 'Atomiser' perfume spray. Both from
Quant's makeup range with their original packaging, c.1966-1967.

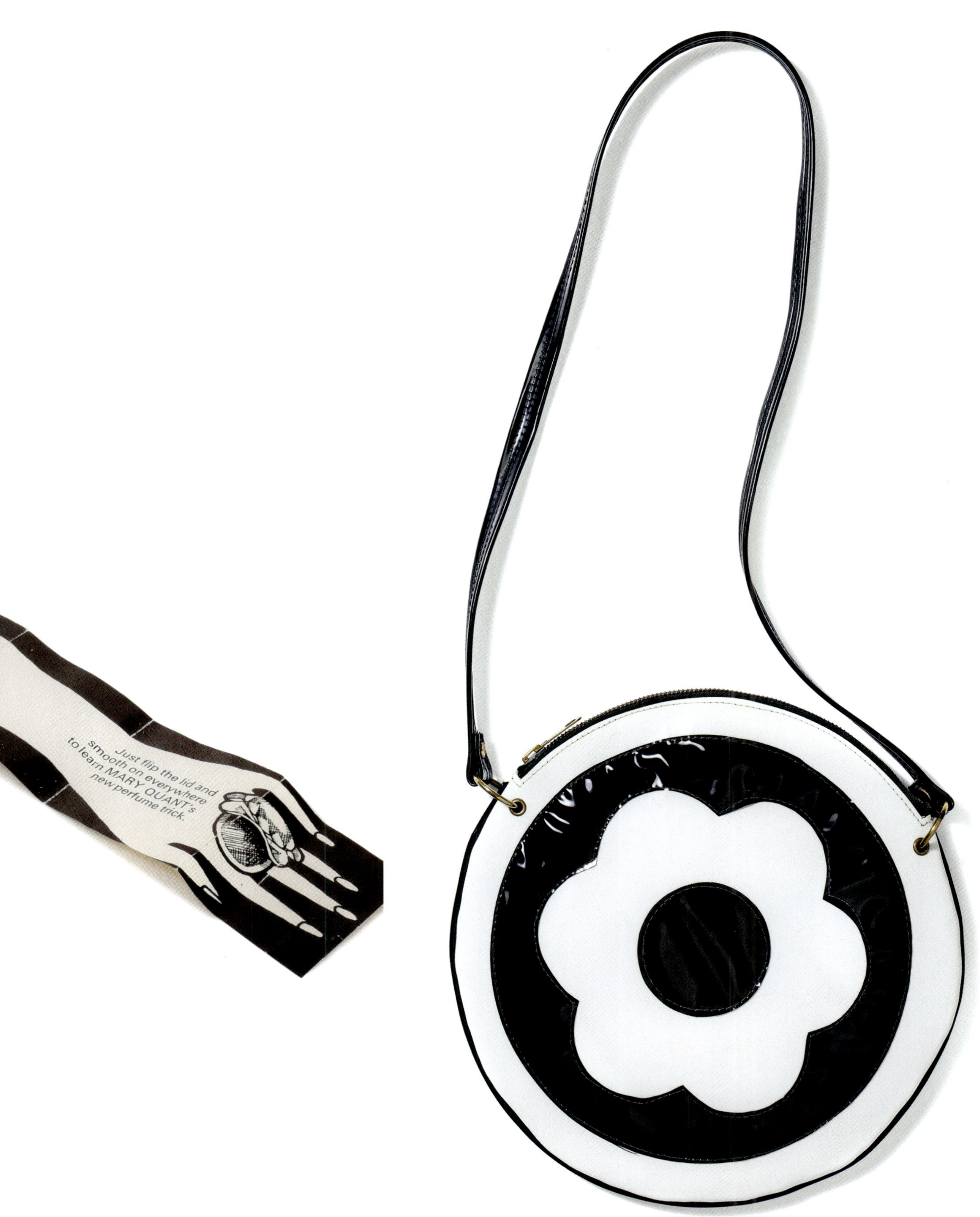

Op Art Daisy Shoulder bag made in PVC. Quant wrote that
this was her first design for a bag, 1965.

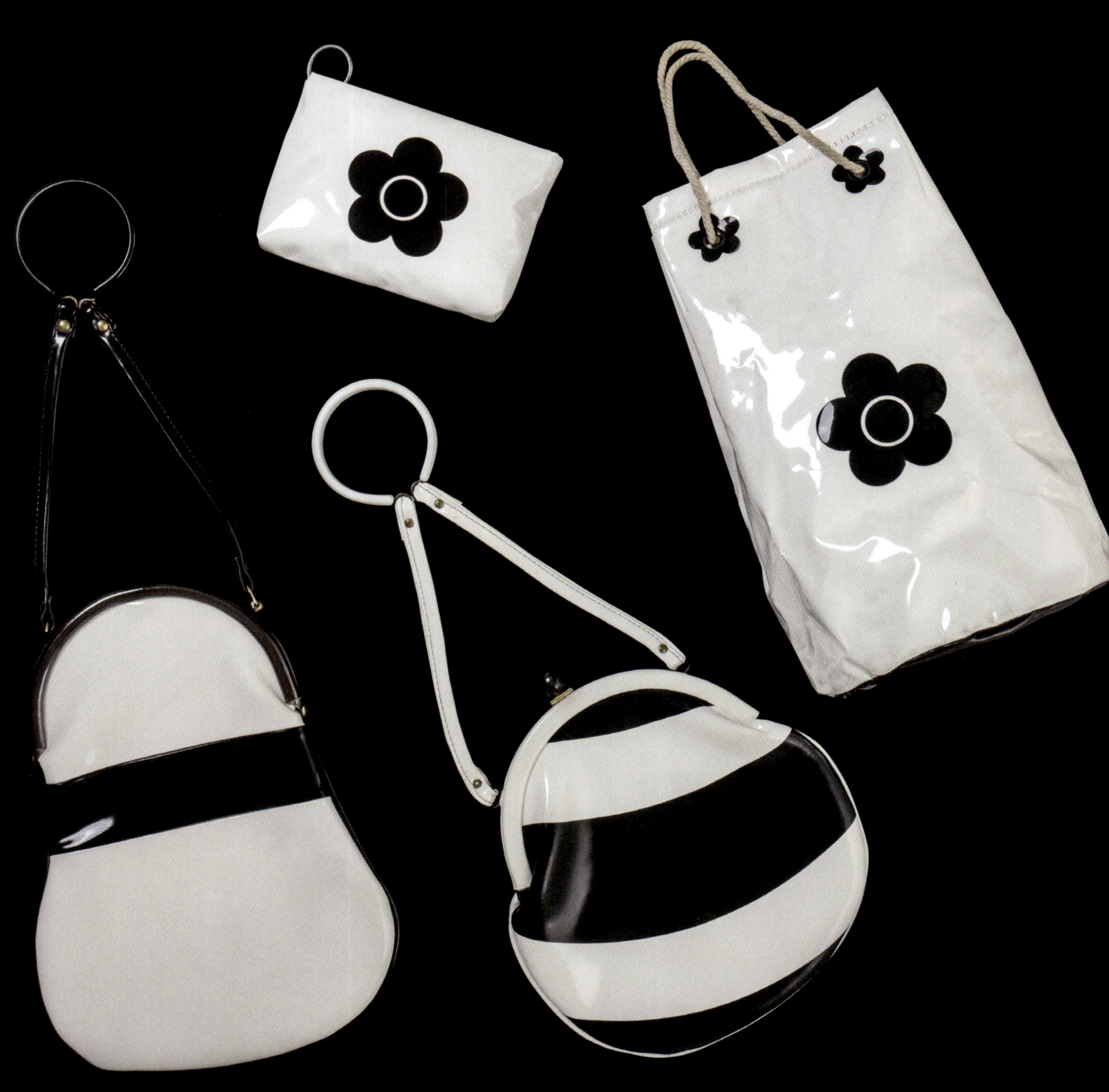

Group of Op Art hand and shoulder bags in PVC, all 1965-1966.

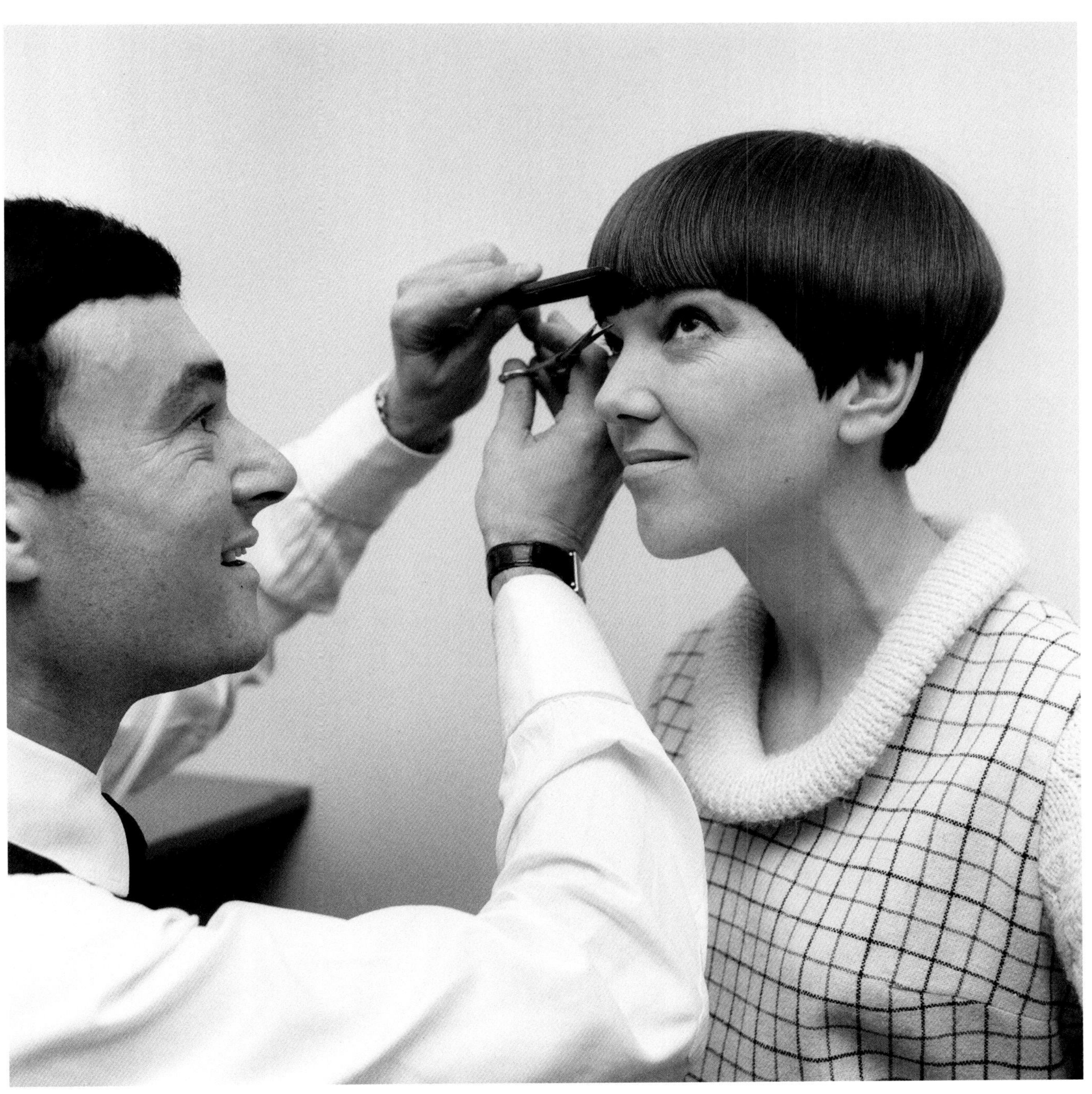

Quant being given the famous 'Five Point Cut' hairstyle by Vidal Sassoon, 1964.

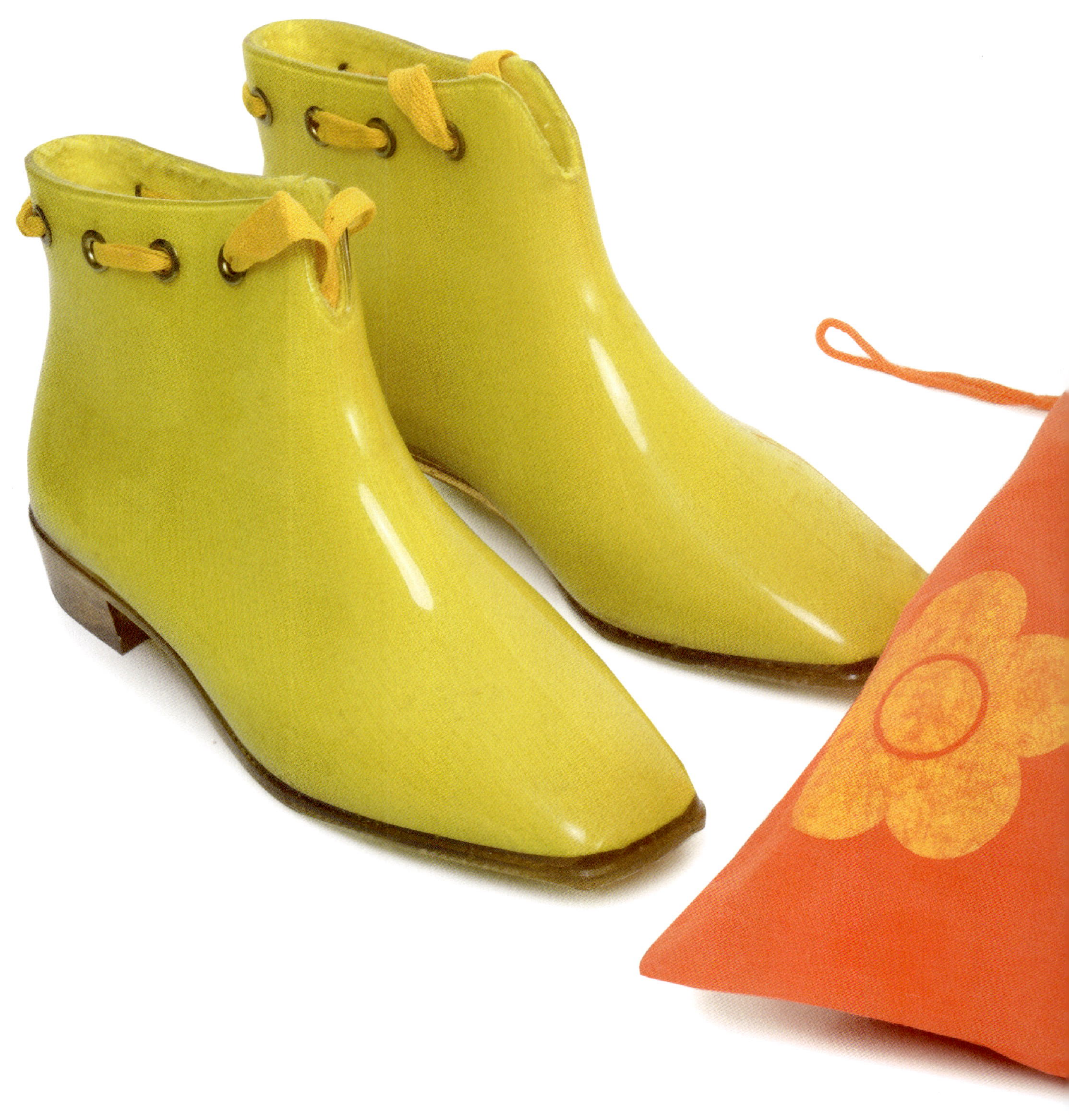

Quant Afoot plastic boots and packaging.

Quant with a group of models at the launch of the Quant Afoot range of
extruded moulded plastic shoes, 1967.

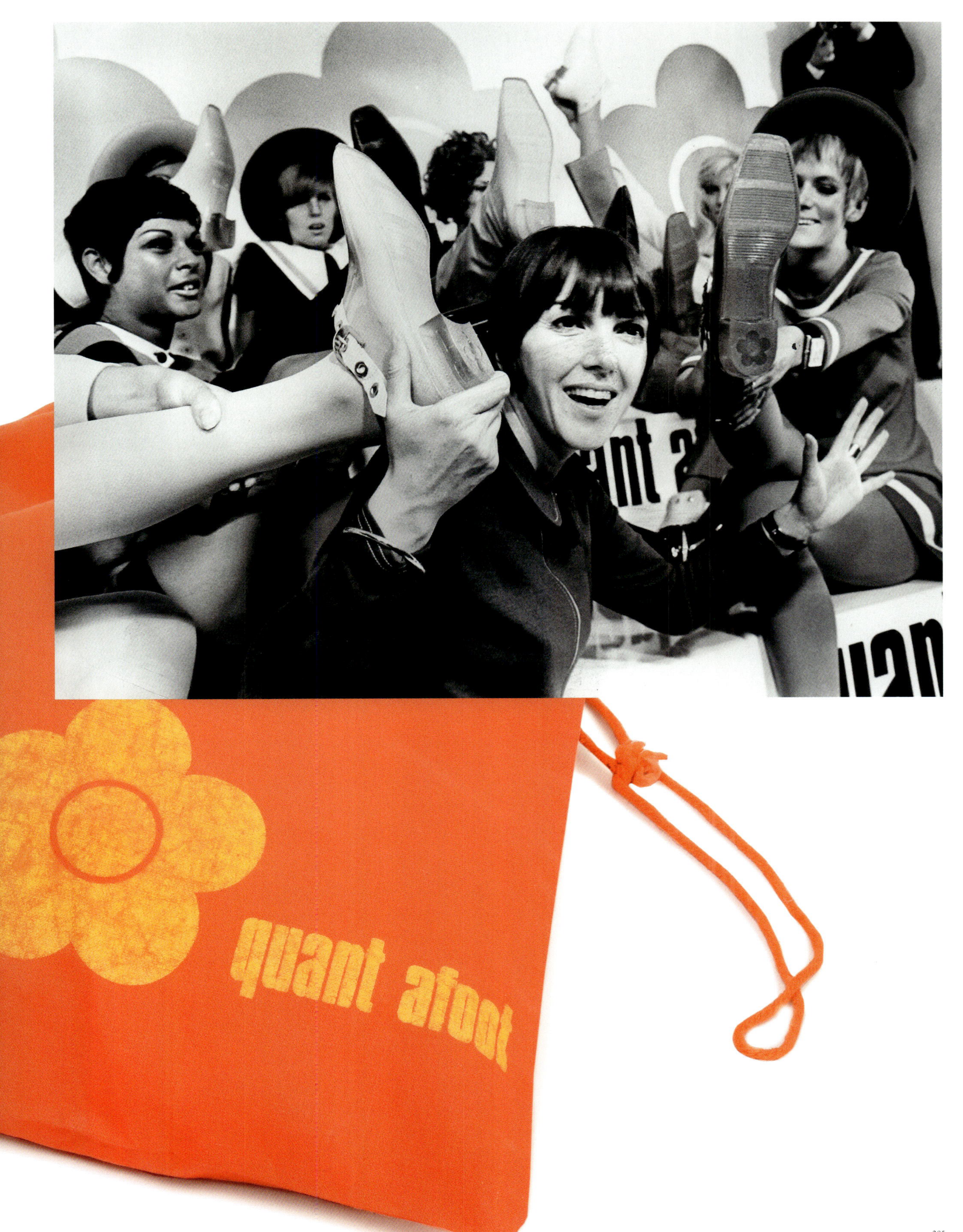
quant afoot

TERENCE CONRAN:
HABITAT 1964–1970

LIKE QUANT, TERENCE CONRAN spent much of the late 1950s and early 1960s extending and consolidating the various components of his nascent empire. Conran Fabrics and the Conran Design Group were added to Conran Contracts in 1956. The Design Group worked across the board, from graphic, product and furniture to exhibition and interior design, a diversity of talent which eventually enabled Conran to realise his personal vision of the 'good life' through the vehicle of Habitat. In 1961 Conran moved his offices and the Design Group's studio to a new base in a former school in Hanway Place, located in central London near the junction of Oxford Street with Tottenham Court Road. Part of the site was used as a showroom for the company's new designs, many of which were intended for both the domestic and contract markets.

THE FINAL INGREDIENT necessary to complete this powerful corporate mix was added in 1963 when Conran relocated the company's manufacturing base to a new purpose-built factory in Thetford, Norfolk. The factory was built for him by the London County Council (LCC) under the Expanding Town Scheme, one of many attempts by the authorities to persuade business and industry to relocate outside the overcrowded metropolitan area. The incentive in Conran's case was this factory, built by the LCC to his requirements, which was then rented out to him on a 99-year lease. An additional bonus, necessary to cement the deal, was new housing, again built by the LCC, enabling the relocation of 80 of Conran's more essential employee's and their families in Thetford. Perhaps surprisingly, on the occasion of the new factory's formal opening, Paul Reilly, then Director of the Council of Industrial Design, an organisation not always in tune with Conran's approach to design, perceptively expressed the view that Conran's work was as 'invigorating as Mary Quant's in female fashion'. Now, with both an effective business structure and a modern and efficient means of production to hand, he was at last able to initiate his concept of Habitat, the germ of which he had steadily nurtured ever since the revelation of French culture had overwhelmed him on his first visit there with Michael and Cynthia Wickham in 1953.

THE RELATIVELY SHORT period of time Conran allowed to lapse between the relocation of his manufacturing base to Thetford in 1963 and the opening of Habitat in May 1964, is probably indicative of his eagerness to at last realise his retail vision, which, for him, had been a long time coming. Having first secured finance for the project and convinced others to support it, he needed above all to identify and secure the right location for a retail outlet. His final choice was in a newly built development of flats and shops, situated at Brompton Cross, on the junction of Draycott Avenue with London's Brompton Road and the Fulham Road, then mainly a fashionable, up-and-coming residential area, which was also, importantly, within easy walking distance from the King's Road, Chelsea.

THE POSITION CONRAN chose for the first Habitat, a location initially without the busy passing footfall usually considered necessary for a successful retail business, is indicative of his vision of Habitat as a specific venue for destination shopping, rather than just another high street store. Quant had set the precedent when she opened Bazaar in the King's Road, then, in the mid 1950s, a commercial backwater and most unlikely location for a radical new fashion venture. Similarly, in 1964, Barbara Hulanicki set up her first Biba boutique in a former chemist's shop, which was situated some way down Abingdon Road, in what was largely a residential area off Kensington High Street. Quite as fearless, Quant's male counterpart, John Stephen, after his first boutique for men burnt down, opened his second, His Clothes, in 1957, then the one bright spot in an otherwise dirty, dingy and rundown Carnaby Street. Like them, Conran did not spend a great deal on advertising, he didn't really need to. Instead, he dealt as deftly with the media as he had with *House & Garden* at the beginning of his career. More importantly, through his numerous influential contacts, a large element of word of mouth was involved in spreading news of Habitat to the right target group. That way he ensured Habitat was always very much 'in with the in-crowd'. The same aspirational young cohort that wore Quant's clothes generally shared a new irreverent view of the world and were beginning to lead a very different way of life to that of their parents and grandparents, one indeed very similar to Conran's own. They were the target group Habitat was primarily intended for, 'switched on people,' young, affluent and largely urban, the readers of the new colour supplements and lifestyle magazines such as *Nova* and patrons of the bistros and brasseries then mushrooming around London.

SELECTING THE STOCK for Habitat must have been pure joy for Conran; although others were involved, it was chosen, as he put it, 'with one pair of eyes.' [49] If Quant had initially visualised Bazaar's stock as a 'bouillabaisse,' a rich and piquant mix, it was surely the merchandise for Habitat which more relevantly fulfilled that brief. Conran's selection was strongly influenced by memories of his first 'overwhelming' encounter in 1953 with daily life in France, particularly: 'the simple unpretentious but abundant displays on stalls and in shops ... everyday things – stoneware, terracotta, pottery, pots and pans affordable by all.' [50]

HE ESPECIALLY REMEMBERED the joy he had experienced at the 'plenty' of those ironmongers shops in France back in the early 1950s and also of the French warehouses he had visited in his search for products; he wanted to try to recreate that feeling in Habitat.

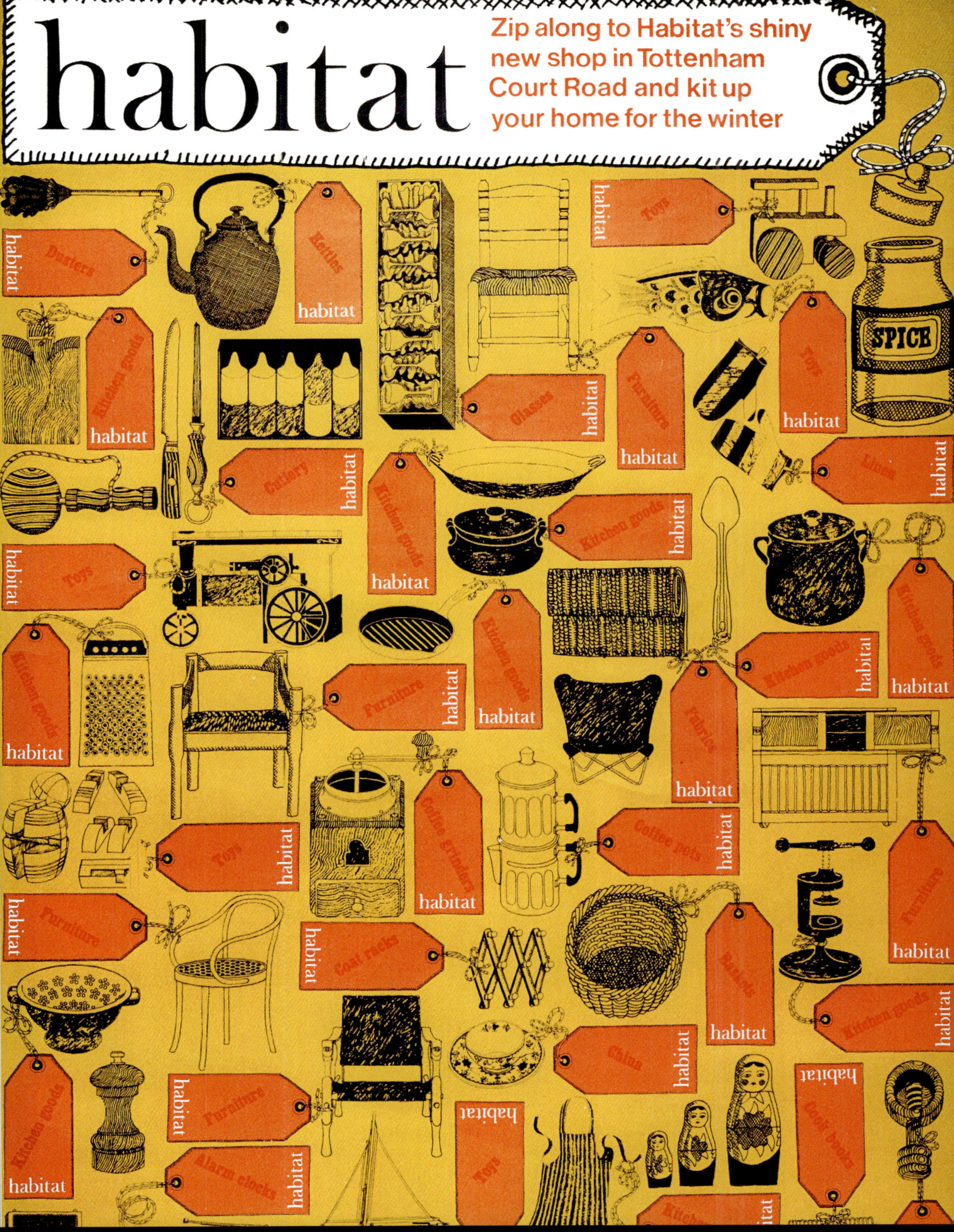

Advertising poster for Habitat, designed by Virginia Clive-Smith and illustrated by Juliet Glynn Smith, 1965.

ALTHOUGH CONRAN OFTEN expressed his appreciation for the work of the Bauhaus, ever since Bryanston and the influence of teachers like Charles Handley-Read and Don Potter, who taught him sculpture, pottery and metal work, he'd had something of an affinity with the Arts and Crafts movement. It is perhaps necessary to understand Conran's realisation of his vision in founding Habitat to, arguably, see him and his work as part of a continuum from William Morris and Christopher Dresser to Arthur Lasenby Liberty in the nineteenth century and Ambrose Heal to Gordon Russell in the twentieth. All, like Conran, were inspired retailers with a vision of something more than mere shopkeeping, and most had themselves been professional designers and hands-on makers. Fiona MacCarthy succinctly placed Conran within what is an essentially British approach to design and lifestyle when she wrote:

'I think Terence likes the simplicity of the Bauhaus and its vision of improving society, but he also has an English sense of comfort. There is a generosity and feel for the Mediterranean in him, just as much as there is a Northern European Bauhaus influence. That taste is expressed in his own home.' [51]

HABITAT WAS ORIGINALLY very much an expression of Conran's personal vision, the retail environment as 'Gesamtkunstwerk', a total work of art. It was simultaneously an ever-changing installation and a 'happening'. As in Quant's Bazaar, shopping in the first Habitat stores was an improvised event in which customers and staff were self-consciously both actors and audience in a performance of incident and event, without either a defined plot or narrative. This was also true of London's other well known Pop emporiums, whose locations such as Carnaby Street, the King's Road and Portobello Road, provided vivid backdrops for the street theatre and carnival that was Swinging London.

HABITAT'S ETHOS WAS light and bright with the 'free to browse' and 'serve yourself' ambience of the then relatively new phenomenon of the supermarket. The store's revolutionary overall style was derived from that of a wholesale warehouse, in particular, one located amid the bustle, colour and movement of a traditional marketplace. Above all, informality was the word. Displays of household goods and kitchenware, punctuated by heaps of brightly coloured enamel teapots, mugs and saucepans, were cheerful, colourful, intriguing, thought-provoking and generally stacked high and plentifully, with little or nothing held in reserve in stockrooms.

TRUE TO CONRAN'S great interest in the culinary arts, among the more memorable items of Habitat's extensive range of kitchenalia – such as the notorious 'chicken brick' – was an impressive assemblage of Elizabeth David's *Batterie de Cuisine*, suitably displayed in the catalogue on and against a rustic nineteenth-century French dresser. He also stocked her classic cookery books and her series of mini booklets on particular aspects of culinary skill. These were complemented by a group of highly original restaurant guides for

London, Paris and New York called *À la Carte*, which consisted of facsimile menus from the great restaurants of those cities, which were printed on the reverse alongside the classic recipes with which each restaurant was famously associated. All were loosely held together in Pop styled folders. The guide for London was compiled by Conran's then wife, the cookery writer and journalist Caroline, who was later to be a great influence and support when Conran set up his series of acclaimed restaurants in the 1970s and 1980s.

THE VARIOUS DIVISIONS of Conran's organisation, more used to fulfilling external contracts, now came together to realise his ultimate design project. At the core of Habitat's stock were the various ranges of domestic furniture, conceived by Conran with the Design Group and made at the Thetford factory. Most, such as the radically simple Summa range, were of 'knock-down' construction and came flat-packed, an important innovation which both brought down prices and made transportation and storage simple and easy. But in the early Habitat stores, furniture was usually shown fully made-up and displayed in imaginatively designed room settings, which enticingly suggested not only where and how items might be used, but also with what. Against the generally pale woods or paint of the furniture, the bright upholstery glowed and the entire *mise en scène* was enhanced by the vivid Pop textiles, specially commissioned for Habitat by Conran Fabrics from talented designers such as Juliet Glynn Smith, Gillian Farr and Natalie Gibson. A plenitude of Pop posters were also available, from the decadence and eroticism of *fin de siècle* artists and illustrators like Aubrey Beardsley and Toulouse-Lautrec to the high Pop Art sensibility of Robert Indiana. Cheerfully scattered throughout the general displays were pieces of often provocative but amusing Pop paraphernalia, like the red and gold painted Victorian tin heater for Saveloy Sausages or 'fun' toys such as the Mamod fully working steam tractor and its various wagons, although there was a certain ambivalence about who it was intended for, the caption accompanying it reading: 'When father allows it, ideal for a boy aged 8 to 16 years'.

RIGHT FROM THE START, Conran also sourced and stocked many international design classics. Among them the Thonet bentwood chair, used in 1925 by Le Corbusier in the interior of the Pavillion de l'Espirit; the now-revered laminated rosewood and leather Armchair 670 and Ottoman 671 by Charles Eames, and, preportedly, Conran's favourite, the Karuselli by Kukkapuro. A somewhat more frivolous addition to the Habitat stock was the Peacock chair, hand-woven in rattan and bamboo. According to Conran's ironic sense of humour, it would apparently make 'even the poorest hovel seem like an oriental throne room'. [52]

THE DESIGN CLASSIC now especially associated with Habitat is Vico Magistretti's rush-seated Carimate chair of 1959. Often mistakenly called 'the Habitat chair', it proved so popular that Conran produced it under licence at the Thetford factory until the 1970s. While predominately available in red, it could also be purchased in several other colours or with a natural wood finish. Originally conceived as a vehicle for the expression of Conran's vision of the 'good life', one bought a lifestyle from Habitat, not merely a chair.

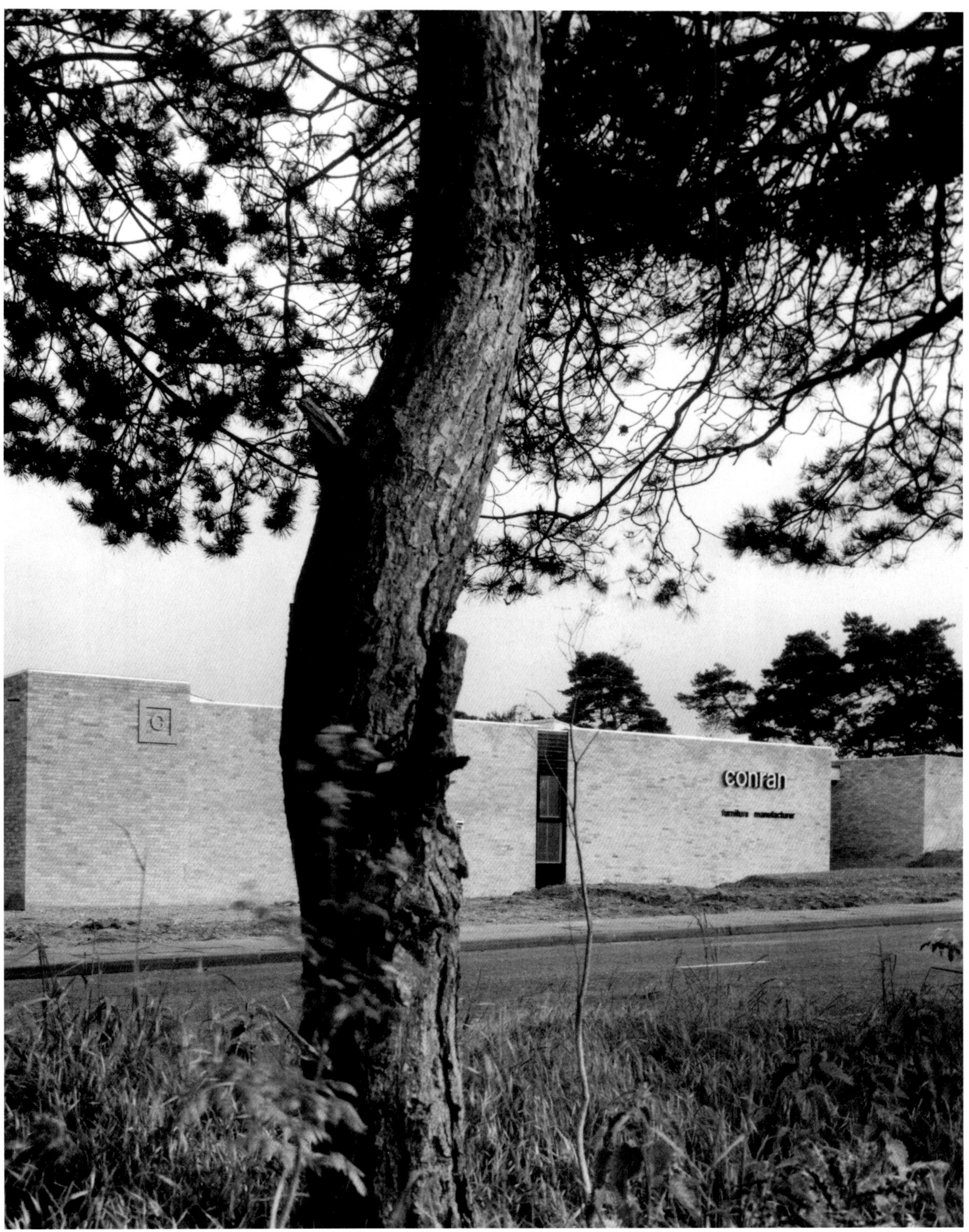

Conran's new factory in Thetford, Norfolk, opened in 1963.

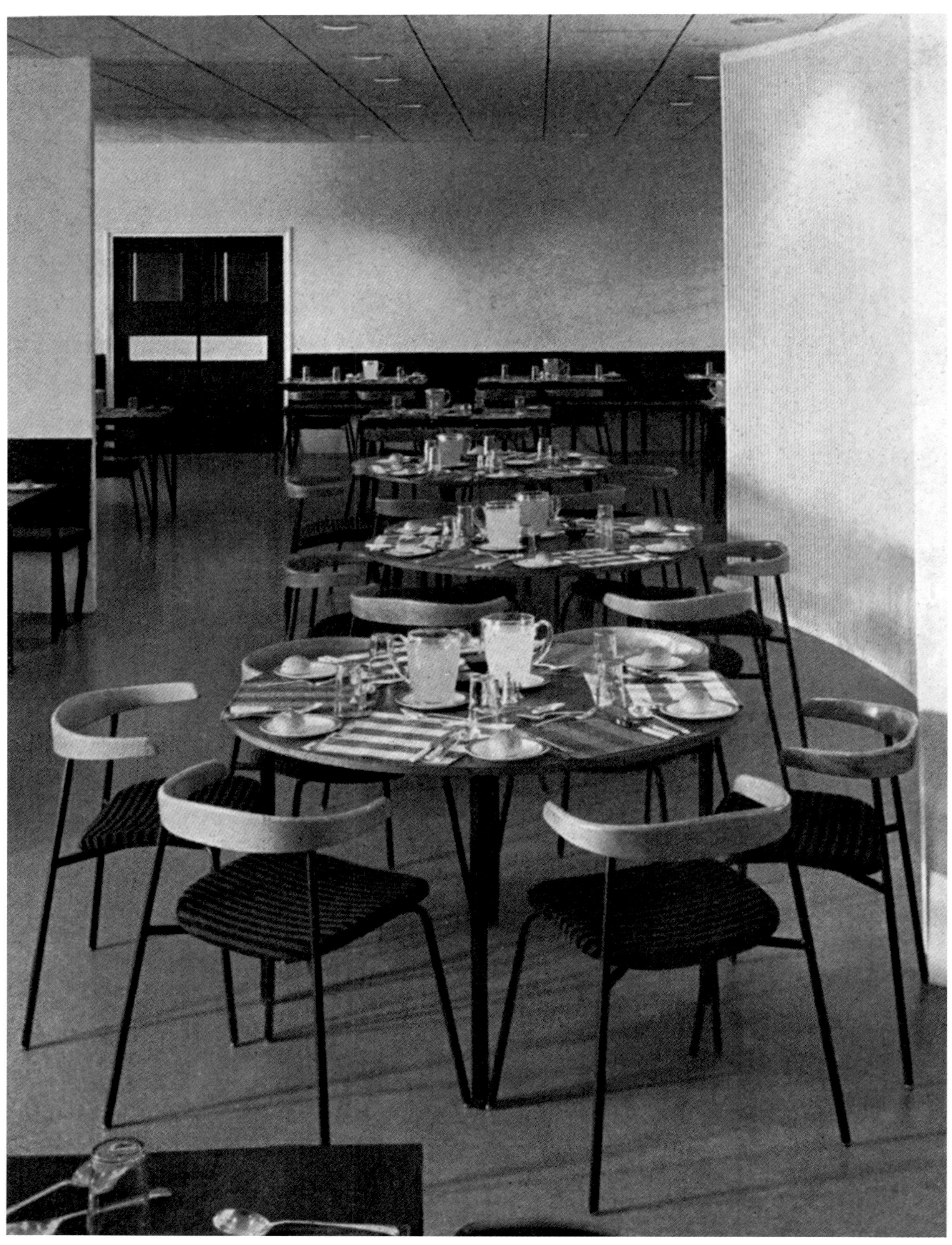

Interior of the Executive Canteen, the Gillette building, Isleworth. The Conran Design group, 1961.

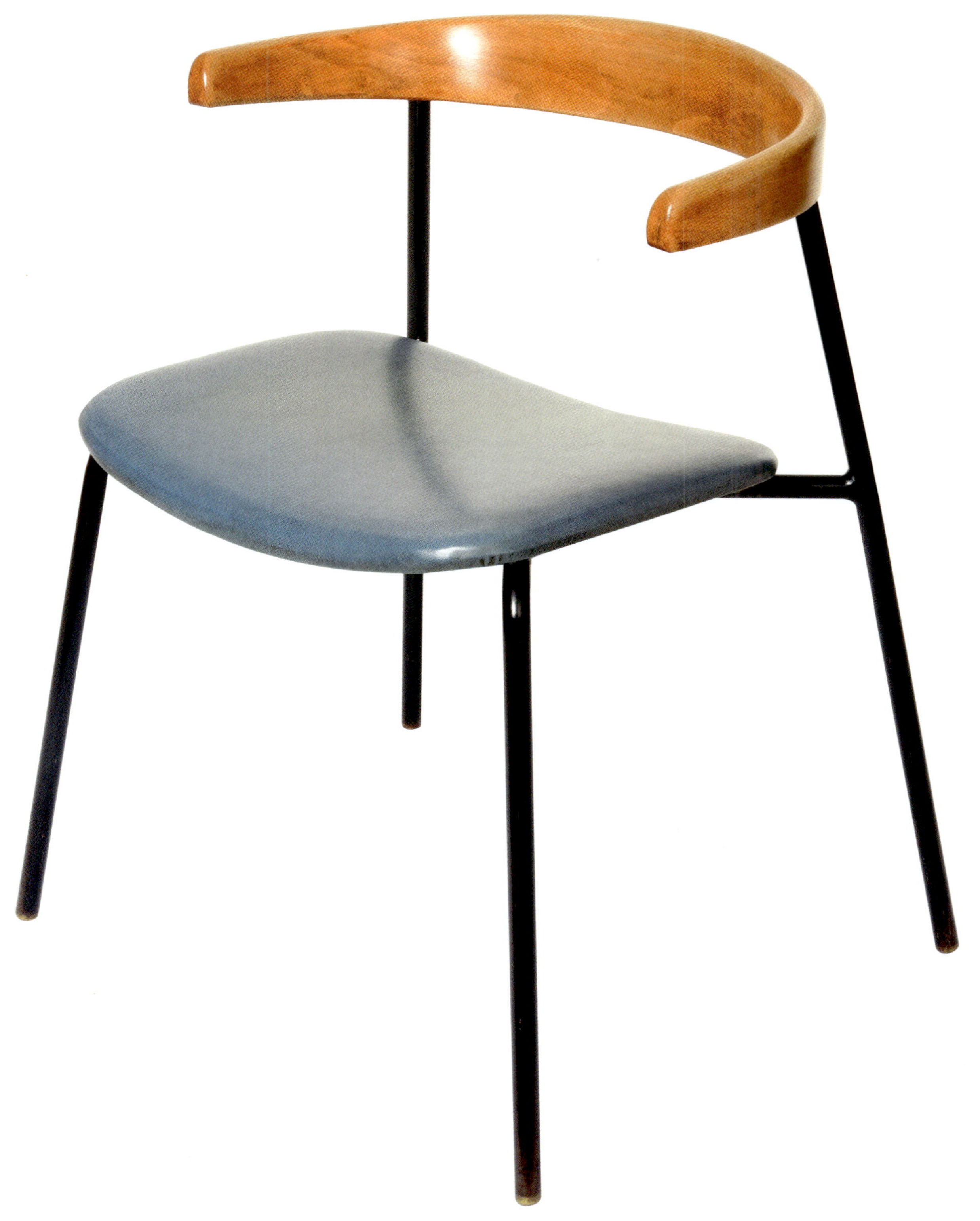

The C.20 stacking chair used in Gillette's Executive Canteen. Designed by Terence Conran and the Conran Design Group for Conran Furniture, c.1958. The chair was advertised in *House & Garden*, February 1959.

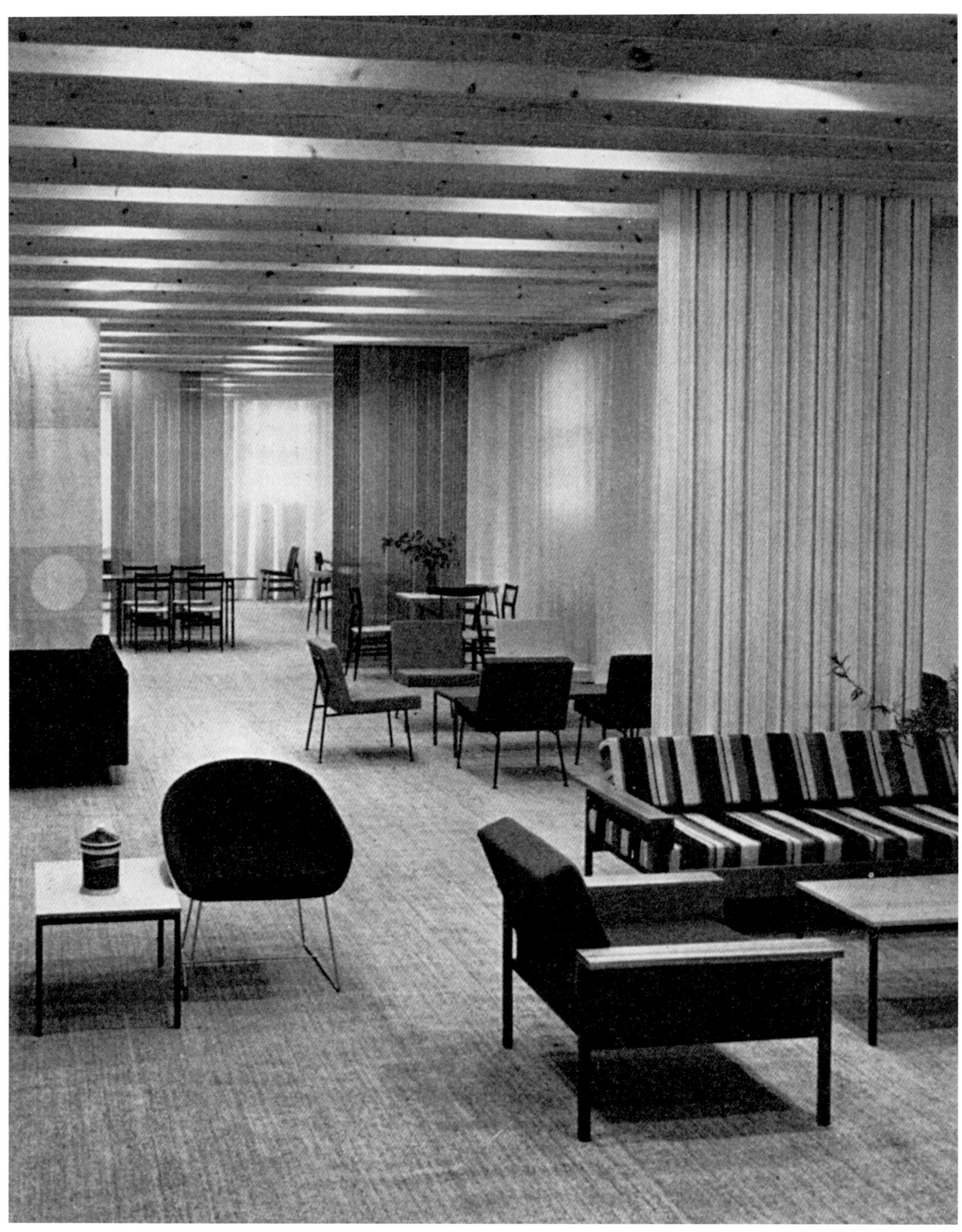

Interior of the Hanway Place showroom of Conran & Co. Ltd, 1961.

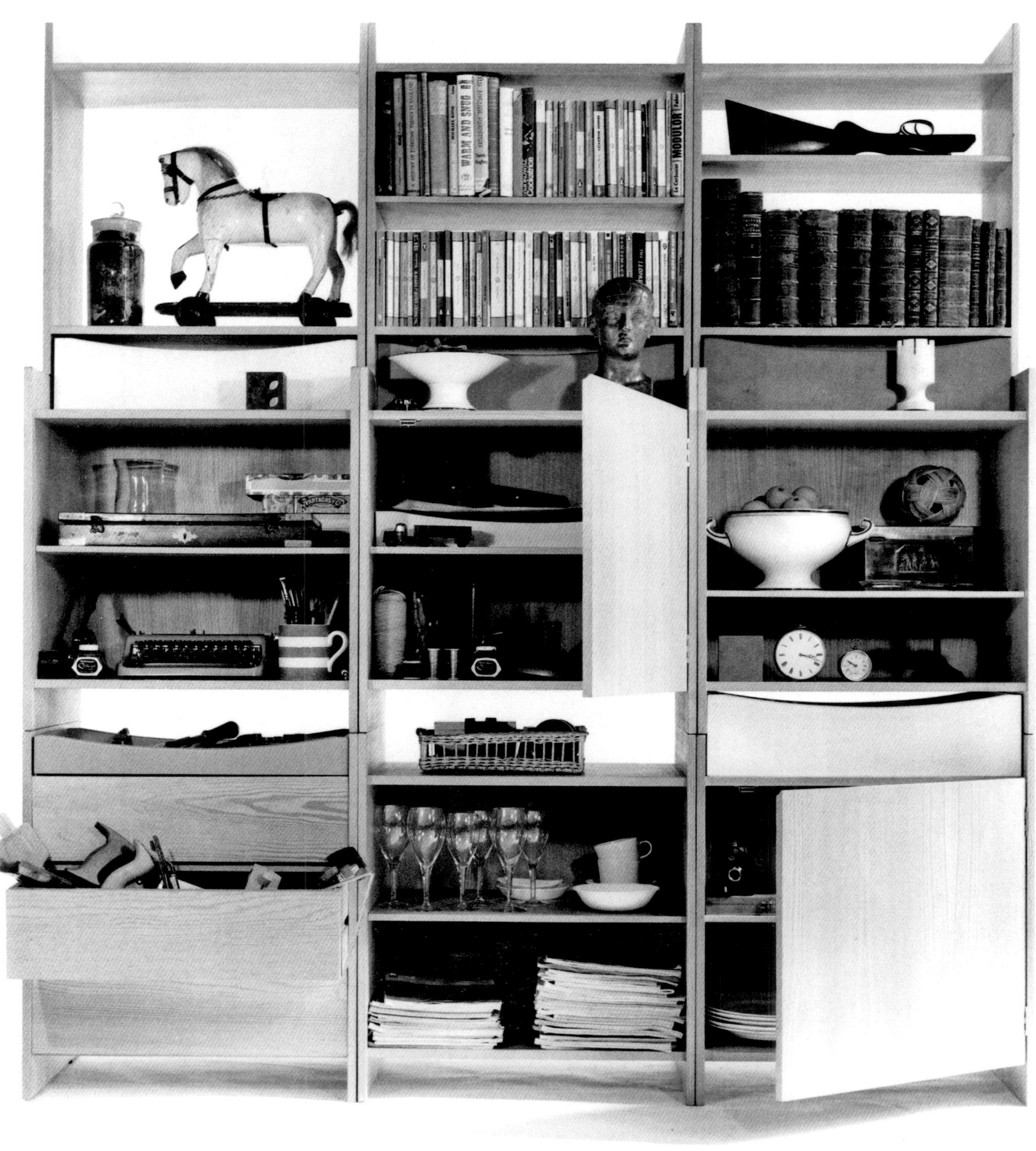

Knock-down storage units from the first Summa range. Designers: Terence Conran and the Conran Design Group for Conran Furniture, c.1962.

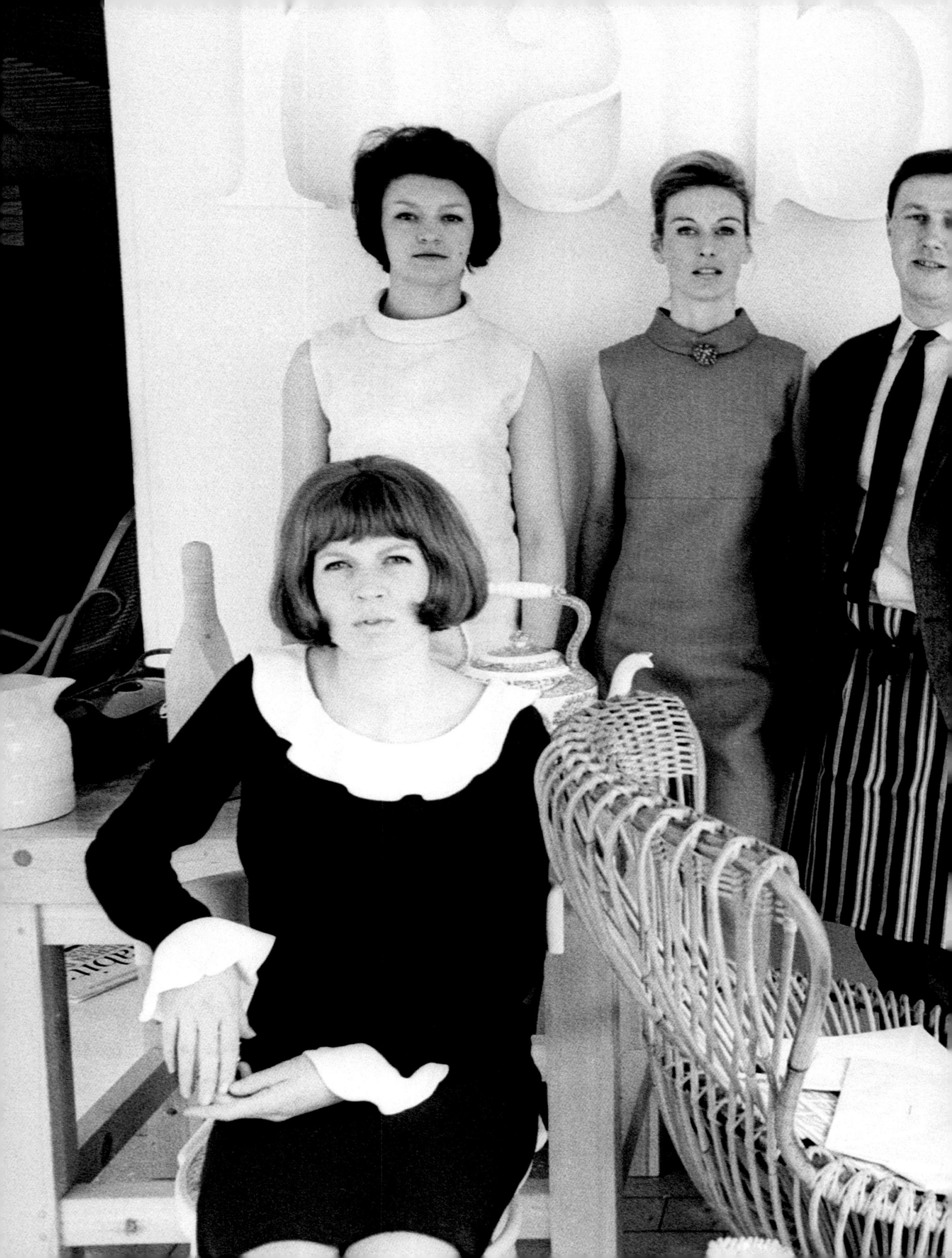

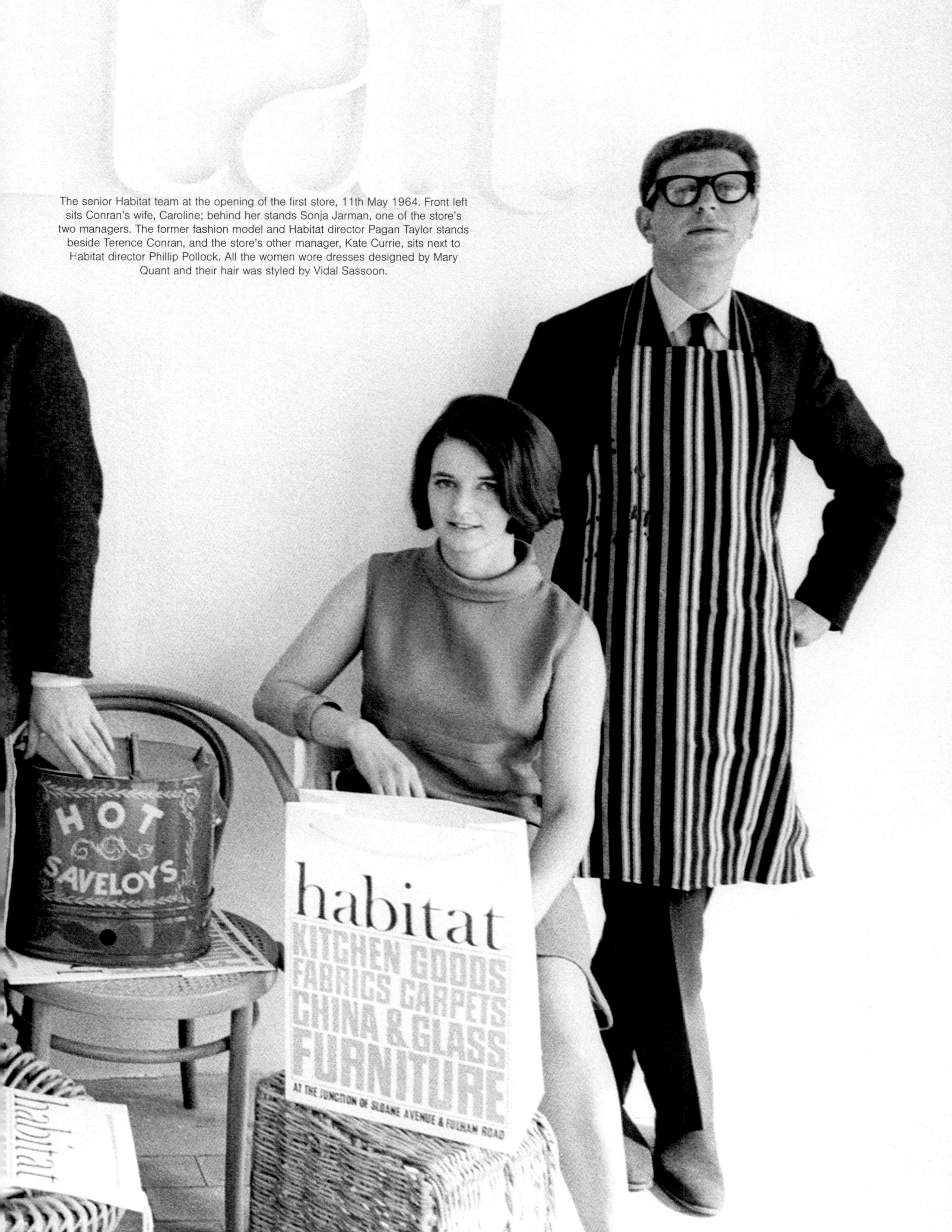

The senior Habitat team at the opening of the first store, 11th May 1964. Front left sits Conran's wife, Caroline; behind her stands Sonja Jarman, one of the store's two managers. The former fashion model and Habitat director Pagan Taylor stands beside Terence Conran, and the store's other manager, Kate Currie, sits next to Habitat director Phillip Pollock. All the women wore dresses designed by Mary Quant and their hair was styled by Vidal Sassoon.

Conran Furniture and Fabrics

This is the furniture that Conran makes. This is this furniture that fits the rooms that fill the flat or add up to the house where YOU live. It offers you who rent the flat (or bought the house) the chance to change and change your minds. Because this is the sofa that's also a bed, and these are the shelves for wherever you choose. And these are just some of the things that Conran make; send for our catalogues and see more designs and where to get them. Conran, Stephenson Way, Thetford, Norfolk.   Thetford 2441

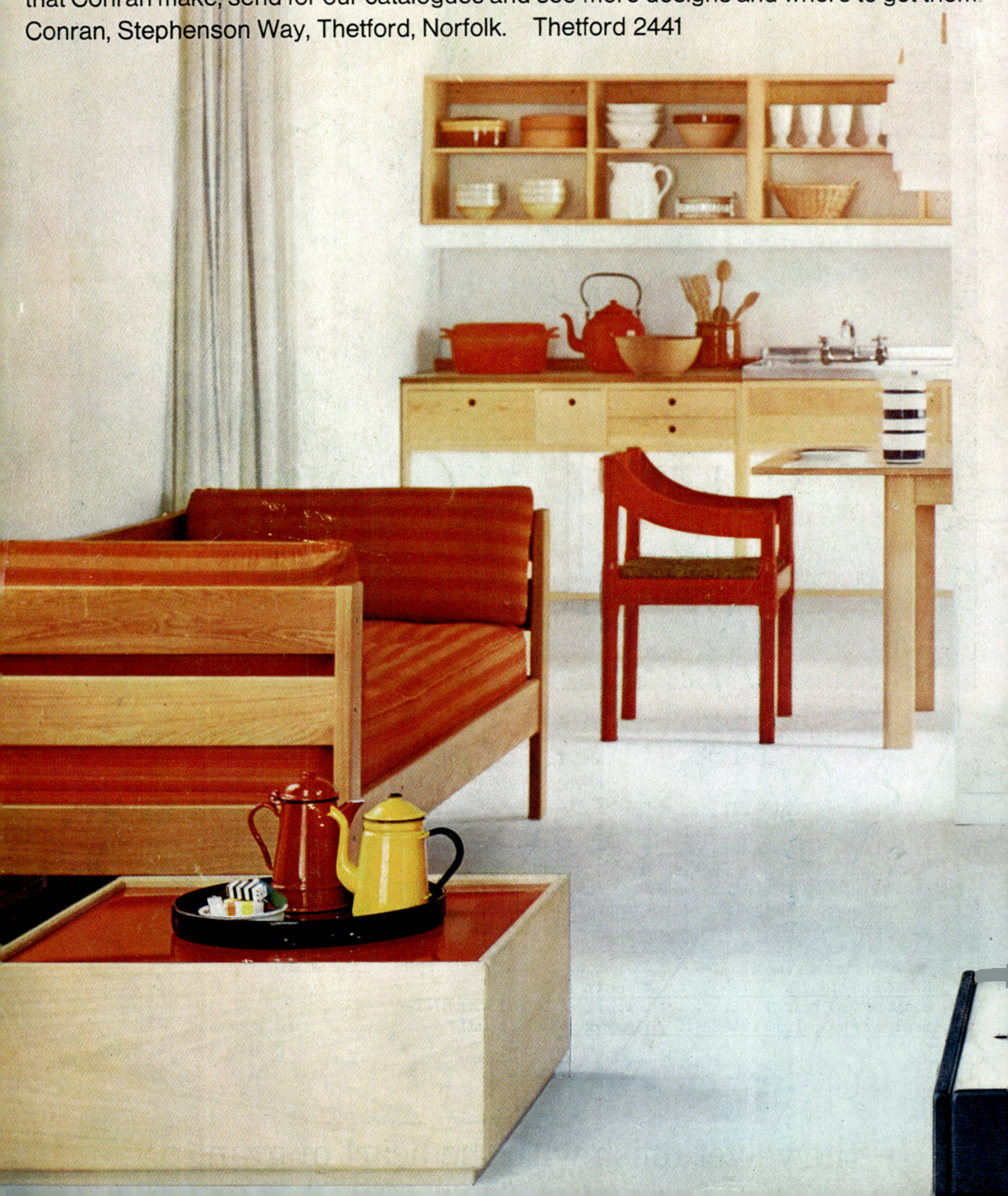

The front cover of *House & Garden* for August 1966, cleverly combined with the back cover, an advertisement for Conran Furniture and Fabrics. Together, they provide a perfect image of the look, style and atmosphere of the first Habitat. Appropriately the photography is by Conran's close friend and mentor, the photographer Michael Wickham.

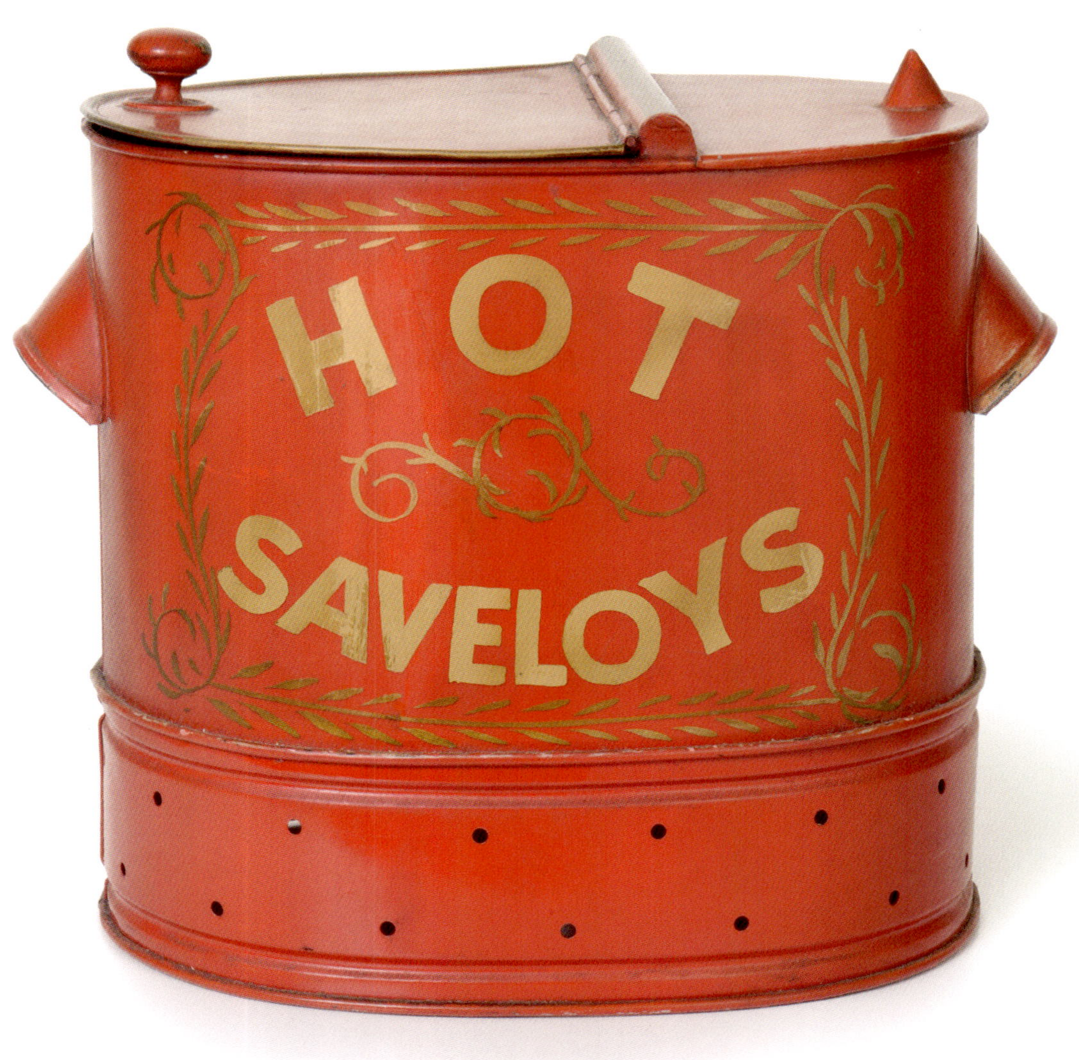

Victorian tin 'Saveloy' Heater. A classic piece of Pop paraphernalia, Conran had this heater reproduced for sale in the early Habitat stores.

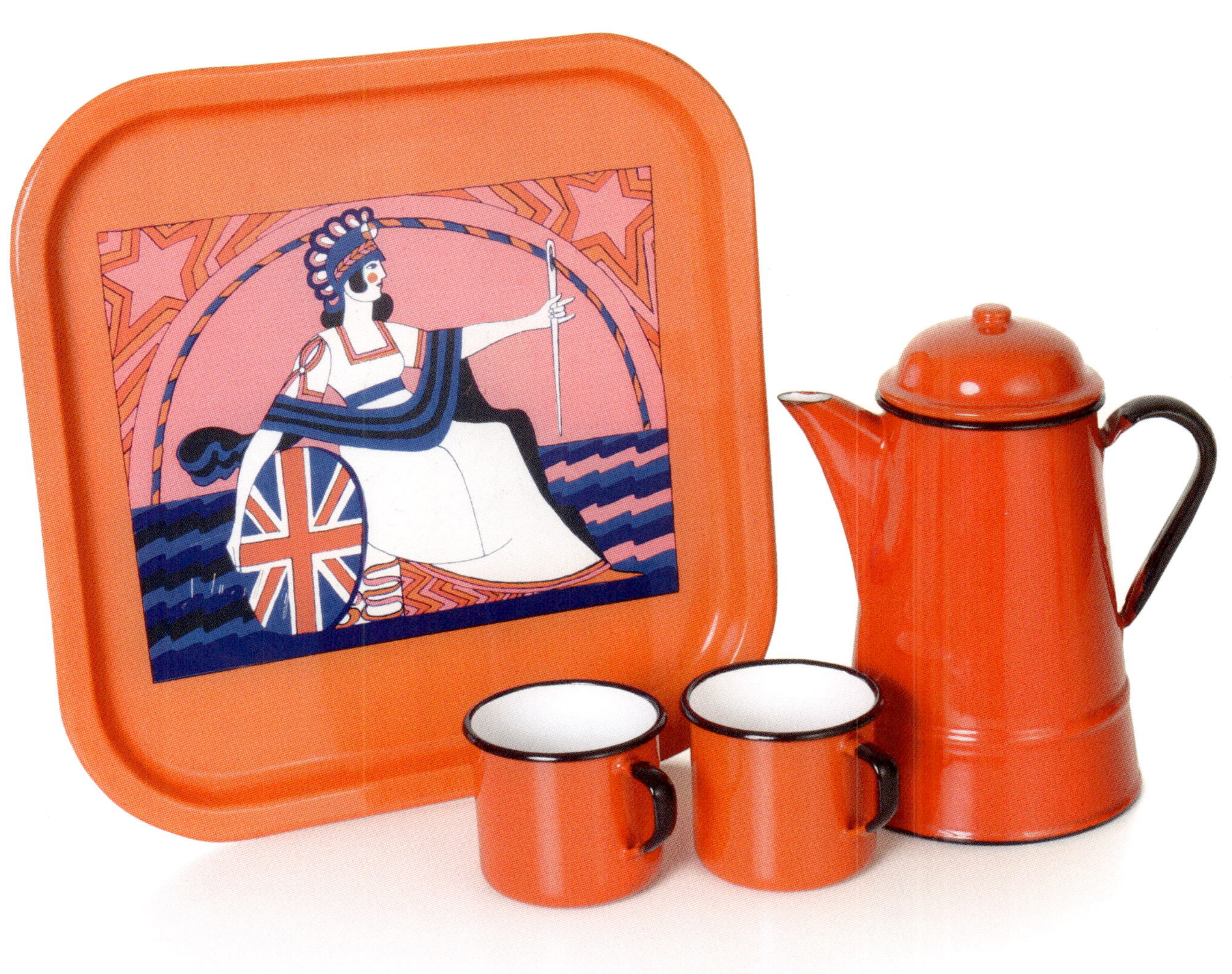

Group of enamelled tin ware. A ubiquitous and inexpensive material, tin was, alongside paper, the perfect expression of the throw-away Pop aesthetic. Habitat's range of inexpensive brightly coloured enamelled tin ware became a distinctive feature of the store. The tray was designed by Juliet Glynn Smith in 1966.

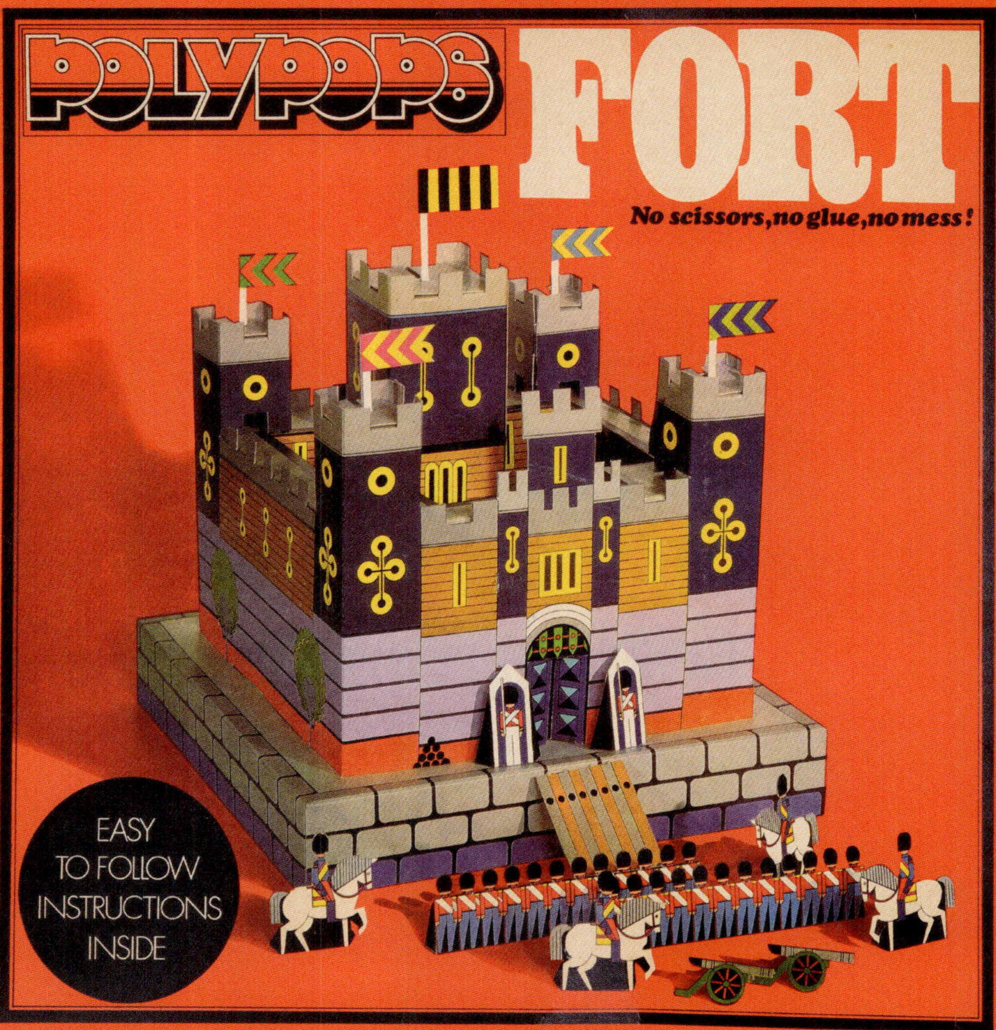

Self-assembly cardboard toy fort by the designer Cliff Richards for Polypops, 1969. Richards, one of the leading Pop designers of the 1960s, specialised in the use of paper and cardboard, creating brilliantly coloured products, from self-assembly toys to cardboard gift boxes. Many of his products were sold not only in Habitat, but also in Carnaby Street emporiums and many stores across the country.

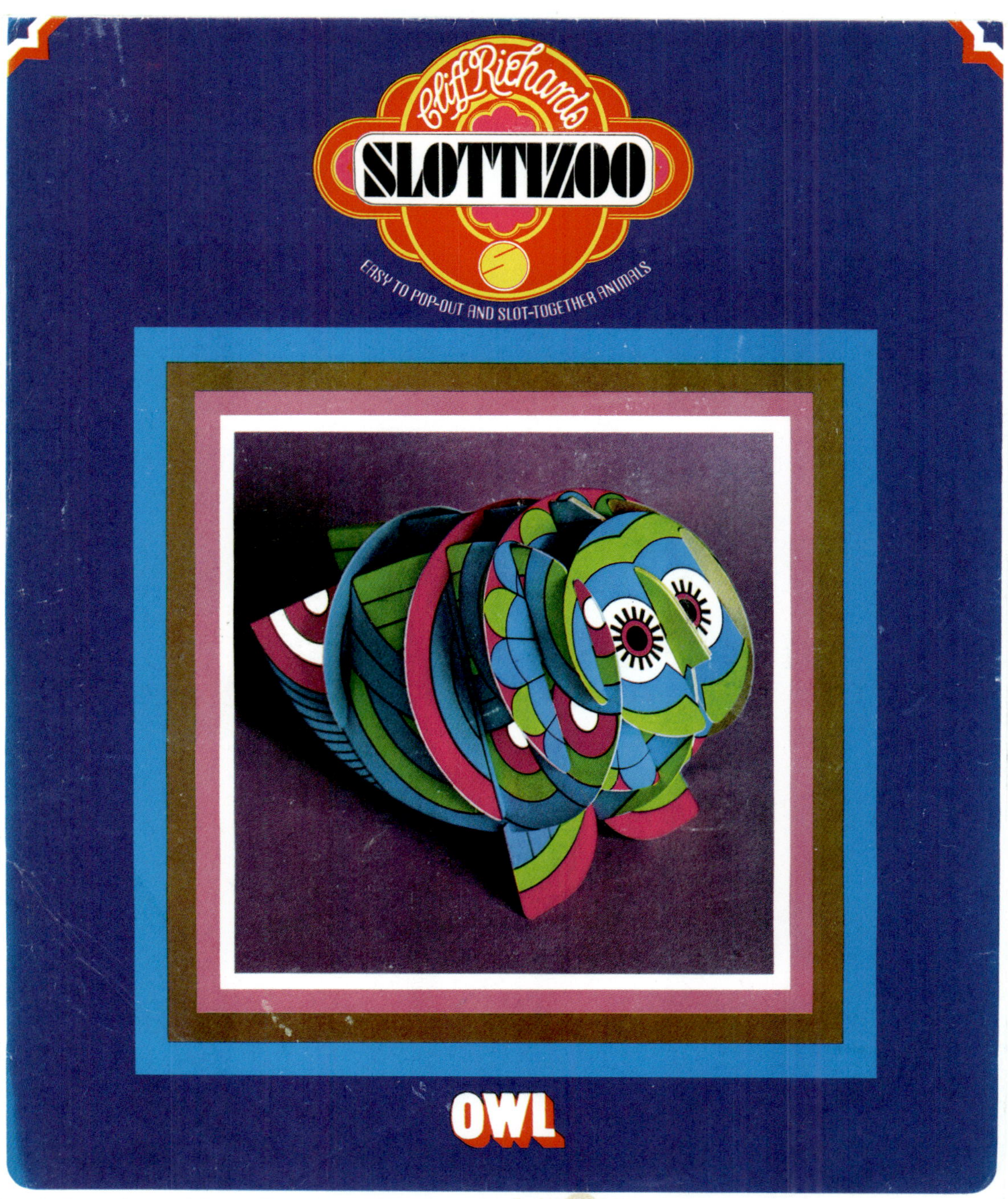

Cardboard owl from Cliff Richards' range of self-assembly Slottizoo toys, designed for Michael Stansfield Products, 1967.

Overleaf: Textile, 'Master Tuggies', screen-printed cotton. Designer: Gillian Farr for Conran Fabrics, 1963-1964.

Textile, 'Prince of Quince', screen-printed cotton. Designer: Juliet Glynn Smith for Conran Fabrics, 1965.

Textile, 'Jacks', screen-printed cotton. Designer: Juliet Glynn Smith for Conran Fabrics, 1964.

Textile, 'Tiddlywinks', screen-printed cotton. Designer: Juliet Glynn Smith for Conran Fabrics, 1964.

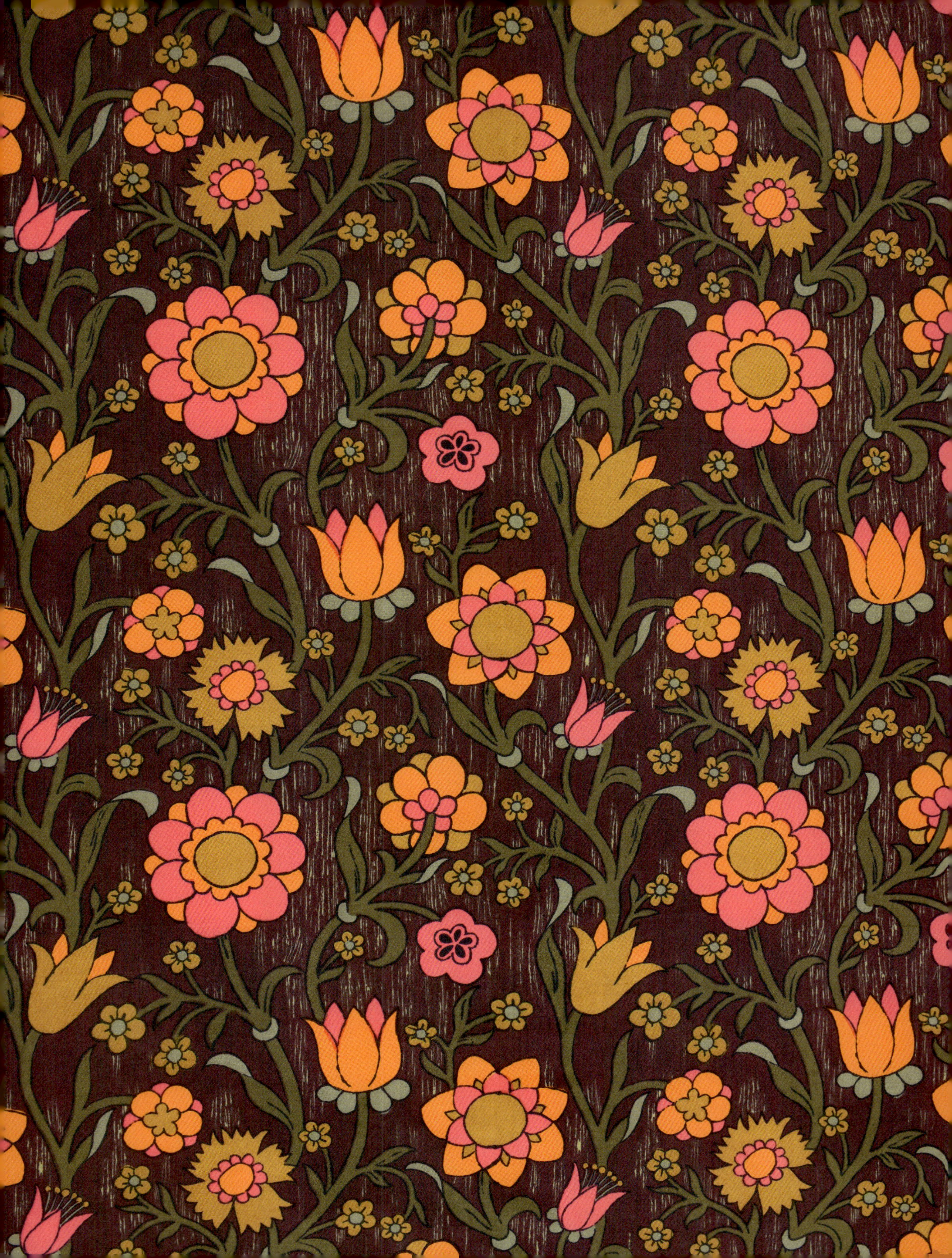

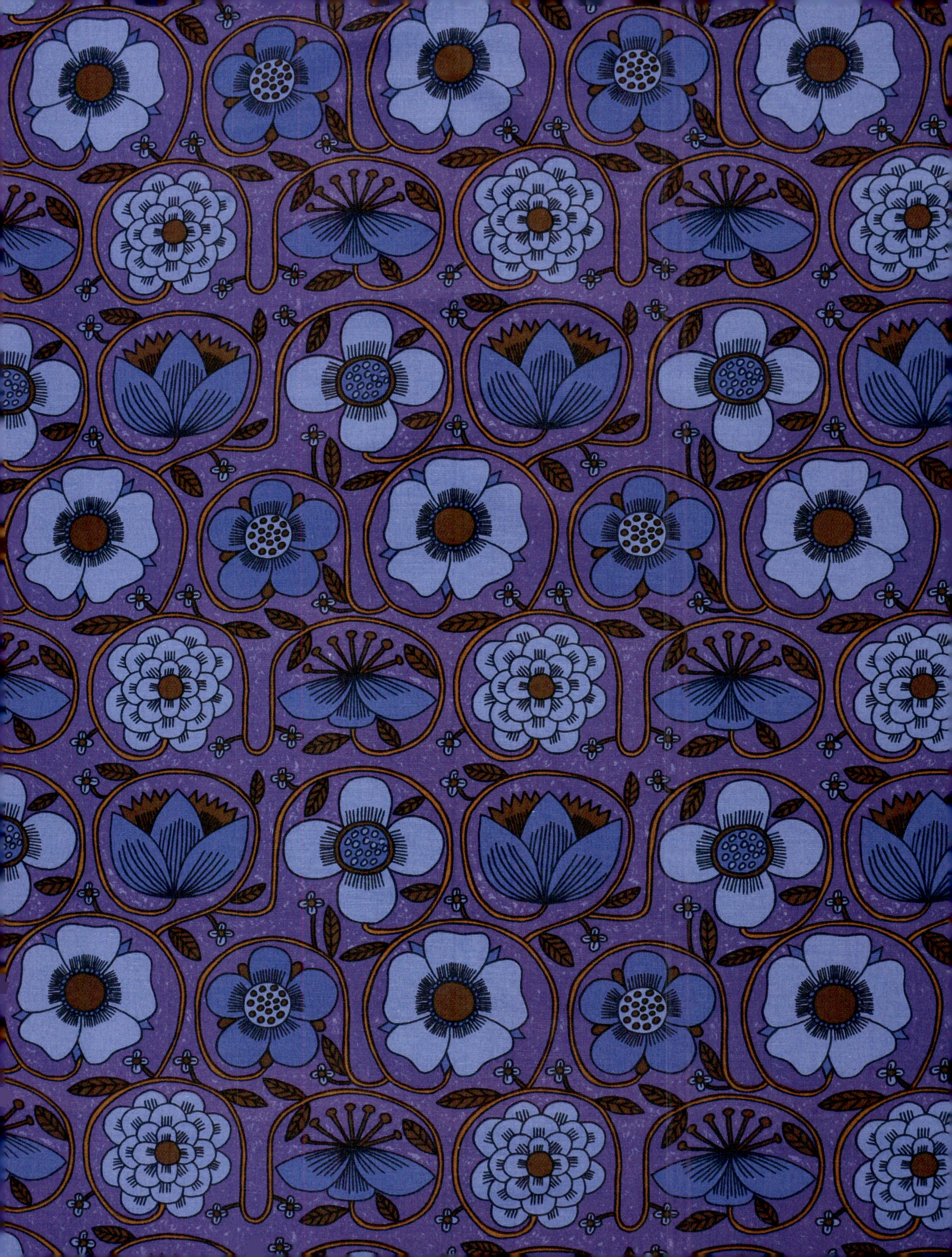

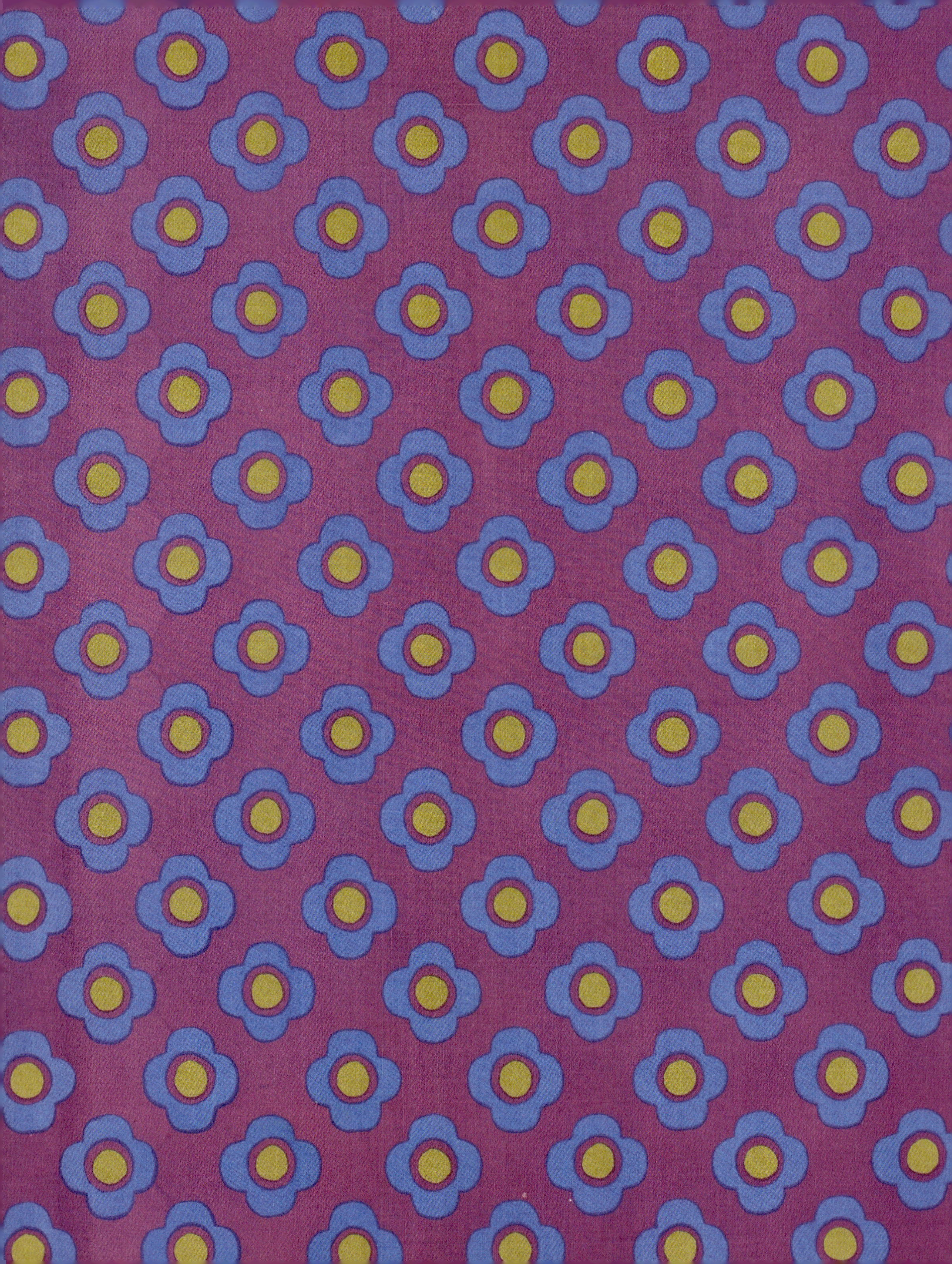

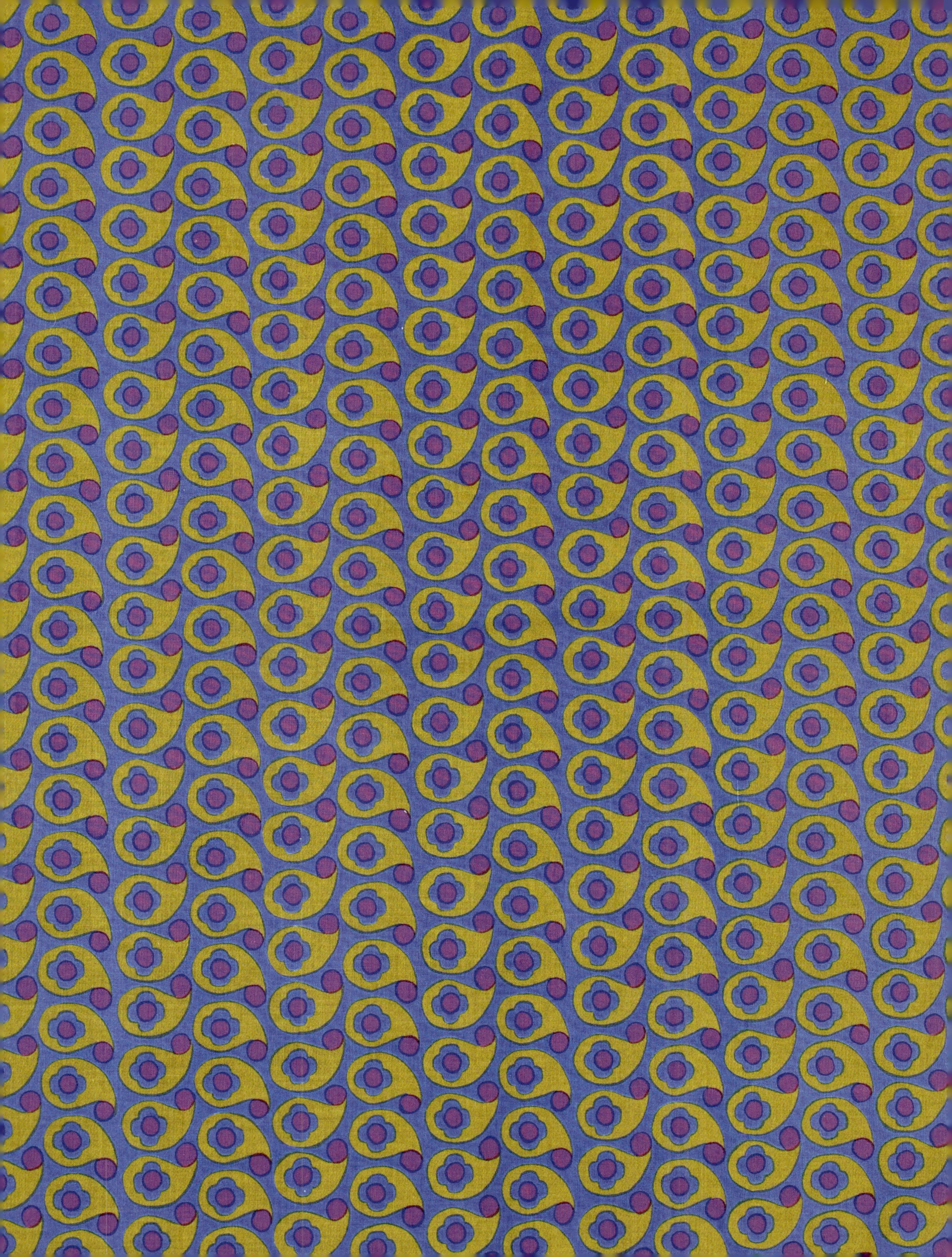

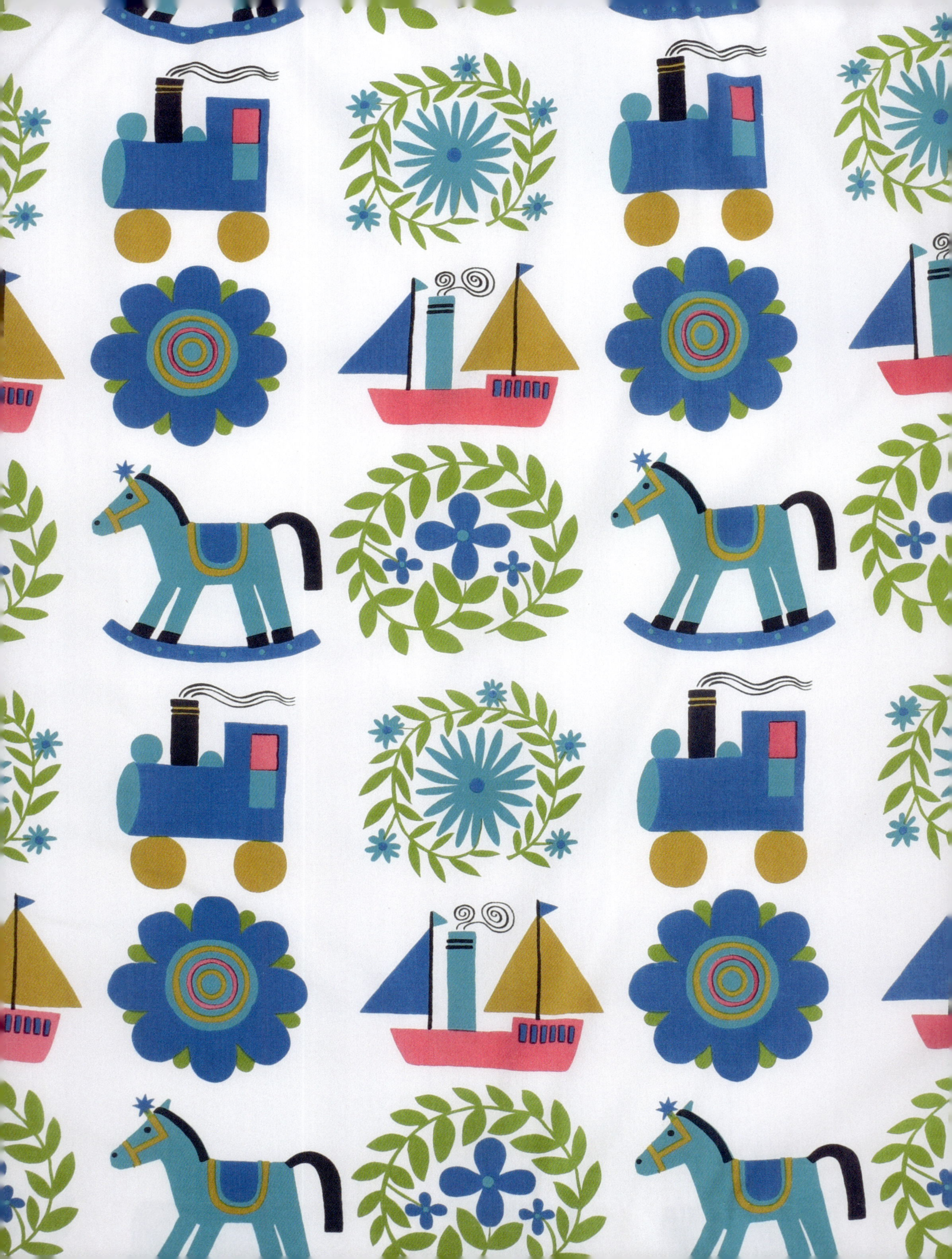

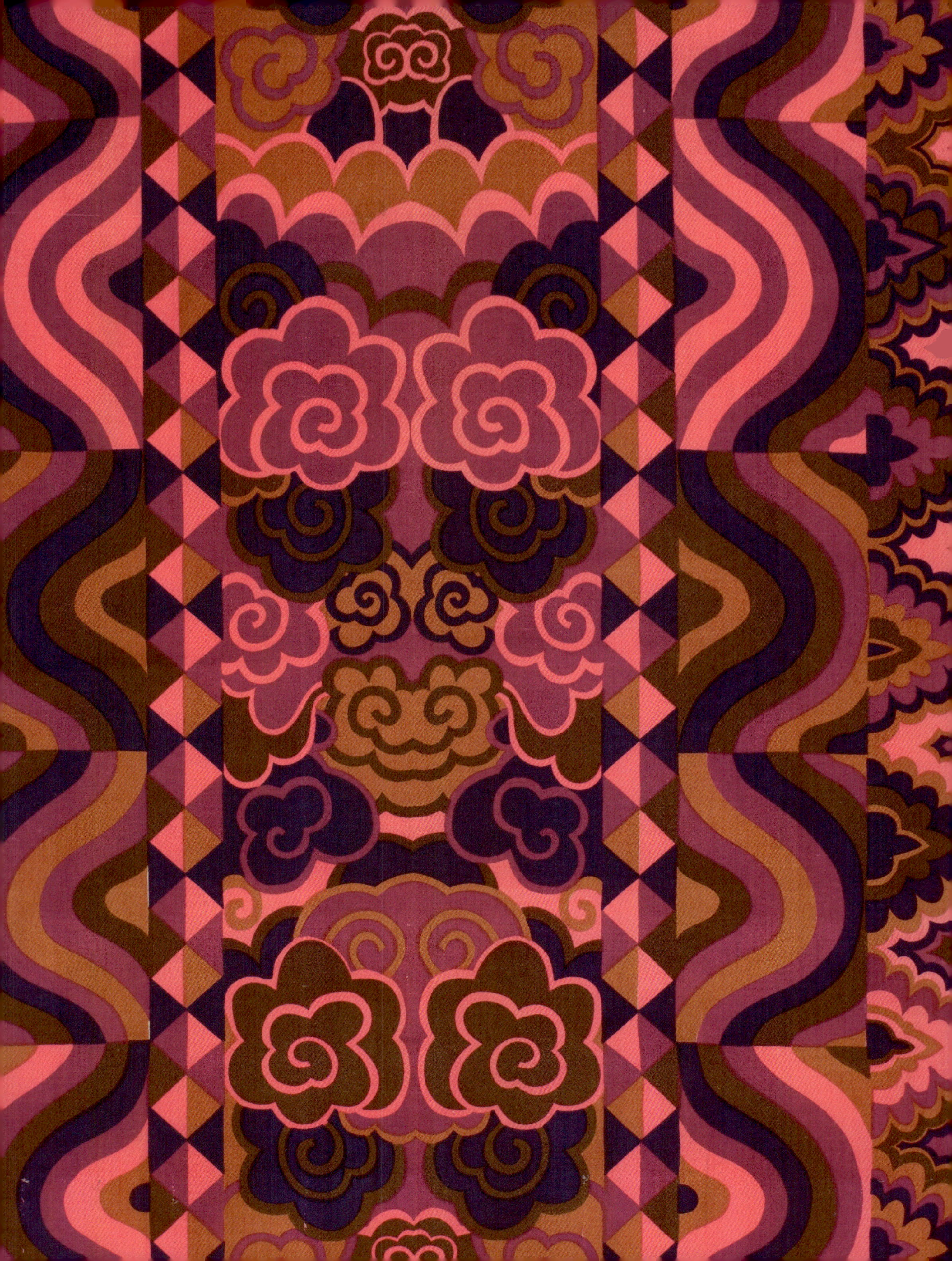

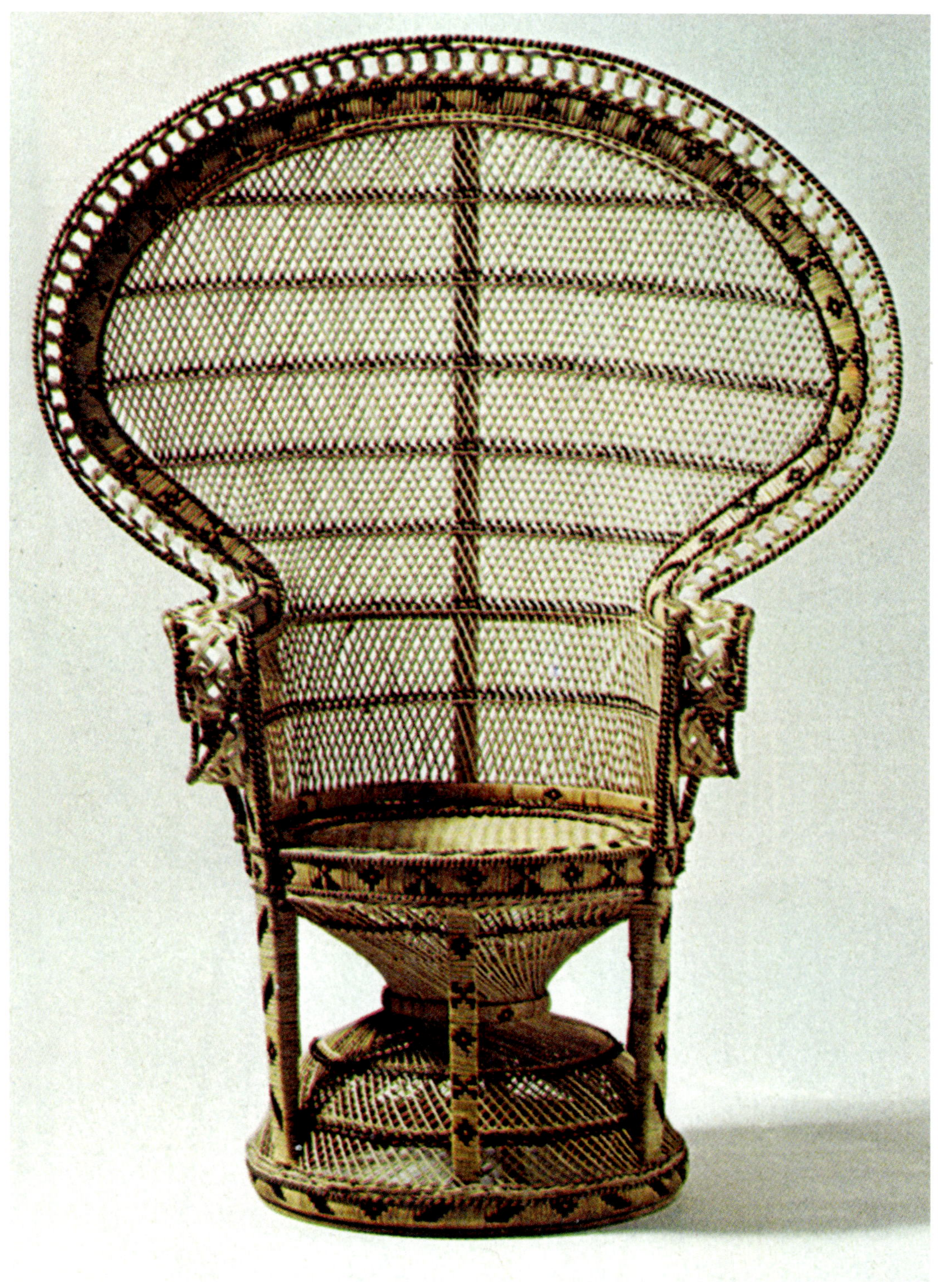

Peacock chair. A traditional hand-woven bamboo and rattan armchair, originally from the Philippines. The Habitat catalogue claimed it 'made even the poorest hovel seem like an oriental throne-room.'

Opposite: Textile, Shimmy, screen-printed cotton. Designer: Natalie Gibson for Conran Fabrics. 1967.

Previous spread: Textile, 'Jack-a-Napes', screen-printed cotton. Designer: Juliet Glynn Smith for Conran Fabrics, 1966.

Textile, 'Toy Cupboard', screen-printed cotton. Designer: Juliet Glynn Smith for Conran Fabrics, 1966.

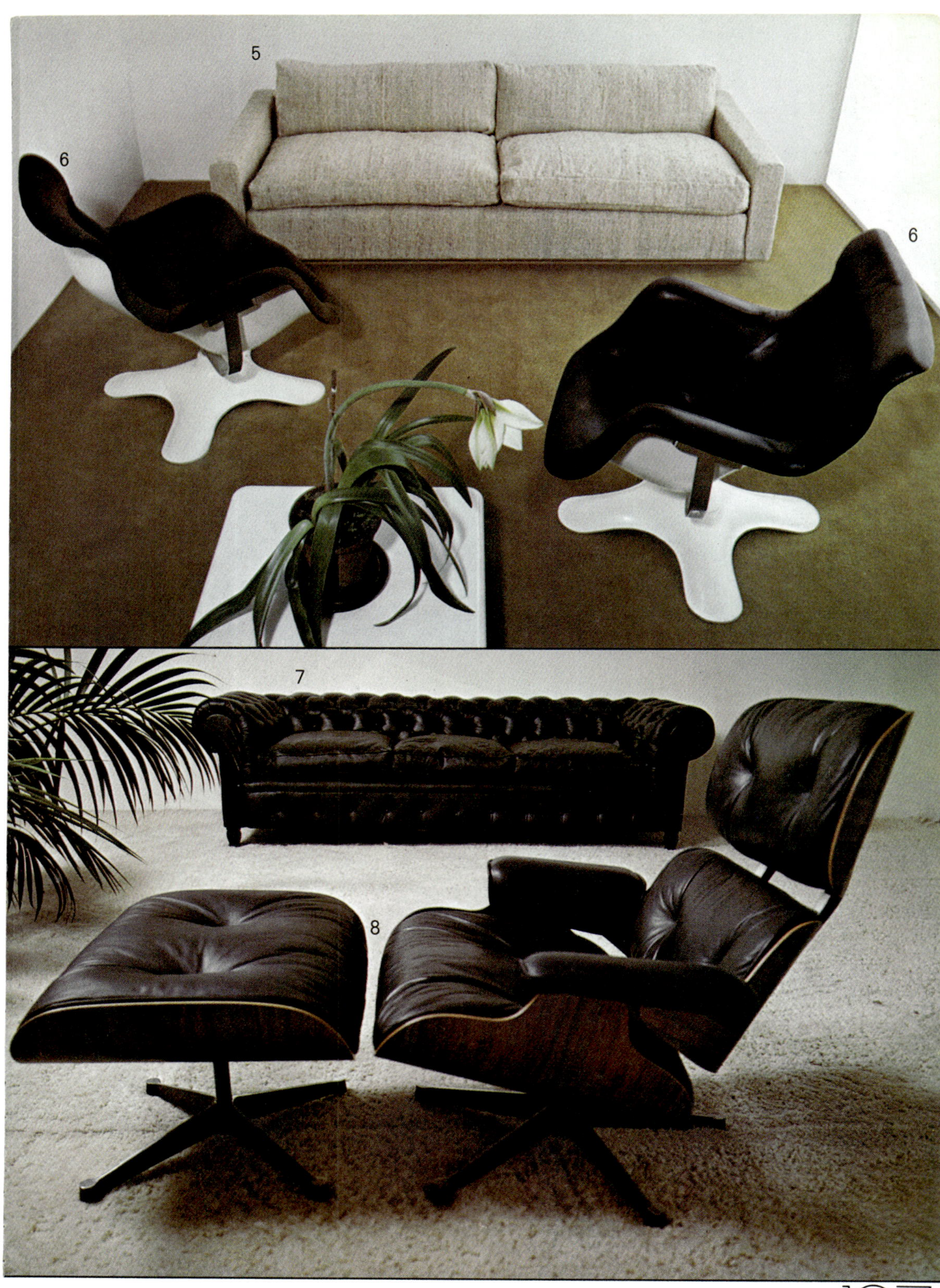

CLASSIC+MODERN FURNITURE 127

Charles Eames's Lounge Chair, 1956 and Yrjo Kukkapuro's Karuselli Chair, designed 1964, pictured together in the Habitat catalogue for 1971. Conran always retailed major design classics in Habitat, a shop that catered for purses of all sizes. The Karuselli was a personal favourite of Conran's, who has owned several.

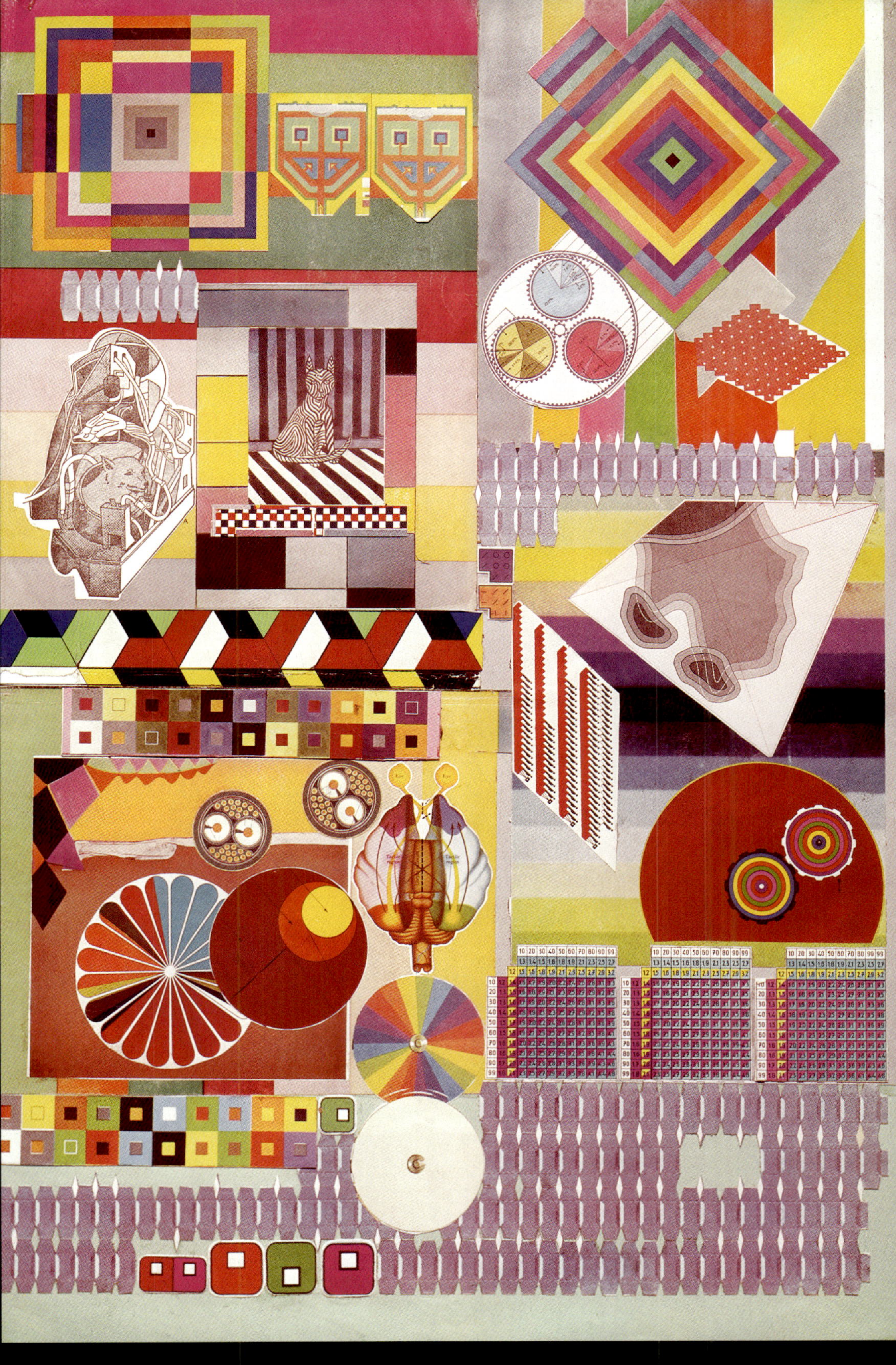

The artwork of Eduardo Paolozzi's poster for the opening of the King's Road Habitat in 1973.

VALEDICTION

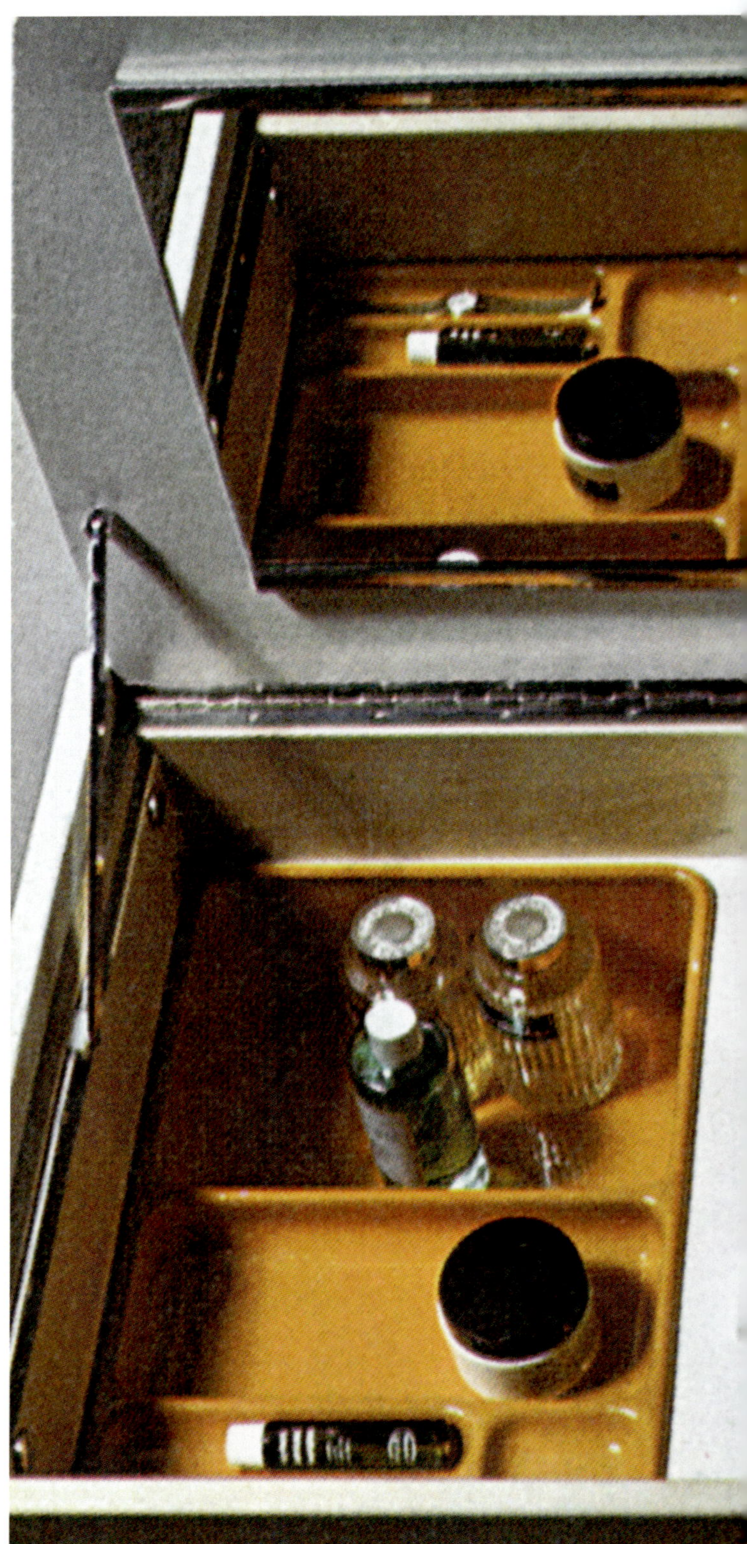

Mary Quant's range of makeup displayed on a vanity unit from the Serendipity range of bedroom furniture in a Habitat catalogue for 1971.

A S THE 1960S, that extraordinary decade, drew to a close, the dazzling brio, verve and extreme chutzpah which characterised it began to wane and the sharply defined vision and almost missionary fervour of many of Pop culture's leading proponents began to dissipate. Yet throughout the era, Conran's friendship with Quant and Plunket Greene remained as strong and as mutually influential as ever. This was made very apparent at the opening of the first Habitat store on 11 May, 1964, when most of the women present, both staff and guests, wore Mary Quant dresses. Habitat subsequently hosted at least one fashion show for Quant, and on the occasion of the opening of the first store, Conran told the *London Times*: 'We see ourselves as the Mary Quant of the furnishing world'.

EVEN AS LATE AS 1971, photographs in the Habitat catalogue show a vanity unit in the 'Serendipity' line of bedroom furniture blatantly decked out with Mary Quant's ranges of make-up – the unmistakable black, white, and silver packaging embellished with her daisy logo prominently to the fore. [53] Yet this example of friendly product placement makes no mention of Quant's name; it just wasn't necessary, the daisy said it all to the Pop generation. This remarkable symbiosis of the Habitat brand with Quant's is indicative of the powerful position they then jointly held in the public's mind in relation to the lifestyle revolution and deep cultural changes their work and ideas had such a major part in bringing about in the 1950s and 1960s, and which continue to shape the way we live now.

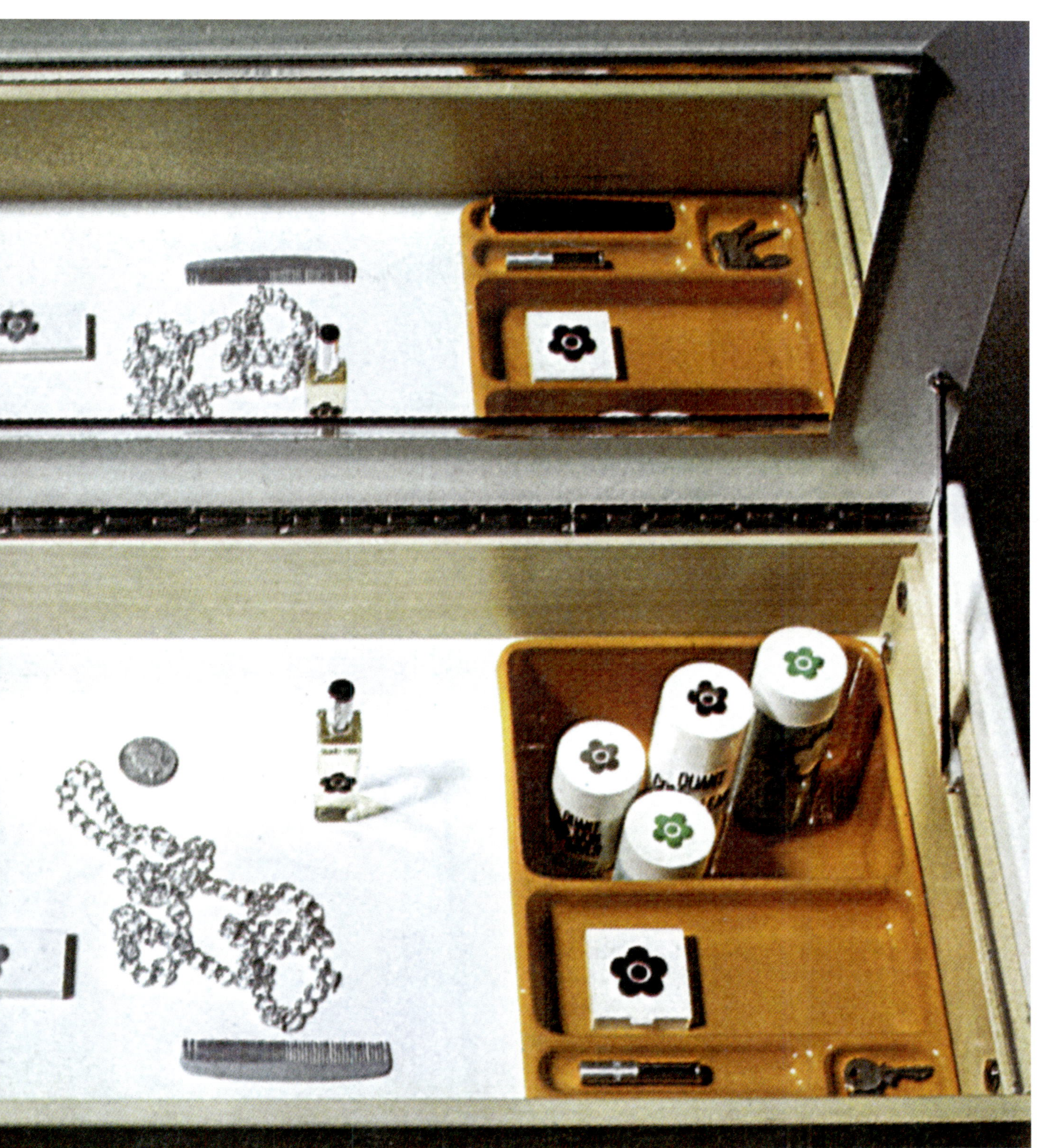

Notes

1. Mary Quant, *Quant by Quant*, Pan Books Ltd, 1st paperback ed., London, 1967, p.40.
2. Robin Day, Foreword in *Austerity to Affluence, British Art and Design 1945 – 1962*, Merrell Holberton, London, 1997, p.6.
3. Ernestine Carter, *Mary Quant's London* (exhibition catalogue), The London Museum, 1973, p.4.
4. George Melly, *Revolt into Style*, Allen Lane: The Penguin Press, London 1970, p.145
5. Mary Quant, *Mary Quant Autobiography*, Headline Publishing Group. London, 2012., pp.4-5.
6. Mary Quant, *Quant by Quant*, op. cit., p.34.
7. Ibid., p31.
8. Ibid., p.31.
9. Barty Phillips, *Conran and the Habitat Story*, Weidenfeld and Nicolson, London, 1984, p.6.
10. Mary Quant, op. cit., p.33.
11. Ibid., pp.39-40
12. Ibid., p.40.
13. Robert Hughes, *The Shock of the New: Art and the Century of Change*, Thames and Hudson, London, 1991, chapter 3.
14. Terence Conran, *A Sort of Autobiography*, HarperCollins Publishers, London, 2001, p.41.
15. Nicholas Ind, *Terence Conran: The Authorised Biography*, Sidgwick & Jackson, London, p.81.
16. Mary Quant, *Quant by Quant*, op. cit., p.41.
17. Joel Lobenthal, *Radical Rags*, Abbeville Press, New York, 1990, p.13.
18. Mary Quant, *Autobiography*, op. cit., p.55.
19. George Melly, op. cit., p.146.
20. Mary Quant, *Quant by Quant*, op. cit., pp.48-9.
21. Mary Quant. *Quant by Quant*, op. cit., p.91.
22. Barty Phillips, op. cit., p.14.
23. Mary Quant, *Mary Quant Autobiography*, op. cit., p.57.
24. Catherine Moriarty and Victoria Worsley, *Indoors And Out. The Sculpture and Design of Bernard Schottlander*, The Henry Moore Institute and the Design Institute, University of Brighton, 2008, pp.3-4.
25. Nicholas Ind, op. cit., p.99.
26. Terence Conran, *Printed Textile Design*, Studio Publications, London and New York, 1957, p.32.
27. 'Something for the Weekend – Barbara Jones', www.bibleofbritishtaste.com, 9/5/2013
28. Nigel Whiteley, *Pop Design: Modernism to Mod*, The Design Council, London, 1987, p.123.
29. Ibid., p.120.
30. Nicholas Ind, op. cit., p.102.
31. Ibid., p.95.
32. Ibid.
33. The title of the second volume of the 'All and Everything' trilogy, *A Quest for Spiritual Truth*, by the Greek Armenian Philosopher and spiritual teacher G.I. Gurdjieff. First English translation, Routledge and Kegan Paul, 1963.
34. Terence Conran, *A Sort of Autobiography*, op. cit., p.37.
35. Carlton Lake and Françoise Gilot, *Life with Picasso*, McGraw-Hill, 1964.
36. Nicholas Ind, op. cit., p.58.
37. Alastair Grieve. *Constructed Abstract Art in England: A Neglected Avant-Garde*, Yale University Press, New Haven and London, 2005, pp.17-27.
38. Nicholas Ind, op. cit., p.69.
39. Ibid., p. 70.
40. Nicholas Ind, op. cit., p.74.
41. Author's interview with Sir Terence Conran, 2005.
42. Martin Wood, *Laura Ashley*, Frances Lincoln Limited, London, 2009, p.32.
43. Terence Conran, *Printed Textile Design*, op. cit., p.36.
44. Mary Quant, *Quant by Quant*, op. cit., p.117.
45. Marnie Fogg, *Boutique: A '60s Cultural Phenomenon*, Mitchell Beazley, London, 2003, p.22.
46. Mary Quant. *Autobiography*, op. cit., p.78.
47. Mary Quant, *Quant by Quant*, 1st hardback ed., Cassell, London, 1966, p.156.
48. Ibid., p.107.
49. Nicholas Ind, op. cit., p.141.
50. Terence Conran, *A Sort of Autobiography*, op. cit., p.41.
51. Ibid., p.132.
52. *Habitat Catalogue*, Autumn 1971, p.125.
53. Ibid., p.90.

Select Bibliography

BOOKS

Buruma, Anna. *Liberty and Co. in the Fifties and Sixties: A Taste for Design*. ACC Editions: Woodbridge, Suffolk, 2009

Carrier, Robert. *Great Dishes of the World: The Robert Carrier Cook Book*, boxed paperback edition, Sphere Books Ltd: London, 1967

Conran, Terence. *A Sort of Autobiography*. Harper Collins: London, 2001

Conran, Terence. *My Life In Design*. Conran Octopus: London, 2016

Conran, Terence. *Printed Textile Design*. The Studio Publications: London and New York. 1957

Conran, Terence and Stafford Cliff. *Terence Conran's Inspiration*. Conran Octopus: London, 2008

Cotton, Michelle (ed.). *Nigel Henderson & Eduardo Paolozzi Hammer Prints Ltd 1954-75*. Firstsite: Colchester, 2012

David, Elizabeth. *A Book of Mediterranean Food*. John Lehmann: London, 1950

David, Elizabeth. *French Country Cooking*. Paperback ed., Penguin Books Ltd: Harmondsworth, 1959

Fogg, Marnie. *Boutique: A '60s Cultural Phenomenon*. Mitchell Beazley: London 2003

Garlake, Margaret. *New Art New World: British Art in Postwar Society*. The Paul Mellon Centre: Yale University Press, 1998

Garner, Phillippe. *The Contemporary Decorative Arts From 1940 to the Present Day*. New Burlington Books, 1980

Garner, Phillippe. *Twentieth-Century Furniture*. Phaidon: Oxford, 1980

Grieve, Alastair. *Constructed Abstract Art in England A Neglected Avant-Garde*. The Paul Mellon Centre, Yale University Press: New Haven and London, 2005

Harling, R., A. Kroll and Olive Sullivan (eds). *The Modern Interior – House & Garden*, London, 1964

Hinchcliffe, Frances. *Fifties Furnishing Fabrics*. Webb & Bower: Exeter, 1989

Hulanicki, Barbara. *From A To Biba*. Hutchinson & Co Ltd, 1983

Ind, Nicholas. *Terence Conran: The Authorized Biography*. Sidgwick & Jackson: London, 1995

Jackson, Lesley. *Modern British Furniture Design Since 1945*. V&A Publishing: London, 2013

Jenkins, Steven. *Midwinter Pottery: a revolution in British tableware*. Richard Dennis: London, 2003

Jones, Barbara. *Follies and Grottoes*. Constable & Co. Ltd: London, 1953

Jones, Barbara. *The Unsophisticated Arts*. The Architectural Press: London, 1951

Lobenthal, Joel. *RADICAL RAGS Fashions of the Sixties*. Abbeville Press Inc.: New York, 1990

Mauries, Patrick. *Piero Fornasetti Practical Madness*. Thames & Hudson: London, 2015

McLaren, Graham. *Ceramics of the 1950s*. Shire Publications Ltd: Princes Risborough, 1997

Melly, George. *Revolt Into Style: The Pop Arts in Britain*. Allen Lane, The Penguin Press: London, 1970

Peat, Alan. *David Whitehead Ltd, Artist Designed Textiles, 1952-1969*. Oldham City Art Gallery: Oldham, 1993

Peat, Alan. *Midwinter: A Collectors' Guide*. Moffat (Cameron & Hollis), 1992

Phillips, Barty. *Conran and the Habitat Story*. Weidenfeld and Nicolson: London, 1984

Quant, Mary. *MARY QUANT Autobiography*. Headline Publishing Group: London, 2012

Quant, Mary. *Quant by Quant*. Cassell & Co Ltd: London, 1966

Rayner, G. and R. Chamberlain (eds). *Austerity to Affluence British Art and Design 1945 – 1962*. Merrell Holberton: London 1997

Rayner G., R. Chamberlain and A. Stapleton, *Artists' Textiles 1940 – 1976*. The Antique Collectors' Club: Woodbridge. 2012

Ross, Alan and John Minton. *Time Was Away: A Notebook In Corsica*. John Lehmann: London, 1948

Sassoon, Vidal. *Sorry I kept You Waiting Madam*. Cassell & Co.: London. 1968

Twiggy, *TWIGGY – an Autobiography*. Mayflower Books Ltd: St Albans, Herts, 1975

Walsh, Victoria. *Nigel Henderson: Parallel of Life and Art*. Thames and Hudson: London, 2001

Whitely, Nigel. *POP DESIGN, Modernism To Mod*. The Design Council: London, 1987

Wood, Martin. *LAURA ASHLEY*. Frances Lincoln Ltd: London, 2009

MAGAZINES, PERIODICALS AND CATALOGUES

The Architectural Review, vol. 112, July – December 1952. London

Butterick Home Catalog, Fall 1967. The Butterick Company Inc. New York

Catalogue of Mary Quant Dresses in the Exhibition 'Mary Quant's London', held at the London Museum, Kensington Palace. November 1973 – June 1974

Design, The Council of Industrial Design, London, 1949 – 1970

'Dynamic Design: The British Pottery Industry, 1940 – 1990', catalogue and book accompanying the exhibition. Niblett, Kathy. Stoke On Trent City Museum and Art Gallery, 1990

Furnishings from Britain, The National Trade Press Ltd: London and Manchester, June 1951

Habitat Catalogue, 1971. Habitat Designs Ltd, Wallingford

Indoors and Out The Sculpture and Design of Bernard Schottlander. Moriarty, Catherine and Victoria Worsley. Henry Moore Institute and the Design Archives, University Of Brighton. Publication accompanying an exhibition of Schottlander's work. 23 September 2007 – 9 February 2008

J.C. Penney catalogues: 1965. 1968, 1969. J.C. Penney Co. Milwaukee, Wisconsin

Nova. The International Publishing Corporation (IPC) London. 1965 – 1970

The Studio Yearbook of Decorative Art. The Studio Publications, London and New York, 1950 – 1970

The Sunday Times Supplement/Magazine, 1962 – 1970

Vogue, Condé Nast Publications, London, 1955 – 1970

Acknowledgements

The Ashley Family Foundation.
Anna Buruma, the Liberty Archive.
Sue Breakell, University of Brighton Design Archives
H. Kirk Brown.
Sarah Campbell.
Lucie Cash, Royal Mail Group Limited.
Trevor and Elaine Chamberlain.
Stafford Cliff.
Sir Terence Conran.
Michael Eftihiou.
Anna Emms, ACC Art Books.
Steve Farrow, ACC Art Books.
The staff of the Fashion & Textile Museum, London.
Liliane Fawcett, Themes & Variations.
Julia Gahlin, née Schottlander.
Natalie Gibson.
Orlando Plunket Greene.
Alison Hart, ACC Art Books.
David Kewn, Gordon Maxwell Conservation.
Jonathan Knight, Gordon Maxwell Conservation.
Paul Liss, Liss Llewellyn Fine Art.
Stephen Mackinley, ACC Art Books.
Dr Catherine Moriarty.

Kitty Morris, Textile Conservation.
Dennis Nothdruft, the Fashion & Textile Museum, London.
Neil Parkinson, the Royal College of Art.
Andrew McIntosh Patrick, the Fine Art Society Plc.
Terence Pepper.
Annamarie Phelps
Heather Tilbury Phillips.
David Queensberry.
Dame Mary Quant.
Tony Raymond.
Jonathan Richards, Fototheme.
The Royal Mail Group Ltd.
Mat Riches.
Peter Salmon, Upstage.
Emma Shuckburgh, née Ashley.
James Smith, ACC Art Books
Pippa Stockdale, the Fine Art Society Plc.
Yuki Tintori, Fornasetti.
Toby Treves, the Paolozzi Foundation.
Andrew Whittaker, ACC Art Books.
Dr Lesley Whitworth, University of Brighton Design Archives
Lisa Wood, the Fine Art Society Plc.
Jill A. Wiltse.

Image Credits

Alamy Stock Photo p.158 (**Keystone Pictures USA**), p.168 (**Pictorial Press Ltd.**), pp.178-9 (**Peter Horree**), p.180 (**V&A Images**), p.185 (**Everett Collection Historical**), p.205, p.203 (**Trinity Mirror/Mirrorpix**)

The Ashley Family Foundation: p.126, p.130, p.131 (**Photo by Priscilla Conran**), pp.132-37

© **Terence Conran:** p.17, p.21, pp.30-1, p.36, pp.63-6, pp.78-9, pp.80-4, p.88-91, p.94, p.98, p.96, pp.100-1 (cover photograph by Priscilla Conran), pp.102-3, p.122, p.231, p.229

Permission Terence Conran: p.16, p.18, p.90, p.209 (Photo by John Pantlin), p.210, p.212, p.213 (Photo by John Maltby)

© **Terence Conran/The Paolozzi Foundation:** p.115

© **Terence Conran/Mary Quant:** p.232

Photograph by Anthony Denney: p.99, p.112

Design Archives, University of Brighton © Julia Gahlin née Schottlander: p.15; p.108

Photo by Terence Donovan: pp.214-15

A Eames Ò Lounge Chair and Ottoman, Designed by Charles Ray Eames, 1956: p.230

Courtesy of Fornasetti: p.56 (**Photo by Uglo Mulas**), pp.57-8

© **Julia Gahlin, née Schottlander:** p.39 (inset), p.109

Getty Images: p.61

© **Natalie Gibson:** p.228

Granger Historical Picture Archive/Alamy Stock Photo: p.50

Photo by Sharok Hatami: p.39 (main image)

Photo by JAY (Elsbeth Juda): p.73

George Konig: p.43

Yrjo Kukkaparo: p.230 (Karuselli Chair)

Courtesy of Michael Mott: p.173

© **The Paolozzi Foundation:** p.59, pp.67-9, pp.70-2, p.231

Terence Pepper Collection: p.9 (Photo by Vic Singh), p.11; p.12 (Photo by Vic Singh), p.33 (Photo by John Cowan), p.46 (Photo by Vic Singh) p.139, p.144, pp.176-7

Photo Arts: pp.40-1

Permission Mary Quant: p.35, p.42, p.44-5, p.47-8, p.51-3; pp.145-48, p.160-63, p.167, p.171, p.181-4, p.186-7, p.188 (Stamp design: **Royal Mail Group**), pp.189-91, p.197, p.200-02, pp.204-5

© **David Queensbury:** pp.93-4

© **Tony Raymond:** pp.74-5

© **Clifford Richards:** p.220-21

© **Royal College of Art/Bridgeman Images:** pp.22-7

Photo by Joe Santoro: p.49

© **John Sayers:** pp.128-9

Photo by John Walcott: pp.149-150, p.152

© **Denny Wickham:** p.19

Photo by Michael Wickham. © Denny Wickham: back cover (left), p.6, p.62, p.85, p.105, pp.106-7, pp.110-11, p.119, p.120, pp.216-17

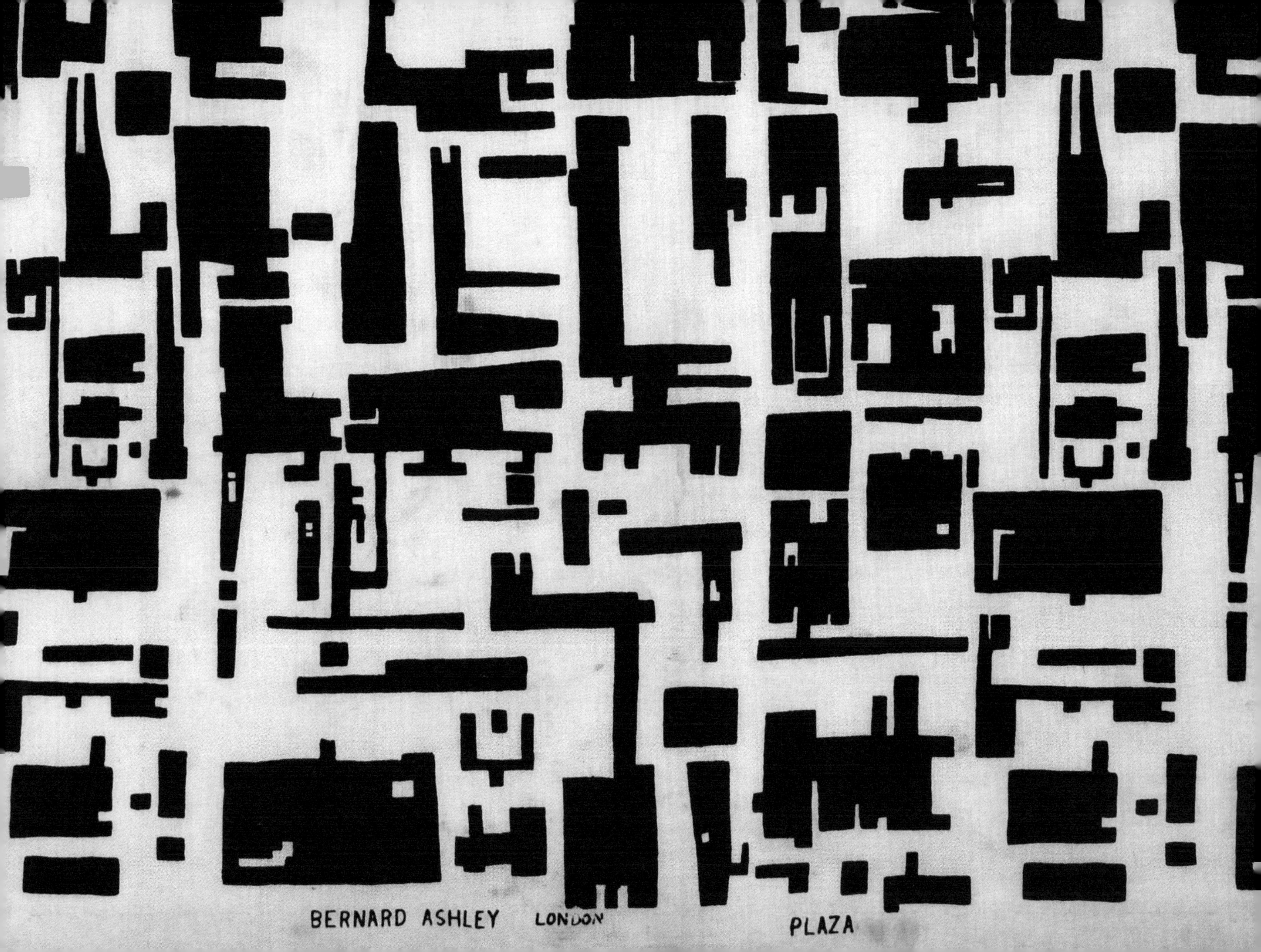

BERNARD ASHLEY   LONDON   PLAZA